Newcastle, February 21, 2005

for Richard,

with gratitude for
your hospitality —
again!

Phil

# The Music of European Nationalism

## Cultural Identity and Modern History

PHILIP V. BOHLMAN

A B C ● C L I O

Santa Barbara, California    Denver, Colorado    Oxford, England

Library of Congress Cataloging-in-Publication Data
Bohlman, Philip Vilas.
The music of European nationalism : cultural identity and
modern history / Philip V. Bohlman.
p.  cm. — (ABC-CLIO world music series)
Includes bibliographical references and index.
ISBN 1-57607-270-3 (hardcover : alk. paper)  ISBN 1-85109-363-X (e-book)
1. Music—Europe—History and criticism.  2. Nationalism in music.
I . Title. II. Series.
ML3580.B64   2004
781.5'99'094—dc22
2004005429


04  05  06  07  ⁊  10  9  8  7  6  5  4  3  2  1

This book is also available on the World Wide Web as an e-book.
Visit abc-clio.com for details.

ABC-CLIO, Inc.
130 Cremona Drive, P.O. Box 1911
Santa Barbara, California 93116-1911

*Design by Jane Raese*
Text set in New Baskerville

This book is printed on acid-free paper.
Manufactured in the United States of America

*for Christine*

. . . du nur, du wirst immer wieder geboren:
weil ich niemals dich anhielt, halt ich dich fest.
**—Rainer Maria Rilke**

# Contents

# Musical Examples on Compact Disc

1. "Tzarina Milica and Duke Vladeta," Boro Roganović

2. "Kantele," sung by Anni Kiriloff

3. "Maailman synty" ("The Birth of the World"), sung by Iivana Onoila

4. "Radnalied" ("Radna Song"), Banat-German Romanian Pilgrims

5. "Medjugorje Song," composed by Leander Prinz

6. Tambores del Bajo Aragón: "Desperadoes y toque procesional"

7. Karelian wedding song, "Kylä vuotti uutta kuuta" ("The Village Awaits the New Moon"), Värttinä

8. "Kárpáti menyasszony" ("The Fiancée from the Carpathians"), Kati Szvorák

9. "Khused" (Hassidic wedding dance), Gheorghe Covaci, Sr. ("Cioata") and Gheorghe Covaci, Jr.

10. Village Wedding Dance, Rom Band of Gheorghe Covaci, Jr.

11. "Trip Jig," arranged by Anish and Aibhlín Dillane

12. Die Tanzgeiger: "Bläserweise" and "Ländler"

13. "Wiener Fiakerlied" ("Viennese Coachman's Song"), Gustav Pick

14. "Jedlička," Laxblech

15. "Ve Skalici na rínečku sekajú sa o d'ívečku," Skaličan

16. ". . . Nach Großwardein" (". . . To Großwardein"), Hermann Rosenzweig and Anton Groiss

17. Yiddish folk song, "Ani maamin" ("I Believe"), Gheorghe Covaci, Sr. ("Cioata"), and Gheorghe Covaci, Jr.

18. "Máramosi Tánc" ("Dance from Máramoros"), Béla Bartók

19. "Oláh Nóta" ("Walachian Song"), Béla Bartók

*For additional information on each track, see CD Notes and Commentary.*

# Series Foreword

*When Philip Bohlman,* professor of ethnomusicology at the University of Chicago, and Alicia Merritt, acquistions editor at ABC-CLIO, first approached me in 1998 to ask if I would serve as editor for a new series of books on world music traditions, the prospect excited me greatly.

At that time, the monumental, ten-volume *Garland Encyclopedia of World Music* was on the verge of publication. Several academic publishers, including the University of Chicago Press, had developed extensive and impressive ethnomusicology lists. A handful of quality textbooks designed for introductory world music survey courses were already available, and a few other promising ones were on the way. In short, in conjunction with the dramatic rise in the overall popularity of world music (a subject to which I will return), the related literature was growing rapidly and expanding on several different fronts all at once.

But for all of this growth and expansion in ethnomusicology and world music publishing, one special kind of book remained surprisingly rare: the accessible yet substantive introductory text on a specific world music region or area—and this was exactly the kind of book to which ABC-CLIO was now proposing to devote a series. I therefore enthusiastically accepted their series editorship invitation.

As I had expected, my enthusiasm for a series of such books on the world's diverse musical cultures and traditions was widely shared by my colleagues in the ethnomusicology/world music studies community. In short order, several leading experts, most of them teaching at major research universities with leading ethnomusicology programs (University of Chicago, University of Pennsylvania, University of Florida), were under contract to contribute volumes in their respective areas of expertise. This was a Dream Team of scholars, but even more importantly, these were highly gifted authors who were up to the series mission challenge that ABC-CLIO and I set before them: Write a book that is accessible to the non-specialist reader, that is highly informative without being overly technical, that is brought vividly to life by its illustrations and accompanying compact disc (CD), that conveys your own passion for the music it explores and the world in which that music lives, and that will engage the interest of a wide readership composed principally of high school and undergraduate nonmusic students.

Beyond these requirements, the authors were asked to conceive of their works in accordance with a structured yet flexible model that directed each book through a telescopic progression from broadly general to increasingly specific vantage points, starting with a general introduction to the selected music area and topic covered, then moving to a more narrowly defined regional focus and an emphasis on key themes and issues, and finally concluding with an in-depth portrait of a particular musical community or phenomenon, a portrait based on the author's own principal field research. The model was developed with three specific objectives in mind: achieving a high level of consistency of presentation between volumes, striking an appropriate balance between comprehensive breadth and focused depth within each volume, and engendering in readers an intimate sense of personal engagement with the music and its world. It has been highly satisfying for me as series editor to see these objectives splendidly realized in each volume to date.

Underlying the concept and vision of this series since its inception have been two important issues: the dramatic ascent of world music in recent years and the rather paradoxical term "world music" itself. Since these issues in a sense prefigured and continue to shape the ABC-CLIO World Music Series vision, I would like to devote the remainder of this foreword to a brief discussion of their significance.

## The Dramatic Rise of "World Music"

The popularity of world music has grown by leaps and bounds here in the West in recent decades. It was not so long ago that the sounds of Indian sitars, Indonesian gamelans, Chinese pipas, and the like were largely unknown to the vast majority of Western listeners. Today, such sounds are to be heard just about everywhere: on the radio, on the Internet, in record stores, at concerts and festivals, even in shopping malls, supermarkets, and elevators. Whether or not you know how to identify the source of the distinctive, "otherworldly" melody on your favorite Beatles or Ricky Martin CD as a sitar, it is there, permeating your consciousness and affecting your musical sensibilities. And that infectious Janet Jackson dance groove? Perhaps it's the one enlivened by a heavily processed, digitally sampled Balinese gamelan orchestra. Then, of course, there is the internet, where thousands upon thousands of world music recordings and "sound file" sources are available at the click of a mouse to everyone, from major record producers and dance club DJs to soccer moms and teenage computer hackers.

Some of the musical traditions that fall within the eclectic domain of world music represent continuations and developments of musical practices and repertoires dating back centuries or even millennia, such as Indian *raga* and Japanese *gagaku*. Others, such as "world beat" and various cross-cultural fusion genres, are of recent origin or are emerging at this very moment, as music makers blend together resources, ideas, and musical materials from a variety of sources and inventively forge them into new expressions of their unique identities as individuals, as members of communities, societies, and cultures, and as human beings in the broadest sense of the term. All points on this spectrum are embraced within the pages of each volume of the ABC-CLIO World Music Series.

But what exactly *is* world music? There is no easy answer to this question. In actuality, *all* of the world's music traditions, or *musics,* as ethnomusicologists like to call them—past and present, traditional and modern, familiar and unfamiliar, Western and non-Western, classical and popular, folk and tribal—should rightly fall within the category of world music. Since all of the world's musics exist in the world, it makes sense that either all of them should be categorized as world music or that none of them should be. Any scheme that includes some musics within the category while excluding others is simply arbitrary.

And yet the popular meaning of the term "world music" is just that: arbitrary. It rose to prominence as a convenient catch-all classification for types of music that did not fit conveniently into existing Western categories (jazz, rock, classical, etc.) and was subsequently embraced by bewildered record store owners seeking an appropriate designation for bins displaying such material. The "world music" category, as it is usually applied, includes only those musics that do not fit within the conventional categorical boxes that identify the Western musical "mainstream" (another slippery and ever-malleable term that today encompasses, among other musics, classical, jazz, rock, country and western, easy listening, rap, and hip-hop). Traditional musics of African, Asian, Aboriginal Australian, Native American, Central and South American, and Eastern European cultures are the prime candidates for inclusion. Western-influenced popular music styles built upon the roots of traditional musics of non-Western origin are also usually included, sometimes under the aforementioned subcategory of world beat. And certain musical traditions of North America and Western Europe—Irish traditional, Cajun, and so on—fit the bill of world music according to some people's lists but not others'.

The philosophy underlying the ABC-CLIO World Music Series, in step with current directions in the discipline of ethnomusicology and important recent publications such as *The Garland Encyclopedia of World Music,* endeavors to move away from the arbitrary inclusions and exclusions that are so often invoked by the term "world music" and to approach the study of world music instead simply as an exploration of selected musical traditions from around the world, wherever that exploration may originate and wherever it may take the reader along its multidirectional pathways. The geographical and cultural "hubs" of given musics—the places identified with their origins, the principal cultural groups with which they are connected, the musicians recognized as their leading representatives—are most certainly accounted for, but so too are the complex, intersecting webs of geography and culture that situate these musics in more broadly global, that is, in *world,* contexts.

Thus, for example, Philip Bohlman's volume on music and European nationalism privileges neither rural Eastern European folk music nor concert works by the well-known nineteenth-century Czech composer Antonín Dvořák one over the other, devoting serious attention to both; Carol Muller highlights the inextricable ties between indigenous Zulu musical traditions, Christian hymnody, and the global configuration of the modern popular music industry in her book on South African music; and Henry Spiller finds an essential continuity between the centuries-old tradition of Javanese *gamelan* music, on the one hand, and the Western pop music–inspired Islamic didacticism of the Indonesian *dangdut* genre on the other. In all cases, the concept of world music is treated by these authors not as an invitation to divide the world up in West-versus-the-rest style, but as a point of departure from which to explore musical traditions both at their most localized levels of identity and within the context of broad, overarching processes of globalization and modernization.

It is a great pleasure to bring this exciting series to your attention. I hope you enjoy reading these books as much as I have.

*Michael B. Bakan*

# *Preface*

*The Euro might be the first currency in history
to be choreographed and introduced with music.*
—*National Public Radio, 1 January 2002*

In January 2002, as I sketch out the final stages of writing this book, many nations of Europe embark on the initial stages of one of the most sweeping attempts to bring unity to the continent: The **Euro** has become the single legal tender for twelve of the fifteen nations of the European Union, replacing completely the national currencies of those nations and supplanting all previous attempts to create common currencies, such as the short-lived **ecu** in the early 1990s. The Euro is both a common currency (banknotes are the same denominations and display the same images) and a means to preserve the unique identity of individual nations (each nation can print an image of its own on coins, thus individualizing and nationalizing their exchange).

During the decade-long preparations for the Euro, debates about its advantages and disadvantages turned around several critical issues. Would it actually stabilize peace and unity after a century of world wars and colonialism? Would it provide Europe with a global financial edge, especially in competition with the American dollar? Would the Euro strengthen the strongest European nations, especially France and Germany, at the expense of the smaller and financially weaker nations? Would it make a nation's citizens feel more like Europeans than Spaniards, Greeks, or Belgians? What about the European nations that delayed employment of the Euro—the United Kingdom, Denmark, and Sweden? And what about the several nations of Eastern Europe that would gladly accept the Euro and all other advantages of the European Union but remain, nonetheless, outside the circle?

Symbolically, the introduction of the Euro draws our attention to many of the issues that serve again and again as the main themes of this book. The Euro is an emblem that is profoundly contradictory. On one hand, it is about Europe and the potential for its wholeness; on the other, it is about the individual nation and the potential threat of

*Euro banknote, with symbolic portal on the front and symbolic bridge on the back*

nationalism to European unity and sovereignty. Historically, the two hands have worked against each other far more often than they have joined in cooperation, thus making it necessary to invent Europe again and again as a composite of myths, histories, and icons. Take the Euro banknotes and coins themselves as a case in point. All denominations, from five to five hundred, have images of doors, windows, or archways on the recto side, with a bridge on the verso side. Each bridge enters the banknote in the upper left-hand corner and crosses the bill toward the right, which is covered with a map of Europe. The monumental forms on the Euro bills narrate an architectural history, beginning with Rome on the five-Euro banknote (a triumphal arch on the front, an aqueduct on the back, together symbolizing the European unity achieved through conquest and administration of resources) and reaching abstract modern forms on the 500-Euro bill.

The banknotes juxtapose geography, history, and art. The iconography of the doors, windows, and other entryways consciously projects the Euro as a currency representing the power to cross borders through welcoming passageways. Ironically, however, these passageways are virtual and not real. Rather than depicting doors and arches that really do allow Europeans to cross the borders that separate them, the Euro invents its images of unity. The bridges are stripped of national character and drafted in such a way that it would be impossible to ascribe an exact identity or location. The question the Euro raises, then, is whether its use of imaginary images solves the problem of access and exchange across real national borders.

Such questions are not merely rhetorical. In fact, they provide the narrative stuff of which the history and political economy of European nationalism is made. To invent unity, the Euro eliminates its enemy, the other side of the coin, metaphorically speaking, nationalism. The inventors of the Euro have erased the icons of the nation from the bills, the faces of national heroes, politicians, soldiers, artists, and musicians who achieved great things for the nation. Scenes of historical importance or buildings of national significance no longer appear on the verso side. In fact, individuals of every kind have disappeared from the Euro banknotes. The European currency is devoid of Europeans; it remains an open question just who will pass through these doorways and cross these bridges? The coins provide us with one answer to such questions, for each nation adopting the Euro is allowed to mint coins with faces of national heroes or leaders on one side, preserving a measure of national pride and contributing to the exchange of coins across Europe. The Dutch and the Portuguese will encounter no problems should a coin with Austria's Empress Maria Theresa stamped on it turn up in their coin purses. The nationalization of Euro coins, thus, is a concession, one trumpeted by every public announcement designed to quiet public complaints about the loss of national identity.

The introduction of the Euro provided ample opportunities to celebrate Europe and the European nation with music. At the Euro ceremonies on New Year's Eve in 2001 the European Anthem ("Ode to Joy" from the final movement of Beethoven's Ninth Symphony; see Chapter 1) provided the counterpoint for new works, most rather banal rock jingles that crammed lyrics from as many European languages as possible into a single song. Music and money, however, have long been companions in Europe. Indeed, the faces of musicians have graced banknotes of many nations: Claude Debussy on the French franc, Clara Schumann on the German mark, Béla Bartók on the Hungarian forint, George Enescu on the Romanian lei (see Bălaşa, forthcoming). Such musicians are of both national and nationalist significance. None would be used as Beethoven is on the hologram of the Eurocard, the common ATM card of the 1990s. Whatever its political stance, wherever its geographical position on the map of Europe, the iconic representation of musicians made specific statements about European nationalism.

It is significant that several nations have not yet embraced the Euro or, for that matter, joined the European Union. Some countries still resist entry into the EU (for example, Switzerland and Norway), in part because of issues such as a common currency. At the same time, other countries (Slovakia, Romania, and others that already fix their currencies to the German mark or the American dollar) clamor to join the EU, eager to gain the economic benefits of a common currency. The

Euro, nonetheless, has been very much in evidence since the 1990s in prices given just about everywhere in Europe, even in Switzerland. The celebrations of the introduction of the Euro, which are under way as I write this preface, have cause to be both real and virtual.

Can something like the Euro, with both symbolic and economic value, really mitigate the negative aspects of nationalism and undergird the positive aspects of Europe as a community of nation-states? The issues generated by questions such as this run through the present book. The nation is both necessary for what Europe is and responsible for many of the dilemmas and traumas that have destabilized Europe. European musicians depend on the nation but struggle to liberate themselves from its symbolic borders. Both at home and abroad there is capital to be had, but there is also great danger in investing in the nation, not to mention nationalism. Music, as a context for the nation, serves all of the contradictory ends that the Euro represents. Borders— real, imagined, invented, and virtual—shape and reshape the ways in which music represents the nation and enhances its worth. Music can make the issues of nationalism more real and at the same time complicate them by shrouding them in myth. The introduction of the Euro on 1 January 2002, as I write these lines, symbolizes a sort of ethnographic present for this book, in which Europe competes with its constitutive nations. Music marks this ethnographic present, all the more so because it reminds us so powerfully of the past, the fact that Europe has been here before, competing to overcome the nationalism upon which it depends. As we listen to the music of Europe and its nations, therefore, we experience both the historical past and the ethnographic present, and the ways they interact as music and nationalism combine in the making of modern Europe.

Europe does not lend itself easily to ethnomusicological examination as a single global region distinguished by cultural unity or a unified history. Indeed, one of ethnomusicology's paradigmatic shifts in the mid-twentieth century, which was in many ways crucial for shaping its modern identity as a scholarly discipline, was a turn away from Europe. Much, if not most, previous scholarly attention mustered for what was then called **Vergleichende Musikwissenschaft,** or "comparative musicology," took European music as the yardstick for measuring all other musics of the world. The historical processes of European music, say, the belief that music becomes more complex as history unfolds and societies develop, were used to impose notions of civilization on other cultural areas. European concepts and categories of music were applied to other music cultures, and European musical scholars accompanied colonial armies and Christian missionaries as they spread about the globe discovering "folk music," the pride of a European metaphysics of authenticity. By the end of World War II and the onset of the postcolonial disintegration of European military and political dominance of the rest of the world, European concepts for measuring the world's musics were exposed as threadbare, not just for so-called non-Western music but also for European music itself. European ethnomusicologists began increasingly to turn inward, to their own regional and, especially, historical traditions, and Europeanist ethnomusicology devolved into a constellation of national institutions, many espousing nationalist agendas.

With this volume in the ABC-CLIO World Music Series I return to Europe as a whole, that is, as a cultural and musical area that deserves our attention for what it is as much as for what it once was. The debates and ideological issues unleashed by the introduction of the Euro are not anachronistic symptoms of a continent in cultural death throes but signs of cultural vitality and the ongoing struggle to reimagine Europe as a region with contemporary global significance. The Euro might well succeed in providing new financial and cultural glue for Europe, and it may help to heal the wounds remaining from a century when Europe's internal and colonial struggles were devastating for most of the world's peoples. More important than whether the Euro engenders European unity is whether it draws attention to the ways in which wholeness might be achieved at some level. It is to determine just how music symbolizes that wholeness, and more actively contributes to its formation and maintenance, that this book examines the ways in which music and nationalism interact to make modern Europe. These two foci—music and nationalism—are powerfully implicated in Europe's past and in the shaping of its future.

Approaching Europe as a cultural and musical whole is a daunting task for the ethnomusicologist. Does one write a volume that is representative in some way, giving equal coverage to as many nations and musical cultures as possible? Or does one, in contrast, plead for the special role that certain types of music and musicians, say, folk music or nationalist composers, play in the construction of the nation? Does one aim for the semblance of an all-encompassing approach, or does one admit to the necessary compromises and state one's disclaimers from the beginning? Frankly, my own approach might be described as "none of the above." Instead, I am adopting and adapting ethnomusicological approaches that grow from historical discourses about Europe's wholeness and respond to contemporary debates about Europe's unity. By focusing on both music and nationalism, I approach Europe as an historian and an ethnographer.

As with other volumes in the ABC-CLIO World Music Series, this volume is shaped by on-the-ground encounter with musicians and music cultures and reveals the methodological pitfalls and potential that accompany ethnography. From the outset, it is necessary to recognize that no ethnomusicologist can undertake fieldwork across an entire continent. Clearly, I know some parts of Europe better than others, and my familiarity with repertories and the contexts of music-making is stronger in some European nations than in others. The challenge of music ethnography is not one of whether the fieldworker has spent any time in Latvia or Portugal, or if the Iberian Peninsula receives the same amount of space in the ethnography as do the Balkans. The fieldwork experiences that lead to a book that takes Europe as a whole as its topic are different, indeed radically different, from local ethnographies, which are in-depth and long-term in a single place. To illustrate why this is so, I might schematically sketch the ethnographic work upon which I have drawn for the present book:

- Intensive studies of European Jewish communities, beginning in 1982
- Collection and analysis of European folk songs, beginning in the mid-1970s
- Community-based studies of folk religion and religious revival since 1989
- Participant-observation on five major foot pilgrimages, accompanied by numerous ethnographies of shrines, from the late 1980s to the present
- Fieldwork at urban sites of street music throughout Europe, beginning in 1989
- In-depth studies of the multicultural border region (Burgenland) shared by Austria, Hungary, and Slovakia, beginning in 1990
- Field trips to the Carpathian Mountains of Romania, 1996 and 1998
- Diaspora studies of European Jewish communities in Israel, beginning in 1980

- Diaspora studies of European ethnic traditional music in North America, ongoing from the mid-1970s until the present
- Integration of European folk, popular, and classical traditions into my own musical performance in the Central European community of Israel, button-box accordion studies in the mid-1990s, establishment and artistic direction for the European Jewish cabaret ensemble, the New Budapest Orpheum Society
- Popular-music research in the institutions of European broadcasting and recording, including irrepressible fandom in annual studies of the Eurovision Song Contest, beginning with the victory of the UK's Buck's Fizz in 1981

These ethnographic experiences may or may not cover enough European turf. Far more important for the consideration of a modern ethnomusicology and an ethnomusicology of modernity is that these experiences arose from and were responses to a set of questions about music and culture that are not primarily connected to older notions of geography and identity. Rather than concerning themselves with musicians and musical life in villages or the performers of specialized repertories and genres, the new questions recognize that many of Europe's musicians are on the move and that they freely incorporate new styles from the mass media. Rather than fixing the language of authenticity, the new questions interpellate the troubled histories that the belief in authenticity has imposed on the culture of modernity, especially the destruction resulting from the Holocaust and colonialism in the twentieth century.

Ethnography and fieldwork have been crucial in this book for another, very simple reason: It is impossible to listen to European music without encountering nationalism. As I argue throughout the book, nationalism contributes fundamentally to the ontology of European music, that is, to music's "ways of being" in Europe. However, I have avoided, assiduously so, stating that all European music is nationalistic. Much is, much is not, but that's not the point. Surely some European musicians have distanced themselves from nationalism, say, composers of the nineteenth and twentieth centuries who strove for what they imagined to be autonomy in music. In quite different ways, there have been nationless musicians (see Chapter 6) in the twentieth century who skirt the borders of national style because of the real physical violence it might bring upon them. But even here, that is, even in the conscious attempts to move away from national identity in music, the specter of nationalism haunts modern practices of folk, popular, and classical music, and that specter travels under the name of "Europe." In a very real, practical sense, it is because of that specter that nationalism shapes the ethnographic field in which we encounter European music today.

The musical encounters upon which I have drawn in shaping this book have not only been ethnographic. Since my first studies of musical practices owing a large measure of their identity to Europe, research on Irish- and German-American musics (see, for example, Bohlman 1980 and Bohlman 1985) and European-Jewish musics that survived the Holocaust (see, for example, Bohlman 1989 and Bohlman 1992), I have consistently worked with archival and historical sources. In particular, I have approached the music of Europe at the intersection of and through the interaction with oral and written traditions. Discovering and collecting musics transmitted orally in the late twentieth century, I have traced tradition through written sources to document history with as much detail as possible. My concern for historical processes shaped from the oral-written nexus has taken me to more archives than many ethnomusicologists. If my ethnographic and historical projects often intersect, they also lead me, often insistently, to projects such as this book on nationalism and music, in which diachronic and synchronic approaches, history and ethnography, past and present, are just as insistently forged together.

The archives in which I have worked are sometimes national and international, for example, the Deutsches Volksliedarchiv in Freiburg im Breisgau, Germany, or the Jewish Music Research Centre at the Jewish National and University Library in Jerusalem. Written sources also occupy regional and local institutions, such as the city and village records that I have visited and revisited in the border regions between Central and Eastern Europe. At even deeper community and personal levels, the research leading to this book has depended on the ways in which musicians and the sites in which they perform—choral ensembles and public stages, dance bands and synagogues, village entrepreneurs and festivals—have shared with me the evidence that allows me to connect their pasts to the changing landscapes of European nationalism. Nationalism cannot, I believe, extricate itself from music history any more than from European history as a whole.

The whole of Europe can only be approached through its parts, indeed, by gathering fragments that do not so much yield a more complete picture of the whole as provide new and unexpected perspectives on the whole. It may well be that Europe has always been approached in this way, with fragments representing the whole. Ancient and modern travelers—Caesar writing his *Gallic Wars,* the Christian diplomats who wrote of their travels into the Ottoman Balkans, the youngest generation of travel writers journeying into Eastern Europe since the fall of communism—assembled images of Europe as viewed from the roads and paths, images that allowed them to reimagine the encounters of those who had passed before. Like the mariner's map charted almost entirely from the ship passing along coastal waters, the whole emerges from the perspective of the journey itself, and it is precisely the whole that does emerge: It was the mariner's map, ultimately, that first brought entire continents into view. The crucial issue I have repeatedly encountered as my research has led me in search of fragments has been one of experiencing Europe on the move, not as a static, bounded continent of discrete nations, but of constant cultural movement and shifting cultures. The nationalism we witness through encounter, therefore, accompanies a long history of complex multiculturalism and mixing and subaltern resistance to the hegemony of the nation-state.

If this book couples music and nationalism to forge a view of Europe as a whole, it also depends on the historical centrality of cosmopolitanism. Europe is a culture of cities, and city culture is crucial to European identities, not least among them, national identities. It is not by rhetorical accident that historians begin discussions of European history with the "city-state" and end with the "nation-state." The city consolidates the nation, but it also provides the geographical conditions that invite the most extensive cultural mix; it supports the institutions central to the state yet requires the constant in-gathering of immigrants from the provinces and beyond to run the institutions.

As an exporter of colonialism and empire, Europe came to depend on the city in ever-changing ways. The spread of European culture to its own peripheries was made possible by routes that connected nodes provided by cities, be they the Hanseatic cities, such as Bergen or Königsberg, that imported Early Modernism to northern Europe or the Habsburg imperial cities, such as Kraków and Czernowitz, that transplanted the Baroque to Eastern Europe. As a final element in the cosmopolitan mix of European nationalism, the city is home to the nationless, not just the new immigrants or the guest workers, but also ethnic, racial, and religious groups consciously excluded from the state, perhaps by denial of land-owning privileges, perhaps by denial of citizenship rights, often by both. European Jewish culture and European Jewish music are perhaps the most obvious case of the dissonant relation between cosmopolitan nationalism and urban culture. Historically, the European city was both utopian and dystopian for its nationless peoples; the city was the symbol of the nation's greatest potential and most immediate danger.

We find the music of the European nation not only in the center but also at its many peripheries and borders, and in the course of the research for this book I have frequently plied boundary regions in order to listen more acutely. The boundary-crossing that ethnography and encounter make possible also has a parallel in the approaches I bring to European music itself. In short, I take all musics of Europe as the topic of this book, and in this way the book offers a conscious departure from most studies of music and nationalism. Most commonly, scholars seek the national in music in one genre or repertory or another, in the overwhelming majority of studies, either in art music or in folk music. There are reasons for such approaches. From a global perspective, that music which we call "European music," particularly in historical, literate contexts, provides the paradigm for "art music," that is, elite traditions. Art music depends to some extent on national institutions, and it frequently furthers discourses about national history, which accordingly generate music histories that elevate art music to "classical music," in other words, to an emblem of a classical, authentic past. Much of the attention given to nationalism and music, it follows, has been devoted to art music, especially traditions of national opera, or to composers who plumb folk music in a small nation that wishes to resist the hegemony of a larger nation or empire (see, for example, Taruskin 2001, especially the bibliography). That other invention of European musical discourse, "folk music," provides the counterpart for identifying and exploiting the national in music. Folk music becomes the property of the nation and the language of national discourse, but only after it is collected and anointed as a canon, the product of age and the icon of agelessness, as a manifestation of the classical.

In this book, both art and folk music retain their importance as discourses of the national center, but I turn also, indeed, above all, to the musics that proliferate at the national peripheries. I examine popular and religious, mediated and authentic musics; I regard the ephemeral as no less crucial for shaping nationalism than the classical; I challenge the reader to consider music that resists nationalism no less than music that celebrates the nation-state. Indeed, I exclude no music from the possibility of serving as a source for national identity. More to the point, I find nationalism in music at the borders between repertories, genres, and practices. These are the sites of hybridity and contested identities; it is here that the landscapes inhabited by displaced and nationless peoples take shape; it is at the borders between musics and nations that the pressing battles over identity are most viciously fought. Music mobilizes the nation and provides a language for its invention. Ultimately, it may well be the true measure of music's significance for nationalism that it provides so many and such fluid contexts for the nation itself.

Ethnography, encounter, and border crossing also raise fundamental questions about competition and confrontation, both of which appear repeatedly in the book. At one level, I examine musical competition in very literal ways. Chapter 1 opens, for example, with a competition, the **Eurovision Song Contest.** The Eurovision is a mass-mediated event that takes place on a musical stage to which all Europeans, at least theoretically, have access. Throughout Europe, there are countless competitions for composers and chamber musicians, military and minority ensembles, folk musicians and rock bands, and in these competitions musicians compete against each other, often to gain the privilege of representing the nation, that is, their nation. I consider the ways in which competitive frameworks generate and channel movements that rally new and different genres to represent the nation, such as the choralism that permeates the Celtic Fringe along the Atlantic and the Baltic states of the northeast. Most of these competitions culminate in international contests in which musicians from one nation compete against those of another, often on stages before international television audiences.

At another level, I consider competition in more metaphorical terms. The myths and narratives of folk music may represent competition between cultures and nations at prehistorical moments, when the **Niebelungen** were not yet German, and the **Kalevala** was not yet a Finnish national epic. Modern competitions, too, provide contexts for musical practices that symbolize the nation and the desire to demonstrate superiority. Music, such as national anthems, is inevitably present when nations compete on the athletic field. War and colonialism, as violent competitions between nations and empires, engender musics that reproduce military competition, for example in the marches or bagpipe repertories that lead nations to war. The metaphorical presence of music at competitions of all kinds notwithstanding, the fundamental point is that music gives metaphor specific functions, which in turn assume concrete forms. Competition, in most basic terms, transforms the national into the nationalist (compare chapters 3 and 4).

Nationalism is a process that is on the move. Thus, when we experience it in the swirling constellation of musics staged in the name of the nation, we are observing it in various stages of transition. Music enhances the mobility that allows nationalism to find lodging in so many different places on the national landscape. Because it is always changing, nationalism has contributed in many ways to the making of modern Europe. I emphasize both the process of making as more construction than construct, that is, as dynamic, creative, activist, and also politically assertive. Modern Europe, too, is constantly changing and responding to the events of the past and present. We may well be able to locate the beginnings of the history of modern Europe, but the process of making modern Europe is ongoing, indeed, intensely so at the beginning of the twenty-first century, when nationalism and music intersect to shape the New Europe, whose forms change even as I describe and address them in this book.

As I trace the intersection of music and nationalism through the historical counterpoint of the book, I deliberately avoid treating nationalism as a single, monolithic force that is somehow "out there." The approach in this book therefore differs from many studies of nationalism because it does not regard nationalism as exceptional: It is not a question of nationalism that exists or does not exist, that one nation turns on and another off. Nationalism is not the marker of some musics while remaining entirely absent from others; it does not simply become extreme at some historical moments but recede at others. Nationalism has many different shades, and by considering many different genres, repertories, and practices of music we attune ourselves to those shades. We experience—and hear—nationalism in the many musics that together give Europe a wholeness that has historically been hegemonic and fragmented, that has forged cultural cooperation and fostered competition, and that has struggled for the very unity that appears in one form on the front of its Euro banknotes, and in another form on the back.

*Philip V. Bohlman*

# Acknowledgments

*Ethnomusicologists encounter* nations and nationalism early in their careers, often early in their lives. There are the nations whose music entices and fascinates; there are the nations whose nationalism earns admiration and contempt. Early travels generate life-long passions, and the chance concert or a recording discovered by accident unleashes an unstoppable desire to collect and learn everything there is to learn, and then some. Fulbright and IREX fellowships (if we're American) take us to other nations, and they do so in the guise of American nationalism (even if we aren't American). The musical relationships we develop with nations and nationalism are positive in the best of times, but there are many times when nations and nationalism intervene to make foreignness an unpleasant liability. For most ethnomusicologists, the early encounters with nations and nationalism follow them for many years to come, often throughout their careers. It's a love-hate relationship, which means that it can't simply be dismissed.

My own encounters with nations and nationalism have been no exception to the rule. The moment I made the decision to embark on a career in ethnomusicology, I confronted the need to chart the world's musics in one way or another, and the map that settled out after I followed paths across various musical landscapes was scored with the ciphers of nations. It was also scarred with the remnants of nationalism. How to sort all this out? How to make sense out of the musics of ethnic Americans (as we called them in the 1970s) and the German-Jewish community of Israel (as I called it in the 1980s)? How to perceive the ways music gave voice to the residents of a New Europe (as we began to call it in the 1990s)?

I do, in fact, have answers to these questions, answers that provide the stuff of these "Acknowledgments." I was fortunate to learn early on that the encounter with nations and nationalism was most meaningful when most human and personal. My journeys to Europe—for research, for lectures, for teaching, for pleasure—are by now literally countless. Those to whom I owe thanks—for advice, for sage wisdom, for criticism, for lessons learned the hard way—are also countless. I've met so many musicians in so many places; I've joined with so many pilgrims on sacred journeys to their shrines; I've knocked on so many doors in search of someone who might have the key to a synagogue or have special insight into the boundary regions between past and present; and I've taught so many students, whose lives have become emblems of New Europeanness. I'd like to thank them all personally, but space won't permit. There are two measures of appreciation that I do, however, want to offer. First, there is this book itself, which would have been impossible without them. Second, they should know that my engagement with music and nationalism in Europe is ongoing; the lessons they taught me are still a vital part of my life and work as an ethnomusicologist.

I am not a European, and I have yet to allow anyone to convince me that I am a Europeanist. I am an outsider, a non-European, with no ethnic, national, or nationalist ties to Europe. None of the musics I discuss in this book is my own, even the several styles, genres, and repertories that I play as a musician. Still, had I not found various homes in Europe, the book would have been very different. My temporary homes in Europe are several, but those who made me feel at home, even temporarily, are legion. My first European home, as this book amply makes clear, was the German Folk-Song Archive (Deutsches Volksliedarchiv) in Freiburg im Breisgau, where I learned about German (and Jewish and Alsatian and Yiddish and Austrian and Turkish—so much for the DVA's nationalism) music from Barbara Boock, Jürgen Dittmar, Ali Osman Öztürk, and Michaela Zwenger. Most of all, Freiburg has become a home because of Otto Holzapfel and Inge Holzapfel, who so brilliantly and warmly confuse friendship and collegial relationships.

My second home in Europe has been and will be Vienna, most of all because it is a city where one can feel at home but never be at home, as a foreigner. Friendships and intellectual exchange, therefore, become all the more intense. Home in Vienna became the Institut für Volksmusikforschung und Ethnomusikologie and the Institut für Musikwissenschaft, the first at the Universität für Musik und darstellende Kunst, the second at the University of Vienna. Faculty, staff, and researchers at those institutions, especially Oskár Elschek, Franz Födermayr, Gerlinde Haid, Ursula Hemetek, Emil Lubej, and Michael Weber were and are marvelous colleagues. Roland Mahr and Rudolf Pietsch have been far more than colleagues—not only friends but mentors who drew me into music at Europe's center. Two years after her death, I still mourn the passing of Franziska Pietsch-Stockhammer, whose gentle voice speaks to me so powerfully of what Europe must be.

Other temporary homes have allowed me to draw closer to Europe. In Italy, that most non-European of European cities, Venice, now seduces me year after year to its window on the East. The Fondacione Ugo e Olga Levi flings that window open, and Tullia Magrini and my colleagues in the International Council for Traditional Music Study Group for the Anthropology of Music of the Mediterranean join me as we consider Europe from the shores encountered by its Others in Africa and Asia. In recent years, I have visited London and Newcastle upon Tyne with some frequency, in part for conversations with UK colleagues such as Paul Attinello, Michael Berkowitz, Ian Biddle, Julie Brown, Ann Buckley, Stefano Castelvecchi, Martin Clayton, Victoria Cooper, Ruth Davis, John Deathridge, Alex Knapp, Richard Middleton, Paul Nixon, Goffredo Plastino, and Henry Stobart. With new and renewed European invitations to Berlin, Copenhagen, Newcastle upon Tyne, and Vienna, it seems that I'll be a visitor for years to come.

I doubt, nonetheless, that I'll settle into domestic comfort, for so much of what Europe is for me lies along its borders. Again and again, I take my research to the boundary regions, where I encounter the soft underbelly of European nationalism. In Burgenland, I traverse the borders with Walter Burian and Gabi Burian, also with Roland Mahr, Martina Blaschek, and Sepp Gmasz. Whether Ute Bosbach and Hansrainer Bosbach really travel with me to geographical borders is not the question; generation after generation—three and counting—their German family is part of my own. My Carpathian sojourners make an extended appearance in Chapter 6, but let me here again acknowledge Rudolf Pietsch, Tamás Repiszky, and Roland Mahr. It is in Romania that a *Grenzgänger* of a different sort lives and works, when he is not in Chicago. Together with my Romanian friend and colleague Marin Marian Bălaşa I have so many sojourns lying before me.

Historically, the University of Chicago has been friendly toward one of the "two Europes" I discuss in Chapter 1 but not toward the other. Western Civilization, Great Books, and European art music have been standard fare, while those displaced by the spread of empires, oral tradition, and folk and popular music have been treated often with distaste. The situation has shifted dramatically during my seventeen years at Chicago, and this book bears witness to that sea change. I am indebted to many for the change, especially my many student-mentors whose thinking always challenges me to look to the future. In the course of writing the book, moreover, my debt has increased to my colleague, Martin Stokes, that other non-Europeanist Europeanist in the music department. I have been extremely fortunate to benefit from the watchful eye of my unpaid research assistant and Berlin correspondent, Andrea F. Bohlman, who plies me with a steady stream of references from the internet. Jeffers Engelhardt, Aibhlín Dillane, David Hunter, and Jacqueline Jones assisted me in the final stages of writing, enriching the bibliography and thinking through the CD as a musical, not simply musicological, document.

One does not visit and revisit Europe as often as I have without the generosity of fellowships and foundations. I gratefully acknowledge and thank the American Academy in Berlin, Alexander von Humboldt Foundation (Research Fellowship and Transatlantic Cooperation Grant), the National Endowment for the Humanities (Summer Stipend and Fellowship for University Teachers), Council for the International Exchange of Scholars (Fulbright Guest Professorship at the University of Vienna), Internationales Forschungszentrum Kulturwissenschaften in Vienna, DAAD (Deutscher Akademischer Austauschdienst), and IREX (International Research and Exchanges Board).

The ABC-CLIO "World Music Series" was the brainchild of Alicia Merritt, and she wisely turned to Michael Bakan as an ethnomusicologist with the appropriate vision and the necessary hard questions to make its potential so great. Had anyone else approached me to suggest an ethnomusicological monograph on some aspect of the whole of Europe, I'd surely have found it too daunting. I still find it too daunting, but Alicia and Michael have helped me muster the ideas necessary to make the impossible challenging and very exciting indeed.

Whenever I accomplish anything, it is because Andrea, Ben, and Christine were there with me. This book is no exception. I've lost count of the times we spent a month, a summer, or a year in Europe together. Andrea and Ben have had to endure German and Austrian schools; they have had to indulge their father in places where every language we spoke was foreign; they had to ride on my shoulders at circuses, parades, operas, and seemingly endless performances of nationalism. I never got tired, and I have the feeling they did not either, for both are about to take off for sojourns of their own in Europe as I write these lines. At every stage of this book's preparation Christine endured even more than the rest of us. If we were outsiders and foreigners, she bore the brunt of what that really meant. It's for that reason, however, that she asked the hardest questions and became the keenest observer. Christine—always—was there, also during the extended period of serious illness that paralleled my work on the final chapters of this book. Her courage and love inspired this book, just as it has always inspired me.

# Note on Translation and the Glossary

All translations, transliterations, and transcriptions are those of the author unless otherwise noted. Some translations appeared first in translations into non-English languages other than the original, and these in turn served as an intermediary prior to the author's translation into the English that appears in the book. Transliteration decisions emphasize consistency in the English spellings whenever possible, thus necessitating occasional adjustments when using contradictory rules.

For the most part, English words that appear in the glossary are italicized only when they first occur in the text, though occasionally upon their second or even third occurrence, particularly if several chapters have intervened and if the word or concept is especially uncommon or important.

# Chapter One

# Music and Nationalism

## *Why Do We Love to Hate Them?*

### The Eurovision Song Contest
### at the Beginning of Our Millennium

*I love the Eurovision Song Contest. I love it for its magnificent foolishness, its grand illusion that it brings together the diverse peoples and cultures of Europe on one great wing of song, when all it makes manifest is how far apart everybody is.*
—*Terry Wogan (Gambaccini et al. 1998: 7)*

As I begin to consider the path along which this book will pass on its way to completion, the annual crescendo of competition and hype that precede the 2002 **Eurovision Song Contest** is well under way. The national broadcasting networks of the **European Broadcasting Union** (EBU) have announced most of the national entries, and the local, national, and international websites are abuzz with rumors, predictions, and the politics of the largest popular-music competition in the world. The Forty-Seventh Eurovision Song Contest (ESC) on 24 May 2002 marks a watershed. This year for the first time ever, the ESC is taking place in Eastern Europe—in Tallinn, Estonia, whose national entry won the ESC in 2001. When the ESC was founded in 1956, one of the most crucial years of the Cold War, the "Europe" of the Eurovision Song Contest was Western Europe. It was not until after the Velvet Revolution in 1989 that Eastern European nations other than West-leaning Yugoslavia (winner of the ESC in 1989) would begin to take their place on the competitive stage of European popular song. With Estonia's victory for Eastern Europe the circle was complete. Song has unified Europe, achieving a unity that even the European Union itself has

1

yet to achieve. The Eurovision Song Contest has twenty-four participants, the European Union still only fifteen. Musically, the ESC has
also fostered a sense of common culture that the European monetary
system has yet to manage, the promise of the Euro notwithstanding.

*National Entries in the 2002 Eurovision Song Contest*

Austria—Manuel Ortega: "Say a Word"
Belgium—Sergio & the Ladies: "Sister"
Bosnia-Herzegovina—Maja Tatić: "Na jastuku za dvoje"
Croatia—Vesna: "Everything I Want"
Cyprus—One: "Gimme"
Denmark—Malene: "Tell Me Who You Are"
Estonia—Sahlene: "Runaway"
Finland—Laura: "Addicted to You"
France—Sandrine François: "Il faut du temps"
Germany—Corinna May: "I Can't Live . . ."
Greece—Mihalis Rakintzis: "SAGAPO"
Israel—Sarit Hadad: "Light a Candle"
Latvia—Marie N: "I Wanna"
Lithuania—Aivaras: "Happy You"
Malta—Ira Losco: "Seventh Wonder"
Macedonia—Karolina: "Od nas zavisi"
Romania—Anghel & Pavel: "Tell Me Why"
Russia—Prime Minister: "Northern Girl"
Slovenia—Sestre: "Samo ljubezen"
Spain—Rosa: "Europe's Living a Celebration"
Switzerland—Françine Jordi: "Dans le jardin"
Sweden—Afro-dite: "Never Let It Go"
Turkey—Safir: "Leylaklar Soldu Kalbinde"
United Kingdom—Jessica Garlick: "Come Back"
    (*Eurovision Song Contest Tallinn 2002*, 2002)

At no other moment during the year does Europe come together as
completely as during the Eurovision Song Contest. ESC organizers and
promoters both within and outside the sponsoring organization, the
European Broadcasting Union, make much of the event's potential to
unify, repeatedly trotting out an array of statistics that document ESC
audiences at well over 100 million, larger than for any other cultural or

athletic event in Europe. Particularly in small nations, for whom the stakes of a good showing are very high, it is not uncommon for the entire country effectively to shut down so that everyone has an opportunity to watch the broadcast—at home, in a tavern or at a dance hall, or on one of the massive screens erected in stadiums and other public spaces, often on the grounds of governmental buildings.

> *I could die for you,*
> *Look into my eyes and know it's true.*
> —Antique: "Die for You"
> 2001 Eurovision entry for Greece

To witness the ESC is to be swept into one of the most ecstatic experiences of music and nationalism, riveted by the transnational imaginary of global music-making. The baldly commercial nature of much pre-ESC hype notwithstanding, the events leading up to the final broadcast make it almost impossible to escape the allure of a nation symbolized through its music. Riding the bus through the countryside or cruising the suburban shopping mall, Europeans hear the competing entries played over and over, increasingly stirring up hopes that their own nations will win and that competing nations will have a poor showing. On the night of the ESC, nations come virtually to a halt, say, as the Irish take to the pub, gathering in front of its television as if captured in the trance of a techno-session, or as Israelis come together at the close of the Sabbath in the traditional religious ritual of *motze shabbat,* this time with family and friends intent on sharing the ritual broadcast of the ESC.

The experience of listening demands a deeply physical response to the nation. It is unthinkable to watch the ESC alone. Plans are made to gather together, more often than not in some public space. Some, like the pub, are intimate, but others, like the mammoth broadcast screen at the end of a major public square in Europe's largest cities, are imbued with the energy of full-blown spectacle. It is equally unthinkable not to join with fellow viewers who share some measure of belief that song can stir a common national pride. Watching the ESC is not unlike viewing an international soccer match: The quality of play or performance, athleticism or musicianship notwithstanding, in the end it's all about winning. In the public squares of Tallinn, Berlin, and Barcelona, alcohol flows and crowds become rowdy. In the taverns where Irish,

Croatians, or Romanians gather, the rise and fall of national vocal fortunes produce wild mood swings—unmitigated celebration some years, the stupor of disappointment in others. Dispassionate reaction to the ESC virtually does not exist. Even those who reject its overt display of kitsch and patriotism make no bones about the fact that they love to hate the ESC.

The broadcast of the ESC, therefore, is a moment of high nationalism. Staged in one of the largest concert facilities of the host country, the winner from the previous year, the broadcast unfolds over the course of a Saturday night in May as a series of vignettes about national entries and their countries, performances of national entries, and commentary about past winners and historical trends. ESC hosts, for example, England's Terry Wogan, are themselves sometimes greater stars than the musicians who perform. The ESC, nevertheless, has the potential to change all that, for it has launched its share of international stars, among the most notable, Abba, Ofra Haza, and Céline Dion. It is not lost upon most viewers that the Big Night of the ESC has many of the trappings of a beauty pageant or Academy Awards ceremony. Host nations, nonetheless, leave their own imprint on the presentation, as in 2001, when the Danish hosts recited the whole evening's presentation in verse reminiscent of an epic. In 2002, the Estonian hosts interspersed the live performances with "postcards," each one of which portrayed a fairytale in a modern Estonian setting, cleverly mixing myth and nation with cultural tourism. The medium itself, a competition broadcast from a stage, is surely inseparable from the message, popular music as national pride.

Competing nations may or may not invest heavily to support their nations. Winning nations, however, usually commit themselves to considerable expenses. For the 2002 competition it was necessary for Estonia to build an entirely new concert center—"necessary" because the contest would have stayed in Copenhagen another year if Estonia had not been able to host it. Originally, the Estonian broadcasting network fell short of the necessary commitment of almost $4 million by 25 percent, but within months of its 2001 victory, the Baltic state known for its "Singing Revolution" at the end of the communist era was able to display its national pride and capitalist prowess. In 2002, with an East European national host and national broadcasting authority in place, the unity of the Eurovision Song Contest is complete. The entries from Eastern Europe are already in place, among them Bosnia-Herzegovina,

Croatia, Macedonia, Romania, Russia, and Slovenia, and of course the Baltic states, Estonia, Latvia, and Lithuania.

*If for one second you'd remember me,*
*and I would break free from the chains*
*that are wrapped around me.*

—Nusa Derenda: "Energy"
2001 Eurovision Entry for Slovenia

In spite of the enormous popularity and visibility of the Eurovision Song Contest, not to mention its complex history paralleling that of the Cold War and the revolutions that have yielded the New Europe of the past decade, the ESC is never mentioned in discussions of European nationalism. Though participating musicians and national broadcasting networks flaunt national labels, many skeptics dismiss the ESC as globalized pop designed to make money in the name of the nation. Skeptics commonly argue that the songs, the musicians, and musical styles that cut across the international entries have little to do with the nation and even less with good taste in music. If one talks about the Eurovision to academics in Europe (as I have), one is greeted by smiles and snickers, and not infrequently by dismissive derision. How could such insipid songs evoke nationalism? What about the frequent drafting of non-national musicians, such as Canadian Céline Dion for Switzerland in 1988 and Afro-Caribbean Dave Benton for Estonia in 2001? Is there any meaning at all in the frequent use of texts filled with nonsense syllables, such as the Italian Domenico Modugno's 1958 "Nel blu dipinto di blu" with its refrain, "Volare, wo ho ho ho," which nonetheless remains one of the most memorable of all Eurovision entries?

It is easy enough to counter the skeptics, making the case for the presence of the nation and nationalism in ESC songs. Without question, there are songs whose message begins and ends as a love song, and these songs often win or place very high in the final standings. There are also songs that have a powerfully political message, which usually means that they place very low in the final standings. Since the mid-1990s, when the Balkan nations managed to submit entries despite ongoing war with Serbia, they have woven clear political statements into their songs, abandoning reasonable chances of winning. Minority politics often seem to have been erased from the ESC entries, but then there was the recent occasion in 1999 when Sürpriz, a singer from Germany's large Turkish labor force, represented Germany. The real question, then, may not be why there is or is not nationalism at certain moments in the ESC, but rather why music and nationalism interact in such remarkably varied ways. In some ways, this is the question that unifies this book.

> 'Cause God knows I love you so,
> so much I'm going to die!
> . . . Tell me, would it be all right
> only to be alive?
>
> —Nino Prceć: "Hano"
> 2001 Eurovision Entry for Bosnia-Herzegovina

If we are willing to listen, the half-century history of the Eurovision Song Contest tells us a great deal about Europe and its modern history. At virtually every crucial moment of European history, the ESC was present, revealing something about the national politics of the moment. The years 1956 and 1989 were critical in European history, specifically in the history of the Cold War, and they were for the ESC as well. In 2002, as Middle Eastern political and military violence escalate beyond control, the Israeli entry, Sarit Hadad's "Light a Candle," an encomium for peace, has stirred up the greatest controversy as the European Union struggles to broker power between Israel and Palestine. The very real conflicts between European unity and nationalist disunity play out again and again on the stage of the ESC, sometimes during the same evening that love-song crooners and hard rockers are plying their trade with entries devoid of political or national content.

> Whoever lives love will never die.
> Whoever lives love is never alone.
>
> —Michelle: "Wer Liebe lebt"
> 2001 Eurovision Entry for Germany

Is it a matter of musical style? Yes and no. Some national entries consciously employ a style associated with specific nations. Others avoid national style entirely. Still others negotiate national styles because they choose to perform in one of the international languages preferred, but since the early 1970s not required, for Eurovision entries.

ESC musical styles follow several different paths, all of which place the nation on the competitive stage in distinctive ways. At one extreme of a continuum are the nations that prefer a song style that will be understood as their own. Folk music serves such ends quite effectively, but basing an entry on folk-music style deprives the entry of any chance of winning. As a compromise, specific markers of national style might be woven into a song texture that is otherwise global. Bosnia-Herzegovina's 2001 entry, Nino's "Hano," employs both Serbo-Croatian texts and samples of a Turkish light-classical orchestra to mix the European and the Middle East, the Christian and the Muslim. Sometimes nationalist hybridity of this kind offers advantages. Audiences and judges expect an Irish entry to sound Irish, though similar expectations do not extend to, say, Swedish entries. At the other end of a stylistic continuum we find songs that borrow from global-pop and worldbeat vocabularies, not least among them past and present African American musical styles. A mixture of such styles spread across the national entries in 2000 and 2001, and the domination of that mixture unquestionably heightened the chances for Estonia's Tanel Padar, Dave Benton, and 2XL, whose winning entry, "Everybody," mixes Jamaican dancehall with African American Southern vernacular styles. The growing presence of African American and other styles, however, is not primarily a sign of globalization but a vehicle for opening the ESC to the New Europe's multiculturalism (see Chapter 7).

At one end of the continuum African-American styles function not so differently from folk music at the other. The musical styles of the Eurovision Song Contest are therefore remarkable because of their comprehensiveness. It is possible to come to the ESC with virtually any style of popular music and to draw from a staggering range of repertories. Both Europe and its constituent nations find their place in these styles in different ways, and they negotiate the relation between the national and international by making conscious and subconscious choices. The stylistic diversity also complicates questions about what winning as a form of nationalism really means. The most political songs, say those entered by Balkan nations at war, achieve victory even by reaching the ESC stage. In a different way, Estonia's 2001 victory was of enormous nationalistic significance, for the nation and for all of Eastern Europe, and if a celebratory song in Jamaican dancehall helped a Baltic nation-state achieve that end, we must also understand it as a case of wearing nationalism on the nation's sleeve. This was a nationalism that could hardly be lost on the audiences and judges of the Eurovision Song Contest.

> *Come on everybody, let's sing along,*
> *and feel the power of a song.*
> *Come on everybody, let's feel the spark,*
> *that always burns within our heart.*
>
> —Tanal Padar, Dave Benton, and 2XL: "Everybody"
> 2001 Eurovision Entry for Estonia and "Grand Prix" Winner

Though it contains moments of the highest nationalism and the lowest kitsch, we should not forget that the ESC is also spectacle, and therein, too, lies its power to unify. The contest's spectators feel themselves a part of their nations when they are watching the performances. They indulge in regional biases and reinforce national prejudices. Hated enemies earn the usual scorn (such as that between Greece and Turkey), and perennial favorites receive their perennial sympathy votes, the merits of their songs notwithstanding (for example, the Baltic states). There are spectators who might wish that the entrenched powerhouses such as the UK would give smaller nations a chance, but then the powerhouses prove yet again how and why they win with such frequency.

Significantly, spectators are not just passive viewers. They, too, participate in the arbitration of music and nationalism that culminates annually in the ESC. Initially, they can play various roles on the local and national levels, participating in the official and unofficial voting that eventually leads to the decisions made when the national competition takes place. They listen to entries on the radio, buy demos and cover versions, click on websites, and generally make their voices known. Participation at the local and national levels differs from country to country. Israelis, as I learned during 1980–1982, when I lived in Jerusalem, are deeply involved; Austrians, as I learned in 1995–1996 and 1999, when I lived in Vienna, are generally unaware of the decision-making process. When the competition moves to the national plane, however, spectator involvement increases exponentially. At this stage, the national broadcasting authorities assume active control over the entries, and they enter into a stage of musical diplomacy with their sister organizations. Managing the ESC from its earliest years in the mid-1950s, the European Broadcasting Union facilitates the musical exchange and border-crossing that acquire more and more European trappings.

*I can fly over mountains, over seas.*
*I've never felt so free in the choices of my life.*
—Michelle: "Out on My Own"
2001 Eurovision Entry for the Netherlands

Finally, there is the ESC's Big Night in May, when the number of EBU networks connecting each nation's citizens to the spectacle of European performance is the greatest. One by one, the groups are presented, first as sympathetic and loyal citizens of their nations, and then as performers with the potential to become international pop stars. After the performances, the voting begins. Throughout much of its history, ESC voting was undertaken by national committees, who called in their results after the final performances. Each committee ranked the performers, leaving its own national entry out of the ranking. More recently, the national committees respond to the voting of their own national audiences, who vote using various electronic media, including internet polls that are both official and unofficial. All forums for the voicing of public opinion yield results that the national committees total, then read off in televised phone calls from Madrid, Dublin, or Helsinki. Every attempt is made to project fairness and decision-making based on musical qualities.

As the votes are tallied, Europe is exercising a cultural democracy more universal and grassroots in character than any of its election rituals. The European Song Contest, one might fairly argue, depends on greater democracy and more committed unity than the European Union. The fissures, however, begin to show as the vote totals come into view. National pride and nationalist prejudice go hand in hand once again. As in all competitions, it is not necessarily the best song that wins, but rather one that articulates the historical moment. European unity is not affirmed; a more historical fragility, however, is. And so, the popular music performed at the European Song Contest aspires once again to portray Europe itself, capable of celebrating its present and future, but in so doing, the ESC reveals that the old fault lines are still present, with new ones coming into view as the real possibility of victory spreads to the Baltic states and someday beyond. The question that remains to be posed and answered in this book, then, is how song consciously endowed with the potential to pull Europe together in unity contributes to the nationalism that endangers that unity, today no less insistently than it has during the course of modern European history.

Before turning to that question, however, I pause momentarily on 25 May 2002 to acknowledge the winner of yesterday's Eurovision Song Contest in Estonia: Latvia's Marie N, who sang "I Wanna." There can be little question that the nations of Eastern Europe have fully embraced the implicit and explicit nationalism that attends the ESC in the twenty-first century.

> *I'd like to go away, but it's easier to say*
> *that you know all the tricks that make me stay. . . .*
> *Today you think you are the winner,*
> *today you think you are the king.*
> —Marie N: "I Wanna"
> 2002 Eurovision Entry for Latvia and "Grand Prix" Winner

## Music, Nationalism, and "The Voices of the People in Songs"

*Song loves the masses, the combined voices of many: It requires the ear of the listener and a chorus of voices and all that is joyous.*
 —*Johann Gottfried Herder* (**Volkslieder** *1778–1779: 167*)

A remarkably diverse cast of characters gathers on the stage of history to give voice to music and nationalism in the making of modern Europe. The Eurovision Song Contest, as we have just seen, requires not just hundreds of performers and thousands of organizers, but also millions, even hundreds of millions, of Europeans willing to gaze upon the musical performance of nations. The ESC, however, is hardly an isolated phenomenon. Nations are collectives, and music often musters a collective at the moment of performance. If music truly does shape the nation by resonating with what Johann Gottfried Herder, in the first volume ever devoted to folk music and modern nationalism (Herder 1778–1779), called the "voices of the people in songs," then both quantity and volume combine forces to articulate the modern nation. On the eve of modernity, that is, in the Enlightenment of late eighteenth-century Europe, it was not the music of the few but rather of the masses that sang of the nation in its most fully recognizable form.

Discussions of music and nationalism most often focus on the elite or the marginal, in other words, the castes of composers and ethnic or racial outsiders whose music consciously or unconsciously represents the nation or challenges the nation. Nationalism in music, according to Carl Dahlhaus, one of the most influential music historians of the late twentieth century, is evident in the nebulous qualities of the nation, "the spirit of the people in musical sound" (Dahlhaus 1980: 101). In a magisterial survey of nationalism and music Richard Taruskin expands upon Dahlhaus's nineteenth-century and Austro-German themes, extending them to Eastern Europe and to a more variegated range of ideologies that generate forms and repertories of musical expression, particularly in the twentieth century, among them colonialist nationalism, tourist nationalism, and neo-nationalism (Taruskin 2001).

In the present book, nationalism assumes much more down-to-earth forms, and the people who employ it to express national identities do so much more actively. It is their voices we hear, their actions we witness. They dance the folk dances and rally to the military marches. They join together in choruses, and they form communities of worshipers mobilized through song. Their songs fill the volumes gathered by nineteenth-century collectors, and their votes determine the winners of competitions at twentieth-century folk festivals. They take songbooks on pilgrimages and to war. Their spectatorship each May is fundamental to the overwhelming popularity of the Eurovision Song Contest.

If we experience music and nationalism in the voices of the people, not just in their spirit, we also recast the ways in which music participates in the making of modern Europe. Just as there are more individual European people involved, so too are there more European musics. The question is not which genres or repertories are nationalist, but how musicians weave their own national identities in the many musics they create and reproduce. Nationalism no longer enters music from the top, that is from state institutions and ideologies; it may build its path into music from just about any angle, as long as there are musicians and audiences willing to mobilize cultural movement from those angles. In this book, I am far more often concerned with the multitude of angles than I am with the top-down trajectories that motivate most scholars to address European music and nationalism by considering operas, tone poems, and character pieces that borrow what they might imagine to be authentic languages from the nation's people. Folk music, too, finds its way into discussions of music and nationalism, but again as a cultural artifact that is appropriated for the loftier purposes of representing the nation-state.

It is the thesis of this book that we can experience nationalism in any music at any time. Music is malleable in the service of the nation not because it is a product of national and nationalist ideologies, but rather because musics of all forms and genres can articulate the processes that shape the state. Music can narrate national myths and transform them to nationalist histories. Music marks national borders, while at the same time mobilizing those wishing to cross or dismantle borders. Music enhances the sacred qualities of the nation, and it can secularize religion so that it conforms to the state. There is, then, no single place to experience the interaction of music and nationalism.

Quite deliberately, I have begun by examining a competition at which the national entrants perform popular music, probably the most frequently overlooked domain of nationalism in music, at least in Europe. The reader should be forewarned that the ESC is only the first of many unexpected places to which I journey in this book. Already in the first chapter, we make brief sojourns at street festivals, museums, and international anthems. These places of intersecting music and nationalism chart a complex musical and ideological landscape across Europe, a landscape that each chapter represents in different ways until, with the final chapter, we encounter a New Europe that often staggers under the weight of its own nationalist heritage. At that point, our own ethnographic present, new musicians step in, combining music and nationalism to shape a New Europe.

Ethnography, encounter, and border crossing raise fundamental questions about competition and confrontation, both of which appear repeatedly in the book. At one level, I examine musical competition in very literal ways. I consider contests in which musicians compete against each other, often to represent the nation. In several chapters we examine the ways in which competitive frameworks generate choral movements. I also set the historical stage with the international contests, such as the Eurovision Song Contest, in which musicians from one nation compete against those of another.

At another level, I consider competition in more metaphorical terms. The myths and narratives of folk music may represent competition between cultures and nations at prehistorical moments. Music, such as national anthems, may be present when nations compete on the athletic field. Musical competition between nations may result from the different types of colonialism in the nineteenth and twentieth centuries. Competition, in most basic terms, transforms the national into the nationalist. Finally, I turn frequently to competition because, though on its surface it is about those who "get into the nation," it reveals a great deal about those who are marginalized or, even more critically, have been historically excluded.

The people whose voices give rise to modern Europe's songs have historically occupied a very crowded political and ideological landscape. Frequently, they have had to compete for land, a competition that often instigated border disputes, unleashed war, or spawned imperialism. Figuratively and literally, the competition for land in Europe also spills over into other forms of competition, not least among them the musical competitions that fill the pages of this book. Sometimes, competition means that the voices of some people will drown out those of others; at other times, competition may provide a means for opposing voices to coexist; almost always, competitions provide ways of accommodating large numbers of people in times of national crisis or celebration. The competition, finally, is the musical and cultural event that levels the differences between the people of the nation. Class distinctions are not eliminated but perhaps put on hold, religious and sectarian conflicts subside, and the social gap between center and periphery is narrowed, all to make audible the voices of people in songs.

## Music between the Two Europes

*When we speak about Europe today and attempt to establish just how this great and famous continent came to be, we must not forget that there are two Europes. In addition to the classical West European, grandiose and museumized, historical and pathetic, Europe there lives a second Europe, humble and cowering in the corner, for centuries repressed at the peripheries.*
*—Miroslav Krleža (Wieser 2001: 6)*

Two Europes have historically competed for the music of the nation. The two Europes assume many forms, which in turn enhance the degree and ways in which they compete for the music of the nation. The general shapes and functions of the two nations, nonetheless, have certain attributes that make them recognizable wherever and whenever we encounter them. In their different ways they compete for music by yielding musical practices, repertories, and identities that are both national and nationalist.

The first Europe is the Europe of the whole. The names and labels given to the first Europe draw attention to some aspects of wholeness. The first Europe is foremost a continent with geographical unity. Its religious history, in practical and idealized forms, also demonstrates unity, principally as the product of Christianity. The first Europe asserts itself through claims to a common culture at a continental level, be it more global, as in "Western Civilization," or more bounded by Europe itself, as in "European art music," which is for all intents and purposes also "Western art music."

The second Europe is the Europe of parts. The names and labels given to the second Europe stress the ways in which the parts do or do not fit together. Unlike the unity of the first Europe, geography parses the second Europe into regions and zones: East and West; North and South; Mediterranean and alpine; Nordic and Slavic; Romance and Germanic. Civilization and culture also assume regional, often parochial, forms, which reflect a sense that competition for European history or music can produce winners and losers. Religion in the second Europe is more diverse. It splits into many more sects and denominations, many of which exhibit extensive intolerance, particularly at the borders at which religions have met and for which they have competed. Religious strife, much of it generated by Christianity's claims to Europe, has repeatedly ripped apart the seams of the Balkans, transforming southeastern Europe into the classic region of the second Europe. The adjective "European" is rarely explicit as a denominator of cultural practices in the parts of the second Europe, partly because of the desire to diminish indebtedness to other parts or to the first Europe itself, as when the English claim that they are not really Europeans. If the term "European" occurs rarely, one nonetheless finds frequent use of terms from the second Europe itself, such as "balkanization," which in international parlance refers to conditions of dysfunctional divisiveness.

The two Europes assume many other forms that, to greater and lesser degrees, reflect the distinction between a whole and parts. Economically, for example, there is a Europe that has unified mercantile and industrial strength, which has historically afforded it the role of the "First World." All Europeans, even most Europeans, however, have not been the beneficiaries of such economic might, leaving them in the position of a "Fourth World." The division between first and fourth worlds produces other divisions, for example, between South and

North, East and West. Europe's compass distinctions, moreover, have been among the most persistent rubrics for separating the two Europes. To the West go attributes such as industrial might, colonial power, and, for our purposes in the present book, "Western music." It is not that the same attributes are absent in the East, but there they fail to cohere, largely because of a persistent need to compete with the West for them.

At the turn of our own century, from the twentieth to the twenty-first, the differences between the two Europes seem, if anything, more pronounced than ever. At the very least, cultural and political institutions functioning under the public rubric of "European" remain committed to supporting, even exacerbating, the existence of two Europes, often in the cause of unity. From its earliest formation as a post–World War II trade and defense organization, the European Union has both supported and divided the continent. During the Cold War era, the European Union and its predecessor, the European Economic Community, represented the West but not the East, which was unifying in other ways, particularly the international socioeconomic alliances of Communism. European unity failed to come swiftly to the European Union, and it is hardly surprising that refining the processes of real unity today remains a highly contested political issue. In 1952 there were only six countries in the proto-EU, but even a half-century later, at the time of this writing, the total had expanded only by an additional nine to reach the current total of fifteen. That total pales in comparison with the more than twenty European nations that are not members of the EU (the exact number depends on whether countries such as Cyprus or small nations such as Liechtenstein are or are not aligned with Europe). Most of the non-member states lie in Eastern Europe, though there are the notable holdouts in Western Europe, such as Norway and Switzerland.

The political philosophy of the EU and the institutional structures that put it in play represent and emphasize the persistence of the two Europes. John Pinder notes that "the phenomenon of the Community and the Union" can be explained in two ways. The first of these locates European unity at the economic, military, and cultural borders between individual nation-states. Problems of unity are therefore more pragmatic, and for that reason Pinder calls proponents of this model of unity "realists" or "functionalists" (Pinder 2001: 6). Those who turn to larger European institutions for solutions to the many problems that extend far beyond inter-nation-state relations often go under the name "federalists" (ibid.: 7). They concern themselves primarily with the articulation and enforcement of principles, such as the EU requirement that member states have democratically elected governments. The history of the EU unfolds in fits and starts because of the shifting influences of and quarrels between the realists and the federalists. It is unlikely whether one or the other will ever win the day, and it is thus equally unlikely that the two sets of conditions they espouse will succeed in unifying Europe in ways that will reflect real compromise. To move ahead, the EU, too, has had to accept the presence of two Europes.

The question that remains open is whether the EU effects unity or whether it generates historical and political demands that exaggerate the conditions that rip Europe into two parts. Arguably, even the introduction of the Euro has the function of bringing about some forms of unity while at the same time exacerbating the absence of unity. Indeed, there are nations almost desperate to join the EU, but there are also movements within the most stalwart EU member states (such as France and Germany) as well as more maverick states (Austria, Denmark, and the UK, for example), that openly espouse withdrawal from the EU. The EU may well successfully navigate these currents and countercurrents, but to do so it must address—and accept—the tendency for Europe to persist in two parts. That tendency, as the several examples here illustrate, is fueled by nationalism.

### Why Do We Love to Hate and Hate to Love Nationalism in Music?

I do not believe that I have ever encountered anyone who is simply ambivalent toward nationalist music. Some love it; many more hate it. Some welcome it for its potentially positive attributes; others vilify it for its destructiveness. When I lecture about nationalist music, say, about the Eurovision Song Contest, I am seldom spared responses that dismiss it as trite and unworthy of scholarly attention. More often than not, someone in the audience is willing to punctuate discussion with pronouncements like "this is crappy music"—indeed, one of the tamer judgments. The point is not simply that many who dismiss Eurovision songs have never heard them—they have not—but rather that they imagine that, because the Eurovision Song Contest panders to nation-

alism in so many ways, it must be dreadful. After all, doesn't nationalism bring out the worst in music? It is shockingly easy to dismiss music
that possesses and expresses any elements of the nation and nationalism. Nationalist music embarrasses and infuriates us. We laugh at it
and we become angry at it. Almost perversely, we love to hate national
music.

Our love-hate relationship with nationalism and music is not simply
relegated to popular-song contests such as the Eurovision. The moment folk music enters the national sphere, which it does with great
frequency, it too loses the luster of authenticity. Once folk music is up-
rooted from its pristine world and put on the stage of the nation, perhaps as a national collection in the nineteenth century, a repertory
available for the virtuoso display of an Eastern European army ensemble, or as the competitive underpinning of folklike hits for scores of national broadcasting companies, it loses its natural beauty and accrues
the ugly messages of national ideologies. The great collectors of European folk music recognized this, while at the same time they attempted
to steer clear of nationalism in folk music.

European art or classical music is no less endangered by the pollut-
ing impact of contact with the national. Composers tainted by the national spirit are lesser talents, mere mortals incapable of ascending to
the pantheon of godlike beings whose greatness results from their ability to recognize that art music is autonomous, moving in the course of
modern European history toward **absolute music.** European art music
should be the product of a universal spirit. There is, of course, the nag-
ging historical problem of composers who did write with a musical vocabulary that meant to draw attention to the nation. Like the fans
watching the Eurovision Song Contest, there are listeners who truly do
like the music of Antonín Dvořák, Edvard Grieg, and Manuel da Falla,
not to mention Béla Bartók and Arvo Pärt. It is possible to skirt the
problem by pointing out that such composers did not really quote folk
melodies or that they really aimed their compositions at international
audiences.

We might turn briefly to the case of Antonín Dvořák (1841–1904),
whose place in European music history has been secured in spite of an
unsettled criticism of his musical nationalism. A composer whose
oeuvre undeniably contains many works drawing extensively and explicitly upon Czech historical and musical themes, Dvořák enters the
discourse of European music history as a victim of nationalism. For

those who champion him, he is a victim of the Central European domination of modern music history. Take, for example, the first three sen-
tence fragments in the entry on Dvořák in the most authoritative English-language music encyclopedia: "Czech composer. With Smetana,
Fibich and Janáček he is regarded as one of the great nationalist Czech
composers of the nineteenth century. Long neglected and dismissed
by the German-speaking musical world as a naïve Czech musician, he is
now considered by both Czech and international musicologists as
Smetana's true heir" (Döge 2001: 777). He was lost but now he's
saved, but not through amazing grace. Quite the contrary, Dvořák
saved himself from the very historical oblivion to which his desire to
say something Czech was doomed to condemn him.

Just how did Dvořák save himself? His champions offer a convincing
register of explanations. First of all, if the great composer chose the
path toward nationalism, there had to be a reason, and according to
his staunch defenders, it was his desire to resist the political hegemony
of the Austro-Hungarian empire in the nineteenth century. He used
dance forms in his orchestral and chamber works and national imagery in tone poems to show the Germans and the Austrians that a
Czech nation really did exist, even though it was not yet independent.
Second, although his ear was attuned to Czechness in music, his pen
was never a slave to that Czechness. His greatest works, so we often
read, do not use folk melodies, but rather they merely take an idea of
folk music and use that as the point of departure for true invention
and creativity. Third, if the Austro-German tradition could not appreci-
ate Dvořák for the universal meanings embodied by the Czechness in
his musical language, the rest of the world, unfettered by the need to
repress Czech nationalism, recognized his greatness. His success and
renown were the results of invitations to England in 1883 and to his
three years in the United States (1892–1895). Fourth, though national
markers are everywhere in his compositions, they are not overtly nationalist. Dvořák remained in control of his nationalist impulses, employing them to serve his ends, not their own. And so a great composer
resists the seduction of nationalism by turning it on its head through
the power of music to make its own claims on European history (cf.
Beckerman 1986–1987; Döge 1991; Beckerman 1993; Plantinga
1996; Döge 2001).

Dvořák, however, was one of the lucky ones, one of the few lucky
ones. Nationalism does something to music that many of us—listeners,

critics, philosophers, and historians—find unacceptable. On one hand, there are reasons internal to the music, reasons that are textual and aesthetic: Music should not give way to the base influences of the ideologies and politics of nationalism. The assertion that music could and does exist in a metaphysical domain separate from cultural forces such as nationalism is, undeniably, the product of European modernity. On the other hand, at a very basic, gut level there is the belief, predicated on contextual and cultural grounds, that nationalism cannot be good, or rather that it can only be bad. Music influenced by nationalism thus takes on all that is bad about nationalism and is ultimately sullied by it.

Ironically, claims that nationalism does something unacceptable to music do not parse into what might seem like obvious ideological categories, such as liberal or conservative. Ardent nationalist composers may create with an agenda pointing to the right or left. Folk musicians may insist on the authenticity of their national repertories by confining them within stylistic boundaries or pleading for universality. In the course of modern European history, governments from across the political and ideological spectrum turned passionately to nationalist music to support the machinery of fascism, communism, or democracy. Therein lies the irony: Even though so many find nationalism's impact on music unacceptable, uncoupling nationalism from music has served the interests of no nation. More, rather than fewer, nations clamor to participate in the Eurovision Song Contest.

### Nationalism and Music—Uneasy Bedfellows

So it is with love-hate relationships. As much as we think we know the rational grounds for separating ourselves from them, the attraction they engender proves too powerful to overcome. It is never easy to sort through the passions that lead to love-hate relationships, but in the course of this book I do my best to make sense out of the reasons that nationalism and music repel and attract each other. To begin the process of making sense, which itself has a necessarily ironic ring about it, I should like to lay some groundwork in very schematic terms. I should like to hypothesize that there are really three general reasons that the impact of nationalism on music leaves so many uneasy and is utterly irresistible to others.

First of all, there is the unwillingness to accept the fact that music—folk, popular, art—can be used in the service of the nation-state. In the cultural history of modernity, music should have more **autonomy,** especially in modern Europe, where the history of music has been interpreted as leading toward greater independence from its cultural and political contexts. Accordingly, nationalism masks and destroys—trumps—the deeper beauty and meaning of music. Nationalism draws attention to the nation-state and supports its function while in the same process drawing attention away from the music itself. Similarly, nationalism disrupts the "real" functions of folk and popular music, be they ritual or entertainment. Ultimately, any semblance of authenticity is erased.

Second, nationalism ultimately trivializes music, exaggerating all that we find most repulsive and ugly. Music that might otherwise represent individual, local, or regional traditions must undergo a process of aesthetic leveling, in which it speaks in the language shared by the broadest cross-section of a nation's population. Once leveled, tradition communicates itself as kitsch, as banal love songs at the Eurovision Song Contest or folk dances rendered as character pieces by hack composers. It is not, however, only a process of eliminating difference to find a cultural common denominator, but rather taking on new markers of the state that affirm its presence in aesthetic language. It is precisely these markers that are most embarrassing of all.

Third, when music is mustered in the service of the nation-state, it mobilizes all that is dangerous and destructive. This is a case of rejecting nationalism because it represents racism and prejudice. Nationalist music serves the state at the moments when its violence may be the greatest, often in war, and even in genocide. Nationalist music plays a role in erasing the voices of the nation's internal others and foreigners. In state rituals, nationalist music is that which is loudest and which makes no room for alternative and resistive voices. It is impossible to deny that openly nationalistic music accompanied modern Europe's most horrific moments: The Holocaust against European Jews and **Roma,** and ethnic cleansing after the breakup of Eastern Europe.

It would be almost easy to hate nationalism in music. But then we run up against those who love national and nationalist music, and they remind us that it is one thing to hate nationalism and another thing to hate music. Hating music, ultimately, is an alternative that those espousing autonomy and the universal spirit rarely consider, for it undermines the very premise of their elevation of music to a special, aesthetically unique marker of European modernity and modernism.

### Good Music/Bad Music

13 May 1999. The Jewish community of Vienna celebrates *Yom ha-Atzmaut,* Israeli Independence Day. What had been for years a street festival near the City Temple in the First District has been promoted to a day-long festival in the Palais Liechtenstein in the Ninth District. It is a day of high nationalism, staged on the grounds and in the palace belonging to the royal family of one of Europe's smallest nations, Liechtenstein, which nonetheless lies not in the Danube Valley but rather the Rhine Valley, at the opposite end of Austria. Music orchestrates the events; more to the point, the day itself is one long performance of music by Jewish musical ensembles—local children's choruses, Eastern European **klezmer** bands, and Central Asian ensembles such as the Bukharan band that for years has come to be the official symbol of easternness for Vienna's Jewish community.

The musical potpourri notwithstanding, the hit song on this day proclaims the anniversary of a nation-state many understand to have been founded by exiles, refugees, and survivors from Austria itself. The hit song is "Diva," the winning entry in the Eurovision Song Contest from the previous year. On this day of national independence it seems as if no one can get enough of "Diva," which had been sung at the ESC by the transsexual Dana International. Every musical group had its own version, and even the city's chief cantor, backed up by members of the synagogue chorus, chanted a version of the song about multiple identities—Maria, Victoria, Aphrodite—on Israel's national day. The huge crowds cheered for more, and they received more. "Diva" was the song that Dana International proclaimed would bring the nation together. In one week, it would bring the Eurovision contestants and EBU cameras to Jerusalem for the 1999 Eurovision.

Not everyone in the crowd liked "Diva." Musicians, many of whom knew me from my years of research in the Jewish community of Vienna, approached me to assure me that "Diva" was a terrible song and that it surely did not represent Jewish music in Europe. I should know, so I was told repeatedly, that there is no accounting for the bad taste that accompanies nationalism. I pointed out, however, that "Diva" was not the only Eurovision winner that was punctuating the celebrations on this national independence day. Had they forgotten that Milk and Honey's "Halleluja" had been Israel's breakthrough entry, the first hit song to secure Israel a place in the pantheon of popular-music nationalism? They had. Still, "Halleluja" had become more than just a Eurovision winner. Hadn't it? It had survived, a testament to the fact that it was good music. Wasn't it?

> *Halleluja, hand in hand,*
> *Halleluja, all over the land,*
> *Halleluja, let's try from the start,*
> *and sing with our heart, halleluja!*
> —Gali Atari & Milk and Honey: "Halleluja"
> 1979 Eurovision Entry for Israel and "Grand Prix" Winner

We expect and want the music of Europe as a whole to be good; however we understand "good" in banal aesthetic terms as a condition of culture between the efficacious and the beautiful. Music that is good is more likely to elevate than entertain, or to effect unity rather than disarray. We embrace music that is good as our own, while we dismiss music that fails to aspire to some level of goodness. Whatever "good music" is, we sense that it is important when programming concerts, preparing syllabi for teaching music-appreciation and music-history classes, and deciding on the CDs and radio broadcasts that accompany us through the day. The alternative is not even worth considering. Who would want to go to a concert of bad music? Quite deliberately, I have reduced one of the most common measures of European music to an aesthetic category that is almost entirely meaningless. It may well be meaningless, though it is often invoked as a means of judging and expressing the qualities that distinguish the canon of European music. Invoking the capacity of music to be good drives a wedge between the music of the two Europes like no other aesthetic category.

How often, in contrast, do we hear that the music of nationalism is good music? Nationalism drags music down and sullies it in such a way that music no longer possesses the intrinsic capacity to rise above insipid melodies and simple forms. The badness that threatens music from beneath, however, need not be taken seriously, for as an aesthetic quality it offers us no real lessons. We do not program concerts of bad music, nor do we teach courses about it. We push bad music to the periphery, wondering how anyone could possibly listen to it. Remarkably, though, bad music does not go away. If the songs of the Eurovision Song Contest are bad, why do so many European listeners tune in the annual broadcast extravaganza? Why do people line the streets of every European nation to hear military bands play one hackneyed march after the next?

Separating good music from bad music is not easy. Private tastes, more often than not, are publicly made and mediated. This is where competitions often prove to be immensely useful. Songs and symphonies that weather the competitions established by national broadcasting stations or transnational foundations and recording labels immediately acquire an aura of being good. Accordingly, there should have been a much broader consensus on Israel's Independence Day that "Diva" was good music. There are, however, other forms of competition, some of them populist, others driven by the media or revival, such as the Central European "Grand Prix der Volksmusik." If it were just a matter of uneducated masses of European citizens going to their telephones to vote for "Diva," then there would be no reason not to accept claims it is bad music.

The competition between good and bad, between the music of one Europe and that of the other, is not simply an aesthetic exercise. Its stakes are high, and competition makes them even higher. The stakes for the 2002 Israeli Eurovision entry, Sarit Hadad's "Light a Candle," are very different from those for "Diva." At a time of war, the Israeli Broadcasting Authority is sending a song about peace to the Tallinn competition, deliberately picking up on the image of light rising from darkness that runs symbolically through Estonia's "Singing Revolution." In the mythical competition between good and bad, it is light that symbolizes the former and darkness the latter. In the politics of nationalism, however, the musical aesthetics of good and bad are at least as modern as they are mythical.

Music helps make the nation by altering our perception of time. More skillfully and subtly than other forms of artistic expression, music finds its way into the temporal boundaries where the myth and history of the nation overlap to create complex myths about what we want a nation to be and what it is. Myth and history constantly interact in the chapters that follow, so much so that it may seem that there is no real difference between the two. The musical representation of the nation, however, constantly reminds us that there is a difference between national myth and history. Music allows for the juxtaposition of myth and history, insisting that they cohabit the ways nations represent themselves to their own citizens and others. Music multiplies and enriches the stories about the nation's past. In this book we encounter the proliferation of national myths and histories with each new musical genre and each new location on the European musical landscape. In each case the nation assumes a new shape, both similar and different from other images of the nation. Before we explore these myriad shapes, let us pause and visit a place where nations attempt to render them roughly similar: the museum of national music. It is in such museums that myth and history are most richly woven into a counterpoint representing the nation.

## Myth/History: Musical Museums of the Nation

Europe's musical museums come in all sizes and shapes, and one can find them just about anywhere one finds monuments and memorials that make public declamations about a nation's history. Folklore and ethnology museums, locally and regionally, inevitably contain a section devoted to music, as do art and history museums. Open-air museums place musical performance in the context of reimagined village life. Museums also allow the modern pilgrim to trace the stages in the lives of composers, from the seemingly countless Viennese apartments in which Beethoven lived to the equally countless birthplaces of national composers, great and not-so-great. Many of these locales earn only a memorial plaque, but a surprisingly large number turn into museums, perhaps with no more than a musical instrument, a desk, and a few reproductions of representative compositions. Collectors of musical instruments also seek ways to make their treasures available to the public. Some collectors specialize and some save aging artifacts from oblivion; all recognize their special passion as potentially contributing to the greater welfare, often of the entire nation.

It is hardly surprising, then, that the musical museums of the nation weave myth and history together in similar ways. Usually one first encounters the displays of musical instruments that were retrieved from archeological sites, which in turn are followed by and compared with the instruments made by anonymous craftspeople. The historical journey continues through early evidence of music-making at the courts of

minor and major aristocrats, provincial cultural centers, and eventually
in the modern metropole. Dominating the end of the historical journey are the products of literate and industrial music culture, the works
of national composers, publishers, and musical-instrument manufacturers. The museum visitor is asked to compare the items contained in
exhibition cases and told that comparison will reveal that myth and
prehistory are one, and that the nation forms from the similarities that
the displays bring into focus. The sciences of historical musicology,
**organology,** ethnomusicology, and history provide ample signposts for
the comparison, preventing the visitor from straying too far from the
museum's main story, which in turn becomes a thread in the nation's
primary history. Instruments occupy chapters of the story according to
the materials from which they are built and through which they
sound—winds, strings, percussion—while at the same time they find
their way into the cultural contexts of a nation passing through historical transition—string orchestras at court, military bands shipped to the
edge of the empire, pianos in the bourgeois home of an industrial age.
The musical museum of the nation celebrates its heroes, the great
composers and performers whose artistry conveyed the nation's story
to the world, the favorite sons and daughters whose achievements have
acquired mythic proportions.

A nation's musical museums tell us much about the nation and its
forms of nationalism. For this reason we often find particularly important museums near the center of national power. The Music Museum
of Slovakia's National Museum, for example, stands on the grounds of
Bratislava Castle, high atop the bluffs along the Danube River, which
runs between the old city and the new residential districts added during the socialist era. Bratislava Castle itself combines historical functions with state ceremonies, thus using the past to generate the present. Tourists and state dignitaries alike approach the castle only after
passing by the musical instrument museum, whose inviting collections
chart Slovak history in painstaking detail and provide a resource for
performing Slovak national identity, not infrequently in state ceremonies (see Mačák 1995). Whereas the Slovak national instrument
museum provides evidence for the ways the nation is distinct from its
neighbors, especially Austria, Hungary, and the Czech Republic, whose
borders can be seen from the castle grounds on which the museum
stands, the national instrument museum of France, housed in the
*Musée de l'Homme,* or Museum of Man, in Paris, recounts the national

history of empire. In the context of a state anthropology museum, the musical instruments enter the museum from cultures throughout the world, especially from former colonies and present **départements,** semi-independent commonwealth holdings (such as Guadalupe and Martinique). Arguably, the music produced by these instrument collections if and when they are played (they are used for performances of world music) is not French music. It is, nonetheless, music that is inseparable from French national history, and it is, accordingly, inseparable from historical narratives of French nationalism.

The musical instrument museum of Hungary tells yet another national story. Located in buildings shared by the Institute of Musicology of the Hungarian Academy of Sciences, the Music Museum and Bartók Archives sits atop the hills of the Buda side of Budapest, a few minutes' walk from the Mátyás-templom, the cathedral dominating the fortress hills, the former fortress grounds (now an art museum), and the former arsenal and army barracks (now a military museum)—in other words, in the midst of a web of museums representing a variety of national histories. The visitor passes through history more or less according to the stages I have previously outlined. Prehistoric instruments yield to folk instruments that evolve into light-classical instruments that finally reveal themselves as Hungarian precursors to internationally disseminated instruments (such as the transformation of the **tsimbalom,** or large hammered dulcimer, into the piano). Paintings, publications, and printed music sharpen the focus on Hungary, reminding the visitor that, outside (Austrian) or inside (Rom) influences notwithstanding, Hungarian musicians have performed the national myth for centuries.

Almost seamlessly, however, the visitor passes between myth and history, leaving the last room displaying musical instruments and entering the other permanent exhibit of the museum, called "Bartók's Workshop." This exhibit is not so much about Béla Bartók himself, whom modern history has elevated to the status of an unassailable national composer, as it is about how he wrote the story of Hungary through music. In brief, Bartók collected folk songs and dances, from which he derived a new and modern compositional technique; the music of myth became the music of history as the Hungarian folk created a music that Bartók composed into the symbolic sound of Hungarian modernism. The museum cases contain the recording devices used by Bartók the folk-music collector, the manuscript scores and sketches that transformed oral versions into written artifacts, and the publications that would make Bartók's music, crafted as Hungarian music in this workshop of the nation, available to the entire world.

Just as nations put music in museums, they employ music to "museumize" the nation-state, in other words, to preserve and present the very elements needed to realize nationalism through performance in the course of an ongoing history. Museumized music fills national anthologies and complete editions. The multi-volume collections of works by Franz Liszt, to stay in Hungary for a moment, place his output in a museum, and because of their sponsorship by Hungarian publishers and research academies, they make that museum national. The act of nationalizing Liszt has historically been necessary for Hungarians because the composer himself was far more cosmopolitan than Hungarian. A complete Hungarian edition, moreover, recuperated Liszt from the claims of Austria, Hungary's imperial counterpart in the Austro-Hungarian Empire and the national musical culture in which Liszt, in fact, was raised. The museum of the complete edition, such as that published in 1911 at the centenary of his birth, employs a virtual architecture that gives pride of place to the works espousing national characteristics and relegates works without them to lesser galleries, or volumes.

Without national editions of folk song and folk music, the present book would have a rather different shape and a distinctively different content. The national edition of folk song was a product of the nineteenth century, when it became important to designate songs in dialect as German, Swedish, or Polish, thus erecting museums for their storage and for the visitation of the nations increasingly identified as German, Swedish, or Polish. It was not by chance that the tomes of a complete edition actually documented the collections in national museums and archives, many of whom sponsored their publication. Together, the editions and the museums conspired to form unified simulacra of the nation itself.

Festivals and summer academies have similar functions, drawing attention to the nation by moving concerts and academic meetings to the very places in which the music of our own time emerged from the soil of an earlier era. Thus the music of the museum revives the past and presents it to the present, celebrating the passage between myth and history and reinforcing the links between the nation and nationalism.

## The Tale of Two Songs:
## On the Possibility of a European Music

What might a European music really sound like? What might it symbolize as Europe turned away from the competitive divisiveness that reduced it to parts and concentrated on an aesthetics that might undergird its wholeness? At least a few answers to those questions lie in the tale of two songs with which I conclude this first chapter.

Attempts to create a European music have provided one of the historical subtexts of European history since the rise of modernity that began with the eighteenth-century Enlightenment. In the revolutions that led to the establishment of European nation-states, song served as the emblem of unity. It drew the nation together, but even more, it drew the people of the nation into some larger collective of human experience, not uncommonly the male and masculine union symbolized by "brotherhood" and "mankind." Songs of revolution, such as "l'Internationale," called for a resolution to crisis and a leveling of differences that would eventually produce a supernation that was more international than national. The music of the stateless Europe would be given voice from below, symbolically by the foot soldiers of the revolution and those who would replace the machinery of the aristocratic and despotic state with cooperative programs of a utopian and democratic Europe. The song of a utopian Europe was the song of the people, a transformation of the Herderian ideal from myth to history. A chorus constituted from the voices of all nations would take to the stage of European history, making Europe's wholeness palpable and real.

In our ethnographic present, for example, in the song culture of the New Europe, music continues to be seized by those who would move across the borders between nations and aspire to a higher unity than the state. Since 1989 and the velvet revolutions that produced the New Europe, there has been a resurgence of song connected with religious revival, much of it articulated by pilgrims who cross the borders between the two Europes, that is, between the Christian West and the non-Christian (secular, Muslim, and formerly Jewish) East. New songs come into existence, for example, the "Medjugorje Song," the vocal icon for the pilgrimage site at Medjugorje, Bosnia-Herzegovina, which came into existence only in the 1980s but attracts tens of millions of pilgrims each year (listen to CD example 5). The songs of European religious revival—there are, among many others, "Lourdes" and "Fatíma" songs, for pilgrimage sites in France and Portugal—have come to constitute repertories of the subaltern who travel on foot and express their faith to reclaim some measure of Europe's sacred wholeness as their own.

The songs of the several hundred million Europeans who go on pilgrimages each year represent a sort of virtual Europe, which reflects a history of Christianity and turns toward the future, when faith again can unify (listen to CD examples 4 and 5). Zbigniew Preisner portrays a rather different virtual Europe in the musical score for the 1993 film, *Blue,* one of the tricolor films (with *Red* and *White*) produced by Polish filmmaker Krzysztof Kieslowski (Preisner 1993). The screenplay and the musical score of *Blue* juxtapose Europe and the nation, that is, the French nation, whose flag lends its symbolism to the film itself. The plot of the film turns around the several attempts to complete a "Song for the Unification of Europe," which had been commissioned from France's greatest composer, who dies in an automobile accident as the film opens. As the film's major characters struggle to complete the composition for a dedication that will have all the ceremony of an historic moment in the unification of Europe, they find themselves unable to develop the basic theme itself. The compositional struggle continues until the composer's wife, Julie, allows the biblical texts of the song "to speak with the tongues of angels" in the chorus. Real completion, real unification requires transcending the human condition. *Blue* is fiction; nevertheless, it draws attention to the space between Europe's wholeness and its parts, the space into which two very real songs, long controversial in modern European history, lead us: The "International" and the "European Anthem."

Surely the most international of songs to move from the subaltern to the supernational state has been the "International." From its origins in the Paris Commune, a socialist and laborers' living experiment that was brutally suppressed by the French in 1871, the "International," composed by Pierre Degeyter to a text by Eugène Pottier, has played various roles as the anthem of international labor unions and socialist organizations to stints as national anthems, in the pre–World War II era of the Soviet Union and the post–World War II era of the former Yugoslavia. One might say that the "International" has resisted nationalism—both the Soviet Union and Yugoslavia replaced it with more specifically national songs—and that it also does not affix itself to any single political entity (P. Nettl 1967: 113). Its textual emphasis was always unity and the universal, the future when, as the chorus proclaims, "the International will be Mankind," as if the song and humanity were one (see Figure 1.1). The "International" even spread with modernity and industrialization as Europe imposed its own forms of modernity and nationalism through colonialism and globalization. The "International" was and is the song of the working class. Insofar as it is possible to understand the history of modern Europe as proletarian—by following the intersecting paths of the rise of modernity and the spread of industrialization, for example—there is perhaps no more European song.

In stark contrast, the official European anthem, an arrangement of the choral portion of the final movement of Ludwig van Beethoven's Ninth Symphony, became European by dint of epic history and committee decree (Buch 2003). A setting of Friedrich Schiller's "An die Freude" ("To Joy"), Beethoven's Ninth Symphony is regarded by many as the monumental work of the nineteenth century, serving as an ideological link between the Enlightenment, whose spirit the Schiller poem embodies, to the late twentieth-century triumph of European ideals over the destruction of Europe during World War II (see Figure 1.2). The "Ode to Joy," as both the fourth movement and the European anthem have come to be abbreviated, stress unity when *"alle Menschen werden Brüder"* ("all human beings become brothers"), a symbolic goal as lofty as the European Union itself, which adopted the hymn from the European Commission in May 1986 in a gesture that accompanied officially adopting the EU flag, with its blue field on which (then) twelve stars stood in a circle. Again, however, there was resistance from those who insisted that no union sung to Schiller's text—innocuous in its own right, but heavily laden with the historical baggage of German aggression in the world wars—could represent every nation (Clark 1997).

Also complicating the European anthem's official status was the involvement of Herbert von Karajan as the original arranger of a version in 1972. Karajan might have been the most famous conductor of the day, but he had also been a member of the Hitler Youth during World War II. Musicological concerns, too, raised questions about the appropriateness of the symphonic movement itself, which includes a strategically placed Turkish march: Should that represent the exclusion of Muslims from European history or the increasing presence of Turkish guest workers in the Central Europe that produced the symphony? Symbolic unity quickly disintegrated under the weight of the very European history that the European Union wished to supplant with a new

# The International

**Pottier (lyrics) and DeGeyter (melody)**

*Figure 1.1. "The International" (Lyrics, Eugène Pottier; melody, Pierre Degeyter)*

era in which the majesty of European song would rise above nationalist agendas. Against a backdrop of complaint and criticism, full recognition of the "Ode to Joy" as text and music was put on hold. Officially, Beethoven's music remains the European anthem; just as officially, Schiller's text has been excised until a more suitable text can be found.

# European Anthem

Beethoven
(arr. Karajan)

*Figure 1.2.* *"The European Anthem" (opening),*
*based on the "Ode to Joy" in Beethoven's Ninth Symphony*

Europe is left even today with an "anthem of European unification" in which text and music cannot enjoy the unity in which they were conceived (Shore 2000: 48–49; cf. Europäisches Parlament, n.d., which contains the original Karajan recording).

Ultimately, the tale of two songs does not permit me to write a history of European unity. The whole of Europe, onto which I hold tenaciously throughout this book, nonetheless, eludes me, remaining the stuff of myth more insistently than of history. Neither the "International" nor the "European Anthem" has succeeded in providing a song anchored in the experiences of all Europeans. Neither achieved the common ground that was implicit in the myths of their creation and explicit in the histories of their transmission. Rather than symbolizing a single Europe through wholeness or unity, the two songs are pulled constantly toward the two Europes. Each, in its own way, is tainted by the nationalism that accrued to them, as cultural traces or musical inflections, or as themes that spun out of control through the processes of variation. Perhaps it is because their themes are inseparable that they cannot be liberated from the two Europes themselves, which have so often formed a complex counterpoint between the nation and nationalism, a counterpoint that is sometimes consonant and whole, but often dissonant and fragmented.

## REFERENCES

Beckerman, Michael. 1986–1987. "In Search of Czechness in Music." *19th Century Music* 10: 61–73.

———, ed. 1993b. *Dvořák and His World*. Princeton, N.J.: Princeton University Press.

Buch, Estaban. 2003. *Beethoven's Ninth: A Political History*. Trans. by Richard Miller. Chicago: University of Chicago Press.

Clark, Caryl. 1997. "Forging Identity: Beethoven's 'Ode' as European Anthem." *Critical Inquiry* 23 (4): 789–807.

Dahlhaus, Carl. 1980. "Nationalism in Music." In idem, *Between Romanticism and Modernism,* trans. by Mary Whittall, pp. 79–101. Berkeley and Los Angeles: University of California Press.

Döge, Klaus. 2001. " Dvořák, Antonín (Leopold)." In Stanley Sadie, ed., *The New Grove Dictionary of Music and Musicians*. Rev. ed. Vol. 7: 777–814. London: Macmillan.

Europäisches Parlament. N.d. *Europa—da ist Musik drin!* Deutsche Gramophon 445492–2.

Gambaccini, Paul, Tim Rice, Jonathan Rice, and Tony Brown. 1999. *The Complete Eurovision Song Contest Companion 1999*. London: Pavillion.

Herder, Johann Gottfried. 1975 [1778–1779]. *"Stimmen der Völker in Liedern"* and *Volkslieder.* 2 vols. published in one. Stuttgart: Reclam.

Mačák, Ivan. 1995. *Dedičstvo hudobných nástrojov* ("The Heritage of Musical Instruments"). Bratislava: Slovenské národné múzeum, Hudobné múzeum.

Nettl, Paul. 1967. *National Anthems*. Trans. by Alexander Gode. 2nd, enlarged ed. New York: Frederick Ungar.

Pinder, John. 2001. *The European Union: A Very Short Introduction*. Oxford: Oxford University Press.

Plantinga, Leon. 1996. "Dvořák and the Meaning of Nationalism in Music." In David R. Beveridge, ed., *Rethinking Dvořák: Views from Five Countries,* pp. 117–123. Oxford: Oxford University Press.

Preisner, Zbigniew. 1993. *Bande originale du film* Trois Couleurs, Bleu. Virgin Records America 7243 8 39027 2 9.

Shore, Cris. 2000. *Building Europe: The Cultural Politics of European Integration.* London and New York: Routledge.

Taruskin, Richard. 1983. "Some Thoughts on the History and Historiography of Russian Music." *The Journal of Musicology* 3 (4): 321–339.

Wieser, Lojze. 2001. "Ante scriptum." In Renata SakoHoess and Rotraut Hackermüller, eds., *Europa erlesen: Bratislava,* pp. 5–7. Klagenfurt: Wieser.

*Chapter Two*

# The European Nation-State in History

*The histories of the modern European nation-state* and the emergence of modern European music run remarkably parallel courses. In this chapter we examine why and how those courses were parallel, and we turn to the multiple points of intersection at which music came to symbolize and articulate European nationalism. From the outset it is important for us to recognize that music does far more than symbolize and articulate nationalism: music actually participates in the formation of nationalism. The modern nation-state most powerfully came into being when its citizens sang together, embodying what the contemporary theorist of nationalism Benedict Anderson called **unisonality** (1991). Furthermore, music and music making did not simply embody one nation, or even one kind of nation in Europe; their power to mobilize nationalism was recognized throughout the continent. As Europe became a continent of nations and as European history increasingly formed around distinctively nationalist agendas, European music embarked upon new historical paths that were decidedly nationalist.

The European nation-state first took shape in the Enlightenment. The Enlightenment assumed different and distinctive forms throughout Europe, but even such differences were anchored in linguistic and historical distinctions that were, at root, national. After the Enlightenment and the historical events that put its theories into practice, especially the French and American revolutions, and after the rise of French imperialism under Napoleon, the European nation was radically different. For the first time the nation began to embody its citizens. The Enlightenment nation could, and indeed should, take account of its citizens. If the people of a particular historical culture, linguistic region, or common religion were not served by the nation, so post-Enlightenment thinkers and political activists held, one reasonable recourse should be that of creating a new nation.

Modern European nation-states, therefore, formed quickly, often resulting from radical rupture. They needed a new set of national symbols and sounds to give voice to their common culture, however long its history had been. In the wake of the Enlightenment, first during the nineteenth century, with its era of Romanticism and revolution, and then during the twentieth century, with its world wars and radical shifts of national alignment, the nation itself became the central political embodiment of Europeanness, and music made that centrality palpable. Underscoring music's presence in European nationalism, moreover, was its capacity to change and accordingly to accompany the nation as it underwent change from the eighteenth century to the present. In the present chapter we look at the most crucial moments of change and the presence of music as an agent of nationalism at those moments.

### National Music before the Modern Nation-State

Song expressed the aspirations of European nations even before the advent of the modern nation-state. The performers of what we might call "proto-national" genres of music sang tales of great leaders and of the families from which they came; they chronicled the conflicts of power and the battles with mighty enemies; and they charted the landscape of struggles and great events that would inscribe the fate of the nation on its history. The genres of national music that preceded the nation were narrative; in other words, they told stories about the past. Those stories, often passed orally from singer to singer and from community to community, and often local or regional, were also parts of a much larger historical complex, within which the threads of nascent national identity were woven together to form the whole that unified people in the early stages of nationhood.

Among the proto-national genres of music, the **epic** and the **ballad** most commonly possessed the power to transform local stories into national histories, which explains why the narrative genres of folk song have a presence in Europe that is in some ways greater than elsewhere in the world. In narrative genres of folk song we often witness the narrative and national spaces that form between myth and history. We shall return again and again to such spaces between mythology and history, for the meaning of nationalism often occupies such spaces, where it is often volatile and fragile. As narrative musical genres articulate these spaces in their stories, they also create textual structures for representing the nation-state, especially in its premodern forms. Epic and ballad, moreover, reflect different social contexts in the different regions of Europe, generally designating national distinctiveness rather than similarity. We can turn to epic and ballad, therefore, to understand the foundations from which nations formed and to see why some of a nation's oldest stories remain embedded in the narration of its most recent histories (cf., CD examples 1–3).

The epic is the story of the proto-nation writ large through the deeds of a single individual, whose heroism mobilizes the nation and whose leadership provides a metaphor for the nation's own coming of age. The epic's history as a genre of folk song is coeval with the history of Europe, especially Mediterranean Europe, which we witness in its earliest narrative forms in the two Homeric epics, the *Odyssey* and the *Iliad*. The journeys of Odysseus and his followers and the battles for Helen of Troy contained in these epics presage the struggles of early states in the eastern Mediterranean for nationalism in its classical forms, such as the Greek city-states, the early processes of democracy, and the struggle for independence in the conflicts between empires in Europe and Asia. These epic themes have persisted in the epics of the Mediterranean from Antiquity to the present. In many of the regions where the first European epics narrated the history of Antiquity, epics remained in oral tradition well into the twentieth century, when scholars such as Milman Parry and Albert B. Lord collected and analyzed them (cf. Lord 1960).

In epics the nation usually appears as unstable and with varying traces, which in turn are evident in the formal poetic and musical structures of the genre. The basic unit of the epic is the line of text, which, however, grows from internal formulaic structures, usually the division of the line into several phrases and metric patterns that connect text to melody, hence representing the particularity of the language. Epic singers are often specialists, not least because they frequently perform long stories from memory and possess the poetic license to dissect and recombine narrative units to serve their performances. The epic singer's specialty often means that singers acquire special status in their communities, even as local or, if their fame spreads beyond their home region, as national historians. Important for our considerations, moreover, is that the special skills required for performing epics are underscored by music. Epics often require that the singer accompany him- or herself on an instrument, which may provide melodic contour. Melody, rhythm, and meter, moreover, complement the nuance of language, often meaning that the music itself complements the narrative structures of the language. In this way, the music actually acquires the attributes of a poetic language that itself gives specific meaning to the nation at the formative stages represented in the epic.

Historically, epic has dominated the narrative genres of southern, or Mediterranean, Europe. The medieval Iberian *Cid* stories and the Italian musical-dramatic cycle known as *Il Maggio* (cf. Magrini 1992) are both cases of epic. In the Balkans of southeastern Europe, epics by nationalist poets such as the Serb Branko Radičević have sustained the centuries-long conflicts between Christian regions and the Islamic Ottoman Empire. Unifying the otherwise diverse nationalist themes of Mediterranean Europe's epics have been the conflicts between Europeans and non-Europeans invading or colonizing Europe. These conflicts have distinctive religious overtones, usually between Western (European) and Eastern (Asian) religions, and frequently between Christianity and Islam. The historical issues at the heart of epics, therefore, are often fundamentally European, and together the epics provide a remarkably complete and complex history of European protonationalism at the continent's southern and eastern borders (listen to CD example 1).

In central and northern Europe there are also long poetic and musical cycles that narrate early traces of nationalism. The **Edda** myths of Scandinavia, which survived in oral tradition into the twentieth century, and the **Niebelungen** cycles of German-speaking areas of Central Europe are unlike the epics of southern Europe in many ways, narrating instead the distinctiveness of the European regions in which they have circulated and telling of Nordic and Germanic pantheons rather than marking Europe as Christian. We find national and religious conflict, but more often conflict between indigenous pagan forms and the disruptive change brought about as Christianity spread to northern Europe late in the first millennium of the Common Era, in other words, in the centuries surrounding 1000 CE. When we look at and listen to all these epics, recognizing their remarkable presence throughout Europe, we realize that they tell us a great deal about the continent's history as a whole, which nevertheless failed to yield regional and linguistically unified forms. Europe is present in epics both as myth and as history in some of its earliest nationalistic forms.

If epics chronicle the **longue durée,** or the big picture, of a nation's earliest historical stages, ballads speak more often of the individuals and events that together constitute a national mosaic. Ballads are found in most parts of Europe, but in the German-speaking and English-speaking areas they have persisted into the modern era, in large part because of the ways oral tradition has interacted with written tradition, especially the popular print traditions of **broadside ballads** and **Flugblätter** (literally, "pages in flight"). Several ballad traditions also survive in southwestern Europe, where the corpus known as **romancero** contained such genres as the **romance.** Ballads from southwestern Europe, moreover, allow us to witness the ways in which narrative traditions ply the borders that separate modern nationalism from its precursors. Considerable repertories of romances and **romanceros** accompanied the Sephardic Jews in their largely Mediterranean diaspora after their expulsion from the Iberian peninsula in 1492. The Sephardic ballads, sung in **Ladino,** the Spanish-derived language of the Mediterranean Jews, recount historical events from throughout the diaspora, especially the conflicts between European Christians and Muslim empires from North Africa and Ottoman Turkey. The ballad texts concentrate not so much on the great armies and leaders as on individuals whose lives are swept up in the historical strife, which we then understand as emblematic of the Sephardic Jews themselves as well as other powerless people in premodern Europe (see, e.g., Armistead and Silverman 1986).

In the ballad it is not a few great heroes whose deeds are celebrated, but rather the lives of the everyperson and the tragic realities of daily life. Thus the characters of the ballad are often stereotypes, and the narrative of the ballad contains a moral. The structure and form of a ballad also make it possible for a broad cross-section of a society to be familiar with them, if not to participate in their transmission as singers. Each verse of the strophic form sets the stage for a scene in the larger play that becomes the ballad itself. Characters interact with each other, entering and exiting from the verses, with the main characters eventually reaching some sort of denouement, often marked by the tragic confrontation with reality. Printed ballads in Europe, especially from ca. 1600 to ca. 1800, often contained the news of the day, displayed and sold as tabloids might be today, but created for performance as songs. Street hawkers in England or **Bänkelsänger** in Germany might appear in a public square and sing from the ballads they brought with them, hoping that their musically performed reports of the news, often sensationalized, might attract buyers.

The power of epics and ballads to shape the myths of nationalism has not been lost upon modern European nations. In the nineteenth century there were several notable cases of epics that were virtually invented to shape and extend the formative stages of a nation's history. The epic *Kalevala* was created as a patchwork of tales and legends in nineteenth-century Finland but was used by Finnish folklorists, intellectuals, and composers to codify the single narrative of Finland undergoing the transformation from myth to modern nation (see Wilson 1976 and Ramnarine 2003; listen to CD tracks 2 and 3). More infamously, the Germanic myths of the *Niebelungen* were reimagined by German composers, among them Richard Wagner, to appropriate a mythical authenticity of a pure Germanic past for a modern German unity. The modernization of such narratives of the past lent itself to abuse, especially during the first half of the twentieth century, when German fascism rose and eventually led to the tragic racial excesses of the Nazi period (1933–1945) and the Holocaust. Here, too, music provided a template for conflating a nation's myths and history, obscuring the borders separating an imagined past from an invented present. But the historical path from myth to modernity that European music narrated was long and often circuitous, and it therefore behooves us to look more carefully at its initial stages.

## The Birth of National Music in the Enlightenment

Language was the catalyst that connected music and nationalism in the eighteenth century as European nations first entered the historical phase we call modernity. As modern European history supplanted the early modern era, which had accompanied the Age of Discovery, the questions of cultural, social, and political beginnings became crucial. The modern nation was envisioned by philosophers to begin when it recognized what Jean-Jacques Rousseau (1712–1778), for example, called a "social contract," in other words, when it responded to the

common needs of an entire society. Facilitating the political philosophies that espoused the common good of a nation's citizens were further notions about the language and expressive culture that the nation
as a whole might share, not least among them notions of national song.
For the eighteenth-century philosophers and political leaders alike,
music increasingly contributed to the capacity of the nation to achieve
its beginnings—not music in general, but rather song as the highest
and most collective form of language. The nation was to be a collectivity articulated through song.

During the eighteenth century, as the new philosophical movement
known as the Enlightenment spread from one nation to another in Europe, the very concepts of music underwent radical transformations,
which, in turn, connected music to the burgeoning forms of modern
nationalism. Crucial to these transformations were notions about how
music was a part of national origins; we witness the expression of these
concepts in the abundance of philosophical and linguistic treatises
about "beginnings" themselves. Prior to the eighteenth century, most
philosophies of music had held that music was somehow rooted in nature. There were concepts of music that held that music's harmonies
were generated by the physics of nature, moving spheres in harmony
with each other. A different type of naturalness was evident when the
sounds of animals were realized as music. As different as these and
other philosophies of music were from one another, they all located
music's origins in nature. But with the Enlightenment the origins of
music shifted to language and speech. Accordingly, music moved to
one of the domains most essential for new definitions of the nation
itself.

Why did song come to articulate the origins of the nation so crucially? First of all, song had the capacity to liberate music from nature,
thus giving the rational human the possibility of empowering language
to do new things. Language in its elevated forms could be specific to
the nation, and as such it acquired unique qualities. The origins of
song fascinated Enlightenment thinkers such as Rousseau because they
perceived ways in which the origins of nations paralleled and were articulated by the origins of song. In short, it was through song that the
music of one nation came to be different from that of another. In his
famous *Dictionnaire de la musique* (published in English as *A Complete
Dictionary of Music* [1779]) the great French philosopher provides entries for national musical repertories—Italian, French, and German—

and points to the distinctive ways in which the national language requires that sounds be shaped in particular ways, which in turn require that particular melodic patterns result from speech patterns. For Rousseau, whose celebrated claim about the naturalness of the nation held that "the first rule that we must follow is that of national character" (Rousseau 1915, 2: 319), speech more than any other factor, including nature, created different musical structures, and already by the mid-eighteenth century these differences were explicitly national.

The German philosopher and historian Johann Gottfried Herder (1744–1803) also devoted a remarkable degree of attention to the intersection of nation and song. In addition to numerous essays and pamphlets that discussed musical difference along with other national differences, he devoted two books to the potential of song to articulate national diversity. The two volumes, *"Stimmen der Völker in Liedern"* and *Volkslieder* (1778 and 1779), are remarkable for the extent to which they rely on a fundamental impulse of humans to give voice to their distinctiveness with song. The real "voices of the people" were audible in their songs, Herder argues. He took his argument several steps farther, using the two books as an anthology of songs from different nations, several of which would not enjoy political independence for many decades (for example, Estonia and Ireland). With only a few exceptions, the songs in the volumes were published as texts without melodies in German translation; however, the nation of their origin was included. In this way, Herder was the first to use song to chart a musical map of European nationalism.

Herder also employed national song to map two of the most fundamental concepts of the Enlightenment on the nation and thus to connect the nation to European history. On one hand, what he was calling **Volkslieder,** or "folk songs"—it was in these books that the word "folk song" appeared for the first time—had a universal quality: Folk song had the potential to represent all of human culture. On the other hand, folk song possessed the particular power to represent culture in its specific, bounded forms; according to Herder, there was no more commonly specific form than national song. The distinction between the universal and the particular lies at the center of much Enlightenment thought, and it was in the tension between them that history unfolded. By the end of the eighteenth century, the tension had further manifested itself in tensions between Europe, increasingly perceived as the symbol of a universal history, and the nation, the product of a particular history. By claiming that folk song was exceptionally endowed to articulate the universal and the particular, Herder effectively made a case for the historical vocabulary that undergirded the very "voices of the people" that folk songs had become in an era of expanding nationalism.

## Music and the Emergence of Modern Europe

Two sweeping acts of discovery accompanied the Enlightenment, serving to heighten the political potential of philosophical thought. The first discovery was that of the "folk," which for our purposes can be understood as the people sharing the common culture of a nation. The second discovery, which took place at the greatest extreme from the first, was that of Europe itself as a conglomerate of nations. It might seem strange to employ the word "discovery," since both the folk and Europe were present prior to the Enlightenment. However, the discovery of the folk and of Europe relied on another type of discovery with political and nationalist implications, namely the discovery that the folk and Europe were linked by the history of the nation.

In their most abstract, philosophical forms, both the folk and Europe were undifferentiated, even amorphous. It was when they entered the history of the nation, however, that their cultural distinctiveness began to play a critical role. For European intellectuals at the end of the eighteenth and at the beginning of the nineteenth century, identifying the ways the folk interacted with the emerging political collective of the nation required a shift to new forms of history writing. The folk constituted the collective actors of the nation, and the culture they shared— the historical drama they enacted—comprised the history of the nation realized from bottom up. The relation between the folk and the drama of history provided a new basis for folk music, indeed, really the first fully European concept of folk music. Herder had recognized the fact that folk music contained differences, but it was only among intellectuals during the early generations of **Romanticism** that we encounter claims about the power of the folk to create folk music and thus respond with music to the conditions of their own lives. Whereas Herder had argued that the folk were *unpoliziert* ("lacking in social organization"), Jacob Grimm, who with his brother Wilhelm collected folk songs as well as fairy tales, asserted that *das Volk dichtet* ("the people were themselves creative"). Folk song, it followed, allowed them to take

charge of their own narratives and to weave these into the histories of
their own nations.

The discovery of Europe as a continent of nations by the early Romantic intellectuals appears, at first glance, to contrast entirely with
the discovery of the folk. Did not the culture of Europe emphasize the
top while leaving the bottom an undifferentiated mass? In theory, yes,
but in practice during the early decades of the nineteenth century, no.
To understand why this was so, we might turn briefly to the entry of
Russia into the European community of nations and the concomitant
discovery of Russian folk music that grew from the nation's response to
Europeanness in folk music.

### The Russian Shift Westward

Historians have long demonstrated that, until the eighteenth century,
Russia was as much Asian as European, and that its religious, political,
and cultural histories followed paths quite unlike those of the rest of
Europe. With the reigns of Peter the Great (1682–1725) and Catherine the Great (1762–1796), Russia underwent a radical and conscious
shift toward the West. The Russia that had been imagined by other Europeans prior to the Enlightenment as wild and even exotic had become a modern, cosmopolitan nation-state by the beginning of the
nineteenth century. Russia had entered Europe as a member of a community of nations, indeed for many reasons, political and cultural, not
least among them the defeat that Napoleon met in his attempt to bring
all of Europe under a single empire. Rather than providing Europe
with an "other" in the East, Russia's integration into Europe at the beginning of the nineteenth century, as Larry Wolff has shown, created
the first effective cultural division of Europe into East and West (Wolff
1994). In the course of the next two centuries that division assumed
many forms, each of which played a determining role in the larger patterns of European history, most recently of the Cold War and, in the
1990s, the nationalist struggles in the New Europe.

The historical transformations that drew Russia into Europe also
laid the groundwork for its folk music. The burgeoning Russian nationalism of the eighteenth century required the presence of the folk,
and their discovery resulted above all from the actions of a single individual, Nikolai Alexandrovich Lvov (1751–1803). Lvov was both an

aristocrat and a cultural polymath whose many contributions to Russian letters and music explored Russian folk poetry in every possible way (see Taruskin 1997: 3–25). He took as a starting point the themes of the Russian folk epos, the **bilina,** and dissected it in ways that would allow it structurally and thematically to serve eighteenth-century composers, who sought to work with the idioms of folk music. Lvov and his several musical collaborators mapped folk music on the nascent forms of Russian art music, appropriating these first from Western models such as the German *Singspiel* but remolding them so that their Russianness would stand out (for example, in the folk choruses on the opera stage that symbolized the folk as a national collective). Richard Taruskin has observed that Lvov's greatest achievement was combining the aesthetic and the political, allowing music to serve as an emblem for the entire Russian people in collaborative efforts in which "Russia is large and contains multitudes" (ibid.: 24), thus aligning the folk culture of Russia with the folk cultures of other European nations.

Just as the borders between Europe's East and West blurred as the continent's wholeness was parsed by emerging nation-states and national cultures in the early nineteenth century, so too did the boundaries between musical styles and genres blur. Folk-music and art-music repertories overlapped, which is to say that composers, musicians, and folk-music collectors identified the ways in which they overlapped. The early nineteenth-century composer turned to folk-music sources as a matter of course, narrowing the distance between the music of the folk and that of Europe as a cosmopolitan whole. As the distance between folk and art music narrowed, they were drawn into a nationalist tension, the historical implications of which were not lost on philosophers such as Hegel (1770–1831), who crafted new historiographies that viewed Europe as the culmination of a world history that had moved from East Asia to Europe. Today we recognize the full Eurocentric implications of such models of history. But in the nineteenth century they proved enormously provocative as a means of giving Europe a global pride of place. Folk music came to represent the full implications of a history charting the course of the nation's presence in Europe during the nineteenth century. Identifying the nation in the entire spectrum of music, from folk music to art music, was not only possible, it had become a prerequisite for claiming the distinctive history necessary for a nation struggling to find its place in nineteenth-century Europe.

## National Music, 1820–1848

Acts of naming launched folk music along an ineluctable path toward national music. In the wake of Napoleon's defeat and the new partition of Europe into the national entities insisting on self-identity, the traces of the local and the idiosyncratic in folk song, and of the primordial and the anonymous, were supplanted by the name of the nation. By 1820, nations throughout Europe, new and old, laid claim to collectively owned folk musics. In the cases of certain genres, folk music was elevated to national status when local styles were renamed. The name **deutscher Tanz** ("German dance") infiltrated the vast repertories of alpine dances in triple meter; regional Polish folk dances, such as the **mazurka** and **krakowiak,** from the province of Mazur and the city of Kraków, respectively, found their way into Romantic Polish nationalism at a much slower pace than the **polonaise;** local styles of folk dances in duple meter, with angular rhythmic figuration, remained without special designation, whereas those that circulated throughout Europe as symbols of Scottish Romantic nationalism received the names **ecossaise** or **Schottische,** "Scottish" in French and German. It remained an open question just how German, Polish, or Scottish such folk dances really were, but the ambiguity of the acts of giving musical style and repertories names that signified the nation reflected the still-fluid state of European nationalism itself. Nevertheless, it was clear that folk music genres with national identities were proliferating and spreading throughout the entire continent.

Connecting folk songs to the nation with acts of naming was first possible when the songs themselves demonstrated—or were recognized as demonstrating—the traits of a collective. Predicated on some kind of stylistic and linguistic unity, the anthology of national songs possessed some of the same properties of collective cohesion as the nation whose name they bore. At the beginning of the nineteenth century published volumes of folk songs were designated as national for linguistic reasons. Achim von Arnim and Clemens Brentano's anthology *Des Knaben Wunderhorn* (1957), first published as two parts in 1806 and 1808, bears the subtitle, "old German songs." The Germanness of the first editions of *Des Knaben Wunderhorn* lay primarily in their language, which itself was the stylized product of folk poetry in local dialects and variants. Those who had created and transmitted the *Wunderhorn* songs surely would not have thought of themselves as

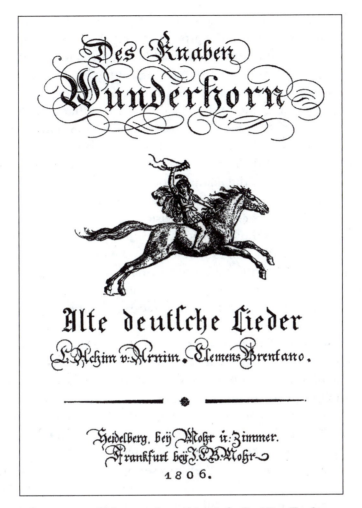

*Figure 2.1. Title page, first edition (1806) of* Des Knaben
Wunderhorn *(Arnim and Brentano 1957)*

"German" in any sort of national sense, but during the course of the
nineteenth century the anthology entered the intellectual history of
Germany through successive editions, constant editing and adaptation,
and by the century's end, ethnographic documentation that identified
the folk songs where the nationalist imagination believed them to be:
in the oral traditions that confirmed the Germanness of the published
anthologies (see Figure 2.1; for a study of the publication history of *Des
Knaben Wunderhorn,* see Schade 1990).

Naming the nation with rubrics attached to music was not limited to
folk songs. It was increasingly important that the acts of naming connected repertories that had previously been unrelated to each other.
The first substantial anthology of "German songs" to follow *Des Knaben
Wunderhorn* was a volume called *Deutsche Lieder für Jung und Alt* ("German Songs for Young and Old"), coedited by Bernhard Klein and Karl
August Groos (1818). Several additional factors enhanced the Germanness of this anthology. First, the texts were only occasionally stylized versions of local dialects, but were more often artifices written in
the style of folk song by the leading poets of the early Romantic period
(Goethe, Friedrich Schlegel, and Ludwig Uhland, for example). Second, most of the songs contained musical settings, in the first edition
usually only melodies, but in a second edition planned for publication
in the 1820s also settings in four voices for chorus (see Feurzeig 2003).
Looking at the early anthologies of German song, we can identify successive stages that transform the folk song from the local to the national, and then recontextualize the national in the trappings of the
folk. The anthologizers, editors, and publishers of the early nineteenth
century imagined "German song" to be something different at each
stage, but in so doing they transposed the history of German song—
the history of a name—into the history of the nation. Gradually much
of the ambiguity accompanying earlier acts of naming disappeared, as
a growing certainty about music's place in the musical life of the nation
undergirded music's role in the political shape of the nation.

Naming the nation through music is inevitably a top-down gesture.
An intellectual and political elite representing the nation appropriates
and consolidates power by extending the nation's name to as many
musical phenomena as possible. In his voluminous studies of Russian
music Richard Taruskin has repeatedly shown that "defining Russia
musically" resulted from conscious acts of assigning meaning through
music that relied on the names, or definitions, assigned by composers
and other intellectuals (see especially Taruskin 1997). The hierarchy
of names, for example, is amply evident in the first great Russian national opera, Mikhail Glinka's *A Life for the Tsar*, the composition of
which in the mid-1830s signaled an entirely new epoch in Russian nationalism. Glinka crafted what Taruskin calls a **style russe** from the
standpoint of a pan-European cosmopolitanism, which relied on con-
tinuous contrast between the music of a Russian selfness, fairly spare
use of Russian folk music, and Polish otherness, usually stereotyped

folklike music in standardized forms. In Glinka's own reflections on the opera he constantly assigned names that connected specific musical gestures to abstract qualities, such as "the soul of Russian music," thus making these less abstract (ibid.: 29). Glinka looked from above and forged his musical definitions from above, thus making it possible for him to achieve with *A Life for the Tsar* "his enthusiastic commitment to the state ideology and his determination to embody it in symbolic sounds" (ibid.). Using the name of the nation, as Glinka so forcefully did and as successive generations of composers would do as they, too, attempted to represent the nation with opera, instigated a crucial change in the nineteenth century. The national became the nationalist. It was not a single nation, but the names of many nations that began to appear in European music from the 1820s onward. As a result, internationalism and nationalism in music came to depend on one another, the names of one bounded by the names of the other.

## 1848: The Struggle for a Populist Nation

Two processes transformed folk song to national song in the decades leading to the revolutionary year of 1848: popularization and politicization. The two processes had been distinct in the 1820s, when the publications of folk songs appeared in greater numbers, but by the 1830s the processes dovetailed, narrowing the distance between folk and national song, and even more significantly, reconfiguring them as populist discourses, that is, as repertories that powerfully connected the aspirations of the working class and a growing middle class to the functions of the nation. The decades leading to 1848, therefore, constituted an era of populism and the politicization of the music culture of Europe as a whole. To analyze just how music gave voice to the struggle for a populist nation, we turn first to those whose voices were raised in song.

More than any other phenomenon, the chorus came to implement the convergence of the popular and the political in folk song and then in national song. During the 1820s and 1830s, choruses grew in number throughout Europe, adopting new repertories and adapting to rapidly changing socioeconomic conditions. The prehistory of the early nineteenth-century choral movement in Europe had followed very different paths in the continent's regions. One of the primary contexts for the chorus had been the church, particularly at the local level. The parish chorus contributed to local music cultures by further ritualizing local sacred practice and expanding the possibilities for literacy on numerous levels. In some regions of Europe there had been long histories of folk-singing with multiple voices singing different parts. The Welsh tradition of choral singing is today the best known of these traditions, but historical records reveal that part-singing was common in many areas of Europe. Folk-singing by choruses spread throughout the Alps, and it assumed a variety of distinctive forms in the Balkans. It was because these pre-nineteenth-century choral traditions were so varied that their consolidation on regional and national levels during the 1820s and 1830s was historically so significant. Consolidation meant that the choruses adopted the new published collections, that they extended their presence from local contexts to the national public sphere, and that they broke down both regional and class distinctions. The chorus was a vehicle for the implementation of power generated from a growing middle class (cf., CD examples 6, 31, and 32).

The choral movement, it follows, was the embodiment of the nation-state as an amalgam of different classes and types of people. This is not to say that many nineteenth-century choruses were openly democratic. The earliest choruses were overwhelmingly male, and in some traditions, notably the German chorus, some distinctions between men's and women's chorus survive even today. The prototypes of the nineteenth century notwithstanding, the choral movement depended upon the acts of innovators and charismatic musical leaders. In Germany the most influential organizer of the choral movement was Ludwig Erk, who actively gathered anthologies, arranged folk songs for choruses, and worked tirelessly to organize choruses in regional and national institutions. Erk pushed the boundaries of the choral movement outward until they were coterminous with the boundaries of the nation. The German chorus served many different types of institutions, ranging from the university to the trade union, the church to the specialized fraternal club. Choruses did invite a growing egalitarian participation from throughout German society. As many German synagogues underwent processes of reform in the early nineteenth century, they, too, came to support choruses, initially men's choruses specializing in Jewish liturgy, but by mid-century many mixed choruses that were no less active in the public sphere (at mass choral conventions or competitions) than Christian organizations or choral groups with no religious affiliation whatsoever.

What did the choruses of the nascent choral movement include in their repertories? A remarkable mixture of styles and genres, but not simply a cross-section of everything available at the time. The choral repertory might seem eclectic at first glance, with its juxtaposition of folk songs, religious and classical compositions, and operatic arias and choruses. Nonetheless, the parts of the repertory were combined in very specific ways to emblematize the collective and political nature of the chorus. By underscoring the collective and its expression through a repertory sharing the literary language of a nation, choral repertories were unified by their common service to the nation.

### Canonizing the National Repertory

The very concept of a national repertory itself underwent a transformation in the early decades of the nineteenth century. A number of songs, referred to in several languages as "hymns," competed with each other to represent the nation. Among the most frequently rallied competitors in the states of German-speaking Europe were "God Save the King," "Marseillaise," and its variant, the "Internationale" (all in German translation), as well as the more regionally meaningful "Deutschlandlied" ("Germany Song") and "Ein' feste Burg" ("A Mighty Fortress Is Our God"). There were other notable competitors also, but these five illustrate that the "nation" was realized in vastly different and seemingly unrelated ways, ranging from a hymn symbolic of German Protestantism to one that has come to represent international socialism (see Kurzke 1990).

By the mid-nineteenth century, however, the "Deutschlandlied" had begun to nudge out the other competitors, leading us to think that it might have been more "German" than the other hymns all along. But such was not the case. The "Deutschlandlied"—also called "Das Lied der Deutschen" but known best to non-Germans today through its first line, "Deutschland, Deutschland, über alles" ("Germany, Germany, above all else")—is a setting of a poem by the Silesian-German poet August Heinrich Hoffmann von Fallersleben, with the four-part "Emperor's Hymn," which first appeared as a quasi-choral setting in one of Franz Joseph Haydn's Op. 77 quartets (CD example 34). (See Figure 2.2.) The melody itself comes from a Croatian folk song that circulated in oral tradition around the Hungarian Esterházy court in Eisenstadt, a

Figure 2.2. *"Das Deutschlandlied," Franz Joseph Haydn and
August Heinrich Hoffmann von Fallersleben, nineteenth-century version
(courtesy of the Deutsches Historisches Museum)*

largely Jewish small city in the border region shared by Austria and
Hungary (CD example 33 is a field recording of a modern performance of the Croatian folk song, "Jutro rano sam se ja stal," which survives in oral tradition today in the area around Eisenstadt; see Hemetek 2001). Hoffmann von Fallersleben wrote the text while in exile on
Helgoland, then a British island in the North Sea.

In the midst of all these competing symbols, where is the German nation? In fact, that is the question that the song itself answered by specifying the rivers, mountain ranges, and landscapes that constituted the historical geography of Germany. Germanness also assumes musical form, specifically in the repetitions of the first line of melody, yielding the common German folk-song and hymn structure known as **Bar-Form** (AAB). The "Deutschlandlied" is not and never was a stable set of images and symbols that could stand in for Germany itself. Its nationalism lent itself to consolidation at mid-century because its meanings, instead, were fluid. For the history of national song we examine in this chapter, moreover, it is significant that the fluid meanings in the "Deutschlandlied" did not disappear in the twentieth century, when the song was interpreted in vastly different ways, as a potential text for fascist imperialism or as simply a means of celebrating common national culture with a nostalgic hymn (Knopp and Kuhn 1988). Already in the mid-nineteenth century meaning upon meaning was accruing to this national hymn and to those of other European countries, at once politicizing the ways in which choruses did or did not perform the nation into being during an era of growing revolutionary instability (CD track 35).

## National Music, 1850–1914

### "Republick von 1848"

1. You citizen, swear hand-in-hand,
To live in the beautifully shining fatherland,
Free from worries,
With hearts loyal
To the Republic.

**REFRAIN**
Take joy in life,
Because freedom now blossoms,
Because the banner
Glows with three colors.

4. And everywhere around the globe
The people make a pact of freedom,
Without self-interest,

Dedicated to protection and defiance,
To standing side-by-side.
> —Broadside ballad printed on 24 February 1848 in Strasbourg
> (see Deutsches Volksliedarchiv)


"Ausgleichslied von 1867"

1. Who now feels at home with us?
Who now feels at home with us?
The Hungarians and the Bohemians, the Hungarians and the
    Bohemians.
They now feel at home with us.


3. Oh, despite everything, is it still home?
Oh, despite everything, is it still home?
In the best way you can imagine, in the best way you can imagine,
Oh, despite everything, it's still home.


4. And at home, what do we call this?
And at home, what do we call this?
We've all become the same, we've all become the same,
That's what one calls it at home.
> —transcribed from *Das ist mein Österreich*, n.d.


Two popular songs open this section, in which we consider the flood of nationalism that swept across Europe in the second half of the nineteenth century in the wake of the revolutions of 1848 and 1849. The "Republick von 1848" ("The Republic of 1848") was itself an immediate product of the revolution. It appeared as a broadside on the streets of Strasbourg on 24 February 1848, the final day of the storming by students and workers of the Palais Royal in Paris, which led to the abdication of Louis Philippe and brought down the French government, with its persistent traces of monarchy. Throughout the revolutionary year of 1848, citizens, workers, and the growing bourgeoisie of Europe found themselves emboldened to throw out the prevailing government structures and to storm the barricades erected by the aging empires in order to bring new nations and new forms of governing them into being. By and large, the revolutionary actions began among the relatively powerless and moved from the bottom up. By and large, they were also bloody and, by the end of 1848, almost entirely unsuccessful.

Whether or not reformed governments and more extensive populist control did gain a real foothold in the nations of Europe in 1848, the citizens of nations throughout Europe had come to recognize the potential of taking nationalism into their own hands. They recognized, furthermore, that the citizens of other European nations were doing the same, which meant that the freedom and self-rule for which they were calling in their own countries would not be isolated phenomena. In the coming half century their aspirations toward the nationalism of a new order would multiply, as would their attempts to effect that new nationalism. An explosion of national songs accompanied the new order, and nationalism itself began to motivate more and more musical practices and the groups that undertook them.

The proliferation of national songs accompanied the expansion of the "discourse networks" of national culture and action (Kittler 1987). Songs appeared, often spontaneously, to record a specific set of events, then broadsides, newspapers, and song pamphlets picked up and disseminated the new songs. A new text, with its highly politicized references, would be crafted to fit a preexisting melody, often one with functions and symbolic associations similar to the new song's message. When "Republick von 1848" appeared on the streets of Strasbourg, its anonymous poet/publisher indicated that it should be sung to the 1793 freedom song, "Freut euch des Lebens" ("Take Joy in Life"), the opening of which comes back repeatedly in the new song's refrain. "Republick von 1848," therefore, immediately entered a network of national song with a hit song from the late eighteenth century, but also with the welter of **contrafacts** and parodies of a song that collectively symbolized the nationalistic revolution.

The second song in this section, "Ausgleichslied von 1867" ("Equality Song of 1867"), responded to a different set of national struggles and entered a different network of national songs, these in the Eastern European regions of the Austro-Hungarian Empire. The "equality" to which the song's title refers—**Ausgleich** might be better glossed as "the result of being made the same"—came from a series of laws enacted in 1867 that would offer other national groups in the empire many of the same rights as the Austrians. The 1867 laws emanated from the top, that is from the Habsburg rulers, with the design of quieting much of the nationalistic fervor that had been unleashed in 1848, when Hungarians had taken the lead in agitating for independence from Austria. However, the "equality" in the "Ausgleichslied" was effectively an empty promise, and the song makes fun of the 1867 laws through parody. It circulated through the empire as a folk song, surviving at the beginning of the twenty-first century in oral tradition. Its network of nationalistic discourse acquired additional meaning through its use of dialect, which powerfully emphasized that the political reality for the Eastern European nationality groups, "despite everything," was still not the home to which those groups were aspiring.

### Inventing National Song

In the second half of the nineteenth century national song participated in the forging of new expressive symbols and practices, such as the formation of standardized literary languages and the creation of national folk-song collections, and in the transformation of these into national musical canons. Accordingly, much of the ambiguity that characterized national song in the first part of the nineteenth century gave way to practices that were more widely shared. Movements for political independence were accompanied by a new wave of choral movements, which relied on repertories whose boundaries were relatively fixed and whose use of literary language heightened the nationalistic import of song. National languages took shape in many of the areas of Europe that were striving for cultural and political rights. Intellectuals and cultural politicians in Romania, for example, redoubled efforts to create a modern Romanian language, which would at once enhance the rootedness of Romanian in Romance-language predecessors and purge the language of many of the traces that modern Romanians might regard as not belonging to the Romanian language, especially Slavic and Hungarian words.

Jewish intellectuals in Romania, as elsewhere in Eastern Europe, turned toward the production of a literature in literary Yiddish, and it is hardly surprising that the bulk of what we today consider to be classic works of Yiddish literature, by writers such as Sholem Aleichem, appeared in the second half of the nineteenth century. At mid-century there had been little evidence to suggest that the canonization of Yiddish had nationalist implications; after all, Yiddish speakers were dispersed across all of Eastern Europe and parts of Central Europe, and the emigration of Jews from Europe was beginning to accelerate. By the end of the century, however, the situation was very different. Yiddish folk-song collections were appearing in greater numbers by the 1890s, and in 1901 Shaul Ginsburg and Pesach Marek published an anthology of Yiddish songs in St. Petersburg that quickly became the core repertory for emerging forms for Jewish nationalism, not least among them Zionism (see Ginsburg and Marek 1901). The Ginsburg and Marek anthology provided a modern source of Yiddish songs to which Jewish folk-song publishers would turn for the next forty years, and the network of songs and song publications that the Russian collection inspired served to connect Jewish communities throughout Europe and to make the musical symbols of Jewish nationalism meaningful in dramatically new ways (cf. Kaufmann 1920 and Bohlman 2003).

Choruses of all sizes and shapes also provided crucial connective tissue for the expanding national song networks. Although they appeared as broadsides or entered oral tradition as folk-song parodies, national songs emphasized the collective, and performance as a collective clearly underscored the metaphorical meaning of the songs for the nation itself. Charismatic leaders were often responsible for transforming loose confederations of choral ensembles into choral leagues and unions whose activities consciously symbolized the nation. In mid-nineteenth-century Denmark, for example, Nicolai Frederik Severin Grundtvig (1783–1872) drew inspiration from a broad range of Danish folklore sources and molded them into concerted cultural activities, among them Danish choral repertories and choral activities embedded in a new system of nationalized education for the common person. Grundtvig's activities were highly political, responding above all to the German military and administrative presence in the southern part of Denmark. The choral repertories that emerged from the organizations that N. F. S. Grundtvig founded, bolstered by the establishment of a national program to publish Danish folk song by the end of the century, whose general editor was Svend Grundtvig (1824–1883), remain cornerstones for Danish national identity even today, when conflict and competition with Germany has largely subsided (see Grundtvig 1881; cf. Holzapfel 1993).

By the turn of the twentieth century national song and the music of nationalism were ubiquitous phenomena throughout Europe. Newly independent nations could claim national repertories and musical styles no less than those whose identity stretched into the premodern history of Europe. Most important, ethnic, linguistic, and religious groups wishing to make national claims against the old empires had

fully recognized the corpus of powerful symbols that music provided to
them. As the twentieth century began, a new era of European national-
ism-mustering national music was quickly taking shape, a national music that would challenge and undermine the old order forever.


## The Implosion of European Empires

As distended empires—England, France, Germany, Austro-Hungary,
Russia—competed for the national spaces of Europe and the colonial
spaces beyond, the nationalism that sustained them became increasingly bloated in the closing decades of the nineteenth century. Tension
grew within the empires, impelled by a new form of nationalism: ethnicity. Ethnicity was a counterforce to nineteenth-century nationalism,
and it relied on the concentration of cultural, linguistic, and often religious difference within the inchoate nation. To transform the inchoate
into the full-fledged, independent nation, difference would need to
undergo an elevation to a canonized, unified culture, and music—ethnic music as we would call it today—appeared as an alternative language, inspiring and aspiring toward the **ethnonationalism** of **fin-de-
siècle** Europe. Within the European empires the distinctiveness of
ethnic groups was increasingly sharpened as the symbols of ethnicity
became tangible aspects of everyday life. Folk songs previously circulating in dialect and oral tradition were collected and set as art songs in
the national language, indeed, encoding the national language
through song. In the waning decades of the nineteenth century, the
national musics of empire and the ethnic musics of growing ethnonationalism were competing for many of the same spaces. By the early
decades of the twentieth century the strain produced by that competition was no longer tenable, producing instead the implosion of European nationalism that led to World War I.

No European empire had depended more on a nationalism that
could embrace and thus contain ethnic difference than had Austria-
Hungary. At the political and military core of the empire was a power-
sharing system that allied the aristocracies of Vienna and Budapest and
the cultures of Central and Eastern Europe. At its most extensive, the
Austro-Hungarian Empire stretched from the Alps in the west, across
the Balkan states in the southeast, into Romania and Ukraine in the
east, and into Poland and the Czech lands in the north. The empire

exhibited its own brand of expansionist nationalism, which endeavored both to tolerate and to integrate the ethnic and religious cultures in the lands it had subjugated. The German and to a lesser degree Hungarian national cultures at the center should thrive side-by-side with the ethnic cultures at the peripheries. New cosmopolitan cities, such as Czernowitz in modern Ukraine, grew rapidly at the periphery, bringing not only the German language and cultural life from the core to regions of complex cultural mixture. Large Ukrainian, Romanian, and Yiddish-speaking areas intersected at Czernowitz, and these areas accommodated several additional minority groups. In turn, the cosmopolitanism at the periphery, with its universities, literary institutions, and intense musical life, funneled elements of the empire's ethnic amalgam back to the center (see Figures 2.3 and 2.4, both from the western Ukraine, near Czernowitz, and published in a volume of folk songs and ethnic costumes, or **Trachten,** given to Empress Elisabeth as a wedding gift in 1854; see Mraz 1997).

By the turn of the century the national culture sought to domesticate the peripheries, for example, by instituting in 1904 the encyclopedic project *Das Volkslied in Österreich* ("Folk Song in Austria"), in which single volumes would encompass the folk song of each Austrian province (Deutsch 1995). By the turn of the century, ethnic musics had found their way into many parts of the Austrian and Hungarian music traditions, so much so that any concept of Austrian music in the twentieth century must account for the presence of ethnic difference. From operetta to the avant garde, Austrian composers sought space for the sounds of national others, which in turn unleashed the virtually unchecked stylistic variation that we now call musical **modernism.** All this occurred as the nationalist demands of ethnic minorities searched for the political and military means to disentangle themselves from the center. By the second decade of the twentieth century ethnonationalism in Austria-Hungary could no longer be domesticated. A Serb nationalist's assassination of the Austrian Archduke Franz Ferdinand in 1914 while he was visiting Sarajevo ignited the impending implosion and started World War I.

Music secured the foundations of ethnicity within European nationalism in contrasting ways. Just as choral groups had centralized German nationalism in the early and mid-nineteenth century, they mobilized ethnic groups as aspiring national movements in fin-de-siècle Europe. In eastern Spain, for example, Catalan ethnonationalism found an en-

*Figure 2.3. The song representing Galicia, in "Ruthenian" (Ukrainian) and German, in Empress Elisabeth's Wedding Gift of 1854 (Mraz 1997)*

tirely new outlet in a choral movement that used music to articulate resistance against Spanish dominance (see Macedo 2002). Among the best-known choral traditions were those of the Baltic states, especially of Estonia. Estonian choruses had drawn inspiration from German influences through centuries of **Hanseatic League** trade connections, but by the twentieth century they were following distinctively Estonian routes. At every level the Estonian singing emphasized the mass chorus, a phenomenon to which all Estonians could and should contribute. Lo-

*Figure 2.4.  Folk costumes from the Bukovina (Czernowitz region),*
*in Empress Elisabeth's Wedding Gift of 1854 (Mraz 1997)*

cal choruses were community undertakings, and the mass choral gatherings provided chances for thousands of singers to perform the repertories of the nation itself. In the course of the twentieth century, as Estonia achieved and lost independence on several occasions, the mass
chorus provided one of the most important symbolic forms of national
unisonality, both in Estonia and in Estonian communities in the diaspora, keeping the nation intact through its choral music itself.

The tension between ethnicity and nationalism also intensified in the
musical culture of diaspora. Irish music, for example, underwent the
transformation from regional folk-music dialects to a nationalized
canon not in an Ireland under English domination, but rather in the
immigrant communities of the United States, where the common cul-

ture of a historically unified tradition could be sutured together. The core repertory of modern Irish folk music was collected in Chicago by Francis O'Neill, a captain in the city's police force, who encouraged his fellow Irish immigrants to perform, then published transcriptions and detailed discussions of Irish music in a series of publications (e.g., O'Neill 1913). O'Neill's publications appeared—and were exported to Ireland—during the period of Ireland's greatest and eventually success-ful struggle for independence from the British Empire. As the Irish na-tion itself took leave of the empire that had encumbered its ethnona-tionalism, it could and did embrace Francis O'Neill's volumes of Irish music, which today are one of Ireland's national icons (see Chapter 3).

### National Music and the Recording of Difference

The cataclysmic historical events that culminated in World War I en-gendered a fear that the European nations of the nineteenth century had fallen victim to history. Already during the war, musical scholars joined other intellectuals in wondering if the fragments of the nation might somehow be retrieved, perhaps even placed in the new historical museums of modernity to preserve them for the future remapping of European nationalism. The museums of modernity, moreover, were not primarily anachronistic institutions, but they often depended on the new technologies of the early twentieth century. For the scholars concerned with the musical soundscapes of nationalism, the new tech-nologies were primarily the products of revolutionary developments in sound recording. Sound recording offered the possibility not only to collect the fragments of the broken nation, but also to classify them in such a way that they could be reassembled. The new technologies, therefore, engendered a conviction that authenticity was inscribed in these fragments of the past and that recorded sound enhanced the power of music to preserve the nation, even as the bits and pieces of the past.

Astonishingly, the Great War opened opportunities for several of our greatest recording experiments. Prior to the war, the world's fair had gathered musicians from nations throughout the world and offered in-ternational audiences the possibility of hearing all the world's nations performing in a single space. During World War I, prisoner-of-war camps did exactly the same thing. Teams of scholars—anthropologists, linguists, folklorists, and musicologists—were commissioned to enter

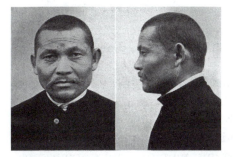

*Figure 2.5. World War I recording project. Carl Stumpf and Georg Schünemann with Tatar Musicians (Doegen 1925)*

the camps and gather prisoners from individual nations, who would then provide interviews about their own traditions, tell stories, and perform the music that they had brought with them to the field of battle. Early German ethnomusicologists were among the most actively engaged fieldworkers in prisoner-of-war camps, and some of the most distinguished scholars of the early twentieth century, including the comparative musicologists associated with the University of Berlin, participated in these projects. After the war several major publications documented the recordings made in the camps, and several remain classic works of early twentieth-century comparative musicology (see, for example, Doegen 1925 and Schünemann 1923). The situation was no different in the Austro-Hungarian prisoner-of-war camps, where even Béla Bartók (1881–1945) contributed his ethnographic expertise to recordings that gathered songs from soldiers. Figure 2.5 comes from just one of many publications based on the wartime recording projects.

The wartime recording projects relied on a belief in a triangulated calculus with three sets of coordinates: authenticity, inscription, nation. By recording the music of prisoners-of-war, the wartime ethnographers elevated local musical practices to the level of the nation. The prisoner from Russia performed music that stood for Russia; the prisoner from Italy sang Italian songs; the prisoner from Romania brought Romanian music with him to the battlefield. Music provided the connective tissue that bound the individual soldier to the nation-state. The musical repertories of different nations, moreover, were comparable, and the individual nation became audible in all the different musics of its soldiers. As we study the wartime collections today and increasingly have the opportunity to listen to the wax-cylinder recordings now re-released on digitized CDs, we are also struck by the extent to which the nations that emerge from the classifications belong more to the twentieth century than to the nineteenth. Empire, as we have seen, dominated the nineteenth century, especially in the struggles for control over Eastern Europe. The wartime recordings, in contrast, admitted more nations, even before these had gained any independence from the empires still at war (listen to CD example 35).

## Sounding the Nation into Being

The experiments with sound recording provided a new vocabulary for imagining and inventing the nation. One of the boldest projects to inscribe an authentic nation with music as a surrogate for the real political nation was Abraham Zvi Idelsohn's (1882–1938) transformation of his field recordings of Jewish musicians in Jerusalem into musical monuments for a modern Jewish state. Armed with a wax-cylinder recorder and financing from the Austro-Hungarian Academy of Sciences, Idelsohn undertook extensive fieldwork in Palestine, working intensively from 1908 to 1911 and then more sporadically until the eve of World War I. Idelsohn transcribed his recordings of Yemenite, Iraqi, Persian, Moroccan, and Central Asian Jewish musicians, then he published them in the ten volumes of the *Hebräisch-orientalischer Melodienschatz* ("Thesaurus of Hebrew-Oriental Melodies"), which appeared from 1914 until 1932. The volumes comprise a deliberate classification scheme, with repertories distinguished according to Jewish ethnic community, but Idelsohn constantly draws on the comparative methods of linguistics and ethnomusicology. The ten volumes appeared during the era of deepening Zionism and accelerating anti-Semitism in Central Europe, and it is hardly surprising that they came to represent a Jewish nation as a whole, albeit with many distinctive parts. Gathered as individual recordings (or drawn from individual manuscripts and anthologies in the concluding volumes for Central and Eastern Europe), the *Thesaurus* renders the whole of a modern Jewish nation audible, reassembling its fragmented past and the centuries of diaspora as if they cohered as a nation in the present.

New technologies were not the only means of authenticating national history to be sanctioned in the period between the world wars. One of the most ambitious of all nationalist song undertakings was a forty-two-volume anthology of German folk songs initiated by the German Folk-Song Archive in 1924 and executed over the course of the next half century. The volumes were to contain *landschaftliche Volkslieder* (literally "folk songs from their landscapes"), whereby a "landscape" was a province or linguistic region within Germany or a former German-language colony, region, or linguistic island elsewhere in Europe. The individual song volumes, therefore, signified Germany within its post–World War I boundaries, but also the areas of German settlement lost during the war, especially those in Eastern Europe.

Nationalism assumed many forms in these volumes, but there could be no question that the inscribed songs, with accompanying illustrations, relied on a national sense of sonic authenticity basic to folk songs in the German language. Folk songs contained sonic markers that came to sound like an original Germanness. That authenticity extended to "Middle Poland" and to the Volga German settlements in Ukraine and to the **Gottschee colonies** of modern Slovenia. By the 1930s, the volumes suggested a new capacity to mobilize authenticity as a means of reclaiming regions the German fascists believed belonged to the German nation, and the symbolism of authentic folk song underwent a transformation to a military agenda of German national expansion (see Figure 2.6). Notwithstanding the obvious ways in which the folk-song volumes served German racist and military agendas during the Nazi period, the *Landschaftliche Volkslieder* project continued after World War II, with the final volume appearing in 1971. A different nationalism is evident in the Cold War volumes, but what emerges is more basic: the need to achieve a sense of closure to make the nation "musically whole." In purely symbolic terms the forty-two

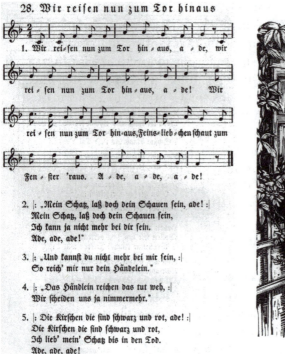

*Figure 2.6. "The Soldier's Farewell,"* Oberschlesische Volkslieder,
*volume devoted to Upper Silesia (Czech and Polish border area)*
*(Deutsches Volksliedarchiv 1938: 40–41)*

volumes represent Germany at various stages of struggle with its own
sense of historical nationalism, a contested "folk-song landscape" of
tragic twentieth-century history (Bohlman 2002b).

## World War II and Music's Nationalist Transgressions

As Europe's fascist nations consolidated power and hardened their political ideologies during the 1930s, nationalism entered a new phase,
in which its forms were reduced to the most banal stereotypes. The nationalism that Germany and Italy fabricated to implement fascist, expansionist ends during World War II relied on a hardened view of European history, in which an extreme view of self and other prevailed.
As nationalism came to serve the goals of the fascist nations, it collapsed Europe into an old model, in which nationalism fed upon intol-

erance and came to trade in symbols so powerful that entire nations could be rallied to undertake unspeakably egregious acts in the name of the nation. And music was there, implicated in the violence and violation of human rights and dignity that was justified by nationalism.

As fascism strengthened its foothold in Germany and Italy during the early 1930s, the old vocabularies of musical nationalism gave way to new ones. Outwardly, the nationalist musics of the fascist governments were no different from earlier forms of musical nationalism. Folk music again grew in importance as the symbol of a nation's authenticity. Music history acquired greater nationalist potential by being recast as canonic repertories that formed from the works of composers whose nationalist pursuits in the past were seen as presaging the present. If nothing else, the distinctions sharpened between music in the service of the nation and music with no real nationalist functions. There was less room for equivocation about which musics were nationalist and which were not. As fascism enveloped more aspects of daily and public life, there was less chance that any given musical repertory or practice could escape the stereotyped labels explicit in the new nationalism. There were no neutral options, no compromises: Music either was or was not nationalist.

If stereotype and banality overwhelmed musical nationalism in the fascist nations of Europe, this does not mean that there was anything simple about the ways in which music could represent the nation to the aggrandizement of self and the denigration of other. Nationalist musics of the 1930s and 1940s exposed numerous layers of prejudice that had been historically inseparable from nationalism. The meaning of "German" in fascist and Nazi discourses about music provides one of the most brutal cases in point. Already by 1933, when the Nazis ascended to power in Germany, the concern for "German music" was expanding rapidly, inculcating many different public discourses about music itself (see, e.g., Potter 1998). The concern for Germanness in music was not new, but the extent to which it displaced other issues of identity was (cf. Applegate 1992). So powerful and pervasive was the need to pursue the question of Germanness that a new science of musical nationalism quickly asserted itself.

Musical nationalism, in other words, was no longer simply a matter of constructivist views of the past but rather the result of what its exponents claimed to be scientific experiments. The new musical "science" relied extensively on some of the crassest of all German nationalist concepts, among them **Blut und Boden** ("blood and soil"). The racializing and racist implications of the first part of this nationalist calculus are obvious: The German in music is that which is racially German, in other words, that which is biologically pure and unpolluted (cf. Linke 1999). Racial purity manifested itself in the diatonic intervallic structures of German modality and in the retention of the pure harmonic relationships in German tonality. In major works of German racial musical science, musicologists sought to demonstrate that interval size and harmonic structures correlated with the size and shape of the human skull. The fact that major-minor tonality characterize German music to a greater degree than any other national music, racialized musical science went on to argue, was clearly evident in the distinctive shape of the skull in the "Nordic races" (see the essays in Waldmann 1938, especially Fritz Metzler's). Racial scientism in musicology extended without theoretical encumbrance to history, with the evolution of major-minor tonality paralleling the history of German dominance in Europe (Frotscher in Waldmann 1938).

### Multiple Forms of Musical Nationalism

To the extent that music historians have concerned themselves with musical nationalism in Europe during the 1930s and 1940s, they have tended to imagine a rather sharp divide between musical nationalisms that were evil and those that displayed a measure of virtue. The danger in casting musical nationalism in such dichotomous terms during World War II is that history itself would seem to dissipate into stasis, with nationalism capable of rationalizing every historical development. Far more important for the larger historical argument of the present chapter is a recognition that musical nationalism did indeed become more important when World War II approached—more central in national debates about political and military action—but it also became much more complex. The use of music to mobilize national military action, to take an obvious case, expanded proportionally to the expansion of the war. Volumes of military songs appeared in exponentially greater numbers, and these were disseminated as popular music through the nationalized radio and other broadcasting media. Throughout the 1930s and 1940s, musical programs on the radio were designed to bring the nation into the home (Currid 1998).

Art-music composers, too, created works that chronicled the nation's historical struggle. Dmitry Shostakovich, for example, remained in Leningrad (St. Petersburg) during most of World War II, including the years of siege by the Germans, an experience that led him to compose a series of symphonies (for example, the Seventh in C, Op. 60, known as the "Leningrad Symphony") that narrated the struggle and eventual victory of the Soviet Union. But such works do not portray nationalism monochromatically. They raise questions about the relation of national identity to other forms of identity. On a particularly tragic level, we witness the search for identity in the powerful works of Jews incarcerated and later murdered in concentration camps. For those few musicians who were able to continue creative activities for several years, usually before being transported to death camps, there was sometimes an almost radical turn toward creating "Jewish works," in other words, compositions with Jewish themes or texts in Hebrew or Yiddish. Distinguished composers, such as Viktor Ullmann (1898–1944), who had never used music to examine questions of Jewish identity, created works such as the apocryphal *Emperor of Atlantis* (1943) that complicate the problem of musical nationalism by narrating disturbing counterhistories of the European nation (Bohlman, forthcoming a).

Music's capacity to narrate the European nation intensified during World War II, although the war brought about the collapse of several pillars of nineteenth-century nationalism. Within years of the war, European colonialism would largely collapse, leaving only vestiges of the extensive empires that had once undergirded European hegemony. The war also brutally reduced several of Europe's most significant nationless peoples, notably through Germany's racialized elimination of Europe's Jews and Roma. These acts of extermination, too, left indelible impressions on European nationalism and the musics that bore witness to its excesses. The Europe that survived World War II had a dramatically different national configuration, and music quickly underwent dramatic alterations of its own to take account of the new form of nationalism produced by the reconfiguration of Europe.

### The European Nation in East and West

With the defeat of Germany, Italy, Japan, and their allies in World War II, nationalism entered a new phase. Internationally, the emergence of a nationalism followed in the wake of the war, acquiring momentum from the contributions to the global war effort by regional and national groups. The colonies had fought alongside large European empires, and the moment had arrived in which they would insist upon their independence from those empires. Within Europe a new nationalism arose in the years following the war, with a number of nations in Eastern Europe that had suffered extensively under the German occupation insisting on their right to consolidate political identity as a nation. If the vestiges of imperial power had been erased in many areas of Europe, a new tension took shape that would channel the several paths that postwar nationalism would follow: the political and ideological fissure that would divide the continent's nations between East and West for the next forty years. Even as the individual identities of European nations multiplied between 1945 and the early 1950s, the necessity to model nationalism on either the democracies of Western Europe or on the socialist democracies in the East hardened.

Was the new nationalism that followed Europe's division into East and West really new? Rather than seizing the opportunity to herald the new nationalism as the milestone for a journey into a future untrammeled by the past, the governments and ideologues of nations in both East and West turned toward the past. They plumbed the past, as if obsessed with the pressing need to reimagine and reconstruct national history to explain if not heal the scars of the war. Music, so thoroughly implicated in national history, proved to be one of the most effective means of tapping the past and remapping it on the present. As postwar nationalism increasingly relied on **historicism**—the use of the past to imagine and construct the present—music contributed substantially to the vocabularies and public culture required for the new era of the European nation that began in about 1950 and continued for the next four decades, an historical moment we have long since called the Cold War. The historical tension implicit in the Cold War was limited to neither East nor West. To understand the ways in which music characterized the new nationalism, therefore, it behooves us to examine historicism in all parts of the continent.

The Eastern European nations established, or reestablished, after World War II turned to music to unravel twentieth-century histories that were extraordinarily complicated. Nations such as Hungary and East Germany were successor states to the fascist governments of World War II, and many of the republics of socialist nations in the East, such as Slovakia, Croatia, and Ukraine, had largely joined ranks with Germany as it invaded the East. In order to erase the immediate past, many Eastern European nations sought a more distant past that took precedence over the war years. In folk music the new nationalist historicism found an ideal vocabulary. The folk-music scholars of the German Democratic Republic (GDR), for example, launched a sweeping campaign to redefine the canon of German folk song so that it would provide the historical script for what Wolfgang Steinitz called German folk songs with "democratic character" from the previous six centuries of German history (Steinitz 1978). Whereas Steinitz adapted widely held claims about the functionality of song in the lives of workers, thus imbuing all workers' songs with a degree of historical specificity, he employed the prevalent historiography of the socialist dialectic in the GDR to give folk song a new meaning for the interpretation of the past. The German folk song, in its most historicized form, was also "oppositional," in other words it voiced criticism and channeled social action against the hegemonic forces of labor and the state. Steinitz did not simply pick random folk songs that would serve his three-volume history, but rather he drew from the standard collections (e.g., Erk-Böhme 1893–1894) and archival sources, above all the German Folk-Song Archive in Freiburg im Breisgau, since the partition of Germany in the West. His folk-song history, which proved enormously influential for Central European folklorists and historians, served not only, or even primarily, as the history of the GDR as a nation, but rather as a history of a six-century course of nationalism that had reached its apex with the founding of the GDR.

### Folk Music and Modern European Nationalism

Folk music flourished in the socialist nations of Eastern Europe, and it penetrated every level of society. To be a folk musician chosen for a local, regional, or national ensemble in an Eastern European nation was to enjoy a degree of prestige and financial well-being that relatively few others enjoyed. The official performance of folk music gave the nation a public face as it turned within and outside its borders. Folk-music activities were scaffolded on an extremely intricate hierarchy, with local organizations at the bottom and administration from cultural agencies at the top (see a schematic representation of this hierarchy for Romania in Nixon 1998: xv). The hierarchy provided a high degree of mobility for talented musicians, and those with sufficient ambition might launch their careers locally with the intent of participating at higher levels in the hierarchy, each of which would intensify their participation in musical practices connected more directly with the state. In many countries, annual competitions facilitated such career trajectories toward the national levels of the hierarchy. In Yugoslavia, for example, the musicians who participated in the traditional **tamburitza** ensembles might win national acclaim and positions in state-sponsored ensembles by first entering local competitions and then winning at the subsequent regional competitions, until they eventually reached the national levels (see, e.g., Forry 1986). By the end of the twentieth century the tensions of the Cold War were relaxing. National folk ensembles of Eastern European nations were distributing recordings in Western Europe and North America, and many had even begun to tour internationally. Among the best-known national ensembles were those of Bulgaria, whose state women's chorus had won international acclaim already in the 1980s (cf. Rice 1994 and Buchanan, forthcoming). By the turn of the millennium, the historicism of the socialist nations of Eastern Europe was a familiar sound throughout Europe.

Folk music was also crucial to the new paths of national history in Western Europe. Rather than state sponsorship or official hierarchies, however, the primary impetus for national historicism in Western Europe was the **revival** movement. Folk-music revivals were anything but lacking in ideology. The revivalists in Germany, England, Sweden, and elsewhere mined local and regional repertories, often asserting that it was only at the level below the national that history was truly enacted by the nation's people. The ideal of folk song became, therefore, dialect song; folk dance, they argued, should employ local instruments and their variants; and national repertories should represent the past only insofar as they had accounted for as much cultural difference as possible.

The advocates of folk revivals espoused, often openly, a kinship with the ideologies of folk music in service to the socialist state that dominated the new nationalism of Eastern Europe (see, e.g., Lloyd 1967). Folk music in the Western European nations had thrived in a premodern historical stage, before the hegemony of modern expansionism and colonialism. The revived folk musics were not the only national musics of the postwar era in Western Europe—there were also national ensembles dedicated to other repertories and with other nationalist

functions, to which we turn in later chapters—but the folk-music revivals were critical for shaping the historicism that turned the national
music cultures of the Western nations inward. Accordingly, the historicist reconfiguration of the new nationalisms was not confined to one
nation or one type of nationalist movement but became a European
phenomenon. The nationalism embedded in the musical practices
that rescripted the past stretched across the entire continent, under-
girding music's connection to nationalism throughout the Cold War.

### The Rise of Neo-Nationalism in the New Europe

"Unblocked" proclaims the title of a three-CD set released by the
world-music label Ellipsis Arts in 1997. "Music of Eastern Europe," the
subtitle continues, clarifying for the consumer just what had been unblocked. The text on the back of the CD case elaborates: *"Unblocked* is a
spellbinding, ear-opening exploration of the multicolored patchwork
of languages, religions and musical traditions that extends from the
Baltic Sea to the Balkan Mountains." The rhetoric of this world-music
CD producer is tinged with exotic references to New Age as the potential listener is led to expect "vocals that range from the sensual to the
sublime" (*Unblocked* 1997). If *Unblocked* contains sounds enabling the
postmodern listener to experience a "long sequestered heritage of music and culture," there is even a degree to which the recordings are, in
effect, liberating. The nations of Eastern Europe—or the Soviet Bloc,
as it was commonly known in the political rhetoric of the Cold War—
had imprisoned the musics that *Unblocked* was about to free, particularly folk music, with its obscure instruments; popular music, which
had already aspired to the fusion of the West; and religious music, secure as "ethereal church chorales" despite the presumed repression of
socialist governments. It would seem as if nationalism had disappeared
during the process of unblocking, as if music that had been hidden in
a vault of pure sound and authentic traditions could now rise out of
the states that had imprisoned it.

Nationalism, if unblocked, quickly takes over, providing again the
mediating landscape as the cuts on the three CDs and on the single-CD
companion released a year later unfold, representing nation after nation after nation (cf. *Unblocked* 1998). In volume one the listener
makes a figurative journey from Belarus and Ukraine across the Baltic

states, one by one, tradition by tradition. The producers attempt to give every successor state in the Balkans its due in volume three; Bosnia and Macedonia are given signposts on the musical journey, even if it was too early in 1997 to realize just how Kosovo's history would assert itself in the coming years. The producers of *Unblocked* have allowed the language of nationalism to provide the basic text for the examples they include, but they search for alternative representation of the contexts. Religion, instruments that ignore borders, shared pan-Slavic and regional histories, and the omnipresence of nationless peoples all provide suggestive surrogates for the nation. But even these alternatives cannot escape the national traditions into which history has placed them, and they, too, are expected to perform in the service of the state. The closer one listens, the more difficult it is to determine what it is that has been unblocked. The diverse musics of the CDs confirmed what many had suspected and feared: nationalism was on the rise.

By the final decade of the twentieth century, with the closing of the fissure between East and West, nationalism had become one of the most vaunted and feared forces within the **New Europe.** The collapse of socialist governments and communist political ideologies in Eastern Europe that had begun in 1989 and accelerated through the early 1990s generated a sense of hope and belief in a unified Europe, the New Europe. The **European Union** gained strength and gathered nations into a community that would be one as soon as the conditions for membership could be fulfilled, which most often meant purging the state of the old political functionaries and laying the groundwork for a functioning centralized economy. As demanding as the conditions for membership in the New Europe were, they shared a common concern for the integrity of the nation. Many believed that the New Europe could only be as strong as the individual nation-states that constituted it. The nationalist vision for the New Europe was hopeful, even heady—at least until the mid-1990s, when the hopefulness of the early decade began to fall victim to conflicting visions of European history, still dissonant and contested by neo-nationalism in a New Europe.

## New Nationalisms in the New Millennium

Throughout the chapters of this book, we witness the extent to which nationalism—as ideology and statecraft, as cultural bulwark and military excuse—was one of the most highly contested buzzwords in the New Europe. Europeans lived with nationalism, and most either loved it or hated it. Europeans either turned to it for what they could gain from it, or they shunned it, pointing out the damage it had done to their neighbors or to regions still severed from Europe's path toward unity. But there was no avoiding nationalism. Opinions about nationalism's impact on the New Europe were inevitably extreme. The nation-state was either essential, meaning that history would depend on the capacity of European nations to heal their historical ills, or it would bring about the end of European history itself, with regions collapsing into chaos as the millennium approached.

By the end of the twentieth century it was also becoming more and more difficult to extricate European music from nationalism. Some of the ways music's nationalist underpinnings surfaced again in the New Europe were subtle, but most were not. European composers of art music, for example, acquired national labels, some unfairly, but again most justifiably. The composer Arvo Pärt, who had lived for decades in Germany, where he had crafted an international style shaped particularly by a broadly ecumenical engagement with religious symbolism, was labeled an Estonian composer in the 1990s. Performances and recordings of works by Pärt emphasized his Estonianness, and he did little to resist efforts to equate him with a postmodern Estonian national tradition, even though he remained in Berlin as a German citizen. Nor did the art-music composers in Western Europe take collective steps to reject nationalist labels that had accrued to them. The cultural capital of the New Europe depended on intensifying nationalist connections to the officially sanctioned internationalism that seemed to provide the best hope for a truly European music culture.

Europe's musical neo-nationalism of the 1990s was counterpoised against numerous alternatives, which together only served to strengthen nationalism. The cultural policy of the European Union, for example, officially stressed regionalism as a means of softening nationalism's less favorable impacts. The cultural commissions of the EU fostered recording projects that would gather regional musics as anthologies. Projects such as Austria's *Musik der Regionen* ("Music of the Regions") canvassed the diverse regional repertories and practices of a nation, then anthologized them in ways that deemphasized the national core. The globalizing strategies of world-music producers also used recording projects to look beyond the nation to the region. The label "Northside," for example, draws upon the diverse repertories of Scandinavia to market it as "the single hottest region for interesting and exciting world music development" (*Nordic Roots* 1998). Throughout the liner notes a national flag accompanies the description of each cut on the *Nordic Roots* CD, even an unofficial Saami flag (together with the official Finnish flag) in the notes describing traditional Saami *yoiking* (see Chapter 6).

In the New Europe, regionalism has often become a strategy of hypernationalism. Music that locates an ethnic, linguistic, and religious group in the culture of a region also possesses the power to represent the region at national and international levels. In no European region have the political ramifications of regionalism demonstrated more nationalist potential than in the Balkans, with its tragic history of intra- and interregional strife. Still, where musical style had largely not bounded national practices even prior to 1989, increasingly hardened national music repertories dominated the Yugoslav successor states in the New Europe. Whatever form nationalism and neo-nationalism have taken in the New Europe, music has shaped it and formed a receptacle in which its symbols are most quickly accessible (see Chapter 7).

### European Music at the Intersection of Past and Present

As I write this book at the beginning of a new millennium, the historical present dovetails with the ethnographic present. History has refused to go away, even as I reflect upon and write about Europe in its own present. The ethnomusicological monograph that I write to account for European music "today" is, the temporal distance from various yesterdays notwithstanding, no less a "history of the present," to borrow the title of Timothy Garton Ash's essays on the New Europe (Ash 2000). In the ethnographic present, encountering the music of European nationalism in its variegated forms in the present, I cannot escape European history itself, even as I witness Europeans using music to engage in what Eva Hoffman, also writing about the New Europe, has called an "exit into history" (Hoffman 1993).

As we conclude a chapter devoted to history and the historiography of European music, it might seem as if we had put a series of historical moments behind us. The history that this chapter has narrated, however, does not lend itself to being relegated to the past. One of the unifying threads that has connected the successive sections in the chapter to each other has been the way in which nationalist ideologies consistently turned to the past to find the symbols necessary for constructing the present. The past justified the present, whether it was through nostalgia or with acts of violence. But the past was never simple or singular, it demonstrated many forms and multiple meanings. Music, in the service of those constructing the present from the past, made the meanings of the past seem even more trenchant and history even more powerful.

The power of European music to give meaning to the nation, therefore, lies in its ability to juxtapose historical and ethnographic presents. The nation lies at the intersection of those presents, fragile and temporal, despite the ways in which both forms of the present reinforce each other. At the intersection of these historical presents, moreover, we see that European history is teleological, with various events engendering others. And European nationalism may be the product of a jerrybuilding of the past from parts that are made to fit. Given historical moments may remind us of the past, but to suggest that they repeat the past is to misunderstand the intersection of historical and ethnographic presents. History is never so banal that it merely takes shape from such simple and simplified pasts.

European nationalism relies intimately on the meanings that music can draw from the past precisely because the nation possesses presents that are both historically and ethnographically imagined. Nationalist music not only captures past meanings, but it has the power to mobilize those whose actions give the nation its successive forms. Music closes the gaps that abound in Europe, again both the historical gaps and ideological gaps that characterize moments of disintegration. As we have seen in this chapter, music was employed to reach across the gaps separating past from present, whether as historicism or revival, or in narrative genres, or driven by technologies that created the illusion of authentic pasts.

Even though this chapter devoted to music in the history of European nationalism draws to a close, we do not leave history behind us. The history of European nationalism is far too stubborn for that. As subsequent chapters examine different forms of music's presence in European nationalism today, we should never take these to be snapshots or cross-sections. Instead, we should realize that history is changing at a dizzying pace, and that nationalism, whatever the reader's

personal stance toward its positive or negative attributes, is also proliferating at a dizzying pace. European nations continue to reimagine
themselves, and the continent's many forms of nationalism incessantly
reshape Europe itself. There is and will be nothing random about such
historical change, nor is there anything predictable. We can expect
only that history will continue to connect European nations in various
ways to multiple pasts, and that music, through its power of unisonality,
will render meaningful the representation of national identity that
forms when the nation's past is recast as its present.

## REFERENCES

Applegate, Celia. 1992. "What Is German Music? Reflections on the Role of
    Art in the Creation of the Nation." *German Studies Review* (Winter): 21–32.
Armistead, Samuel G., and Joseph H. Silverman, with Israel J. Katz. 1986.
    *Judeo-Spanish Ballads from Oral Tradition: Epic Ballads.* Berkeley and Los
    Angeles: University of California Press.
Arnim, Achim von, and Clemens Brentano. 1957 [1806 and 1808]. *Des
    Knaben Wunderhorn: Alte deutsche Lieder.* Munich: Windler.
Ash, Timothy Garton. 2000. *History of the Present: Essays, Sketches and Despatches
    from Europe in the 1990s.* Harmondsworth: Penguin.
Bohlman, Philip V. 2002b. "Landscape—Region—Nation—Reich: German
    Folk Song in the Nexus of National Identity." In Celia Applegate and
    Pamela M. Potter, eds., *Music and German Nationalism,* pp. 105–127.
    Chicago: University of Chicago Press.
_____. 2003. "Before Hebrew Song." In Michael Berkowitz, ed., *Nationalism,
    Zionism and Ethnic Mobilization of the Jews in 1900 and Beyond,* pp. 25–59.
    Leiden: E.J. Brill.
_____. Forthcoming a. *Music Drama of the Holocaust: Opera and Performance in
    Theresienstadt.* Cambridge: Cambridge University Press.
Buchanan, Donna A. Forthcoming. *Performing Democracy: Bulgarian Music and
    Musicians in Transition.* Chicago: University of Chicago Press.
Currid, Brian. 1998. "The Acoustics of National Publicity: Music in German
    Mass Culture, 1924–1945." Ph.D. dissertation, University of Chicago.
Deutsch, Walter. 1995. "90 Jahre Österreichisches Volksliedwerk: Dokumente
    und Berichte seiner Geschichte 1904–1994." *Jahrbuch des Österreichischen
    Volksliedwerks* 44: 12–50.
Doegen, Wilhelm, ed. 1925. *Unter fremden Völkern—Eine neue Völkerkunde.*
    Berlin: Otto Stollberg, Verlag für Politik und Wirtschaft.
Erk, Ludwig, with Franz Magnus Böhme. 1893–1894. *Deutscher Liederhort.* 3
    vols. Leipzig: Breitkopf und Härtel.

Feurzeig, Lisa, ed. 2002. *Deutsche Lieder für Jung und Alt*. Middleton, Wisc.: A-R Editions.

Forry, Mark E. 1986. "The 'Festivalization' of Tradition in Yugoslavia." Paper read at the 31st Annual Meeting of the Society for Ethnomusicology, Rochester, N.Y.

Ginsburg, Shaul M., and Pesach S. Marek. 1901. *Evreiskie narodnye pesni v Rossii* ["Jewish Folk Songs in Russia"]. St. Petersburg: Voskhod. Reprinted 1991: Ramat Gan: Bar-Ilan University Press.

Grundtvig, Sven. 1881. *Danmarks gamel folkeviser*. Copenhagen: Thieles bogtrykkeri.

Hemetek, Ursula. 2001. *Mosaik der Klänge: Musik der ethnischen und religiösen Minderheiten in Österreich*. Vienna: Böhlau.

Herder, Johann Gottfried. 1975 [1778–1779]. *"Stimmen der Völker in Liedern"* and *Volkslieder*. 2 vols. published in one. Stuttgart: Reclam.

Hoffman, Eva. 1993. *Exit into History: A Journey through the New Eastern Europe*. New York: Viking.

Holzapfel, Otto. 1993. *Das deutsche Gespenst: Wie Dänen die Deutschen und sich selbst sehen*. Kiel: Wolfgang Butt.

Kaufmann, Fritz Mordechai. 1920. *Die schönsten Lieder der Ostjuden*. Berlin: Jüdischer Verlag.

Kittler, Friedrich A. 1987. *Aufschreibesysteme 1800/1900*. 2d ed. Munich: Wilhelm Fink.

Klein, Bernhard, and Karl August Groos. 1818. *Deutsche Lieder für Jung und Alt*. Berlin: Realschulbuchhandlung.

Knopp, Guido, and Ekkehard Kuhn. 1988. *Das Lied der Deutschen: Schicksal einer Hymne*. Frankfurt am Main: Ullstein.

Kurzke, Hermann. 1990. *Hymnen und Lieder der Deutschen*. Mainz: Dietrich'sche Verlagsbuchhandlung.

Linke, Uli. 1999. *Blood and Nation: The European Aesthetics of Race*. Philadelphia: University of Pennsylvania Press.

Lloyd, A. L. 1967. *Folk Song in England*. London: Lawrence and Wishart.

Lord, Albert B. 1960. *The Singer of Tales*. Cambridge, Mass.: Harvard University Press.

Macedo, Catharine. 2002. "Music and Catalan Nationalism in Fin-de-siècle Barcelona." Ph.D. dissertation, University of Oxford.

Magrini, Tullia, ed. 1992. *Il maggio drammatico: Una tradizione di teatro in musica*. Bologna: Analisi.

Mraz, Gerda, ed. 1997. *Österreich-Ungarn in Lied und Bild: Ein Hochzeitsgeschenk an Kaiserin Elisabeth 1854*. Vienna: Christian Brandstätter.

*Nordic Roots: A Northside Collection*. 1998. Northside NSD6016.

O'Neill, Francis. 1913. *Irish Minstrels and Musicians, with Numerous Dissertations on Related Subjects*. Chicago: Lyon & Healy; Dublin: M. H. Gill.

Potter, Pamela M. 1998. *Most German of the Arts: Musicology and Society from the*

*Weimar Republic to the End of Hitler's Reich.* New Haven, Conn.: Yale University Press.

Ramnarine, Tina K. 2003. *Ilmatar's Inspirations: Nationalism, Globalization, and the Changing Soundscapes of Finnish Folk Music.* Chicago: University of Chicago Press.

Rice, Timothy. 1994. *May It Fill Your Soul: Experiencing Bulgarian Music.* Chicago: University of Chicago Press.

Rousseau, Jean-Jacques. 1977. *A Complete Dictionary of Music.* Reprint of the 1779 edition. New York: AMS Press.

———. 1915. *The Political Writings of Rousseau.* 2 vols. Ed. C. E. Vaughan. Cambridge: Cambridge University Press.

Schade, Ernst. 1990. "Volkslied-Editionen zwischen Transkription, Manipulation, Rekonstruktion und Dokumentation." *Jahrbuch für Volksliedforschung* 35: 44–63.

Schünemann, Georg. 1923. *Das Lied der deutschen Kolonisten in Russland.* Munich: Drei Masken Verlag.

Taruskin, Richard. 1983. "Some Thoughts on the History and Historiography of Russian Music." *The Journal of Musicology* 3 (4): 321–339.

———. 1997. *Defining Russia Musically: Historical and Hermeneutical Essays.* Princeton, N.J.: Princeton University Press.

*Unblocked: Music of Eastern Europe.* 1997. Three-CD set, with accompanying booklet. Ellipsis Arts CD3570.

*Unblocked: Music of Eastern Europe.* 1998. Ellipsis Arts CD3574.

Waldmann, Guido, ed. 1938. *Zur Tonalität des deutschen Volksliedes.* Wolfenbüttel and Berlin: Georg Kallmeyer.

Wilson, William A. 1976. *Folklore and Nationalism in Modern Finland.* Bloomington: Indiana University Press.

Wolff, Larry. 1994. *Inventing Eastern Europe: The Map of Civilization on the Mind of the Enlightenment.* Stanford, Cal.: Stanford University Press.

*Chapter Three*

# National Music

## Music in the Image of the Nation

Music is a particularly malleable means for shaping a nation's many images. It is the question of music's malleability—the many ways in which it can and does represent the nation—that we examine in the next two chapters. Each chapter allows us to gather a larger set of perspectives on how music itself represents the nation. In the present chapter, we examine national music, and we follow that with a chapter on nationalist music. It will quickly become apparent that the distinctions between and among these two relations between music and the nation are both great and small, sometimes coarse but more often subtle. The genres and repertories that constitute national and nationalist music overlap at times, but at other times differ sharply from one another. In each case, nonetheless, the use of music to shape an image of the nation is conscious, and in both chapters we find that those who turn to music to shape that image do so because they recognize the power of music to enhance the power of the nation.

The differences between national and nationalist music reveal themselves in a number of ways, including the ways the nation uses music to draw attention to its borders. In national music, reinforcing borders is not a primary theme, whereas nationalist music often mobilizes the cultural defense of borders. In both instances, as we shall see in the case studies that constitute the final sections of the next two chapters, the producers and consumers of national and nationalist music are distinctive, as are those who collect, disseminate, or even study and write about them. Each nation in Europe can claim repertories of national and nationalist music, but the ways in which those repertories interact with each other are specific to the nation, as well as to the particular historical moment in which music is defining the nation.

Despite the differences and distinctions, there are many ways in

which the interrelation between national and nationalist music is very
European. We witness that Europeanness in the national characteristics of folk music, for example, or in the remarkably related nationalist
functions of national anthems. European nations, individually and as a
collective, also express a belief in the capacity of music to be international. In historical moments such as the early twenty-first century,
when great emphasis is placed on strengthening European unity, time
and money are expended on the canonization of music suitable for international venues—for example, determining a piece worthy of serving as the European anthem. The difficulties with which the national
can be extricated from the nationalist again make it abundantly clear
that there is very little music in Europe that does not bear witness to
the idea and ideals of the nation in one way or another.

National and nationalist music assume their functions, and even acquire their aesthetic and sonic characteristics, from the ways in which
they connect history to the nation. In the following discussions of the
musical connections between history and the nation I draw upon concepts from a wide range of literature on nationalism, in particular
Prasenjit Duara's critical vocabulary for an examination of nationalist
narratives in modern China, to which he refers as "rescuing history
from the nation" (Duara 1995). We might tinker with Duara's concepts in the next two chapters, suggesting that national music rescues
history for the nation and nationalist music rescues the nation for history, but neither really rescues history from the nation.

History is more oblique and malleable in national music, which possesses the potential to shape it and make it more tangible in narrative
form. In nationalist music, history is not the least bit oblique, primarily
because the nation is insistently mapped on the narrative functions of
music. In both relations between music and the nation we realize that
music articulates a sort of imbalance resulting when history or the nation put each other at risk. When it becomes national or nationalist,
music also assumes a new sort of power, which can redress the imbalance, but to various ends. That imbalance is one of the primary reasons that rescue, in one form or another, is so critical.

## Folk Music as National Music

Let us begin, then, with national music. Defined most simply, national
music reflects the image of the nation so that those living in the nation

recognize themselves in basic but crucial ways. It is music conceived in the image of the nation that is created through efforts to represent something quintessential about the nation. The quintessence of the nation exists prior to its imagination through music; hence the task of national music is to represent that preexisting entity through music. The preexisting nation is more indefinite than definite, and it becomes the task of national music to bring out as much of the definition as possible. The nation that national music evokes may be most evident in nature or the natural landscape and boundaries, in a national or proto-national language, or in a national people, whose collective character may be abstract, yet historically and linguistically unified. Characteristic of the preexisting nation and what national music represents are the common narrative and historical experiences of a people. The preexisting nation emerges as a set of intangibles reimagined as specific traits, which music might ultimately have a special power to represent. National music in this sense does not attempt to represent by competing but rather by sharpening focus on the national quintessence.

The linguistic, cultural, and historical path traced by national music is from the bottom up. National music must capture some measure of the nation's quintessence, establishing the foundations of the nation musically. National music, therefore, frequently turns to folk music, laying claim to its authenticity. In national opera, for example, the authentic nation appears on the stage, acting out scenes from village folklife at the earliest stirrings of national history, but also connected to that very history because of the elaboration of the music itself. Bedřich Smetana's *The Bartered Bride* (*Prodaná nevesta* 1866) provides a clear example of national opera, further representing what we might call a peasant opera, in which the Czechness of the work lies in the peasant world portrayed by the people of the nation, even before they are themselves "national" (on Czechness in music see Beckerman 1986–1987). In essence, the music translates peasant culture to national culture.

Not infrequently, weddings occupy a very central position in peasant operas, where they symbolize the ways in which proto-national culture is reproduced and folk culture perpetuates itself through ritual and music. The symbolic use of the peasant wedding is by no means limited to national opera, and we find it in a wide range of genres that employ music to narrate the ritual events of folk culture, such as Karl Goldmark's five-movement symphony, *Rustic Wedding* (*Ländliche Hochzeit*, op. 26, 1876). National folk-dance troupes in Eastern Europe have traditionally staged weddings, so much so that their canonic presence remains standard fare long after the Velvet Revolution, when national troupes (for example, Hungary's Honvéd Dance Theater; see below) are often called upon to perform for tourists. The peasant culture of the wedding extends its authenticity to the nation through the musical language shared by folk and national cultures.

National music often provides a narrative template for history, creating a place for history through association with a specific geographical place. Folk song and dance often seem to depend on their association with specific places, whether it is a region determined by nature or linguistic and musical dialect or a place determined by natural or cultural geography (e.g., the essays in Stokes 1994). Until very recently, folk-music scholars have privileged the survival of song repertories in isolated geographies, which depended on national geographies (for example, remote islands off the coast of Ireland, fjords in Norway, or mountain valleys in Austria). The village, with its cultivation of folk-music practices displaying extensive unity, also depended on establishing close connections between music and a specific sense of place.

Place does not afford identity to national music because it remains entirely fixed while music may acquire the attributes of migration from one place to another. National music, accordingly, follows a journey that implicitly charts the landscape of the nation, beginning in the remotest core and reaching the end of the journey in the national metropolis. Again, Smetana, as one of the first Czech composers to concern himself explicitly with the nation, provides us with a well-known case of national music's capacity to map the place of the entire nation. The "Moldau" ("Vltava") movement from Smetana's orchestral tone poem, *My Fatherland* (*Má Vlast*, 1880–1894), represents the nation when the music's representational narrative flows from its "source" in the mountains through the country, culminating in the city. The journey through national history is implicit in each of the cases we examine in this chapter, and in several cases (for example, in the concluding sketch of the Soviet film musical *Volga, Volga*) it is explicit.

It is perhaps critical to the bottom-up trajectory of national music that its quintessential forms do not themselves have a history prior to the journey upon which they embark. It may be, instead, their use by composers or folklorists that establishes a connection to history. Bartók's notion of the "Old Style" and other Hungarian notions of music stretching into a pre-European past are prime examples. By stressing origins in the **Finno-Ugric-** and Turkic-speaking regions in Central

Asia, the Hungarians stripped Hungarian folk music of European history and opened it up for a distinctively Hungarian history.

One of the chief differences between national and nationalist music is the fact that competition with the music of other nations plays only a secondary role in the formation of national music. Competition for geography and history, therefore, is not fundamental to national music. Through its inscription of place and national narrative music makes the state internally meaningful and serves as a symbol of national pride.

When competition shapes national music, it moves along the trajectory from the the bottom to the top. The first stages of a folk-music competition might be in the local village, the next stage in a regional or provincial capital. Only for the final stage do musicians from throughout the nation compete in the national capital. The journey from local to regional to national competitions has benefited from the growth of mass media on a national level, so much so that the media themselves commonly provide most of the stages for the competitions, all the while enhancing the national character of the competitions. The crucial issue remains representing the quintessential and just how one does that effectively through, say, staging folk music or choral ensembles.

The border between national and nationalist music may well be very blurry at times, while at times the national and the nationalist may overlap so extensively as to form a hybrid. To the extent that the product of music has the potential to be both national and nationalist, depending on interpretation and use, contexts and historical perspectives may distinguish one from the other. In the nineteenth century it became increasingly important for nations striving toward nationalism to have national folk-song collections. The motivation for these nineteenth-century collections, coming from the top-down, was decidedly nationalist, even though the contents were supposed to be national. As we see with several cases in the next two chapters, national music always has the potential to become nationalist, especially as its trajectory from the bottom, the point of a nation's quintessence and prehistory, reaches the top, the pressing history of the present. To understand just where the distinctions between national and nationalist music fall and why those distinctions are important, it is first necessary to examine the diverse ways in which music in the image of the nation acquires its potential to rescue history for the nation.

### Rescuing History for the Nation, Making Music National

*This music [Norwegian **slåtter**], which is handed down to us from an age when the culture of the Norwegian peasant was isolated in its solitary mountain-valleys from the outer world, to which fact it owes its originality, bears the stamp of an imagination as daring in its flight as it is peculiar.*
*—Edvard Grieg in the "Preface" to his **Slåtter**, op. 72*

We begin where most studies of national music begin, with folk music, but our point of departure, not to mention the path followed upon departure, will be different. Rather than anchoring the nation to a mythical, unknown past, the folk music that concerns us is dynamic, changing, even unstable, all qualities necessary if folk music charts what I here describe as the national journey. When folk music follows the national journey, it undergoes a transition from representing the immanent quintessence of the nation to representing the nation itself. In doing so, folk music further brings into being an historical dialectic that connects land and language to the nation. The historical dialectic is possible for two fundamental reasons. First, folk song possesses complex narrative properties: The stories it tells are often historical (see Holzmeister 1965). Second, folk dance displays extraordinary mobility, and hence a capacity to map the paths along which the national journey unfolds. In the course of its travels from the land to the nation, folk music becomes suddenly modern, and it is that transformation that makes it profoundly national.

Since the first modern theories of folk music in the late eighteenth and early nineteenth century, concepts of folk music have increasingly responded to a history of ideas that emphasizes the nation. In nineteenth-century collections of German folk songs, for example, there is an historical shift from songs gathered in rural, isolated regions, usually transmitted aurally in the dialects of those regions, to a centralized canon designated simply as "German folk songs." Songs classified as German demonstrated the qualities of a common culture, a nation still in the process of achieving unity. In theories such as Wilhelm Tappert's notion of "wandering melodies" (Tappert 1890), folk songs were imbued with the potential to migrate across vast distances, unencumbered by natural boundaries. The national journey required linguistic and musical changes, all of which produced a more centrally German body of folk music, to which more and more qualities of the national accrued.

The national journey of Hungarian folk music also unfolded along a path from the proto-nation of the isolated village ("Old Style") to the centralized nation of the metropolis ("New Style") to what might be called a post-nation in the cosmopolitan culture beyond the city ("Mixed Style"). At one end of this historical journey, musical traits were themselves isolated, conforming to the Hungarian language (**parlando rubato**) or to dance movement (**tempo giusto**). The Hungarian composers and folk-music scholars Béla Bartók and Zoltán Kodály envisioned the literal and figurative loss of these quintessentially Hungarian traits in the course of the journey from isolated to cosmopolitan contexts. The isolation of musical traits was possible only when singers and other musicians had not traveled, and it is for this reason that women, who were deemed less mobile because of their place in the domestic life of the village, turned up more often than other village residents on the early recordings and in the early collections of Hungarian folk music (see, for example, Bartók 1924 and 1934).

The national journeys of folk music necessarily follow distinctive routes in each nation. The national journey of Austrian folk music, for example, is quite unlike that of German folk music, even though there are surface qualities (such as the German language) that seem more similar than different. The rural origins of Austrian folk music are at several levels quite unlike those in Germany. In Austria dialect in song texts plays a much more powerful role, as does the nation's mountainous topography, which creates a complex geographical underlay of isolated valleys. The modernity of Austrian folk music has also emerged from a distinctive national history.

On the national journey Austrian folk music has been particularly open to the multiculturalism that arises from several historical conditions. First is the multiculturalism of the former Austro-Hungarian Empire, which included large portions of Eastern Europe within its borders (see Chapter 5). Second are the cosmopolitanism and the centralizing influences of cities—not just Vienna, but Budapest, Prague, and scores of provincial metropolises in Eastern Europe—that have transformed cities into places where folk-music traditions arrived from the provinces only to undergo extensive processes of consolidation. Third is the recontextualization of folk-music genres that accompanies modernization. The waltz emerged historically from the **Ländler** in the nineteenth century because the waltz absorbed and responded to the extensive urbanization of musical life, especially in Vienna. The **polka** provided the folk source for many marches in the Austro-Hungarian Empire, and the interaction between the two instrumental forms, one used for dancing and the other for regimented mobilization of the nation (but also for dancing), created a cultural axis from the provincial lands to the cities.

The movement of folk music along the path of the national journey does not simply happen. Human agents undertake the journey and bring folk music with them. Technologies streamline the path of the journey. Specific institutions, moreover, shape and reshape the ways in which folk music moves toward the center, and they do so by providing for the full modernization of folk-music practices. The agents who bring folk music from the periphery to the center of the nation are the musicians and scholars, observers and promoters who traverse the many roads constituting the national journey (e.g., Cooley, forthcoming). Folk dances from the provinces of Austria-Hungary arrived in Vienna during the nineteenth century because musicians, amateur and professional, came to Vienna in search of opportunities.

Several technologies had a direct bearing on the nationalization of folk song, first the printing and publication of folk music, which spread across Europe in the second half of the nineteenth century, and then the use of sound-recording devices beginning at the turn of the twentieth century. Technological developments also influenced folk-music practices directly. The mass production of musical instruments, possible because of the modernization of urban industry, dislodged many musical practices from rural traditions, encouraging not only the expansion of sound production by making larger ensembles possible, but also stimulating the exchange of repertories along the roads forming the national journey.

Many institutions responded to the historical dynamic of the national journey by following parallel channels, in other words, by assuming institutional forms of the journey itself. It is the national music competition that most often serves, in the course of this book, as a metaphor for what I have here called the national journey. In his study of folk fiddling in modern Norway Chris Goertzen (1997) has painstakingly traced the journeys of fiddlers from local to regional to national competitions, a journey that fiddling competitions replicate year after year. The institutions of the competition—the choice of venues and repertories, the designation of stylistic limits and judges to enforce them—pave the way for the journey itself, all the while channeling the competitive roads so that their confluence affords the opportunity, as Goertzen observes, to "fiddle for Norway." The journey of the modern fiddling competition bears striking similarity, historically and figuratively, to the ways in which the Norwegian composer Edvard Grieg (1843–1907) transformed folk music to compositions with explicitly national imagery. The fiddle tunes in Grieg's *Slåtter,* op. 72, are composed realizations of tunes that were "original transcriptions by Johan Halvorsen" of pieces "played on the Norwegian peasant's fiddle." Grieg does not claim that the **Slåtter** *are* folk dances, but rather reflections of folk dances, with the "free arrangement" for piano laying the groundwork for the national journey from peasant culture in the province of Telemark to works of national music. It is, then, at the end of folk music's historical journey that music finally and fully performs the image of the nation.

### Music and the Evolving Nation

By the second half of the nineteenth century music was imagined to embark on other journeys that permitted it to evoke the nation, journeys that led to its acquiring the name "national music." In this section I examine two important works that designated and theorized "national music" itself, and did so by elevating national music to an extraordinarily privileged position in European nationalism. Carl Engel's *An Introduction to the Study of National Music* (1866) and Ralph Vaughan Williams's *National Music* (1934) provide bookends to a period during which the music of the nation aspired to a position of special importance. Historically, the period began as the revolutionary struggles of 1848 subsided and the rise of fascism accelerated. Scientifically, the period reflected the direct influence of evolutionary theory and thought. Musically, the period was marked by a growing conviction that music aspired toward a complexity that was present in its most authentic forms.

Despite their differences these two books devoted specifically to national music share a great deal. Both take as their point of departure the qualities in national music that distinguish it in positive ways from all other musics. National music, both authors argued, should not be at root exclusive, but rather its noble character, expressed in rich and evocative metaphors, should be an ideal that all forms of music can acquire. Almost tautologically, all nations possess national music, whether their musicians or other people know it or not. Accordingly, national music was international and democratic. For Engel in the mid-nineteenth century and Vaughan Williams in the mid-twentieth century, national music formed the plane for world music writ large.

National music was immanent in the lives and musics of a nation's people. On one hand, they simply needed to discover its presence. On the other hand, they needed to recognize an almost patriotic duty to enhance the presence of national music, to make evident to everyone in the nation its importance above all other musics. National music both was and was not folk music, which is to say, folk music formed a crucial factor in the complex calculus of national music. But both Engel and Vaughan Williams deliberately stopped short of claiming one as a synonym for the other. The subtle difference between folk and national music is critical to the historical argument Engel and Vaughan Williams wanted to make: Folk music is always present in national music, engendering the path of evolution.

> Folk-song is not a cause of national music, it is a manifestation of it. The cultivation of folk-songs is only one aspect of the desire to found an art on the fundamental principles which are essential to its well-being. National music is not necessarily folk-song; on the other hand folk-song is, by nature, necessarily national. (Vaughan Williams 1934: 114)

### Stages along the Evolutionary Path of Folk Music

The evolutionary path of national music, according to Engel and Vaughan Williams, unfolded because of the ways in which a people's music and the growing complexity of music dovetailed. Three more general stages characterized the evolutionary path. The first stage was pre- or, more accurately, proto-historical. It was at this stage that national music exhibited the qualities that were most intangible, those of a nation's "soul" or of an almost ageless national body.

> There is generally a remarkable health and freshness in national tunes; the lapse of years hardly seems to affect their spirit and power, and many doubtless attain a venerable age before they fall into decay and die off to make room for others. (Engel 1866: 318)

At this stage, the nation is inchoate, but so too is national music, thus allowing music to signify the nation even before there is a nation to signify. The Romantic arguments used to describe this stage may seem unconvincing to us today, but they were crucial to shaping the early discourses of national music, when, as we have seen in this chapter, it was important to make the origins of music seem at once mystical and real.

The second stage differed quite dramatically from the first, for it was at this stage that history and science became determining factors, that core patterns of notes coalesced as scales and then became melodies that acquired harmony and then the rhythmic organization that served as a template for dance. The growing complexity of national music was not the least bit random, a point that both Engel and Vaughan Williams made clear. Engel organizes his chapters to trace the development from one stage of complexity to the next. Vaughan Williams devotes two chapters at the heart of his book to the same subject, "Evolution of Folk-Song" (1934: 53–92).

The third stage returns again to the intangible, but it is now possible to describe it with a scientific language. A path of development that appeared to be teleological now turns back on itself, using music to claim the preexistence of the modern nation. National music, Engels and Vaughan Williams assert, possesses the qualities of the folk music of an untutored people and of the finest endeavors to create an art music. The journey of national music is complete, but its completion was immanent in the musical materials before the journey even started. Music has finally achieved the privileged position that its inherent national qualities imprinted on its oldest forms, virtually as if such qualities were a national genetic code. It is as if the nation can be heard in the folk music of the village.

> The art of music above all other arts is the expression of the soul of a nation, and by a nation I mean not necessarily aggregations of people artificially divided from each other by political frontiers or economic barriers. What I mean is any community of people who are spiritually bound together by language, environment, history and common ideals and, above all, a continuity with the past. (Vaughan Williams 1934: 123)

Although Engels and Vaughan Williams theorized a national music that embodied what they and many of their contemporaries took to be a full gamut of styles and repertories, there can be no question that their viewpoint originated at the end of the evolutionary chain. The importance they assigned to national music came from the top down. That viewpoint afforded a high degree of democracy and expanded the international horizons of national music itself. Engel, in particular, postulated that national music would become the true music of a modern, nationalist age, and in his concluding chapter he publishes an extensive bibliography of collections of national music, which he ambitiously calls "The Library of the Future" (Engel 1866: 369–421). This library serves not only the nations with long histories, but also those with long national aspirations, for example, the "Basque Provinces" (ibid.: 379), "Transylvania" (ibid.: 418), and Wallachia (ibid.: 421).

The view from the top, however, produces a myopia that makes it increasingly difficult to perceive the difference between national and nationalist music. Vaughan Williams, not in small part because of his own agendas as a composer of art music, began to argue that a nation without national music was also a nation without a real soul. His pronouncement that there is "no work of art which represents the spirit of a nation more surely than *Die Meistersinger* of Richard Wagner" (Vaughan Williams 1934: 129–130) has a chilling ring, following on the heels of a sermon in which he inveighs against American multiculturalism and the ways it encumbers the development of a truly American folk song. Vaughan Williams celebrates the national achievements of the Germans while expressing reservations about the attempts of American composers to transform jazz to art music (ibid.: 127). In 1934, such observations confuse nation and race, juxtaposing both at the borders between national and nationalist music.

### National Folk Song Collections

In 1902, when the Habsburg Monarchy charged its leading musical scholars and Universal Edition, one of the leading music publishers of the world, with the task of collecting and publishing in individual volumes "the totality" of Austria's folk songs, it was adding its imprimatur to a publishing tradition that had been under way since the mid-nineteenth century: the national folk-song collection. The Habsburg endeavor, called simply *Das Volkslied in Österreich* (VÖ), or "Folk Song in Austria," was in many ways similar to previous national collections but notable because of the ways it differed from them.

The spirit of the Habsburg call for a collection that would include everything and surpass anything that had preceded it was but a variant of all other national calls for nation-encompassing collections. The rhetoric of the imperial culture minister was grandiose in its assessment of an Austrian national treasure ("the pearls of Austrian folk song" [ibid.]), but also sufficiently vague in defining what either Austria or Austrian folk song might be. There was room for pushing at the edges of the nation, the empire, and all aspects thereof that folk song might inscribe in a national collection. The VÖ's attempts to draw Austria's finest scholars from the University of Vienna, the first and most prestigious musicology institute in the world, and from the Imperial Academy of Sciences, a path-breaking institution with its own Phonograph Archive founded not even a decade earlier, were also both typical and exceptional when compared to similar attempts in other nations at the turn of the past century.

The VÖ national collection, however, was a phenomenon that we might characterize as too much, too late. In 1902, the collapse of the Austro-Hungarian Empire during World War I was still a dozen years in the future, but the imminence of that collapse was already being felt, and the VÖ collection was already responding nervously to it. "Austrian folk song" should come both from the Austria at the center of the empire—the largely German-speaking alpine provinces—and at its peripheries, where German-language songs were at best sung by a minority of the population. When the first volume of folk songs from the **Gottschee colonies** appeared in summer of 1914, simultaneously with the outbreak of World War I, it projected nine more forthcoming editions with "alternating German and non-German volumes." These would begin with Filaret Kolessa's collection of "Ruthenian folk songs" from the border area with overlapping Ukrainian (the meaning of "Ruthenian" here), Polish, Rusyn, Jewish, and German repertories, and which would conclude with Raimund Zoder's "Lower Austrian dance tunes" from the province of Niederösterreich, which geographically surrounds Vienna.

In its ideology and scope the VÖ national collection grows from nineteenth-century notions of the nation, in which nationalism and imperialism were intertwined. The collection drew the peripheries to the center, but it did so by plotting the center's presence in the peripheries, German songs in non–German-speaking provinces. The very monumentality of the national collection spoke to the fragility of the nation, for it announced its ability to undergird the foundations of the nation. By no means, however, was it coincidental that the national collection began appearing—and then stopped appearing—as the European nations of the nineteenth century slid off the precipice of nationalism into World War I. In four years, the Austria that the VÖ collection was charged to bolster would no longer exist. From the first ten of the projected volumes only three—for Styria, Tyrol, and Lower Austria—would include Austrian folk songs from the Austria of 1918.

When it came to imagining and realizing the European nation with a national folk-song collection, the stakes were very high. They could mean the difference between having the nation or not. The investment of individual, institutional, and national resources in the collecting and publishing of such collections had expanded exponentially throughout the nineteenth century as the stakes for the nation and nationalism themselves grew. When Carl Engel was taking stock of his "Library of the Future" in 1866, he would devote over fifty pages to lists of works that, in one way or another, reflected the impulse to create national collections. On the eve of World War I, when the VÖ project was commissioning its collectors and editors, it would have taken a volume-length annotated bibliography to account for the national collections that had appeared in the previous half century. At the turn of the present century, the production of national collections has assumed a momentum and bibliographical (and discographical) girth entirely unimaginable in the mid-twentieth century.

To understand the concept of a national folk-song collection and the ways it differs from other types of collecting endeavors, a brief historical sketch might prove helpful. National folk-song collections appear at historically critical moments and do so because of the ways they articulate those moments. The consolidation of resources and assessment of the nation with folk-song collections are the most acute at moments (1) when historical circumstances make it necessary to define or redefine the nation or (2) when they contest the nation. The call to create a national collection expresses immediacy and great concern with loss and for rescuing national treasures for the future.

The first national collections of folk song appeared from about 1820 to 1850, in the decades between the defeat of Napoleon and the revolutionary period around 1848, when European nations were retrenching themselves. The most important German collection from this period, Ludwig Uhland's two-volume, 357-song *Alte hoch- und niederdeutsche Volkslieder* (1844–1855), is significant for the ways it connects songs with regional dialects in oral tradition to those in the national literary language, High German. Uhland's collection thus strengthens the nation from within, buttressing the edifice of a common literate musical tradition by demonstrating its foundation in regional and dialect traditions.

In the second half of the nineteenth century, national collections consolidated the nation along both geographical and historical lines. Franz Magnus Böhme completed the publication of Ludwig Erk's life's work *cum* national collection, the three-volume *Deutscher Liederhort* (1893–1894), which includes 2,175 songs, many in multiple variants that cut across genre boundaries and geographical borders. The collection at once reveals a more universal concept of music and a more international image of nation. Both stemmed from the growing national and imperial presence of Germany in Europe following Bismarck's consolidation of Germany in and the realignment of the nation with Prussia and Berlin at its center.

### Contested Borders

Late nineteenth-century collections also emerged from border regions contested by nationalist expansion. Border regions such as Alsace-Lorraine and the Galician-Carpathian area, which today includes parts of Poland, Ukraine, Slovakia, and Romania, produced numerous collections that were no less expensive than they were expansive. Polish (e.g., Kolberg 1964a, 1964b, 1964c) and Ukrainian (e.g., Kolessa 1910 and 1913) collections included songs documenting the same geographical spaces as Austrian and Hungarian collections, one of which we have already encountered in the plan for the VÖ project. In the course of the twentieth century this border region would even turn into a particularly rich and oft-tapped source for Jewish folk songs (see Chapter 6).

Are such collections national or nationalist? To some extent they are both, for they illustrate that folk-song collectors recognized the possibility of multicultural and multinational regions, but that they rarely take the opportunity of a national collection to inscribe that possibility on the image of the nation. Such collections call attention to the ways in which national borders are contested by nationalism, making it impossible to deny that national borders, specifically identified in the songs themselves, are not also implicated in national collections, a phenomenon examined in the section devoted to Germany's *Land-schaftliche Volkslieder* in the next chapter.

The importance of national folk-song collections did not subside in the twentieth century, when they continued to provide powerful means of rescuing history for the nation. The national collection provided the heart of the myriad folk-music research projects supported, often generously, by socialist governments in Eastern Europe from the end of World War II until the early 1990s. Throughout the continent, national collections drove collecting projects and recording projects alike. In the New Europe since 1989, new collections are under way, some supported, for example, by the cultural resources of the European Union that are dedicated to the more extensive documentation of a nation's regional resources.

At the turn of the present century, some national collections have entered, phoenix-like, a new phase of revival and historicism. As if to pick up where the *Volkslied in Österreich* project of the Habsburg Monarchy left off in 1914, a new Austrian national collection, *Corpus musicae popularis austriacae* ("Anthology of Austrian Folk Music"), began to appear in 1993, with its first volume from Lower Austria taking the center as its point of departure (Deutsch 1993). In the New Europe the national collection continues to turn to its national treasures to retrieve the past for the present, again escalating the stakes that accompany rescuing history for the nation.

### The Nation on Stage

During the past two centuries, when the moment has arisen to put the European nation on the musical stage, there has been little doubt who received the part: the chorus. The chorus at once envoices and embodies the nation, giving voice to all its citizens and harmonizing those voices in an emblematic unisonality. The chorus's capacity to serve as a simulacrum for the nation is particularly powerful, furthermore, because of its position on the stage. The chorus connects to the audience, symbolizing for the audience its own selfness, as if to put the audience also on the stage. It is when the chorus sings that the audience feels itself drawn to the edge of the stage, drawn even to the edge of song as it recognizes itself on the stage. At such moments, the audience, too, hears its voice, and in some genres and forms staged choral music freely joins in the performance. The potential to transform the choral performance into a moment of high nationalism is very great indeed. It is a moment the composers of national opera or the organizers of choral revival movements rarely fail to seize.

In this section I turn to several genres and repertories that rely on the ways choruses stage the nation musically. I might have separated these from each other, isolating, for example, pageants, but I have deliberately combined them to emphasize what it is that choral movements, national song and dance troupes, pageants, and national opera share. Each of them captures the quintessence of the nation and reveals it on the stage, heightening the ways the nation on stage reflects the nation at the edge of the stage, that is, the audience. The chorus musically mobilizes the nation, intensifying the sound of the nation's selfness and the ways it is perceived, collapsing the difference between unisonality and uniaurality (cf. Gossett 1990 and Parakilas 1992).

Since 1989, with its sweeping national realignments throughout Europe, choral movements have swept across the continent (see Chapter 7). But nowhere have choruses captured the national limelight and stirred international wonder more powerfully than in the Baltic nations of Estonia, Latvia, and Lithuania, where amassing choruses in auditoriums, stadiums, and singing festivals has produced what many have called a "singing revolution." It is not unusual to hear reports of concerts in which entire cities or much of the nation gathers to sing. As one popular CD claims, "a quarter of the Estonian population has been known to turn out" for festivals in the capital city, Tallinn (*Unblocked* 1997, liner notes: 30). Elsewhere in Eastern Europe, for example in Belarus, choral movements have attempted both to depoliticize and to repoliticize religion by forging sacred repertories that juxtapose Orthodox and Catholic, and by introducing Protestant and Jewish repertories—thus reclaiming sacred music as the music of a new national unity unlike the historical nationalist disunity.

Choral movements have also spread to groups without nations that aspire to a position within other national identities. Jewish synagogue choruses, for example, have multiplied and acquired considerable visibility through their extensive tours and the production of audiocassettes and CDs. Some Jewish choruses seem to arise from a **longue durée** of European Jewishness. The rabbinical academies of Budapest and Moscow were among the first organizations to send choruses on tour after 1989. Other Jewish choruses celebrate their newness, thus the promise of their presence in the New Europe to thwart the nation-alist tendencies of anti-Semitism. Theirs is a Jewishness made possible by the New Europe (see Chapter 7).

The repertories upon which Eastern European choral movements have drawn deliberately juxtapose the traditional and the modern. Tra-ditional components—folk song, mythological imagery, national sym-bols—imbue the choral movement with a sense that choruses have al-ways provided a context in which the nation could realize itself, even during the decades of Soviet domination. Modern components—the integration of popular song, commissioned compositions, experimental sonorities—give new meaning to the nation, staking a claim for the cho-rus's reification of democracy as the nation embarks on its future. East-ern European choruses rely on a vocabulary of historicism and revival, a revival that makes the sound of the nation singular and singable.

Were post-1989 choruses the first attempts to stage the nation, their impact would be much less widespread than it has proved to be. The socialist governments of Eastern Europe fully exploited the national ensemble, allowing it to bring the nation to the people at the center and in the hinterlands of the nation. In Hungary, as in many other Eastern European socialist states, the national chorus and its ancillary organizations served as constituent parts of the army. The Honvéd Chorus and the Honvéd Dance Theater (*honvéd* means, simply, "army") were the premier national ensembles during the period of commu-nism in Hungary from World War II until 1989.

A typical Honvéd performance consisted of a repertory gathered from villages and regions throughout Hungary and integrated into a single historical tapestry. In the course of a Honvéd performance the nation was palpable at the interstices between the local and the na-tional, oral and literate tradition, difference and similarity. Recogniz-ing just how powerfully the chorus and, in this case, its cohabitant on the national stage, dance theater, bring the nation to life, it is less sur-prising that the Honvéd ensembles have survived at the national level in post-communist Hungary. No longer officially associated with the army in any way, the Honvéd ensembles nonetheless continue to per-form national music. The Honvéd Chorus commissions new works, which juxtapose traditional repertories with avant-garde sonorities, and the Honvéd Dance Theater tempers regional folk dance with elec-tronically modified popular elements. The Honvéd ensembles remix Hungary's past on the stage of its future.

### The Pageant

When the chorus takes to the stage, it assumes a narrative function: It acquires the power to portray the history of the nation. Historically, the narrative power of the chorus was first realized by the dramatic genre known most generally as the pageant. Initially a phenomenon of medieval Europe, pageants have lost little of their power to mobilize villages and nations alike as they witness history unfolding before them.

Whether narratives are local or global, pageants are distinctive because of the ways in which they reconfigure local populations, involving them directly in the reconfiguration of the historical stage. There is perhaps no more striking example of the persistent power of the pageant to mobilize a local population than the Oberammergau performance of the life and passion of Christ, with its overwhelmingly national and nationalist implications. The Oberammergau pageant has taken place since 1643, expanding in size to 100 performances in 2000, with approximately 5,000 visitors, or "pilgrims," at each performance. The regulations underlying the pageant's tradition, in contrast, dictate that no one from the outside may act in the pageant, thus restricting the pool of actors, even today, to the 5,200 residents of the Bavarian village itself (Shapiro 2000: 3–15).

Like many pageants, the Oberammergau passion took a turn toward the historical and, by extension, the national through the introduction of new functions for the chorus in 1811, when Rochus Dedler created a new musical score (Heaton 1979: 56–57). Choruses began to fill the passion, conflating national and sacred collectives and engendering the conflicts over the allegorical meanings of Germany (or Bavaria) and Europe's Jews (or Israel). Choruses accelerate the passion play's path toward a full envoicement of the national through the life of the village (for an English translation of the pageant, see Lane and Brenson 1984).

Oberammergau and other pageants seem at first glance to stage arcane, even atavistic, images of the nation. Nations appear inchoate or trapped in allegory. It is not clear whether individual identities mask historical identities or vice versa. Nor is it clear just how the chorus becomes the envoicement of a nation that the singers and audiences themselves experience only in fragments. The pageant, nonetheless, sets the nation in motion through a variety of narrative processes. Those processes acquire a new teleology as they aspire toward a different stage, where the chorus acquires functions both more abstract and more nationalist. It is that stage we encounter when we examine European opera as a setting for national and nationalist music.

## Four Paths to National Music

Folk music forms an axis with national music that generates and is generated by pairs of genres, styles, and repertories. The relation between the members of the pairs is one of contrast formed of what is common to the two of them: They serve as different ends of the national journey and of a national history articulated by folk music. The image of the nation is present in both members of the pairs, yet neither member alone suffices to represent the nation and its history fully.

Throughout this book we witness the ways in which the historical dialectic between folk and national music is particularly striking and persistent in Austrian music. There are at least two reasons that account for the panoply of pairs in Austrian music. The first is so obvious that stating it seems almost banal: Music is one of the cultural goods used most visibly by Austrians to lay claim to Austrianness. Music maps the Austrian nation at every level—from local to regional to national to international—and in every genre—from folk and popular musics to classical and modern musics. The second reason that generic and stylistic pairs are so pervasive in Austrian music derives from the transformation of the modern Austrian nation as a monarchy with substantial imperial claims to a relatively small nation that has withdrawn behind the borders of neutrality. Thus the image of the Austrian nation has undergone a dramatic change during the age of European nationalism. Austria has lost a great deal of land and political potency, but it has compensated by discovering the ways in which Austrian music represents a different national presence in Europe.

Music further articulates Austrianness through a process of centralization: All musical roads—or national journeys—lead to Vienna. Historically, Vienna has been a city that formed around its center, now the First District, with St. Stephen's cathedral at its center. New districts and neighborhoods form around Vienna as concentric rings. Each new ring encompasses what was formerly a village, many of which developed along a stream, a road, or a cultural artery leading toward the center. As the national capital, Vienna both spreads geographically toward the peripheries and culturally draws them toward the center, where their presence becomes more concentrated (see Chapter 5).

The musical pairs that signify the spokes leading from the national center to the cultural peripheries render the national landscape distinctively Austrian. The Ländler, as we have seen several times before, becomes the waltz in Vienna. Both the Ländler and the waltz can lay claim to displaying qualities of the Austrian nation. The Ländler, danced with the courting figures that express its rooted qualities—its connections to the land—contrasts with the waltz, which is danced without figures, employing instead the rapid spinning motion of a couple dance that dislodges its connections to the land and replaces these with the cultural mix of Vienna.

Popular music, too, migrated through processes of urbanization and centralization from the provinces to the center. The music of the popular stage, for example, is first evident on the folk stages of the villages and small cities of the provinces, often performed by traveling troupes of actors and musicians. In the course of the nineteenth century, during the period of Austrian cultural history known as the **Biedermeier Era,** troupes arrived in growing numbers to provide popular entertainment for Viennese taking excursions to the outer districts of the city. We experience the new repertories of popular music on broadsides from the era, such as that in Figure 3.1. On the small stages at the city's periphery, the diverse traditions and repertories of the provinces began mixing together, forming, among others, the new, multicultural genre of cabaret, with its distinctive stock of popular songs and musical theater. Cabaret settled in the inner districts of the imperial capital by the beginning of the twentieth century, quickly establishing itself as a cultural force that would siphon off a growing number of musical traditions from the provinces (see CD examples 12, 13, and 16).

In Figures 3.2 and 3.3 the formation of musical pairs to represent the national journey from the village to the city is explicit, indeed, quite intentionally manipulated in the popular dance music of nineteenth-century Austria, composed here by two of the most notable composers of the century, Josef Strauss and Johann Strauss, Jr. So powerfully symbolic are the two images of the nation that they lend themselves to the iconic imagery of the published versions of the songs. The village life of "Village Swallows" combines nature with family life in the rural village. Arguably, there is no symbol of the preexisting Austrian nation that is absent here. Nature is everywhere. The swallows of the title are complemented by the spring in the lower left-hand corner of the song's cover sheet, with an apparently unending source of water sustaining the harmonious family. The church in the background also sustains the life

*Figure 3.1.*
*"Der Raubmord in*
*Mariahilf"/"The Robbery*
*and Murder in Mariahilf,"*
*Viennese broadside from the*
*late nineteenth century*

Der Raubmord in Mariahilf.

Gedicht von K. J. Hermann.
Arie: die arme Waise.
Druck u. Verlag v. M. Moßbeck Wien Wieden Waaggasse Nr. 7.

Im Zimmer saß beim Arbeitstisch,
Elisen emsig dort —
Sie dachte wohl an ihren Gott
Und an sein heilig Wort.
Denn ihre Züge lieblich hold,
Sie lächeln fromm und mild —
Sie gleichen, unschuldsvoll fürwahr,
Nur einem Engelsbild.

of the village, and lest we forget the role of religion in Austrian nationalism, the swallows draw the eye and ear toward the church tower.

The frames that crowd in upon the cover of "Wiener Blut" could not produce a more contrastive pair. The images of Vienna form around the geographical and religious center of the Austro-Hungarian Empire, St. Stephen's cathedral. As we might expect in a waltz, the images of the national capital push against the borders, blurring some scenes but highlighting others, not least among them the several pairs of lovers, whose cultural differences are mediated by the music. Rather than na-

*Figure 3.2. Josef Strauss, "Dorfschwalben aus Österreich"/
"Village Swallows from Austria," cover of the version for piano solo*

ture and village life, here it is blood that provides the source of national identity formed at the cultural confluence in the center of the empire.

Both songs in this pair are narrative, "Village Swallows" amplifying a novella of the same name, and "Vienna Blood" serving as the title song for Johann Strauss's operetta of the same name. The stories they narrate are historical at many levels, but the levels also share the critical common path that parallels Austria's national journey in the nineteenth century.

## Evreiskie narodnye pesni v Rossii—
### Jewish Folk Songs in Russia (1901)

The two Yiddish songs epigrammatically opening this section (see Figures 3.4 and 3.5) announce the possibility of a Jewish nation—**Eretz Yisrael,** "the Land of Israel"—in quite different ways. In the first, the announcement draws upon biblical imagery: The descendants of King David await his regal blessing on the entire land, which will be blessed by the arrival of the Messiah and the reinstatement of Israel. The

*Figure 3.3. Johann Strauss, Jr., "Wiener Blut Walzer"/"Vienna Blood Waltz"*

## № 12.

*Варіантъ:*

| | |
|---|---|
| מָשִׁיחַ בֶּן דָּוִד זִיצְט אוֹיבְּן אָן, | Moschiach ben Dowid sitzt eibn on, |
| אִין גָאלְד אוּג אִין זִילְבֶּער אָנְגֶעטָאהָן. | In Gold un in Silber ongethon. |
| עֶר הַאלְט אַ בֶּעכֶער אִין דִי רֶעכְטֶע הַאנְד, | Er halt a Becher in die rechte Hand, |
| מַאכְט עֶר אַ בְּרָכָה אִיבֶּער דִי נַאנְצֶע לַאנְד. | Macht er a Broche iber die ganze Land. |
| אָמֵן וְאָמֵן דָאס אִיז וָואהְר: | Omein w'omein, dos is wohr: |
| דִי גְּאוּלָה וֶועט קוּמֶען הַיינְטִיגֶען יָאהְר. | Die G'ule wet kummen haintigen Johr. |
| וֶועט זִי קוּמֶען צוּ רַייטֶען, | Wet sie kummen zuraiten, |
| וֶועלֶען מִיר הָאבֶּען גוּטֶע צַייטֶען, | Welen mir hoben gute Zaiten. |
| וֶועט זִי קוּמֶען צוּ פָאהְרֶען, | Wet sie kummen zufohren, |
| וֶועלֶען מִיר הָאבֶּען גוּטֶע יָאהְרֶען, | Welen mir hoben gute Johren, |
| וֶועט זִי קוּמֶען צוּ גֵעהְן, | Wet sie kummen zugeihn, |
| וֶועלֶען דִי מֵתִים אוֹיף שְׁטֵעהְן. | Welen die Meissim aufsteihn. |
| מִיר וֶועלֶען קֵין אֶרֶץ יִשְׂרָאֵל גֵעהְן | Mir welen kain Erez-Jissroel geihn, |
| וּבָא לְצִיוֹן נוֹאֵל וְנֹאמַר אָמֵן ! | Uwo l'Zion Geeil w'neimar omein! |

А. Д. Пикъ и В. М. Кассель. (Ковенск. губ.).

*Figure 3.4.* "Moschiach ben Dowid sitzt eibn on"/"Moses, Son of David, Is Seated," *Yiddish song from* Jewish Folk Songs in Russia *(1901)*

## № 14.

| | |
|---|---|
| אִין מִימְ'ן וֶועג שְׁטֶעהְט אַ בּוֹים | In mitten Weg steiht a Beim |
| אוּג הָאט זִיך אֵיין נֶעבּוֹיגֶען ; | Un hot sich aingebeigen; |
| פָאהְרְט אַיין אִיד קֵין אֶרֶץ יִשְׂרָאֵל | Fohrt ain Jid kain Erez-Jissroel |
| מִיט פֶערוֵויינְטֶע אוֹיגֶען. | Mit verweinte Eigen. |
| גָאט מַיין גָאט, גָאט מַיין גָאט ! | Gott main Gott, Gott main Gott! |
| לָאמִיר דַאווְנֶען מִנְחָה, — | Lomir dawnen Minche,— |
| בְּשַׁעַת מִיר וֶועלֶען פָאהְרֶען קֵין אֶרֶץ יִשְׂרָאֵל | Bischass mir welen fohren kain Erez-Jissroel, |
| וֶועט זַיין אַ גְרוֹיסֶע שִׂמְחָה ! | Wet sain a greisse Ssimche! |

А. Рейзинъ (Минск. губ.).

*Figure 3.5.* "In mitten Weg steiht a Beim"/"In the Middle of the Road Stood a Tree," *Yiddish song from* Jewish Folk Songs in Russia *(1901)*

journey to Eretz Yisrael is a humbler undertaking in the second song, for Israel is reached only by painstaking trials—in this song a tree lies across the path—that prayer must overcome before it is possible to rejoice at arriving in the promised land. Both songs are hopeful enjoinders to rescue a nation that has been lost. Both appeared in a section of national and religious songs at the beginning of Shaul Ginsburg and Pesach Marek's *Jewish Folk Songs in Russia* (1901), the first comprehensive anthology of Jewish folk songs in Europe, a collection that would profoundly influence virtually every collection of Jewish folk songs—in Yiddish and in other European languages—for the next half century.

Of the many national collections of national folk song from the turn of the twentieth century, it might seem strange to focus on a Jewish collection, since it could not yet represent a nation striving to shore up its modernity by rescuing history from its past. The two songs above, after all, display two quite enigmatic views of the nation, and they seem almost contradictory in their treatment of national imagery: one regal and aristocratic, the other rooted in folk culture. But were we to compare the national songs in *Jewish Folk Songs in Russia,* we would find that the images of the Jewish nation, whether or not geographically located in Europe, were articulated through songs very similar to those in the national collections of the late nineteenth century. It is, in fact, the transformation of more traditional songs about diaspora and separation from the past into a single collection, with multiple variants, that confirms the ways in which this collection characterized the national impetus of its own day.

The editors of *Jewish Folk Songs in Russia* not only knew they were rescuing history for the nation, they stated that agenda openly and directly in the extensive introduction that opens this volume of 376 songs. Ginsburg and Marek were only too well aware of the growing output of national collections, and they forcefully argued that if Europe's Jews did not follow suit, their own national struggle would fall behind or falter. The volume must assume the role of the other national collections, and its methodology and form should reflect those that had served national collections so effectively. The most specific model was, indeed, that used for the three volumes of Ludwig Erk and Franz Magnus Böhme's *Deutscher Liederhort* (1893–1894).

*Jewish Folk Songs in Russia* was further possible because of the sudden appearance of several recent institutional structures that were surrogates for the nation. The best known of these is the Zionist movement, which became the unofficial representative of a national polity through its conventions and cultural undertakings, beginning with the First Zionist Congress in 1897. More culturally than politically motivated, the formation of the St. Petersburg Society for Jewish Folk Song most directly influenced the canonic functions that would accrue to *Jewish Folk Songs in Russia* (cf. Heskes 1998). Finally, an explosion of Jewish music publishing propelled the collection into the forefront of approaches to representing European Jewish nationalism. Virtually every collection of Jewish folk song published in Europe during the next four decades, until the full-blown rise of fascism on the eve of the Holocaust, would make a bow to the Ginsburg-Marek collection (see Bohlman 2004). *Jewish Folk Songs in Russia* was foundational and hence catalytic as an endeavor to rescue history for the nation.

The cultural and national work accomplished by the collection was considerable. The folk songs included in the collection were malleable, which is to say, they lent themselves to molding into a new image of the nation, one which was above all classical. The paradox that folk song not only grew from a classical past but could be molded to reinstate the past as a classically based present was hardly lost on the editors, the St. Petersburg Society, and the musicians and scholars plumbing its contents. The sources for the collection were spread across the diaspora, especially Ashkenazic Europe and the growing immigrant culture of Russian Jews in North America. Underlying the collection's geographical boundaries, then, was the modern dispersion from the **shtetl,** or Jewish village of Eastern Europe, to the cosmopolitan Jewish culture of Central Europe to the complete dispersion that would follow migration to North America. It was a national dilemma of European and international dimensions, and for this reason the only antidote was removal to the folk culture where the fragments of the nation could be gathered and sutured through song.

*Jewish Folk Songs in Russia* was one of the first national collections to serve a European people without a nation. It would hardly be the last. In the course of the twentieth century, not least because of the destabilizing impact of two world wars on European borders, national collections serving peoples in search of their nation's history would proliferate. For the Jews of Eastern Europe, the path toward the nation that the collection generated would become at once more direct and more treacherous as additional collections came to channel it in the course of the next half century.

### Captain Francis O'Neill and Ireland's National Folk Music

*O'Neill's publications are the largest snapshot of this music
ever taken in its 9,000-year history.*
—*Carolan 1997: 60*

What is most remarkable about the hyperbole with which Captain
Francis O'Neill's collections of Irish music are assessed is that few re-
fute it. Whether the history the O'Neill collections gather is 9,000
years old, give or take a decade, or whether they will simply continue as
the "essential reference-point for future researchers" and "an essential
induction to the Irish tradition and a treasure trove of music of the
past for future use" (ibid.) is seldom open to serious question. The
nine volumes of Irish music that Captain Francis O'Neill (1848–1936)
published during his lifetime, with their estimated corpus of over
2,500 tunes, provide a national canon with a singular importance unri-
valed by any other collection of national music. The O'Neill collections have appeared in innumerable reprints and new editions alike
(cf. ibid.: 62–65). After their appearance in published form, traditional musicians copied them in manuscripts, which circulated
throughout Ireland, serving as a parallel national collection, securing
the literate foundations of O'Neill's collection while spinning off a
twentieth-century oral tradition grounded in those foundations.

O'Neill's volumes appeared on the threshold of the modern age of
recording technology, which meant that the earliest recordings of Irish
traditional music for commercial recordings or, after the founding of
Irish radio in 1926, for live radio broadcasts helped to position
O'Neill's volumes as an unassailably influential national collection. It's
a remarkable story that reveals much about the ways in which folk music acquires the power to rescue history—even 9,000 years of it—for
the nation. Most remarkable, Francis O'Neill did not gather his national folk-music collection in Ireland, but rather in Chicago, where he
served as a captain in the Chicago police force.

The volumes of music and music history, the essays and articles, and
the sundry other papers produced by Francis O'Neill bear many of the
earmarks of a national folk-music collection, but their idiosyncrasies
and highly personal attributes also challenge the very premise of claiming that a collection can be typical of the nation, any nation. If
O'Neill's vision and labors are not typical, it is not, however, because of
the personal touch he brought to them. In one way or another, every

national collection I discuss in this chapter is shaped by a personal touch. The nineteenth-century German collections clearly bear witness to the personalities of Ludwig Uhland, Ludwig Erk, and Franz Magnus Böhme. Shaul Ginsburg and Pesach Marek left their imprint throughout the 1901 St. Petersburg collection of Jewish folk songs. There were several powerful personalities behind the Habsburg Monarchy's "Das Volkslied in Österreich" project, the most powerful and quirky of them all being Josef Pommer (see Figure 5.6).

The ways that O'Neill's editorial decisions influenced how he and his publishers—most importantly, Lyon and Healy of Chicago, best known as a firm making musical instruments because of its slogan, "Harp Maker to the World"—presented the music on the page were also both personal and typical. Melodies appeared in generalized forms, stripped of the many embellishments that might reveal local performance practice or individual improvisation. But even if the songs were standardized for the printed page, neither O'Neill nor his publishers attempted to mask the fact that most of the tunes were published in a version played by individual musicians or transmitted through a local tradition (see, for example, Figure 3.6 below, a normalized version of "Chief O'Neill's Favorite," transcribed from the version played by Edward Cronin). Francis O'Neill generally did not make his own transcriptions but learned them from others, played them on the violin, and allowed songs to be transcribed from his performed versions by his police colleague, James O'Neill (1853–1949). The editorial decisions made by O'Neill have been crucial to the reception history of the tunes themselves, allowing performers to repersonalize them, thus drawing on the national collection to create new variants and confirming the canonic functions of the collection.

As we compare the O'Neill collection with other national collections, we also recognize that it is not exceptional in its reliance on the maintenance of a musical tradition from a diaspora as a source for inscribing the national music history. Irish music history, all 9,000 years of it, survives in the diaspora because oral tradition is concentrated in the quintessential practices that diaspora musicians, making their lives in a new world, maintain and use to connect themselves to the past. Music history is genealogical, performed by musicians from the past and the present whose individual efforts coalesce as the national tradition. In addition to his collection and publication of the music performed by Irish musicians in Chicago, O'Neill gathered the biographies of Irish musicians throughout the world and wove them into the

*Figure 3.6. "Chief O'Neill's Favorite"*
*(Carolan 1997. Reprinted by permission of Ossian Publications)*

collective biography that further justified the national collection (see especially O'Neill 1913).

By working in the diaspora O'Neill effectively underscored the national character of Irish music, even when this meant inventing or exaggerating the connections, musical and historical, between traditions that, in Ireland, would never have come into contact. In Chicago, musicians from different parts of Ireland played together, not only in the many immigrant neighborhoods of the city, but also in the religious and social organizations of an ethnic culture. O'Neill was himself serving as president of the Chicago Irish Music Club when he published his first volume, immodestly entitled *The Music of Ireland*, perhaps because its 1,850 individual melodies far outstripped in size any previous collection.

O'Neill was neither the first nor last to turn to a diaspora to determine the canonic repertories for a national collection. At more or less the same historical moment, A. Z. Idelsohn was collecting Jewish music in Jerusalem (see Idelsohn 1914–1932) and Béla Bartók was just beginning to sort out Hungarian repertories from the Hungarian-speaking communities beyond Hungary's borders (cf. Bartók 1913, 1923, and 1954, and 1959–1970). O'Neill's achievement proved to be the fact that he was able to recover the quintessence of the nation in its most localized forms in the neighborhoods of Chicago, where it was reimagined and repackaged as representative of the nation as a whole and rescued in that form for retrieval by the nation itself (cf., CD example 11).

## Volga, Volga

We might wonder how any movie could become "Stalin's favorite film," but that is precisely what Grigori Alexendrov's film musical, *Volga, Volga,* managed during the final decade and a half of the Soviet leader's life. *Volga, Volga* (1938) is a musical comedy, produced at the end of the first great decade of sound film, when national and international film companies recognized the potential of film to put masses of musicians and dancers on the stage, where they spurred the collective imaginations of audiences throughout the world. The international flair of film musicals would seem to be anathema to the **socialist-realism** of the Soviet Union, with its demands on the artist to serve the state directly and without undue embellishment of the national image. Alexendrov's films, many of them musicals, acknowledged the growing cosmopolitanism of international film, but they did so by reworking standard themes of the musical stage so that they would speak to the nation-building projects of the Stalinist era. Alexendrov's films, among them *Lucky Fellow* and *The Circus*, drew widely from the American film musical, in other words, from Broadway and Hollywood, but they also took a conscious bow to European prototypes, not least among them the Yiddish film musical, which was thriving in Poland even on the eve of the Holocaust.

Though such influences might seem to militate against the possibility of winning favor with Stalin, an avid fan of film, instead they won him over. Above all, *Volga, Volga* was a film musical that successfully staged the nation, indeed, that transformed the nation itself into a musical, placing it on a boat that followed the course of the Volga River from the heart of its agricultural regions in Ukraine to the seat of political and cultural power in Moscow (or, perhaps, Stalingrad, which was, in contrast, located on the Volga). Like many of the best Broadway musicals of its day, *Volga, Volga* was about making music and about musicals themselves. Its actors played the roles of musicians, and it transparently borrowed from the great American musical of its day, Jerome Kern and Oscar Hammerstein's *Showboat*. It hardly seemed, at first glance, the stuff of national music in the Soviet Union, which took its national agendas particularly seriously as the specter of European war loomed again.

The Soviet nation, however, runs through *Volga, Volga* like a river, deliberately channeled so that the nation would form along its shores and resonate to the music that issues forth from its waters. *Volga, Volga's* story begins in the countryside, at the site of an agricultural collective, where a ferry bearing Alyosha and his orchestra founders in the middle of the river. Alyosha and the orchestra are on their way to Moscow, where they will compete at the People's Art Olympics, and news of such an event intrigues the diverse workers at the collective, especially

Stralka, the prodigious musician of the region, whose talents seem to have won her a place in all areas of the collective's musical life.

Two ensembles form, competing to win the one spot available for the region at the People's Art Olympics, but there is little doubt about who is who. Alyosha and his musicians are the cosmopolitans, who, while waiting to proceed downstream on a repaired boat, rehearse and re-hearse the orchestral music of "Schubert, Wagner, and Strauss," never, however, getting it really right. Stralka, trying to convince the local bu-reaucrat to send her and the collective's musicians to Moscow, gathers them from their various trades and labors, showing all that they sponta-neously break into song and dance, and that music unites them in com-mon cause. Clearly, the viewer's sympathies—surely also Stalin's—go to Stralka and the chorus and band of natural musicians. But the bureau-crat, seizing the opportunity to bask in the potential victory of Alyosha's orchestra, sides with the cosmopolitans. Authorization to proceed to Moscow, substantiated in the gift of the collective's decrepit steamboat for the Volga journey, goes to Alyosha. Not to be outdone, for she is the guardian of the real music of the Soviet people, Stralka commandeers local workers to fashion a boat, more of a raft made from local timber, for her journey, and she and the collective musicians embark on their own Volga trip, powered more by music than by machines (Figure 3.7).

The Volga and music conspire to bring the people together in their pursuit of the national ideal. Neither boat is sufficiently rugged to make the journey on its own, and it becomes evident to all, if more be-grudgingly to the bureaucrat and Alyosha's orchestra, that true hope lies in combining forces. The catalyst that brings about the unity of the singing nation is a strange song, one that seems at first to come from nowhere, but soon begins to find voice through Stralka. Its beauty is unavoidable, and so too is its potential to provide the winning entry at the People's Art Olympics. It behooves all to learn and rehearse the song, known now as "Dunia's Song," and the musicians on board set themselves to the task of transcribing its melody, for apparently Stralka has formulated the song from oral tradition, and then to the subse-quent task of arranging it for orchestra and chorus. Just shy of Moscow, navigating the river proves too much of a challenge for the makeshift boat, and all copies of the song and its parts are swept overboard into the river. "Dunia's Song" is not to be lost, however, for others traveling to the People's Art Olympics fish the transcribed parts from the river's waters, marveling that the Volga should give up a song of its own, a

*Figure 3.7.   The journey to the People's Art Olympics in Grigori Alexendrov's 1938* Volga, Volga *(courtesy of the Berlin Film Museum)*

song the olympic-bound peoples from all the Soviet republics begin to call the "Volga Song."

*Volga, Volga* ends triumphantly, and in the fashion of the film musical of the day, all the loose ends are resolved, and the male and female leads, Alyosha and Stralka, also resolve the sexual tension between them. At the People's Art Olympics music brings the nation together as "Dunia's Song" becomes "Stralka's Song," which ultimately becomes the "Volga Song." The question of the song's authorship has been supplanted by assurances of the song's authenticity. In the grand finale, with the collective's musicians joined by people from all the Soviet republics, the many strains and arrangements of the "Volga Song" spontaneously unite in an arrangement made on the spot, clearly revealing that this is a song that all people of the Soviet nation subconsciously knew. The musical **quodlibet** that has provided narrative tension to the film now affirms national unity. Though all can sing independently, their great strength lies in their inherent ability to sing together.

In the course of *Volga, Volga* and in many other staged works of national music, it is necessary first to blur identities before they are united again to form a true image of the nation in music. Similarly, we begin to wonder, as we see music used in so many ways to imagine and represent the Soviet Union of the 1930s, whether clear distinctions between national music and nationalist music do not themselves blur. The symbols of national music are all present: music arising from nature, the authenticity of folk culture, and the national journey that anchors national narratives. The symbols of nationalist music are no less present: clearly designated foreign music, competitions, and music as the agent of state agenda. The brilliance of *Volga, Volga* lies in the ways Alexendrov plies both the national and the nationalist. By musically staging the nation on the collective farm, the Volga showboat, and at the People's Art Olympics, he multiplies rather than reduces the number of images that the nation might form.

By multiplying the images of the nation, *Volga, Volga*'s director and the musical arrangers simultaneously dislodged it from the quintessential Sovietness that its title and narrative imply. Filmed to underscore the representational potential of national music on the eve of World War II, *Volga, Volga* quickly assumed nationalist power once the most devastating conflagration of twentieth-century Soviet history was unleashed. Uniting in common historical cause, the national and the nationalist endowed the music of the Soviet film musical with uncommon power to stage the nation.

### REFERENCES

Alexendrov, Grigori. 1938. *Volga, Volga*.

Bartók, Béla. 1913. *Cântece poporale românesti din comitatul Bihor.* Bucharest: Academi Româna Librariile Socec & Comp. si C. Sfetea.

———. 1923. *Volksmusik der Rumänen von Maramures.* Munich: Drei Masken Verlag.

———. 1924. *A magyar népdal* ("The Hungarian Folk Song"). Reprint. Albany, N.Y.: State University of New York Press.

———. 1934. *Népzenénk és a szomszéd népek népzenéje* ("The Folk Music of the Magyars and Neighboring Peoples"). Budapest: Somló Béla.

———. 1954. *Serbo-Croatian Heroic Songs.* Ed. by Albert B. Lord. Cambridge, Mass.: Harvard University Press.

———. 1959–1970. *Slovenské l'udové piesne* ("Slovakian Folk Songs"). 2 vols. New York: Universal Edition.

Beckerman, Michael. 1986–1987. "In Search of Czechness in Music." *19th Century Music* 10: 61–73.

Bohlman, Philip V. 2004. *"Judische Volksmusik": Eine mitteleuropäische Geistesgeschichte.* Vienna: Böhlau.

Carolan, Nicholas. 1997. *A Harvest Saved: Francis O'Neill and Irish Music in Chicago.* Cork: Ossian Publications.

Cooley, Timothy. Forthcoming. *Making Mountain Music: Tourism, Ethnography, and Music in the Polish Tatras.* Bloomington, Ind.: Indiana University Press.

Deutsch, Walter. 1993. *Volksmusik in Niederösterreich: St. Pölten und Umgebung.* Vienna: Böhlau.

———. 1995. "90 Jahre Österreichisches Volksliedwerk: Dokumente und Berichte seiner Geschichte 1904–1994." *Jahrbuch des Österreichischen Volksliedwerks* 44: 12–50.

Duara, Prasenjit. 1995. *Rescuing History from the Nation: Questioning Narratives of Modern China.* Chicago: University of Chicago Press.

Engel, Carl. 1866. *An Introduction to the Study of National Music, Comprising Researches into Popular Songs, Traditions, and Customs.* London: Longmans, Green, Reader, and Dyer.

Erk, Ludwig, with Franz Magnus Böhme. 1893–1894. *Deutscher Liederhort.* 3 vols. Leipzig: Breitkopf und Härtel.

Ginsburg, Shaul M., and Pesach S. Marek. 1901. *Evreiskie narodnye pesni v Rossii* ["Jewish Folk Songs in Russia"]. St. Petersburg: Voskhod. Reprinted 1991: Ramat Gan: Bar-Ilan University Press.

Goertzen, Chris. 1997. *Fiddling for Norway: Revival and Identity.* Chicago: University of Chicago Press.

Gossett, Philip. 1990. "Becoming a Citizen: The Chorus in Risorgimento Opera." *Cambridge Opera Journal* 2: 41–64.

Heaton, Vernon. 1979. *The Oberammergau Passion Play.* London: Hale.

Heskes, Irene, ed. 1998 [1912]. *The St. Petersburg Society for Jewish Folk Music.* N.p.: Tara Publications.

Holzmeister, Johannes, ed. 1965. *Carmina historica: Geschichten im Lied.* Boppard: Fidula.

Idelsohn, A. Z. 1914–1932. *Hebräisch-orientalischer Melodienschatz.* 10 vols. Berlin et al.: Benjamin Harz et al.

Kolessa, Filaret. 1910 and 1913. *Melodiia ukrains'kykh narodnikh dum.* 2 vols. L'viv: Naukova Tovarystvo im. Shevchenka.

Lane, Eric, and Ian Brenson. 1984. *The Complete Text in English of the Oberammergau Passion Play.* London: Dedalus.

Parakilas, James. 1992. "Political Representation and the Chorus in Nineteenth-century Opera." *19th Century Music* 16 (2): 181–202.

Shapiro, James S. 2000. *The Troubling Story of the World's Most Famous Passion Play.* New York: Pantheon.

Stokes, Martin, ed. 1994. *Ethnicity, Identity and Music: The Musical Construction of Place.* Oxford: Berg.

Tappert, Wilhelm. 1890. *Wandernde Melodien*. 2d ed., enlarged. Leipzig: List und Francke.

Uhland, Ludwig. 1844–1845. *Alte hoch- und niederdeutsche Volkslieder.* 2 vols. Stuttgart and Tübingen: J. G. Cotta'scher Verlag.

*Unblocked: Music of Eastern Europe.* 1997. Three-CD set, with accompanying booklet. Ellipsis Arts CD3570.

Vaughan Williams, Ralph. 1934. *National Music.* London: Oxford University Press.

# Chapter Four

# Nationalist Music

*There is indeed no* nation *among all the* European *peoples, whose* music *is so greatly ennobling, as that of the Germans. They have contributed more than anyone else to the expansion and growth of music.*
*—Reimmann 1709: 276; italics in the original*

*An irresistible power drew his spirit back to the [South German] city of his birth, which he had come to regard as a paradise in and of itself; there, he burned with desire to learn music from the ground up.*
*—Wackenroder and Tieck 1979 [1797]: 112–113*

*Instrumental music is the sole possession of the German—it is his life, it is his creative power.*
*—Wagner 1983 [1840–1841]: 160*

As modernity began to make aesthetic inroads into the nation-state in the eighteenth century, a new rhetoric of aesthetics followed suit. The rather immediate result of the aesthetics extolling the emerging nation-state was the growing tendency to claim that the music of one's own nation was better than that of another's. The vocabulary and syntax of the new rhetoric juxtaposed a number of keywords, each one charging the other with greater power to focus identity on the single nation and the grandeur of its music. In short, the crucial argument advanced by the new rhetoric was that "our music is better than anyone else's." The assertion then followed that "our nation is better than anyone else's."

Characteristic of the rhetoric of national aesthetics is that relatively little evidence was necessary to prove it one way or another. Claims that one nation had contributed more to music than another might recognize the volume and extent of one nation's musical activities. Perhaps that nation's composers had been at it longer than another's, thus making for a longer and more notable history. Perhaps it was the complexity and rootedness of the national aesthetics, the quality of a nation's soul that somehow accounted for a better music.

By claiming that "our music is better than anyone else's," the aesthetic rhetoric that accompanied the rise of the modern nation-state also underwent a dramatic shift from emphasis on the national to the assertion of the nationalist. Comparison was crucial to that shift, and competition was critical to its implications. It is perhaps no surprise that the first nation to embrace the shift from a national to a nationalist aesthetics of music was Germany. The three epigraphs opening this chapter do not represent isolated sentiments. Jacob Friedrich Reimmann may have been one of the first to make such sweeping claims for the dominance of German music, but he was hardly the last. In the course of the following centuries, the German nationalist aesthetics became both more general and more specific. In the chapters and fragments of what would become a foundational aesthetic manifesto for Romanticism, Wilhelm Heinrich Wackenroder and Ludwig Tieck draw nationalist distinctions between the cultivation of the visual arts in Italy and of music in Germany, endowing the history of both cultures with an aesthetic discourse that would become formalized in the course of the nineteenth century, when Italian and German nationalism also became formalized in state structures. Music, concluded Wackenroder in the final chapter of *The Outpourings from the Heart of an Art-Loving Friar* (1797), was the provenance of the Germans.

The national chauvinism in Wagner's nationalist aesthetics may not surprise us, but we are less likely to expect that Jewish composers of the early and mid-twentieth century are no less restrained in their recognition of German contributions. The modernist composer Arnold Schoenberg and the aesthetic philosopher Theodor W. Adorno, both forced into exile by the Germans because they were Jews, nonetheless were willing to heap fulsome praise on German music as the dominant tradition of the present and the future.

By no means did the German nationalist aesthetics remain unremarked and unchallenged. If Germans such as Wagner emphasized instrumental music, it fell to the Italians to emphasize vocal music, above all opera and music for the stage. A French nationalist aesthetics claimed an older history, one more classical than anything the Germans could muster (see, e.g., Fulcher 1987). Latecomers to the formation of modern nation-states, particularly Eastern Europeans, sought a rhetoric that would allow them to circumvent the models of nationalist music shaped by Germans and Austrians for their own uses. If at all possible, it was desirable to beat the Germans at their own game, but if it was not possible, then it might be more effective to reinvent the rules in such a way that, should the Germans—or French or English—wish to play, they would necessarily fail.

### Nationalist Music and Competition for the Nation-State

Nationalist music serves a nation-state in its competition with other nation-states, and in this fundamental way it differs from national music. The competition spurred on by a nationalist music may be political, economic, cultural, or even ideological, but for each form of competition there develops an appropriate aesthetic vocabulary. These forms of competition may be either internal or external, bolstering a power elite within the state or the state's own feeling of power in international affairs. The competition may portend that there is more at stake than music itself, thus effectively investing music with a nationalist potential to serve far more than aesthetic ends. When national music undergoes the rhetorical transformation to nationalist music, its competitive potential has the power to undertake an entirely new kind of cultural and political work.

Competition shapes that cultural and political work. Nationalist music appears at those times and places when nations confront each other, or when they compete with each other for the same set of cultural goods. Above all, nationalist music may contribute to the struggle over contested territory such as border regions. Possessing music becomes like possessing land: Necessarily, one must claim it as one's own. To discover nationalist music, we seldom need to look much farther than those places where there are competing historical claims for land.

The rhetoric of nationalist music differs from that of national music. The latter emphasizes the "nation" itself and the images thereof. The former emphasizes the "state" in the formulation of "nation-state," and rather than merely representing the images of the nation, nationalist rhetoric recognizes music in "service" to the state. Certain musical activities, for example, are taken over by state ensembles, especially at moments when the nation-state is competing for its position in history. Thus state ensembles function like the state itself, developing structures and hierarchies that resemble those of the state. The recalibration of the state, for example in the army-based song or dance ensembles in Eastern Europe during the Cold War, serves as a case-in-point for the use of state musical ensembles to transform the status of the state. The cultivation of musical activities by state organizations such as national academies of science, which often support folk-music divisions, similarly invest music with national meaning and the potential to be used to produce nationalist ends. (Listen to CD example 35, in which soldiers of the Austro-Hungarian army sing the national anthem in World War I.)

Whereas a national music might reflect place through its representation of a geography that defines the nation in symbolic ways, a nationalist music relies on the symbolism of structures that define the nation. Nationalist music functions to enforce borders. It enters into public and political ritual, and the trappings of ceremony necessary for statecraft thus come to enter into its structure. Nationalist music not only rescues the nation for history, but it does so by contributing fundamentally to history's articulation of the nation-state (cf. Duara 1995).

Nationalist music comes into being through top-down cultural and political work, just the opposite of national music. Rather than representing something preexistent and quintessential—culturally prior to the nation—nationalist music represents cultural boundaries for the state that have political purposes. Rivers, rather than providing a cultural core to the nation, trace the nation's boundaries. The Rhine River that appears in many German nationalist songs is portrayed as a border against France, even though the Rhine also flows through much of western Germany. Mountain ranges along borders acquire nationalist symbolism when their functions as repositories for traditional folk song are replaced by their potential to block the cultural and political onslaughts of the nations lying beyond them.

At the point when national music becomes nationalist, the symbolic geography of nationalism is no longer common only to a nation's people and their musical culture. The natural, linguistic, cultural, and historical symbols of national music are replaced by those that are abstract. Nature in its purest forms may symbolize the nation, providing a vocabulary for national folk songs. The state may be reimagined as transmitted by blood and soil. History, too, is reduced to struggle, which itself justifies political expansion.

In nationalist songs nature allows itself to undergo a transformation so that it serves the state, for example, when German and Austrian farmers cultivated the soil of Eastern European **speech islands** by reclaiming them for Germany, both before and during World War II, as

**folk-song landscapes.** In the preface to a 1935 collection of German songs from the **Banat** speech island in Romania, the cultivation of the soil affords the German settlers the power to save the land from the neighboring Hungarians through farming and the nation, more German than Romanian.

> One tends to look only at the fertility of the black soil for the raising of wheat, corn, and wine, and to regard it as a true agricultural gift from this region so blessed by climate. But one learns from the residents of today just how much struggle was required of their ancestors 200 years ago, when they had to transform the disease-ridden swamps and impoverished soil into productive fields. And in similar ways, they had to struggle with their soil and land, which the German residents had for even longer before the war had to protect from a relentless policy to make the country Hungarian. (Künzig 1935: 3)

The sixty-one songs that follow the preface of this 1935 collection proceed to claim the Banat region as German, politically wresting it from the Hungarians but not returning it to the dominant population of Romanians. In 1935, these songs, like others from the German collecting project known as *Landschaftliche Volkslieder,* connect the soil of Eastern Europe to Germany, as exemplary models of "the customs and songs of their original homeland" (ibid.).

The state uses nationalist music in several distinctive ways. First, it relies on the malleability of nationalist music to fabricate and create images of itself. The more concrete such images are, the more extensively they endow music with the potential to serve the state. Musical monuments, as we see in this chapter, possess many of the formal characteristics of other state monuments. Second, nationalist music mobilizes the residents of the state through musical ideas. They narrate an historical or political struggle. They identify the entity against which the nation struggles, and they draw the battlelines, both abstract and real. Nationalist music can take the people of the state into battle, for example as military music. Third, nationalist music generates an aesthetic and musical language that allows the nation-state to compete for abstract ideas as well as the specific ideologies.

Competition with other nation-states thus becomes explicit in nationalist music, for example, in folk- and popular-music contests that play out in the nationalized media—television and recordings—of the European nation-state at the end of the twentieth century and the

beginning of the twenty-first. Nationalist music expresses itself in figurative and literal competition. We recognize that these forms of literal
and figurative musical competition, which provide postmodern means
of mobilizing the people of the nation-state to articulate a new rhetoric
of nationalism, constitute more and more of the symbolic language of
nationalist musics of all kinds.

## The Geography and Genres of Nationalist Music

The genres of nationalist music rescue the nation for history at the
places the nation is most contested. Nationalist musical practices form
at the borders of the nation, where they represent many of the issues
that create strife in areas claimed by several nations. Language of folk
song, for example, is one of the most commonly contested aspects of a
border music. National and regional histories, too, leave their impact
in especially direct ways on the musical repertories of border regions.

Nationalist repertories also lay claim to history in distinctive ways,
doing the cultural work of monuments, which occupy particularly distinctive spaces on a national musical landscape. A nationalist musical
monument may on its surface suggest that it is no more than a repertory gathered over the course of many years, but monuments function
to include and exclude certain narratives and memories from the national history. The genres of nationalist music may also rescue the nation for history through the seemingly innocuous forms of competition at which national anthems are played or in which the best folk
musicians from a nation or cultural region perform. But far more is at
stake than the decisions about winners and losers at such competitions.

In the following section we travel across the geography that is most
often home to the genres of nationalist music. In the border regions
and by examining musical monuments and competitions, we experience the ways in which genres form through the musical affinities that
connect the history of a nation to specific geographies.

### Folk Music from Contested Borders

One of the first things the traveler to Alto Adige/Südtirol (South Tyrol) notices is that every village and city, every mountain and valley, has
two names, one Italian and the other German. The two names com-

pete with each other, on one hand because they are different, on the other because they are not entirely different, which is to say that they share many aspects of the same spelling because one name is derived from or intentionally resembles the other (for example, the capital city of the province is Bolzano/Bozen). Names, which is to say, signs bearing names, are everywhere, almost cluttering the landscape of South Tyrol, which is otherwise a relatively sparsely settled mountainous region at the far northeastern frontier of Italy. It shares borders with Austria, Slovenia, and Switzerland, forming one of Europe's most contested border regions.

What seems to be a superabundance of music, especially folk music, also occupies the cultural landscape of South Tyrol. In the rural areas of the mountains, which define the region for its German-speaking residents, German folk-music traditions dominate. The dialects of song texts are ostensibly local, relying on the heavily accented repertory that the region shares with the Austrian province of Tyrol to the north. Instrumental music and folk dance, too, bear witness to cultural exchange with the north. In the small cities of the region, which have formed along rivers (the Alto Adige, also the region's official name in Italian, refers to the upper reaches of a river flowing from the mountains south into Italy), more urban and cosmopolitan religious and popular traditions employ Italian texts. To confuse, or actually to mix up, the situation even more, there is yet another linguistic and historical tradition that forms a network across the South Tyrol, namely traditional song repertories in an ancient Romance language, locally called **ladino** by Italian speakers and *Ladinisch* by German speakers (but not to be confused in any way with the vernacular language of Sephardic Jews, also called *ladino*).

The musical repertories of South Tyrol reveal extremely complex patterns of nationalism. What one sings identifies not only what language one speaks, or what ethnic background one's family claims, but also to what nation one owes allegiance. Those who sing in German and cultivate mountain folk-music practice consciously claim national connections to Austria. In alpine and Central European musical competitions, musicians performing from German repertories publicly represent South Tyrol as if it were a political entity within Austria. German folk-music traditions narrate a particular past, one which has still to be fully severed from the present, even though South Tyrol has not been part of Austria since 1919. Italian traditions directly conflict with the German traditions, though they do not require nearly the same conscious cultivation of the past, the historicist practice called **Volks-musikpflege,** which not only maintains older forms but motivates their frequent revival. Ladino folk-music traditions are not mixed into the multiculturalism of the border region with quite the same goals. They remain, nonetheless, explicit indices of the historical past, and the alternative nationalism that they afford is neither Italian nor Austrian. Instead, Ladino traditions reflect various forms of internationalism, not least among them a pan-European Catholicism predating the modern nation-state about which South Tyrol's borders raise so many questions (see, e.g., Deutsch and Haid 1997).

The nationalist questions articulated by folk music in South Tyrol are by no means unique. We need not travel far along the borders of modern European nations to enter other border regions where folk music also draws attention to the conflicts that simmer there. The mountainous regions of the Balkans begin within a few hours' drive from South Tyrol, and they quickly unfold as a series of border regions, one after another. The historicization of the border conflicts between Austria and Italy in South Tyrol assumes virtually countless forms in the Balkans, though it is critical to trace them along individual political, linguistic, and even musical borders. Again, many places have multiple names. In any given region, there are musical repertories in several languages, which ultimately may be more similar than different, even though it is the difference—say, between the Serbian, Croatian, and Bosnian languages, which have at many times been subsumed under the single designation of Serbo-Croatian—that has played the most public role since the break-up of the former Yugoslavia in the 1990s.

The musical genres of border regions exhibit a very distinctive pattern of rescuing history for the nation. Repertories of folk music may coalesce around a series of historical levels, in which certain musical structures retain the oldest historical characteristics, for example, a scale structure that predates direct influences from the outside, especially the harmonic influences of sacred music beginning with the Early Modern period. The "stratigraphy" of musical structures, as Alica Elscheková has referred to these musically articulated historical levels, establish a scaffold of connections that both respond to more recent nationalist influences and circumvent those influences (Elscheková 1981). The stratigraphy of the Carpathian Mountains provides a particularly striking instance of conflicting musical and political narratives of regional history.

The Carpathian Mountain range stretches from the Danube basin near Bratislava in western Slovakia eastward across Slovakia, Ukraine, and Romania before bending southward into central Romania. There are many ways to attempt to determine the extent of nationalist repertories in the Carpathians. Historically, the national boundaries that crisscross the Carpathians have been determined by outside forces. From the eighteenth to the twentieth century, the Russian and the Austro-Hungarian empires, with occasional forays by Germany and Poland, struggled over the ways the Carpathians provided natural borders between Central and Eastern Europe. Culturally and linguistically, however, the Carpathians juxtapose rather than divide the many linguistic, ethnic, and religious groups populating them. Several languages might be spoken—and shared—in many regions, in rural and urban areas alike (see Wischenbart 1992).

Musical repertories functioned to break down rather than erect borders between the cultural groups of the Carpathians. One of the most striking characteristics of Carpathian repertories is the presence of several languages in the same repertories, or even in the same songs (cf. Krekovičová 1997). In part, this is due to the fluid movement of groups across the Carpathians, for example, pilgrims, who might have combined Latin, German, and Slavic songs and verses to form a common repertory. In the border culture spanning the Carpathian subregion overlapping Slovakia and Ukraine, Rusyns have for centuries forged repertories whose distinctiveness derived from the ways Rusyn, Slovak, and Ukrainian repertories were synthesized with other local ethnic groups, among them Roma, Germans, and Huzuls. What is remarkable about the unfettered diversity that shapes the musical practices of this part of the Carpathians is that it also forms the geographical center of Europe, making it nationally one of the most difficult places in the continent to define with music and to constrain with borders (cf. Metil 2000).

### Musical Monuments

In the wake of the fall of the Ceauşescu regime of Romania, which began with the revolutions of 1989 that led to the reunification of Western and Eastern Europe, markers and monuments of various sizes and shapes began to fill the streets of Bucharest (see Figure 4.1). Bucharest

*Figure 4.1.   Street monument in Bucharest, Romania, 1998*
*(photograph by Philip V. Bohlman)*

has historically been a city defined by monuments. Its architecture was grandiose, and it wore its historical symbolism in very public ways, inevitably making a statement about the past or about Romania's distinctive position at the meeting point of several cultures. During the years of Ceaușescu's communist government, monuments not only proliferated but also expanded in size, with Ceaușescu's pet project, the Palace of the People, aspiring to monumental grandeur as one of the largest single buildings of the world. The memorials to the street battles that toppled the Ceaușescu government assumed the character of shrines, both in their general appearance and in the ways they focused ritual. These memorials would seem at first glance to contrast with the classical architecture of public buildings and the sweep of avenues and boulevards that gave Bucharest its cosmopolitan flair.

More often than not, the new monuments were visited in the evening, when small groups gathered about them, lighting candles, reading texts of various kinds, and making music. The new monuments allowed those who gathered to reflect upon the past and to memorialize it with music. In ways suited to the aftermath of the fall of Romanian communism, the new monuments also encouraged reflection on the monuments of the previous eras, therefore marking publicly the competition between past and present. The contrafacts of Romanian folk songs used at the new shrines and memorials provided counterpoint to the patriotic songs in grandiose arrangements used to ritualize the previous regime. The songs at the new monuments gave voice to those Romanian citizens who had so many years been silenced, empowering them to remember a history that had almost been lost and to rescue that history for the Romania that was taking shape at the end of the twentieth century (cf. Popa 1996).

We have encountered musical monuments throughout this book, and it has been quite remarkable to observe the different shapes and functions that they have as receptacles for the repertories that give the nation its identity. One of the most distinctive qualities of musical monuments is the capacity to embody the past by gathering an enormous repertory of musical works that come to represent the nation. Monuments aim at completeness, and they do so by permitting themselves an almost immeasurable girth. Complete collections of folk songs, for example, should stretch across the repertories of the nation. If indeed a nation's folk-music **Denkmal**—the German word for monument, which is used for comprehensive national collections, such as the *Denkmäler der Tonkunst Österreichs* ("Austria's Musical Monuments")—is to include the national musical heritage, then it should be an ongoing project, retrieving treasures from the past and reaching infinitely toward the future. Monumental publishing projects, in fact, often encounter ideological impediments when attempts are made to terminate them. The collection of German ballads initiated in 1935, the so-called **Balladenwerk,** was planned to conclude with a final volume in the 1990s until voices were raised in protest. Arguing that collection should resume in the twenty-first century, the protesters were less concerned that specific repertories of ballads had been denied entrance than with the unthinkable possibility of a finite monument. The ideological stakes invested in expanding such a German national monument were very great indeed.

Music participates frequently and intensively in the memory work that is crucial to the nationalist functions of monuments. When monuments serve as the focus of public ritual—for example, the parades that fill the most monumental spaces of a nation on the national day of independence—music provides the template for parades and ceremonies that allow the collective nation to remember its past. The dedication of national monuments is usually incomplete without dedication music, a new work composed to mark the entry of the monument into a nation's historical consciousness. The surfaces of physical monuments commonly make reference to music in one way or another, insisting on music's mnemonic power, its capacity to contribute substantially to the human ability to remember. Even more significantly, music endows monuments with the power to retrieve moments of the past when the nation was in danger. Musical monuments have enormous ideological potential to empower a competition over lost spaces, such as sovereignty over land lost in a war.

One of the most remarkable of all monumental spaces reserved for European music is Walhalla, a temple-like structure built to imitate the sacred structures of Classical Greece but placed on a hill overlooking the Danube River valley in Bavaria, not far from the South German city of Regensburg (see Figure 4.2). Walhalla is home to the busts of great German composers who have entered the pantheon of European music history. The prerequisites for receiving monumental space in the temple's space are many and complex, and they have everything to do with nationalism and music. Any composer worthy of a Walhalla bust must qualify as "German" in some way that draws upon the national musical imagination. J. S. Bach won his place in German music history soon after the building of the monument in the late nineteenth century. There was little controversy over Beethoven in the decision-making process, even though he made his career in Austria. Austrian composers, on the other hand, have been almost entirely excluded, with the notable exception of Anton Bruckner, the late nineteenth-century composer of monumental symphonic and choral works whose ideological and aesthetic positions reflected the extreme conservatism shrouding the maintenance of Walhalla as a monument to German music. That Jewish composers from Germany or Austria have yet to win a place for their busts in Walhalla goes without saying. As a temple to nationalist music, Walhalla fails completely to represent Germany since World War II, if indeed the historical moments it memorializes are also inseparable from the extreme forms of nationalism, notably fascism and National Socialism, that led to World War II and the Holocaust. Its very monumentality similarly fails to erase Germany's nationalist past in any way, but succeeds instead in sacralizing it in the present (see Riethmüller 1993).

Music particularly contributes to the temporal dimensions of the memory work that monuments make possible, serving as a framework for what Michael Herzfeld calls "monumental time" (Herzfeld 1991). When public performance shares a monument's space, therefore, it calibrates monumental time by drawing those experiencing music

*Figure 4.2. Walhalla, overlooking the Danube River near Regensburg, Germany
(Riethmüller 1993)*

closer to the historical moment that is being memorialized. They enter the monumental time that allows the history of the nation to become fluid, or "transient" in the theoretical formulation of Rudy Koshar (1998). Music also intersects with the other arts to narrate the mythical past of the nations, shaping the processes necessary for what Stefan Germer calls the "retrospective invention of the nation through art" (1998). One might even go so far as suggesting that music participates in the invention of the nation most effectively when it achieves monumental status (cf. the various ways in which monumental works of art shape the national myths of Europe in Flacke 1998).

Competition underlies many of the ways in which musical monuments rescue history for the nation. The street shrines in contemporary Bucharest compete with Romania's architectural monuments, insisting that the popular struggle for the nation not be forgotten. Each performance of folk song and each ritual event at the street monuments serves as an act of creating monumental time by remembering the past. These monuments remind us that there are voiceless peoples who have not been given national spaces but who instead recognize the power of musical monuments to claim some historical and national space as their own, publicly but fleetingly, through performance. In

Eastern European synagogues, where Jewish communities have never returned in significant numbers since the Holocaust, music similarly is one of the primary means of remembering the past through the reimagination of sacred space at moments when there are special performances of Jewish music (cf. Young 1993 and Bohlman 2000c).

Musical monuments are proliferating in the New Europe, where they signify new nationalisms. When musical monuments blur the distinctions between remembering and forgetting, they further complicate the dilemma of owning national history. Musical monuments reflect this dilemma as simulacra—and in the reunified Europe since 1989, increasingly—by laying claim to a nationalist music in order to rescue it from other claims. The struggle for the European future—the New Europe—may be a brutal competition for owning history and monumental time, but music is crucially present.

### Folk-Music Competitions

On Saturday nights, from late spring well into the summer, the television sets in taverns throughout Central Europe are tuned to the latest round of the "Grand Prix der Volksmusik." Even in many traditional taverns, where there has been live folk-music entertainment during the week, those who have stopped by for an evening's entertainment are watching the broadcast with intense interest. The "folk music" of the Grand Prix is neither rural nor urban—as one might find it in Bavaria or in Munich—but is cast in a popular vein, with electronic instruments, from guitars to keyboards to drumsets, replacing acoustic traditional instruments. More properly, the music broadcast in this competition belongs to the genres known as **volkstümliche Musik** ("folk-like music"), which consciously employ folk music as their point of reference but aim for a more popular, even rock-like sound (see Mahr 2002 for an extensive study of the organization of the Grand Prix of Folk Music).

Paradoxically, both folk and rock components are emphasized as much as possible. Each of the ensembles appears in traditional clothing (**Trachten**), and most songs are performed in dialect, thus emphasizing the local content and style. Lest they seem too local, however, the performers modify their fashion, say, by combining more recent fashions with the *Trachten,* and they alter the sound of their performance by amplifying the bass and throwing in harmonies and improvisatory techniques that have unmistakable rock references. Repertory and performance style conspire to evoke the local and the international, and in the mix of these extremes is unmistakable evidence of the nationalist potential of mediated folk and popular music.

The Grand Prix der Volksmusik, as its name makes clear, is primarily a competition in which folk-like music rescues history for the nation. For those who follow the Grand Prix, the competitive nature of the broadcasts is obvious—a prime motivation for following the various rounds week after week, not only in the tavern but also at home, where the Grand Prix is broadcast on primetime weekend television. By calling the folk-music competition a "Grand Prix"—literally, "grand prize"—the organizers meant to refer to other media competitions, not least among them the Eurovision Song Contest. In a few cases, such as Switzerland's 2002 Eurovision entry, Francine Jordi, musicians have competed first in the Grand Prix der Volksmusik before representing their nation in the Eurovision. More to the point, these musical competitions are all media events, in which radio and television, regionally, nationally, and internationally, create a framework for awarding the region or nation with the winning entry a grand prize: at base, the opportunity to sign concert, recording, and broadcast contracts (see Mahr 2002).

The Grand Prix of Folk Music unfolds much like the Eurovision Song Contest. It begins locally. Any ensemble that wishes is given the chance to represent the local or regional tradition. In the first rounds of the competition, it is more important that the ensembles capture something of the tradition that the judges and audiences understand as their own. The winners move on to subsequent rounds, in each case in a somewhat larger city, which in turn represents a more extensive gamut of local traditions. The expectations of the judges and the audiences, now perhaps also listening through regional broadcasts, are greater. They expect the performers to display a more sophisticated awareness of "folk music" at the national and international levels, that is, in the German-speaking areas of Central Europe. Subsequent rounds take the winning ensembles to national and international competitions, where the audiences and judges are themselves much farther removed from the repertories that the ensembles might perform in local settings, perhaps in the very taverns where the televisions are broadcasting the closing rounds. The local audiences, however, are not cut off from the national and international rounds because "voting" for the winners, particularly since the mid-1990s, is partly determined by the number of calls placed in support of one ensemble or another. In the weeks before the final rounds, the finalists are busily contacting friends and local supporters through web pages and omnibus e-mail requests, urging them to phone in their votes at the appropriate time on the evening of a Grand Prix broadcast.

The Grand Prix of Folk Music does not really become fully nationalist until the closing rounds, when the competitive stakes are the greatest. The context for the final rounds depends on the media of the competing nations, Austria, Germany, and Switzerland. The hosts of the competition itself—the announcers—are chosen to represent the nations through the national media networks that together produce the final television broadcasts. However, the ensembles that perform in the final rounds are not primarily national entries. It is not the case, in other words, that Switzerland has chosen a single entry to perform on its behalf, even if the Swiss host makes his or her preferences clearly known. The winning entries, instead, come from cultural and dialect regions, which occasionally reflect political and administrative regions such as a province or canton, but more commonly suggest that the entries really come from the peripheries of Central Europe rather than its center. In other words, many entries are not, properly speaking, from the three "host nations" but rather from the German-speaking regions beyond their borders. South Tyrol has managed to support a number of excellent ensembles that have reached the final rounds. So, too, have Luxembourg and the Frisian areas stretching from northeastern Holland into southern Denmark. None of these entries is without some political symbolism; German-speaking minorities outside the German-speaking countries clearly intend to make a statement about cultural and national heritage using the most German of all folk-music competitions. For some of these entries, the political stakes of the competition are extremely high. By supporting a winning entry in the German language and with an Austrian folk-music style, South Tyrol intends to make an historical statement about its national allegiance to Austria.

The nationalist imagery of the Grand Prix of Folk Music lies at the borders that many of its entries call into question through music. The competition's nationalist aesthetic rhetoric begins to take shape locally, but it is in the final rounds that it becomes sharpest. It is in the final rounds, moreover, that the competition itself begins to shed traces of bottom-up organization and reformulates an aesthetic from the top down, fueling it with more nationalist musical rhetoric. To a large degree, music competitions throughout Europe undergo this transformation when they undergo the transformations that the modern nation-state imposes upon them. In his study of fiddling competitions in Norway, Chris Goertzen has examined the ways in which the most local level remains far removed, aesthetically and geographically, from the regulations and expectations of the national contest. Historically, the local "contests set the stage and provided a cumulative model for the National Fiddle Contest" (Goertzen 1997: 90), but by the end of the twentieth century the differences that had local meaning were being leveled through a process of turning contests into concerts (ibid.: 90–105).

At the local level, there is relatively little in the folk-music competition that is contested; at the international level, however, folk music has the potential to draw attention to borders and beyond them to the identity politics of linguistic and cultural minorities. In the final rounds of a competition, political questions that may not be of burning interest throughout the area in which the competition is broadcast suddenly become relevant to audiences throughout the area. The nationalist past of South Tyrol acquires contemporary meaning, and the borders that seemingly contained an innocuous folk-music competition are called into question as local folk-music styles are charged with nationalist meaning.

### Music in Competition for the Nation— Folk Music from Alsace-Lorraine

Few European border regions have been as historically contested as Alsace-Lorraine. In the twentieth century, two world wars have emphasized its importance. In World War I Germany used the region, taken from the French through the Franco-Prussian War of 1871, to launch its invasion of France. Retaking the region became one of Germany's primary justifications for invading France at the beginning of World War II. These military struggles concerned themselves, at least on the surface, with land. But the weapons with which the battle for Alsace-Lorraine has been historically waged have also included language and historical tradition. At the juncture of these traditions are the more intangible symbols of heritage and blood, literally and figuratively the re-production of culture through the perpetuation of generations.

Alsace and Lorraine have never constituted a national entity, either as separate region or combined as a common region. The historical struggle that defines them, nonetheless, has been waged according to nationalist terms, those established by France and Germany. The cultural question is not only whether the region is French or German, but the degree to which a distinctive culture of the region itself, with its own language and musical traditions, counterbalances the nationalist with the regional. The language of Alsace-Lorraine is **Alsatian,** which demonstrates the various qualities of an indigenous, vernacular, and literary language. Alsatian is most closely related to German, though only through an extensive linguistic history shared with several dialects of the upper Rhine, especially with **Alemannisch**.

Struggles for political control over Alsace-Lorraine began perhaps in the early ninth century, when Charlemagne gave the western part of the Holy Roman Empire to his son, Lothringen, who then gave his name to the region (in German, Alsace-Lorraine is Elsaß-Lothringen). The lands that became Alsace-Lorraine formed a transit corridor for trade between the Germanic and French lands of Europe, as well as between Europe's southern and central regions. Historically, Alsace-Lorraine facilitated the confluence of many cultures. Its great cities—Strasbourg, Metz, and Colmar—as well as its network of villages and small cities along trading routes attracted cultural differences. These were the qualities that attracted Enlightenment thinkers such as Goethe and Herder, both of whom wrote extensively about the cultural history of the region. Goethe turned to Alsatian villages to engage in some of the first forays into collecting folk songs. His observations about the great age of the songs he collected in Alsace and the fact that they issued from the "throats of the oldest women in the villages" are claimed by many later scholars to have established collection as crucial to the study and analysis of folk music. Already in the eighteenth century, Alsace-Lorraine attracted considerable attention because of its folk music, providing a focus for several of the most influential early theories about the relation between music and nation (see Herder, Goethe, Frisi, and Möser 1983).

For the Enlightenment thinkers, sorting out the cultural mix of Alsace-Lorraine folk song served as a means of transmitting the past. The questions Goethe asked about the cultural make-up of the region ulti-

mately led him and his Enlightenment colleagues to formulate a notion of cultural history: Music, architecture, language, and literature
were the stuff of the historical past. When Louis Pinck (1873–1940)
set in motion the project that would eventually be called *Verklingende
Weisen* (lit., "ever more silent tunes"), his focus shifted dramatically
from the past to the present and then to the future. Pinck took up the
mantle of a folk-music scholar only after wearing the habit of a local
priest in the village of Hambach. In 1908 he had been forced into a
sort of pastoral exile from the cultural and cathedral center of Metz,
the political seat of Lorraine, when he wrote critically of the German
government's administration of the area. His earliest encounters with
folk music, then, were the results of his publicly anti-nationalist stance.
Folk song would provide him with a different medium for addressing
the regional culture of Lorraine, situating it between the national cultures of France and Germany.

By beginning locally and turning to the individuals whose musical
activities constituted the culture of Hambach and the nearby villages,
Louis Pinck did the spadework that would produce the five volumes of
*Verklingende Weisen*. He turned folk songs toward historical ends, determining the ways they would document a cultural position between the
nationalist positions of Germany and France in Lorraine. Pinck's
methodology seems, at first glance, typical of collecting strategies at
the beginning of the twentieth century: Gather as many songs as possible and then transcribe them so that standard forms and specific variants can be published in a representative anthology. The oral transmission of folk song in Lorraine, he suggested at the beginning of his
work, circumvented the nationalist history of the region:

> [The songs in this volume] are old folk songs, and we can prove that
> they were sung in the German-language region of Lorraine already
> before 1870. Many of them, in fact, were transmitted from one gen-
> eration to the next long before recorded history.
>
> These songs have been planted by the father in his son, from the
> mother in her child, as if they were a sacred heritage. In the tavern
> and the spinning room, the songs made the winter shorter, and they
> intensified the humid evenings of summer and contributed to life's
> passions and tribulations. Young men and women were indeed
> proud that they knew many songs, which they were able to use for
> the purest of all song competitions. (Pinck 1926: 9)

*Figure 4.3. Papa Gerné,*
*in Louis Pinck's* Verglingende Weisen, *Vol. 1 (1926)*

Of the many qualities that emerge from the songs of the *Verklingende Weisen* to provide unity to Lorraine, two predominate, both of them demonstrating a figurative rootedness in the land. It is hardly surprising that sacred songs provide one of the unifying threads, for Pinck remained the Hambach priest until his death in 1940, even when he was increasingly honored for his contributions to German folk-song research and, in 1931, awarded an honorary doctorate from the University of Frankfurt am Main. The way in which Pinck encountered his primary informant, Papa Gerné (1831–1923), was typical. In autumn 1914, when he was already eighty-three, Gerné was making his way along the stations of the cross in the Hambach parish church. Pinck was struck by the unusual character of Gerné's performance, and upon making his acquaintance, Pinck proceeded to cultivate Gerné as a representative, we might say, primary, informant. Papa Gerné had acquired a vast repertory by remaining attached to sacred settings and by journeying among the diverse traditions converging in the local vil-

*Figure 4.4.  Louis Pinck recording the 100-year-old Mama Türk
(postcard, 1938)*

lages. The entire repertory contributed by Gerné to Pinck's canon was
inflected in one way or another by sacred traditions, even when Gerné
realized that certain songs would never be sung in religious contexts.

Although he had learned the scientific methods of folk-song research as an autodidact, and through growing collaboration with the
German Folk-Song Archive in Freiburg im Breisgau, Pinck used Papa
Gerné and other singers to formulate a classification system specific to
Lorraine. The names used by Gerné and other singers from Lorraine
to organize their repertories into genres were extended to the entire
repertory, untethering those genres from German classifications but
linking them to other regional styles in Germany and France.

If religion provided one pole for the folk-song traditions of Lorraine, the soil of the region itself anchored the other pole. However, as
we have seen throughout this chapter, it was not the soil itself from
which folk song sprang fully formed but rather the human cultivation
of the soil. The farmers of Lorraine did not themselves transform the
land; they benefited from a power that was greater than the nation.

The songs that conveyed the history of the land as a sacred narrative bore witness to the sacred symbols of the region—for example, the songs about local saints, such as St. Odila, who had unified the common areas of the upper Rhine River as the patron saint for the blind. The very fields that were described by songs in Pinck's five volumes were also marked with shrines and other religious symbols that represented the local and the regional and realized a connection between heaven and earth, the connection evoked so vividly in the song, "The Heavenly Ploughman" (see Figure 4.5).

1. What do we want to sing, and how do we begin?
About a heavenly ploughman,
Indeed, a ploughman!
He hitches the horses and urges them on.

2. He travels across the land, from end to end,
He sows the wheat and grain,
Planting them in the soil,
He places them in the very hand of God, the Father.

3. The tiny bird in the sky,
He provides nourishment for all from the fruits of his labor;
When spring arrives,
All living creatures will be nourished by the farmer.

4. The farmer must also provide nourishment for king and emperor,
He must store away all that he grows for them.
For me, that is just,
We, sisters and brothers, are all their servants.

5. And if there were not a human farmer,
How would it be for the masters with their empty table,
Indeed, with their empty table,
They'd not be able to survive, the masters so great.
    (Pinck 1926)

The political and the nationalist also inflect and influence the canon of songs from Lorraine that Louis Pinck published as *Verkling-ende Weisen.* The collecting project was unleashed by World War I—

*Figure 4.5. "Der himmlische Ackersmann"/"The Heavenly Ploughman,"*
*Alsatian folk song in Louis Pinck's* Verklingende Weisen, *Vol. 1 (1926)*

Pinck encountered his primary informant, Papa Gerné, during the second month of the war—but it stretched across the interwar period and the rise of Nazism in Germany into the first year of World War II. The nationalist and the regional, therefore, form a counterpoint that, by the early 1930s, was already creating a growing sense of tension about what the traditions of Lorraine, appearing first in editions published in France, would signify in an increasingly nationalist era. Nationalist music always has a paradoxical relation to a border region: The border region is inclusive, but nationalist music is exclusive. The five volumes of Louis Pinck's *Verklingende Weisen* were remarkable for their ability to negotiate that paradox during an historical moment when it was at its greatest extreme (Pinck 1926–1962).

### Claiming National Space with Music

"Soldat, du edles Blut"/"Soldier, Your Noble Blood"

1. | : *Jetzt geht der Marsch ins Feld!* : |
*Der Kaiser der tut schlafen,*
*Soldaten müssen wachen,*
| : *Dazu sind wir bestellt.* : |

1. | : Now we march out into the field! : |
The emperor is still asleep,
Soldiers must keep watch,
| : That's what our duty is. : |

3. | : *Soldat, du edles Blut,* : |
*Weil du so hoch geboren bist*
*Aus ein'm so frischen Mut!*
*Hörst du die Kugeln sausen?*
*Soldat, laß' dir's nicht grausen;*
*Wer's Glück hat, kommt davon.*

3. | : Soldier, your noble blood, : |
Because you are born with high estate
From such genuine courage!
Do you hear the shells whizzing by?
Don't let it frighten you;
If you're lucky, you'll escape alive.

4. | : *Jetzt steht die Zahl am Rhein,* : |
*Dazu des Kaisers Töchterlein,*
*Marie Luise, gehörest mein.*
*Ganz Frankreich ist mein eigen*
*Und Österreich auch desgleichen;*
*Behalten muß es sein.*

4. | : Now, the troops stand at the Rhine, : |
The emperor's daughter as well,
Marie Luise belongs to me.
All of France is my own,
And Austria's the same;
We must hold them at all costs.

(Brandsch and Schullerns 1932: 53–54)

*Figure 4.6.* "Soldat, du edles Blut"/"Soldier, Your Noble Blood,"
*German soldier's song from Transylvania (Brandsch and Schullerns 1932: 53–54)*

Two songs and two engravings stand as sentinels at the opening and closing of this section. The song texts and the visual details of the illustrations overflow with the imagery of monuments standing as sentinels to the nation, especially shoring up its borders at times of war and service to the empire. This monument imagery fills the pages devoted to military songs in two volumes of a 44-volume anthology of folk songs, the *Landschaftliche Volkslieder,* "folk songs from the landscapes," which were published under the supervision of the German Folk-Song Archive from 1924 until 1972. Each volume in the anthology stands as a monument to a particular region, about half of them within the boundaries of the present Republic of Germany, about half elsewhere.

As often as not, "elsewhere" here means border regions that include some speakers of German, for example, in eastern France (Alsace-Lorraine) or the western Czech Republic (Sudetenland), as well as

German "speech islands." The folk songs and images that frame this section fulfill many of the functions that accompany the volumes from "elsewhere," in the case of Figure 4.7, because it comes from the speech island of Siebenbürgen, a cluster of cities in Transylvania settled by Germans (see Chapter 6). Figure 4.8 appeared in a volume of songs about Lorraine, edited by Louis Pinck, though it explicitly represents monuments in Strasbourg, the cathedral city and capital of neighboring Alsace. In these examples, then, the songs and images acquire specific historical meanings for Germany, even though they come from and identify monuments in border regions outside Germany that had, nonetheless, been claimed by Germany throughout the modern era of German imperial expansion.

From beginning to end of the publication of the *Landschaftliche Volkslieder*—in other words, from the Weimar period through the Nazi period and World War II until the closing decades of the Cold War—musical monument after musical monument filled the landscapes represented by the volumes. As a single series, the volumes are remarkable not so much because we find songs, not to mention individual editors, whose complicity in politics, say, the fascism of the 1930s and 1940s, was direct, but because of the rather deliberate, consistent progress with which the erection of the individual monuments can be traced.

The volumes do the memory work of German history in the opening (ca. 1924–1932) and closing (post–World War II) phases of the project, while increasingly channeling the energies of nationalist expansion in the middle phase (1933–1945). In each volume, nationalism emerges from regionalism, and it is in the transition from the latter to the former that the monuments of past Germanness contest the territories of the modern German nation-state. The monumentality of the entire anthology depends to a large extent on its comprehensiveness and the capacity of various generations of editors to bring it to completion. Accordingly, it relied on both musical monuments from the past and the monumentalization of the moments of crisis that constituted German history in the twentieth century (cf. Bohlman 2002c).

Each volume musically articulated the monuments from its region in different ways, while contributing to the whole of the anthology because of the overall similarity of its monuments to those of other volumes. The two cityscapes in Figures 4.7 and 4.8 make this abundantly clear. The cityscape of Hermannstadt (today Sibiu in Romania) deliber-

*Figure 4.7. Hermannstadt (Sibiu), Transylvania, the city center*
*(Brandsch and Schullerns 1932: opposite 43)*

ately emphasizes the character of a German city whose medieval walls frame the modern administrative power symbolized by the tower of the city hall in the center of the picture. The cityscape of Strasbourg also mixes old and new, the power of the medieval cathedral tower in the middle of the picture with the soldiers marching off to war.

Both folk-song texts take the long conflict between Germany and France over the lands west of the Rhine, Alsace and Lorraine specifically, as their broad historical subjects. At their heart, however, are more localized issues of nationalism, notably the loyalty of a soldier to home and loved ones or to the nation at war. In the Transylvanian song, nationalism courses through the soldier at the Rhine as through his blood (see Linke 1999 and Ignatieff 1993 for discussions of blood and na-

*Figure 4.8. Engraving of Soldiers at Strasbourg*
*(Pinck 1937: 83)*

tion). "The Strasbourg Song" is one of the most widely distributed of all German military songs, and it is hardly surprising that it is found in multiple variants throughout the *Landschaftliche Volkslieder*, with and without more specific references to German expansionism at the time.

Although my analysis of the immanent monumentality of songs has focused on a selected set—four pages from some 4,000 in the entire anthology—it is important to recognize the extent to which nationalism accrues to folk song because of agency at the top of a highly institutionalized structure. The *Landschaftliche Volkslieder* began as a project of the German Association of Folklore Societies, and scholars at the German Folk-Song Archive, Johannes Bolte, Max Friedländer, and John Meier, set the whole project in motion with their considerable institutional, research, and financial resources. The anthology was meant to serve the nation as a whole. At the middle of organization, individual volumes were conceived, executed, and published at the regional level, even when this meant using publishing houses outside Germany (volume 1, for example, was devoted to songs from Silesia in southwestern Poland and appeared in Breslau, today Wrocław) (Siebs and Schneider 1924).

As the project spread across an increasingly larger area of Europe—by 1932, for example, it included the German speech islands of the Volga River basin in Ukraine (Dinges 1932)—it also became more centralized, with publication and production standardized for each volume. Volume design and conception (for example, the interplay of songs and engravings) were also standardized. Each volume, each musical monument, began to look more like the others. The monumental meaning of each volume, therefore, became less equivocal.

In literal and figurative senses, the songs in the *Landschaftliche Volkslieder* contested place and they did so in the name of the nation. As volume after volume appeared, they used history to make the nation audible and to render its monuments palpable, all the more so in an era of German nationalism that had tragic consequences for most of modern Europe.

"Das Lied von Straßburg"/"The Strasbourg Song"

1. To Strasbourg, to Strasbourg,
A beautiful city,
| : Where there lies buried
A truly handsome soldier. : |

2. A truly, a handsome
And a brave soldier,
| : Who had left his father and mother,
While he was still so young. : |

3. He had left them,
It couldn't be any other way.
| : To Strasbourg and to Strasbourg,
So soldiers must be. : |

4. The father and mother,
They went to the captain's house:

| : "Oh captain, dearest captain sir,
Give me back my son!" : |

5. "I can't give you your son,
For this or that sum of money,
| : Your son must die,
On the long, wide fields of battle!" : |

6. On the long, on the wide,
On the long and wide battlefields,
| : There where the dark young woman
Cries so bitterly. : |
    (Pinck 1937: 86)

## Military Music

Military music mobilizes the nation to undertake action in the name of the nation. Its conscious goal is to generate moments of **unisonality,** when the nation recognizes itself in the collective actions of a military force and, by extension, in the more abstract performance of that collective through ensembles dedicated to the ritual performance of military music. Although it is explicitly nationalistic, military music nonetheless has many functions, and it assumes complex forms. In the broadest terms, military music expresses nationalism on two levels, which literally and figuratively represent the nation through military action. On the first level, we witness the musical practices that accompany soldiers as they go to war. It is music that does not so much represent the nation as literally mobilize the nation. The modern nation-state uses this type of military music to ritualize the ways in which the nation interacts with its armies (see McNeill 1995). The nation establishes ensembles, particularly choruses and wind ensembles whose members are also members of the military, to perform at specific moments that focus the attention of the nation on the conditions of its defense or its entry into combat itself (listen to CD example 37).

The metaphor of the military musical ensemble is remarkably widespread throughout the modern nation-states of Europe, where such ensembles are particularly recognizable because of their use of military uniforms wherever they perform. The music of military ensembles demonstrates universal and national characteristics, but it is surely the more specific traits that are most crucial in their evocation of nationalism. The historical use of pipebands by Great Britain serves as an example of a military music with specifically nationalist symbolism. From the mid-nineteenth century to the present, British military bands have made extensive use of Highland bagpipes. Though the pipeband itself performs the characteristic music of one of Great Britain's more contested areas, Scotland, it came to the service of the nation at the time of greatest colonial expansion.

A number of explanations are mustered for the rise of the pipeband for nationalist functions. First, there is the practical explanation that pipes and drums play at a volume and in a style that can musically overwhelm the enemy. A banal explanation? Perhaps, but precisely the attention to cacophonous music's ability to frighten enemies is found in virtually every account of military music from Thucydides (sixth century BCE) until the present. Second, particular Scottish regiments, notably the Black Watch, have enjoyed several centuries of elite military—and musical—service to the British Empire. Finally, the modern pipeband repertory has itself become a metaphor for military order and competition. Pipebands, military or not, parade with a distinctive sense of discipline, and they perform repertories that stylize music forged from military imagery. Pipebands from throughout the world, especially from the areas of the former British Empire, engage in fierce competitions today, and the competition circuit depends on the cultivation of a full range of traditions that owe their origins to the military uses of pipe music (see Cadden 2003).

The armies of some European nations are notable because their soldiers literally carry music into battle with them. In both world wars Germany made songbooks available to its soldiers at the front, and historical records, particularly the repeated printings during the wars, reveal that these books served German soldiers at the front in numerous ways. The most popular military songbook of World War I was a two-volume set entitled *Volksliederbuch für gemischten Chor* ("Book of Folk Songs for Mixed Chorus"), which was edited by a "Commission for the German Folk-Song Book" (see Kommission für das deutsche Volksliederbuch 1915). Published in chapbook format for easy portability, these volumes were designed to be carried to the front, where they made arrangements for four-part choruses accessible to soldiers at the front. The editorial commission was led by Max Friedländer, a Jewish folk-song collector, scholar, and publisher who would remain active until the 1930s, when the Nazis ascended to political control in Germany. (Friedländer was also one of the founding editors of the series *Landschaftliche Volkslieder,* several volumes of which we have already encountered in the present chapter.) The image of German soldiers' choruses at the Western Front, gathered perhaps in trenches, seems almost too bizarre to be believable, but already by the 1915 printing, in the second year of the war, Friedländer was able to claim in his preface that some 60,000 copies of the two-volume set had been distributed and that there were over 200,000 copies of individual songs in circulation. Each of the two volumes, moreover, contained over 800 pages; together they included 604 songs.

The soldiers' songs produced for German armies during World War II differed from those edited by Max Friedländer in several significant ways. Rather than reaching into the historical past to muster a repertory that narrated a long German history, the songs in Gerhard Pallmann's *Soldatenlieder von Front und Heimat* ("Soldiers' Songs from the Front and the Homeland") focused more specifically on the battles under way in World War II (Pallmann 1940). The publications were themselves not specifically intended for performance at the front; rather they came from the front, where Pallmann served in an artillery regiment and prepared the songs in arrangements for solo voice and piano that "would help to build bridges between the homeland and those serving in their field gray uniforms, and to communicate to the homeland some part of the great events that will provide your sons with substance and memories for their entire lives" (Pallmann 1940: 2).

Of particular significance was the modern and immediate mediation of these songs through the radio, for more than half of the songs were printed from arrangements used for "broadcasts of the Greater German Radio"—in other words, the radio with which Germany was broadcasting music to the lands taken by the German army and beyond. The *Soldatenlieder von Front und Heimat* depended on extensive dissemination through modern forms of the media. The opening song, "Bombs on England" ("Bomben auf Engelland"), for example, was known to soldiers at the front and to Germans at home because it had been used in the airforce documentary film *Feuertaufe* ("Baptism by Fire"), by Hans Bertram (ibid.: 4–5). The imagery of the songs was direct, and their rhetoric was taken from Nazi propaganda; Austria, for example, is referred to as the "Ostmark," as an "Eastern Province" of

*Figure 4.9. Cover of* Soldatenlieder von Front und Heimat/
Soldiers' Songs from the Front and the Homeland *(1940)*

Germany, in songs such as "Lied der Ostmärkischen Landesschützen"
("Song of the Ostmark National Guards") (ibid.: 13). The competitive
stakes could not be clearer in these songs, which narrated each advance of the German army with a music that was as unequivocally militaristic as it was nationalistic (see Figure 4.9).

### Quasi-National Anthems and Unofficial National Anthems

Military music need not be unequivocally militaristic to represent the nation. Military music may have more metaphoric uses in the creation and inscription of national repertories. Accordingly, certain pieces and repertories that came into being with specific military references may accumulate new functions, including those of what I call in this chapter a "quasi-national anthem" or "unofficial national anthem." Unofficial national anthems serve all the functions of a national anthem (sketched in the concluding section of this chapter), but they do not have the top-down sanction to represent the nation beyond its borders. The unofficial anthem enjoys a specific, usually also a wide, range of ritual functions, stretching from performance at the beginning of athletic events (for example, in England, where "Three Lions" rather than "God Save the Queen" is often sung at soccer matches) to the marking of national crises (for example, in the United States after the terrorist attacks of 11 September 2001, when "God Bless America" was more widely sung than "The Star Spangled Banner"). Unofficial anthems also may demonstrate even greater national unisonality than their official cousins, perhaps because they have more immediate historical or modern relevance, or even because they are easier to perform or to sing as a collective. Sanctioned to represent the nation or not, unofficial anthems usually contain particularly powerful historical narratives, which invests them with a common narrative of nationalism.

One reason to speak about unofficial national anthems as nationalist songs is that the narratives of nationalism in unofficial anthems often intersect, which is to say, they reflect struggles over historical turf with neighboring nations. There is, then, an aesthetic and ideological relatedness, and we witness that relatedness to an extreme degree in many unofficial anthems, for example, Austria's "Radetzky March" and Hungary's "Rákóczy March." There is much that is similar about the two works, perhaps most obviously that they are both marches and that both are named after military heroes. Neither has been an official anthem, but this has never prevented either from retaining its public appeal, from the moment of its creation until the present. Even today, when the "Radetzky March" and the "Rákóczy March" are performed publicly, audiences rise to their feet, clapping at the return of the main theme in the first and cheering enthusiastically to punctuate the latter. The two marches continue to popularize nationalism and its historical narratives.

The "Rákóczy March" (see Figure 4.10) is the older of the two unofficial anthems, even though the Hungarian history that it memorializes is inseparable from Hungarian conflicts with Austria. Ferenc Rákóczy (1676–1735) led several Hungarian attempts to throw off the yoke of Habsburg domination at the beginning of the eighteenth century. He was imprisoned and exiled for urging insurrection in 1700–1701, but in the wake of the 1703 peasants' revolt he became Hungary's leader until 1711, when a new alliance with Austria was forged and Rákóczy entered exile for the remainder of his life. Rákóczy did not contribute textually or musically to the march bearing his name. He simply liked the melody, so much so that many Hungarians claimed it to be his favorite piece of music. The reception of the "Rákóczy March" became particularly complicated during the nineteenth century, when it was not chosen as the Hungarian national anthem; instead, Ferenc Erkel's and Ferenc Kölcsey's "God Bless the Hungarians" received that honor as the result of a public competition in 1845 (see Boyd 2001: 669). The "Rákóczy March" was, however, incorporated into a rather broad range of compositions, including those by Liszt and Berlioz, where it intentionally signified Hungary. As conflicts between Hungary and Austria escalated in the second half of the nineteenth century, the march's association with Rákóczy's military actions against Austria was heightened, intensifying its nationalist significance and justifying its continued presence as an unofficial Hungarian anthem at the beginning of the twenty-first century.

Born during Austria's imperial expansion into southern and eastern Europe in the early nineteenth century, the "Radetzky March" provided a nationalist text that accompanied each stage of Austrian history from the mid-nineteenth century to World War II (listen to CD example 36) The "Radetzky March" is modern Austrian history writ large and writ musically (see Figure 4.11). Field Marshall Johann Josef Wenzel Graf Radetzky von Radetz was Austria's greatest military leader during the moment of the empire's greatest expansion, from the retreat of Napoleon from Europe in 1813–1814 until the revolutionary years of 1848–1849. Radetzky led Austro-Hungarian armies to the extreme peripheries of the empire, and he was particularly celebrated for securing northern Italy, and by extension the Balkans on the other side of the Adriatic, for Austria. Radetzky's achievements were mythologized in many ways, particularly through the arts, but it was Johann Strauss, Sr., who composed a march as his opus 228 in 1848 and called it "Radetzky March." It was quite common for march (and waltz) compo-

## Rákóczy March

*Figure 4.10.  The "Rákóczy March"*

sitions of the Strauss era to refer directly to the lands claimed by the imperial armies for Austria (see, for example, *Märche aus der Kaiserzeit*), and to honor individual military figures. Johann Strauss, Sr., moreover, held an official position in the imperial hierarchy, as Musical Director of the Imperial Ball, which placed him in a position as culture broker for the imperial court (see Herre 1981).

# Radetzky March

**Johann Strauss, Sr.**

*Figure 4.11.  Johann Strauss, Sr., "Radetzky March"*

The "Radetzky March" was meant to celebrate Austria at the height of its nationalism; instead, it increasingly became the accompaniment to the nation's decline as an empire and its retrenchment after World War I, when music would serve the nation through ritualized performances of its past (cf. Steinberg 1990). The "Radetzky March" increasingly found its way into performances of the military ensembles posted in the remote provinces of the empire, where the march acquired growing significance through its remarkable capacity to memorialize the grandeur of a past rapidly slipping away. The march appears in countless arrangements, in numerous newly composed works in various genres, and in the arts and literature that Austrians used to mythologize the past during the narrative slide into modernism that could no longer be halted by the beginning of the twentieth century. The great Austrian-Jewish novelist Joseph Roth (1894–1939) employed the "Radetzky March" as the central metaphor for the decline of imperial Austria in his 1932 novel of the same name. As if mesmerized by the monumental meaning of the march, Austrians continue to weave it into modern national myths, through efforts like a national cinema or the annual broadcasts of the Vienna Philharmonic Orchestra's New Year Concerts. When at the end of the performance the "Radetzky March" is played to provide a final historical exclamation mark, the audience inevitably rises to its feet, clapping louder and louder at each chorus, reclaiming the spaces of the empire for the nation as it crosses the Janus-faced threshold into a new year.

### National Anthems

With few exceptions the official national anthems of Europe are less well known and historically much less stable than are the unofficial anthems. Origin myths swirl about the official anthems, generating abundant questionable and often false attributions of authenticity (cf. P. Nettl 1967; Ragozat 1982; Boyd 2001). The anthems of some European nations are notoriously unstable, with version upon version competing for official sanction and trying to keep up with changing governments. Anthems move around from nation to nation, with several notable cases of a trade from one nation to the other; the melody that was first Austria's national anthem, Franz Joseph Haydn's "Kaiserhymne"(CD example 34) was dropped by Austria after World War I, only to be picked up by Germany in 1922. Nor is it uncommon for anthems to be exported as contrafacts, in some cases on the coattails of colonial administrations, but more often because certain tunes have a global popularity, if for military and nationalist ends. We are often left wondering: Just what is and what is not national about national anthems?

Close musical scrutiny of Europe's national anthems fails to turn up answers to that question but leaves us, instead, with the rather perplexing sense that the national anthems sound a great deal alike (listen, for example, to the collection of European national anthems compiled on Swarorski Musik Wattens 1993). Most readers may have been struck at one time or another by the similarities among national anthems, say, during the awards ceremonies at the Olympic Games, when three anthems are played in succession, often generating confusion about which one belongs to which medal winner.

There are many reasons that national anthems are musically ambiguous, even if we imagine that their nationalist cultural work is potentially of great significance. First of all, national anthems do move around, and they often possess the generic characteristics that make melodies suitable for contrafacts, assigning new texts to preexisting melodies (see Kurzke 1990). Second, external forms that together yield the subgenres that fit together as the genre of the national anthem itself are remarkably quite similar. They are either strophic or repetitive in form, using the contrast between an opening theme or chorus and a middle section, usually a bridge of some kind or, in a march, a trio section. Third, melodic themes, leitmotifs, and gestures do seem to migrate from anthem to anthem. The opening of the Irish anthem, for example, uses the same arch-like gesture that begins the German anthem. Fourth, through ceremonial and ritual uses the tempo becomes generalized. In performance, marches do not lend themselves to marching and hymns do not quite possess the sacred aura produced by congregational singing in a sanctuary. Fifth, anthem composers have historically avoided melodies and formal techniques that would exoticize their nations, that might call their Europeanness into question. And Europeanness is very much the issue that Europe's national anthems raise.

The introduction of anthems to the ceremonial trappings of most European nations took place in the nineteenth century. As nationalism became an increasingly important political issue during the century, it was also more important to lay claim to a national anthem, which in turn was employed to lay claim to the nation. However, national anthems were not simply "adopted." In several notable cases, such as Denmark in 1819, Hungary in 1845, and the Soviet Union in 1943, political leaders sponsored open public competitions, and the winning composition was drafted as the national anthem. In other cases, national anthems were dropped, quite unceremoniously, for example, after defeat in war or following the dissolution of an unpopular governing regime. In some nations it is important that the origins of the anthem remain unclear—the subject of myth—whereas in others it is equally important that authority and authorship be linked. Many attributions of authorship are curiously ambiguous as, for example, in the current Austrian anthem, popularly claimed to be a melody by Mozart even though there is no evidence to substantiate the attribution to that quintessentially Austrian composer. Whatever the conditions of adaptation and rejection, national anthems constitute an important discourse in the history of modern European nationalism. There can be no question that they have been and remain crucial to the construction of a nation-state's European identity.

### The Europeanness of National Anthems

Europe can lay claim to some of the oldest national anthems and some of the newest. "God Save the King/Queen," the anthem of the United Kingdom, is probably the oldest national anthem in the world. Its exact origins are unknown, but its first public performances were most likely in 1745, when audiences at several London theaters sang it after the British military defeat at Prestopans. Almost from its first appearance in print "God Save the King/Queen" demonstrated remarkable durability and adaptability. Not only did it serve as the prototype for what a national anthem could be, but it served as the national anthem of a remarkable number of countries from the early nineteenth century to the present. At various historical moments, Denmark, Sweden, Switzerland, and Russia used it; perhaps more understandably "God Save the King/Queen" became the anthem before and after independence in British colonies. Even as its distribution as an official anthem has diminished, "God Save the King/Queen" continues to have remarkable currency as an unofficial anthem of greater or, in the case of the contrafact, "My Country 'Tis of Thee," lesser importance.

If the British national anthem has demonstrated enormous resilience, the Russian anthem, in contrast, has a particularly mercurial history. At the close of 2001, in fact, the often bitter debates about which anthem to use to represent Russia seem hardly close to resolution (for a thorough analysis of these debates see Daughtry 2003). Since the beginning of the nineteenth century, Russia and the Soviet

Union have officially designated at least five different national anthems, including "God Save the King" (prior to 1833) and the "Internationale" from 1917 to 1918. After the dissolution of the Soviet Union in 1991 a textless anthem by the nineteenth-century nationalist composer Mikhail Glinka replaced Aleksandr Aleksandrov's "Unbreakable Union of Free-Born Republics," which had been Stalin's choice almost sixty years earlier.

The dispute over the Russian anthem is a microcosm of the complex issues influencing nationalist music. Glinka's anthem, on one hand, is too ambiguous, largely because it has no text, which makes it unsuitable for certain international forums. Aleksandrov's anthem enjoyed a long and popular history, but it had too many associations with uncomfortable historical moments, including the Stalinist era. The question that arises is: How does the national anthem selectively allow different political and cultural constituencies to return to those moments in Russia's past that it wishes to use for its present? Each of the previous anthems was monumental in its own way, and accordingly all of them crowd in upon the contested landscapes of a New Russia, which in different ways strives to recuperate some of the national monumentality it lost in 1991. The Russian national anthem will not resolve that dilemma itself, but the public debates it stirs up will fuel those surrounding the ideological dilemma of Russian history at the beginning of the twenty-first century.

Are Europe's national anthems more similar than different? Does the fact that their histories intersect—as melodies and discrete musical compositions or as the symbols of political change—exaggerate or eviscerate their contemporary roles as nationalist music? To answer such questions, it may be helpful to think about myths that surround, buttress, and shroud national anthems, and to reflect upon these myths comparatively, much as the origins of European nations have been increasingly portrayed both as myth and history (see, especially, Flacke 1998). At times national anthems chronicle history, but just as often they rely on the narrative ambiguities of myth. If the myths that are woven into national anthems are similar, it may well be a result of the fact that they compete with each other in an international arena. National anthems push many of the questions of nationalism I have raised in this book toward the border regions between nations, that is, toward regions where nationalist music spills over into international music, and the music of the nation is contested by the music of the nationless.

REFERENCES

Bohlman, Philip V. 2002b. "Landscape–Region–Nation–Reich: German Folk Song in the Nexus of National Identity." In Celia Applegate and Pamela M. Potter, eds., *Music and German Nationalism,* pp. 105–127. Chicago: University of Chicago Press.

———. 2000c. "To Hear the Voices Still Heard: On Synagogue Restoration in Eastern Europe." In Daphne Berdahl, Matti Bunzl, and Martha Lampland, eds., *Altering States: Ethnographies of Transition in Eastern Europe and the Former Soviet Union,* pp. 40–69. Ann Arbor, Mich.: University of Michigan Press.

Boyd, Malcolm. 2001. "National Anthems." In Stanley Sadie, ed., *The New Grove Dictionary of Music and Musicians.* 2d ed. Vol. 17: 654–687. London: Macmillan.

Cadden, Jerry A. 2003. "Policing Traditions: Scottish Pipeband Competition and the Role of the Composer." In Martin Stokes and Philip V. Bohlman, eds., *Celtic Modern: Music at the Global Fringe,* pp. 119–143. Lanham, Md.: Scarecrow Press.

Daughtry, J. Martin. 2003. "Russia's New Anthem and the Negotiation of National Identity." *Ethnomusicology* 47 (1): 42–67.

Deutsch, Walter, and Gerlinde Haid, eds. 1997. *Beiträge zur musikalischen Volkskultur in Südtirol.* Vienna: Böhlau.

Dinges, Georg, ed. 1932. *Wolgadeutsche Volkslieder mit Bildern und Weisen.* Berlin and Leipzig: Walter de Gruyter.

Duara, Prasenjit. 1995. *Rescuing History from the Nation: Questioning Narratives of Modern China.* Chicago: University of Chicago Press.

Elscheková, Alica, ed. 1981. *Stratigraphische Probleme der Volksmusik in den Karpaten und auf dem Balkan.* Bratislava: VEDA.

Flacke, Monika, ed. 1998. *Mythen der Nationen: Ein europäisches Panorama.* Munich and Berlin: Koehler & Amelang.

Fulcher, Jane. 1987. *The Nation's Image: French Grand Opera as Politics and Politicized Art.* Cambridge: Cambridge University Press.

Gerner, Stefan. 1998. "Retrovision: Die rückblickende Erfindung der Nationen durch die Kunst." In Monika Flacke, ed., *Mythen der Nationen: Ein europäisches Panorama,* pp. 33–52. Munich and Berlin: Koehler & Amelang.

Goertzen, Chris. 1997. *Fiddling for Norway: Revival and Identity.* Chicago: University of Chicago Press.

Herre, Franz. 1981. *Radetzky: Eine Biographie.* Cologne: Kiepenheuer & Witsch.

Herzfeld, Michael. 1991. *A Place in History: Social and Monumental Time in a Cretan Town.* Princeton, N.J.: Princeton University Press.

Ignatieff, Michael. 1993. *Blood and Belonging: Journeys into the New Nationalisms.* New York: Farrar, Straus and Giroux.

Kommission für das deutsche Volksliederbuch, ed. 1915. *Volksliederbuch für gemischten Chor.* 2 vols. Leipzig: C. F. Peters.

Koshar, Rudy. 1998. *Germany's Transient Pasts: Preservation and National Memory in the Twentieth Century.* Chapel Hill: University of North Carolina Press.

Krekovičová, Eva. 1998. *Zwischen Toleranz und Barrieren: Das Bild der Zigeuner und Juden in der slowakischen Folklore.* Frankfurt am Main: Peter Lang.

Künzig, Johannes. 1935. *Deutsche Volkslieder aus dem rumänischen Banat, mit Bildern und Weisen.* Berlin and Leipzig: Walter de Gruyter.

Kurzke, Hermann. 1990. *Hymnen und Lieder der Deutschen.* Mainz: Dietrich'sche Verlagsbuchhandlung.

Linke, Uli. 1999. *Blood and Nation: The European Aesthetics of Race.* Philadelphia: University of Pennsylvania Press.

Mahr, Roland. 2002. "Von der Aufwärmrunde bis ins Ziel—Der 'Grand Prix der Volksmusik': Eine musikwissenschaftliche Untersuchung des Wettbewerbs als Schlüsselstelle zum Karrieresprung in der volkstümlichen Unterhaltungsbranche." Master's thesis, University of Vienna.

McNeill, William H. 1995. *Keeping Together in Time: Dance and Drill in Human History.* Cambridge, Mass.: Harvard University Press.

Metil, Robert Carl. 2000. "Post–Velvet Revolutionary Cultural Activism and Rusyn Song in the Prešov Region of Eastern Slovakia, 1989–2000." Ph.D. dissertation, University of Pittsburgh.

Nettl, Paul. 1967. *National Anthems.* Trans. by Alexander Gode. 2nd, enlarged ed. New York: Frederick Ungar.

Pallmann, Gerhard. 1940. *Soldatenlieder von Front und Heimat: 1914/1939.* Leipzig: N. Simrock.

Pinck, Louis. 1926–1962. *Verklingende Weisen: Lothringer Volkslieder.* 5 vols. Metz: Lothringer Verlags- und Hilfsverein, and other publishers.

_____, ed. 1937. *Lothringer Volkslieder.* Cassel: Bärenreiter.

Popa, Steluta. 1996. "The Romanian Revolution of December 1989 and Its Reflection in Musical Folklore." In Mark Slobin, ed., *Retuning Culture: Musical Changes in Central and Eastern Europe,* 156–175. Durham, N.C.: Duke University Press.

Ragozat, Ulrich. 1982. *Die Nationalhymnen der Welt: Ein kulturgeschichtliches Lexikon.* Freiburg im Breisgau: Herder.

Reimann, Jacob Friedrich. 1709. *Versuch einer Einleitung in die historiam literariam derer Teutschen.* Vol. 3. Halle an der Saale: Renger.

Riethmüller, Albrecht. 1993. *Die Walhalla und ihre Musiker.* Laaber: Laaber-Verlag.

Roth, Joseph. 1983 [1932]. *The Radetzky March.* Trans. by Eva Tucker. Woodstock, N.Y.: Overlook Press.

Siebs, Theodor, and Max Schneider, eds. 1924. *Schlesische Volkslieder mit Bildern und Weisen.* Breslau: Bergstadtverlag.

Steinberg, Michael P. 1990. *The Meaning of the Salzburg Festival: Austria as Theater and Ideology, 1890–1938*. Ithaca, N.Y.: Cornell University Press.

Wackenroder, Wilhelm Heinrich, and Ludwig Tieck. 1979 [1797]. *Herzensergießungen eines kunstliebenden Klosterbruders*. Stuttgart: Reclam.

Wischenbart, Rüdiger. 1992. *Karpaten: Die dunkle Seite Europas*. Vienna: Kreymayr & Scheriau.

Young, James E. 1993. *The Texture of Memory: Holocaust Memorials and Meaning*. New Haven, Conn.: Yale University Press.

*Chapter Five*

# In the Belly of the Beast

## *Music and Nation in Central Europe*

### The Center of Europe as Musical Marketplace

St. Stephen's Square in Vienna, Potsdamer Place in Berlin: Both are viable candidates for the center of Central Europe. So, too, might be St. Wenceslas Square in Prague or Déak Square in Budapest. Each lies at the center of a capital city in a nation that has employed, in the past and more recently since the Velvet Revolutions of 1989, the "rhetoric of Central Europe." In this chapter we investigate this rhetoric as a political and cultural discourse of claiming authority and privilege at the center of Europe. The fact that all four capital cities use the rhetoric of Central Europe to mean something different is, moreover, characteristic of the shifting borders and changing culture in the middle of Europe. On one hand, the rhetoric of Central Europe is an assertion of power; on the other, it is a recognition that the exact dimensions of the center are illusive, even ephemeral. In some historical moments, the center may result from forces of centripetal change, the concentration of power and culture in the center. At other moments, the center unravels centrifugally, as change redistributes power and culture from the center. Central Europe, as we examine it historically and musically in this chapter, has most often formed from the counterpoint between centripetal and centrifugal forces.

Among the several centers of Central Europe it is on St. Stephen's Square in Vienna we encounter the counterpoint of meanings that are the most explicit. Historically, Central Europe—**Mitteleuropa**—encompassed the lands of the Austro-Hungarian Empire. At the administrative center in Vienna, the culture of this Central Europe was German, which referred not to Germany, but rather to the functions of language to shape and record the arts and politics at the center. Moving away from the center, languages and cultures began changing in the Habsburg *Kronländer,* or "imperial lands." For Austria, Central Europe enveloped these lands, too, indeed embraced them in such a way that they were drawn toward the center. In principle and, as we see in this chapter, often in practice Central Europe came to refer to the multi-culturalism of these nations radiating away from the center.

On St. Stephen's Square, the multiculturalism of Habsburg Central Europe is still striking at the beginning of the twenty-first century. With the massive gothic towers of St. Stephen's Cathedral at its center, the square itself lies at the confluence of many roads, pedestrian walkways, and mass transit arteries, all of them figuratively the spokes gathering at the hub of a wheel. Metaphorically, these spokes extend from St. Stephen's to the farthest reaches of the former empire, penetrating the lands of Central Europe. Even today, that metaphor is still credible, for St. Stephen's Square is filled with musical and cultural activities that juxtapose the symbolic center—the cathedral and its ritual reper-tories of sacred European art music—and the multicultural diversity of the street music that fills the square and the streets that empty into it. On the street, one encounters Moravian, Slovak, and Hungarian musi-cians, playing or singing usually in small groups, most of whom have traveled the hour or so from their respective borders with modern Aus-tria. Other groups of folk musicians have traveled farther, perhaps from the Carpathians on the border between Ukraine and Romania, or from South America, for Andean street musicians are ubiquitous in Central Europe as they are throughout much of the world. There are soloists, too, who return day after day to the same corner, where they patiently wend their way through urban Viennese repertories, accom-panying themselves with the accordion or guitar. Clearly mobile musi-cians enter and exit the urban spaces around St. Stephen's, arriving on the subway, but moving deftly through the crowds filling the streets. These are Roma musicians, most from the larger Roma communities in the neighboring Czech and Slovak republics, but a few from areas of Austria where Roma have lived for hundreds of years.

The music of Central Europe is not only concentrated in St. Stephen's Square: It is accommodated by its urban landscape. Austria no longer controls the lands from which many of these musicians have come or whose traditions they represent—indeed, Austria lost control of its imperial lands after defeat in World War I—but it recognizes that it is these musicians, among others, who realize the heritage of Central Europe. They contribute cultural substance to the ways in which Austria can remember a past that has all but slipped away into nostalgia, but whose traces became tantalizingly recoverable after the fall of the Iron Curtain. After 1989, there was a resurgence, even a revival, of the rhetoric of Central Europe, and Austria's culture brokers, for example politicians such as Erhard Busek, have quickly seized upon music as a means for articulating that rhetoric (cf. Johnson 1996 and Busek 1997).

At the center of Berlin, Central Europe could not look and sound more different. Rather than effecting the metaphorical confluence of diverse music cultures, Potsdamer Place is a landscape scarred by the severing of arteries between East and West. Roads and subway lines reach Potsdamer Place following complex detours and often intersecting there, as if cultural traffic patterns, literal and figurative, had no place else to go. Potsdamer Place was the final station of the West before the fall of the Berlin Wall, and in some ways it has entirely assumed new functions. Brandenburg Gate, a bit farther to the north and east along the fissure in the historical landscape marked by the Berlin Wall, was similarly the end of the line for the East. Since 1989, many efforts have been made to repair the fissure and to restore Germany's rhetoric of Central Europe at the same time (see Ladd 1997). For a Central European culture to emerge again, it would be necessary to heal the wounds at the center. At the beginning of the twenty-first century, the prospects for doing so are still unclear.

The Central European music culture at the center of Berlin remains fragmented and decentralized. Though Germany has depended for decades on guest workers from the Balkans and especially from Turkey in the west, and on day laborers from Poland in Berlin and the east, it has resisted recognizing multiculturalism in any form. Turkish music flourished in the Kreuzberg district, only kilometers from Potsdamer Place, but it was excluded from the cultural debates about Germany's position in Europe, and in particular Central Europe. The streets along the Berlin Wall, or stretching to the east and west from it, do not resonate with street music as the streets radiating from Vienna's center do. The institutions of European art music, the Staatsoper unter den Linden in the former East Berlin and the Berlin Philharmonic in the former West Berlin, stand as they did before the fall of the Wall as sentinels guarding the fissure ripping through the center. Public cultural policy often voices concern about the financial survival of such august institutions at the cultural center. In contrast, the public institutions that stood as guardians to Germany's multicultural musics (for example, the International Institute for Traditional Music) have been forced to dissolve for want of continued funding from the Berlin Senate. In their stead, monumental shopping and commerce buildings, financed by Sony and Daimler-Benz, now occupy Potsdamer Platz.

The music of Central Europe at the center in Berlin sounds very different from that at the center in Austria. The music cultures at the centers in Prague and Budapest, each with public ideological agendas specific to their own historical understandings of Central Europe, are also far more different than similar. In the Czech Republic, the center is constituted of parts both eastern and western; in Hungary, the center looks far more toward the East than toward the West (see, for example, Konrád 1999). The musical repertories and styles that narrate the pasts and presents of the Czech and Hungarian Central Europes are again distinctive, and they grow from rhetorics of Central Europe unlike those we experience in Vienna and Berlin (cf. Dor 1996). Central Europe, clearly, is a product of the national imagination, and the musical rhetoric that shapes that imagination and the European identities it constructs was and is inseparable from an aesthetics of music grounded in the culture of the nation and the politics of the nation-state.

### Shaping Europe's Center

That the culture of Central Europe is changing and its boundaries shifting is by no means a post–Velvet Revolution or postmodern phenomenon. Historically, the identity of Europe's center has been the product of many different ways of determining the nature of place and the cultural relatedness of those occupying that place. Of those different ways, we begin this section by sketching four of the most significant in the historical **longue durée** of Central Europe: geography, myth, language, and politics. We then turn to the historical *longue durée* itself, considering the ways in which the identity of Central Europe today bears witness to its past, particularly to the reimagination of that past in the present.

Although the geographical centrality of Central Europe would seem to be a fact of cartographic coordinates, it is not. In premodern Europe, the center was no more nor less than the unknown land beyond the

*Figure 5.1.  The peoples of European diversity, nineteenth-century folklore table (Österreichisches Museum für Volkskunde)*

Alps. When the Roman Empire pushed north of the Alps, it first gave political meaning to the geography of what would become Central Europe, establishing its primary military and administrative outposts on the rivers of the region, especially the Rhine and the Danube, but also the Mosel (in western Germany, where Trier was an important Roman center). During the first millennium, the center was really the region where Europe's north and south converged and overlapped. At other historical moments, premodern and modern, Central Europe would be the cultural region where East and West would converge. In post-Enlightenment Europe, especially, Central Europe symbolically served as a gateway to Eastern Europe, a political role that both Germany and Austria again assumed in the European Union at the end of the Cold War. The European trade routes connecting north to south and east to west, especially the natural arteries, serve as further definitions of centrality. The Rhine River, flowing from the Alps in the south, moves goods and culture to the north, not just to northern Germany, but to the North Sea and beyond. The Danube River, the continent's largest river, with its source in the Black Forest of southwestern Germany, links Central Europe, Southeastern Europe, the Black Sea, and beyond to Asia. The geography of Central Europe also contributes significantly to its mythology and folklore. The Niebelungen myths rely on and replicate the geographical template of the major rivers, notably the Rhine and the Danube. A Germanic folklore arising from forests and mountains deepens the cultural texture of the center, giving it narrative identities that have been repeatedly historicized up to the present.

The linguistic identity of Central Europe might well seem obvious—Germanic languages, various vernaculars unified by High German in the modern era—but it remains an open historical question whether German was a means for centripetalizing or centrifugalizing the linguistic boundaries at Europe's center. The potential of dialects to decentralize was crucial to premodern Central Europe, and the introduction of minority languages, such as Yiddish, Romany, and Turkish, has challenged modern identities. More to the point, however, is that the German language does contribute substantially to the functions of cultural and political borders.

Central Europe can and does lay claim to a long political history, beginning with the Holy Roman Empire, stretching through subsequent attempts to unify the region politically, and culminating in the attempts at brokering European unity that characterize Germany's politics at the turn of the present century. The political boundaries of Central Europe, both internally and externally, have historically been more unstable than stable, and attempts to shore them up have produced suspicion and fear of expansionism. The situation today is appreciably no different from the early centuries of the Holy Roman Empire, roughly at the turn of the last millennium. At the beginning of our own millennium German attempts to consolidate European Union power in Central Europe, for example by establishing the Central Bank in Frankfurt am Main, are frequently countered by other European nations. Critical to the political identity of Central Europe has been the seeking of ways to curtail Germany's power and contain it within fixed borders.

### Four Historical Phases in the Rhetoric of Central Europe

#### Phase 1, Myth
The rhetoric of Central Europe is heavily steeped in myth, above all in a set of myths about the premodern inhabitants of Central Europe, to

which I refer here as the "Germanic peoples" for lack of an English-language equivalent for **Germanen,** literally the "Germans." What we know about the German peoples is part reality and part myth. There were premodern inhabitants of Central Europe, and there is archeological evidence of late Stone Age and early Bronze Age settlements of various kinds. Whether it is possible to make a case for any kind of common culture for those living in these settlements remains an open question. The imprint that most left on Central European prehistory was local, either through the shaping of early subsistence and trading systems or through the localization of belief systems. The traces of such systems have survived, particularly in local names.

Is there enough unity in the local traces to argue for a Germanic culture in Central Europe? In a recent study of the Germanic peoples, Otto Holzapfel (2001) has answered that question both skeptically and positively. Sorting out the Germanic peoples and their culture from other Bronze Age cultures, notably the Celts, is nearly impossible. Even though comparison of surviving artifacts reveals connections across the region, particularly before the Celts were pushed to Europe's western littoral and the so-called Nordic peoples migrated into what is today Scandinavia, these were probably the result of trade and exchange on relatively local levels, rather than some larger pan–Central European culture.

The myths and histories of premodern Germanic peoples that come down to us today tell a different story, and the question we should pose is, why? Holzapfel answers this question by sorting out an alternative historiography, one that interprets myth as history and interprets history from the perspectives of myth (ibid.: 9–44). It was first the Romans who chronicled encounters with a common culture and people north of the Alps. Although the Romans referred to these peoples as Germanic and Teutonic, they were not concerned with their identity, but rather with the need to defend the boundary between the empire and the region that would become Central Europe. During the course of the first millennium CE the tendency to level differences among the peoples of the region persisted. But the process was imposed by those entering the region, in particular the military and religious forces that would transform Central Europe into Europe's Christian core by the time the Holy Roman Empire was fully established by Charlemagne at the beginning of the ninth century CE.

Most important for the examination of Europe's center in this chapter, however, is the continued production, elaboration, and dissemination of the myths that have entered the rhetoric of Central Europe as Germanic. Perhaps the best known are those that constitute the "Niebelungen" epic cycle. The Niebelungen cycle contains a complex of stories about gods and humans, most of whom occupy the lands bordering major riverways, especially the Rhine and the Danube. For our purposes, the exact nature of these stories is less important than the historiographic fact that they became the substance for countless retellings and reworkings, and that they increasingly tended to provide an integrative image of places and events that together represent Central Europe in forms that Holzapfel describes as "syncretic" (ibid.: 149–161). From premodern Europe to the present day, German folklorists, writers, and musicians, notably Richard Wagner with his four-opera cycle, *Der Ring des Nibelungen,* created variant upon variant of the Germanic myths. Such variants came to shape not only folklore and literature, but also ideology and politics. They provided Romanticism with a common historical core, but they also served as the foundations for the modern myths of racial and cultural purity used by German and Austrian fascists. The Germanic myths have contributed numerous strands to the fabric of modern Central European nationalism.

*Phase 2, Early Modern Europe and the Decentralization of Central Europe*

> *Hunger und Durst, auch Hitz und Kält,*
> *Arbeit und Armut, wie es fällt,*
> *Gewalttat, Ungerechtigkeit,*
> *Treiben wir Landsknecht allezeit.*

> Hunger and thirst, also heat and cold,
> Work and Poverty, as it happens,
> Acts of violence, absence of justice,
> That's what we mercenaries do all day.
>     —Grimmelshausen 1669: Chapter 16

From the end of the Middle Ages until the Enlightenment there were many moments that came to define Central Europe culturally and historically. In the sixteenth century, the Reformation sent forth its first roots in Germany, from which it spread to other parts of Central Europe. In some places, such as northern Germany, it found fertile soil and in others, such as Austria, it was deprived of potentially fertile soil.

The ideological and military battles of the Counter-Reformation were also waged in Central Europe, or by Central European powers elsewhere in the world, leading eventually to one of the most destructive conflagrations of European history, the Thirty Years' War (1618–1648), during which perhaps as many as one third of all residents of Germany died. Due in part to the vast destruction of the Thirty Years' War, the German-speaking areas of Europe developed into one of the major sources for emigration, for both religious and financial reasons, by the beginning of the eighteenth century. In the East, the Ottoman Empire increasingly made headway toward the West, overtaking Hungary and reaching the gates of Vienna by the 1670s, before the combined armies of several European nations, especially Poland, halted what Europe had perceived as one of its greatest threats since the Middle Ages. By the eighteenth century, the Habsburg Monarchy managed to consolidate power, but did so along its eastern frontier only tentatively, leaving for another century the military move toward the East that would define the Austrian model of Central Europe.

Historically, it would seem that decentralization shaped much of the rhetoric of Central Europe during the second phase, a period generally referred to as the early modern era. At its center, Europe underwent considerable fragmentation, with the result that nationalism failed to emerge in any viable form. As the great novel of the Thirty Years' War, Hans Jakob Christoffel von Grimmelshausen's *Simplicius Simplicissimus* (1975 [1669]), makes abundantly evident, the peoples of Central Europe lived in a world that was overrun by chaos and foreign forces, and survival was not infrequently the daily preoccupation of many if not most. Grimmelshausen's title character, Simplicius, survived only by deciding which side was most advantageous at any given moment, though eventually he, too, chose to leave Germany and settle on a utopian island in the Indian Ocean. Europe, Simplicius observes at the end of the novel, no longer offered anything that would sustain civilization (ibid.: 602–603).

At the same time, however, we can observe that an aesthetics of Central Europe did begin to take shape. Already by the seventeenth century, music publishing was flourishing in the German-speaking lands. Not only did the major repertories of the German Baroque come into being, but the architecture and the art of the Counter-Reformation spread across much of southern Germany and Austria. German printers also turned to popular music, using broadsides—the sheet music of the era—to reproduce the news of the day as contrafacts, as new songs based on old melodies. New bridges between orality and literacy formed, which in turn created possibilities for recording the folk music of the day in local, regional, and proto-national repertories. Printed music, whether the sacred works of J. S. Bach or the collections of street songs that Herder would call "folk songs," served not so much as an alternative to the decentralization of the era as a common record. Music accompanied history through its capacity to chronicle it in new forms. It is in this capacity that it increasingly contextualized the repertories of the era as distinctively German, Austrian, and Central European (see Holzapfel 2002).

*Phase 3, Central Europe in the Age of Empire*

With the rise of the European nation-state came a new transformation of Central Europe: It took the shape of empires. In the course of the nineteenth century, both Germany and Austria acquired an increasing amount of territory, which in turn led them to expand their Central European borders and to draw lands both within and outside the geographical borders of Central Europe into its cultural orbit. The German and Austro-Hungarian empires that increasingly encompassed Central Europe were in many ways different, if indeed the accrual of power to the German-speaking center also produced many similarities. The Habsburg Monarchy of Austria-Hungary had the political advantage of having consolidated political power in its center prior to the nineteenth century, thus enabling it to devote its political energies to administering the growing Eastern European lands that it was acquiring, while determining ways to accommodate Hungary's demands for equality within the empire itself. Symbolically, it was the **Ausgleich** of 1867, the legal recognition of Austria-Hungary's multiculturalism as a **Vielvölkerstaat,** that justified the extension of Central Europe from Vienna and Budapest into Eastern, Southern, and Southeastern Europe in the nineteenth century (see Chapter 2). Critically, the recognition of a multicultural empire carried with it certain rights, not least among them the expanded possibilities of cultural exchange between East and West (cf. the essays in Rupp-Eisenreich and Stagl 1995).

Germany faced a different set of political dilemmas as it strove to acquire imperial girth in Central Europe. At the beginning of the nineteenth century there was no centralization of political power within the German-speaking lands; they remained a collection of smaller and larger states, ruled in different ways and capable of different forms of alliance. The attempts to centralize Germany in the first half of the century might have culminated in 1848, but instead the revolution of that year, which briefly installed a parliament in Frankfurt am Main, was thwarted. It was not until 1871, when the Prussians defeated the Austrians along their common frontier, that a new empire under Wilhelm I was proclaimed. Imperial Germany threw itself into the building of its empire with extraordinary vigor, buttressed by military and political zeal. It extended Central Europe first into Eastern and Northeastern Europe, incorporating Polish provinces with larger and smaller German-speaking populations and strengthening its longtime trade relations with the Baltic states. However, the German empire soon found that the territory for its expansion of Central Europe was inadequate, and it turned to overseas expansion, especially but not exclusively in Africa, to fire the engines of colonial desire. The cultural core of the German empire would remain German, as would its arts and especially its music. On one hand, colonial aspirations meant that music-making Others were brought to Germany to perform at international expositions or university research institutes in Berlin. On the other hand, such music-making Others were to define Central Europe primarily through their roles as colonial Others, not as residents of a multicultural Germany.

European colonial expansion flourished well into the twentieth century. It still haunts many parts of the world in its more recent forms, notably post-colonialism and globalization, but the empires that carved out a new presence for Central Europe collapsed in the two world wars. It is important for us to recognize that the empires at the center of Europe were not isolated and that their rhetoric of Central Europe was not only generated by ideologues in Berlin and Vienna. The empires in the center also confronted the empires at their borders, especially in the East, where the Russian Empire and the Ottoman Empire did not yield their historical positions in Europe to the upstart empires encroaching upon their western frontiers. The imperial expansion of Central Europe encountered and then exacerbated cultural tension along the borders in the East, especially as competition intensified for the peoples without modern nation-states, especially those speaking Slavic languages, driven by the deeper competition between religions, those of the West—Catholic and Protestant Christianity—and those of the East—Christian Orthodoxy and Islam. German and Austrian imperial expansion intensified the conflicts between East and West in the nineteenth century, but even more significantly, it translated and transformed those conflicts by locating them in the contexts of the nineteenth-century—thus, the modern—nation-state.

### Phase 4, Central Europe Imploded and Reassembled

At the beginning of the twenty-first century it is the postmodern, rather than the modern, symbols of Central Europe that shape our image of the region and block our memories. The Berlin Wall. Borders torn apart and put on sale. Monstrous Mercedes overtaking minuscule Trabant automobiles in the race to create a single economy for a single *Volk*. Retreating Soviet and Russian occupying forces and advancing NATO forces. "Guest workers" from Turkey and Eastern Europe keeping the economies afloat. Austria's claim to housing more asylum seekers per capita than any other nation of the world and calls from Austria's right-wing Freedom Party to shut out foreigners. Center and periphery have collapsed upon each other in the aftermath of Central Europe's implosion in the twentieth century (cf., CD examples 14 and 15).

The final historiographic phase in the rhetoric of Central Europe has followed a path from ideological and cultural power to disarray and collapse and then—or now, because we find ourselves still in the fourth phase—the struggle to reestablish the power of Central Europe. The final phase emerges from two forms of cultural activity, those spinning out centrifugally from the center and those centripetally gathered at the center to repair the enormous fissure that effectively rent Central Europe into powerless fragments.

It is sometimes customary to divide the twentieth-century history of Central Europe into several stages, one separated from the other by abrupt changes, such as the defeats at the ends of the world wars or the popular revolutions that marked the end of the Cold War. The rhetoric of Central Europe, however, does not unfold in fits and starts, even with fragments and pieces that we can relegate to the past. There is a unity, even a logic, to the rhetoric, because of the ways in which the models of Central European nationalism assume forms that suture the rifts between nations and heal the wounds of twentieth-century cataclysm. We are familiar with the vocabulary of this new Central European nationalism, even if we do not necessarily employ it as a rhetoric: memory and monument, reunification and revival. Music, as we see in this chapter, provides the syntax that connects the elements of this vocabulary in a common rhetoric.

Music mobilized the spread of Central Europe in the early century and monumentalized its retreat in the wake of the century's world wars. It is this power to mobilize that determines less whether a repertory is German, Austrian, Czech, or Hungarian than as constituents in a common rhetoric connecting the end of the past century to the end of our own century. Anchored in the Central European canon and mapped on the landscape coveted through ideology and war, music not only serves as a symbol for the final phase I examine here, but it provides a primary source for the symbols that serve its rhetoric. At the end of the twentieth century, as Central Europe achieves new and old meanings again in the New Europe, music acquires even greater power in the ideological reformation of the present, for it serves to mark the process of healing. Figuratively and literally, it reassembles pieces left from the implosion in Europe's center.

## Musical Discourses of Centeredness

*"God, Protect Franz, Our Emperor"*
—*Opening of the Austrian Imperial Anthem, "Kaiserhymne"*

The "Kaiserhymne" vividly symbolizes the difficulties of creating and maintaining the national core of Central Europe (listen to CD examples 34 and 35). At different places in this book the "Kaiserhymne" has served as a metaphor for understanding how music represents the nation (see, especially, Chapter 2), and we turn to it again at the beginning of a section in which we examine just how music comes to occupy and define the presence of the nation at the center of Europe. We begin with a single performance of the "Kaiserhymne," in fact a recording made in the waning years of the Austro-Hungarian Empire. The performance enacts the Habsburg rhetoric of multiculturalism to an extreme: On the recording (CD example 35) one hears singers from the four "official languages" of the empire—German, Hungarian, Czech, and Polish—performing at once. Even if we were linguistically capable of doing so, it would be virtually impossible to separate more than single words from each of the languages from the multilingual chorus. Understanding the individual language, culture, or region was, however, never the point. Instead, the performance is significant for its wholeness, for displaying a national fabric in which the parts form a whole through their common, yet entirely uncommon, envoicement of the nation in its national anthem made multicultural. The performance draws the parts of the singing nations of Habsburg Europe into the center, where together they sound Central Europe.

There are many other reasons that the performance shapes a metaphysics of centeredness. So obvious that it might be easy to overlook, the performance exploits technologies of sound recording that were still rather new at the time. This performance was not an isolated curiosity, but rather one of many attempts during the first decades of the twentieth century to gather as many sound portraits of the diverse cultures of the empire as possible. The Phonogramm-Archiv of the Imperial and Royal Academy of Sciences in Vienna, founded in 1899, was the first national sound archive in the world, and within only a few years of its founding it was ambitiously sponsoring recording expeditions throughout Eastern Europe and the world to gather its plethora of sounds on recording, so they could be analyzed, studied, and stored in Vienna.

The second sound archive, at the University of Berlin, would be founded within only a few years, in 1900, and its agenda of gathering, analyzing, and storing also developed quickly, albeit following somewhat distinctive directions. The Germans concentrated more on the center itself, taking advantage of musicians and ensembles that were passing through the imperial capital for performances at expositions, fairs, and commercial ventures. In the course of the next century, the two Central European sound archives would compete with recording projects throughout the world to gather more materials and subject them to the analytical techniques of what would be called **vergleichende Musikwissenschaft** ("comparative musicology") and **systematische Musikwissenschaft** ("systematic musicology"), both of which stressed the autonomy of the musical object and the scientific analysis of its meaning as musical and cultural data. The question of music's autonomy as an object was crucial to the formulation of a rhetoric of Central Europe and the ways in which individual works, such as a recording of the "Kaiserhymne" in four languages at the same time, entered the discourses of centeredness.

The question I examine in the present section might be stated most baldly thus: How does music come to demonstrate the qualities that make it represent the core of a national tradition? By extension, how does music come to serve a national and nationalist aesthetics that privileges the power that Central European nations have claimed for themselves? That these are ideological questions goes without saying, but my concern for the next few pages is actually aesthetic rather than ideological. I am concerned primarily with ontological questions, in other words, those questions that philosophers ask about how we understand an object's being-in-the-world and how music creates meaning for those who perform and listen to it (cf. Bohlman 1999b). More specifically, I examine the ways in which certain types of music undergo transformations so that they can more effectively represent the assertions of musical and political power that the nations of Central Europe have claimed for themselves. These changes are not the products of something immanent in music itself, but rather result from aesthetic decisions and actions made by those with a certain degree of power at their disposal, especially the power invested in technologies for the retrieval, recording, and reproduction of music.

In Central Europe music finds its way-in-the-world through processes of collecting, inscribing, transcribing, and in-migration toward the center. These are the ways in which Central European nations come to own music and make it their own, and ultimately, making music one's own is itself critical to the ontology of music, especially music that participates in nationalism. We might even go so far as to say that there is an obsession in Central Europe to stake claims of musical ownership. That obsession is not simply an abstract quality; it is realized through certain mechanisms and technologies as well as the institutions that house those mechanisms and technologies. In Central Europe most of these mechanisms, technologies, and institutions that create musical objects in order to draw them toward the center possess a distinctive relation with the nation-state.

The centripetal pull of music's ontologies in the Central European nation-state begins with the transformation from oral to written tradition. A folk song in oral tradition, for example, is a different musical object from the *same* folk song in written tradition. It is not simply a matter of standardizing notation, tuning, or rhythmic inconsistencies from verse to verse, but rather of creating a version that represents something essential—about a performance or performer, or in the canonic repertories about an expansive tradition. The shift from oral to written tradition assumes various forms, which depend on many different concepts of what an object of music is. There are historical contexts for these concepts, and there are also scientific contexts, but for the most part these have a common goal: Creating an authentic representation of music, the internal properties of which are consistent with the scientific interpretation of culture. It is for these reasons that better and better machines for the transcription and representation of works of music have been so critical to the consolidation of tradition in the Central European nation-state (cf. Kittler 1987). It is under these circumstances that museums for the literal and figurative display of musical works proliferated in the course of the nineteenth century, making music at once public and iconic for the ideological and political acts of the state (see Goehr 1992). For Germany, Austria, and the other nation-states competing on the cultural landscape of Central Europe, it has historically been important to possess music—both of self and of other—and to create spaces for it at the center of the nation itself.

### Finding Music at Europe's Center

The music at Europe's center was variously discovered, explored, invented, and willed into existence. Regardless of the musical path to the center, those who followed it were willing to expend great amounts of energy and money, often to concentrate resources over a period of years and decades. Sometimes, the journey to the center was the undertaking of a single individual whose passion for identifying and translating the essence was both eccentric and extraordinary. For the amateur and professional collectors and scholars who created the canons of German and Austrian folk music, the decision to forge a new path to the center most often resulted from a powerful personal motivation to envoice the folk music at the center so that it would be audible for the entire nation.

Throughout the course of this chapter we encounter several of the most notable of the folk-music scholars who devoted their lives to collecting and editing national collections: Ludwig Erk and Franz Magnus Böhme in Germany, Josef Pommer in Austria. But for the moment we turn briefly to an amateur collector, Konrad Mautner, who entirely devoted his energies to establishing the musical core of alpine music in Austria.

Mautner inherited a traditional view of folk music that had been developing in Austria since the late eighteenth century, namely that the origins and essence of folk music lay in the most remote mountain areas of the province of Styria. The characteristics of the Styrian essence included song in regional and local dialect rather than in the literary language, High German, and dance that retained many of its most distinguishing markers of functionality, such as courting. The performance of Styrian folk music also retained other trappings of the essential, above all, traditional clothing. Mautner spent many years, usually during the summer, living among the residents of the Gößl, a village area farther into the high mountains from Bad Aussee in southwestern Styria, today roughly the geographical center of Austria. From these experiences he published the *Steirisches Rasplwerk* (Mautner 1910), which soon acquired the aura and symbolic functions of a modern canonic repertory anchored firmly in the geography and history of the center itself.

The *Rasplwerk* (see Figures 5.2 and 5.3) contains 372 pages of songs, each one illustrated by Mautner in his own hand. The transcriptions of the songs employ notational style that, while using standard conventions that any reader would understand, are nonetheless specific to the local tradition. The orthography of the textual transcriptions (for example, the use of special superscripts to mark the vowels in Styrian dialect, such as å) marks a further shift from the orthography of the German-language repertory of Central Europe to Styrian German at the core. For Mautner, then, Styrian folk song requires a process of personalized and localized translation. Rather than generalizing a canon for Central Europe, his *Rasplwerk* trims that canon to an essence, the reproduction of which, through mass publication, is culturally channeled.

Konrad Mautner's relentless and passionate pursuit of the center seems on its surface to arise from cultural and national chauvinism. The microcosm that the *Rasplwerk* portrays is almost inaccessible, and in some ways the world in which Mautner had increasingly become a resident was as foreign to the cosmopolitan culture of fin-de-siècle Vienna as the cultural worlds constituting the periphery of Central Europe. Ironically, it was from one of those worlds, the rural Jewish shtetls of Silesia, a region along the Czech-Polish border, that Mautner's family had emigrated only a generation earlier. Konrad Mautner could trace no familial or cultural roots to Gößl; his forebears were Jewish, and they had made their fortunes as textile manufacturers. Mautner himself remained the head of the family industry, and he was actively involved in the business of running factories in Vienna and in the eastern provinces of the empire. His life, as reflected in his biography, was filled with Viennese intellectuals, artists, and literary figures (see Schönfellinger 1999)—people who could not have been less like the figures who fill

*Figure 5.2. Title page from Konrad Mautner's* Steirisches Rasplwerk *(1910) (original in Special Collections, Regenstein Library, University of Chicago)*

the pages of his *Rasplwerk* and the other anthologies of Styrian folk music that he published—and illustrated—during his lifetime.

The Styrian center may have been the focus of Mautner's personal aspirations and imagination, but was also the product of a deeper fin-de-siècle anxiety about the inaccessibility of the center in the Austro-Hungarian empire that was straining at the outer limits of Central Europe (ibid.). Mautner's anxiety was symptomatic of another force fixing Styria at the center, namely modernism, the artistic and aesthetic movement that accompanied the implosion of Central Europe during the twentieth century. At the turn of the twenty-first century, Styria's position as a symbolic center remains seemingly unassailable. Austria's regional CD recording project, "Musik der Regionen" ("Music of the Regions"), which stems from Austria's entry into the European Union in the mid-1990s, not only begins its first volume in Styria, but also in the valley of the Enn River, which geographically distinguishes the southwestern part of the province in which Konrad Mautner had lived and collected a century earlier (*Im steirischen Ennstal* 1996).

*Figure 5.3. Song from Konrad Mautner's Steirisches Rasplwerk (1910) (original in Special Collections, Regenstein Library, University of Chicago)*

## Collecting at the Center

The discourses of centeredness also came about in ways so unexpected that they seem almost surreal in retrospect. During both world wars there were several recording and anthology projects that took the prisoner-of-war camp and, in World War II, the concentration camp as a means of accounting for the diversity that the Central European nations drew toward their center. Again, the ideological stakes of such projects were great, and they attracted an extraordinary range of professional and amateur scholars. The most concerted efforts to emphasize the center by recording prisoners of war from the peripheries of the German and Austro-Hungarian empires took place during World War I, when national musicological and anthropological institutions sent teams of researchers into the camps where captured soldiers were held. Among those drafted for this scientific study of musical difference were leading comparative musicologists from Germany, such as Carl Stumpf and Georg Schünemann. Unlike a center defined by presumably authentic folk music, the center of an empire at war acquired its identity through the accrual of difference. In Germany's prisoner-of-war camps, for example, the recording teams from Berlin encountered the macrocosm of world music reduced to an essence. Recording and transcribing the prisoners, as Figure 2.5 reveals, demanded meticulous attention to detail and highly developed translation skills. The sweeping results, however, were deemed worth the effort. In the eyes of those who published the results of these collecting projects, they founded nothing less than "a New Anthropology" (see the anthology gathering results of the prisoner-of-war fieldwork, Doegen 1925).

The center in Germany, Austria, or Hungary became what amounted to a centralization of the periphery. The music cultures of entire German speech islands, to take a notable example, appeared in print, for among the prisoners of war were German-speaking Russian soldiers from the so-called Volga Colonies. Making recordings for the Berlin Phonogrammarchiv, Georg Schünemann was able to collect 434 songs, which then served as the basis for one of the most influential monographs in early comparative musicology (see Schünemann 1923). Whereas it may seem that the real issue in such projects is not defining the center but rather the periphery, they also served as ideological justification for demonstrating that the center extended outward toward the periphery, ultimately absorbing German music at the frontiers of Central Europe. The prisoner-of-war recordings were the most immediate antecedents, for example, of the nationalistic folk-song project *Landschaftliche Volkslieder,* which I discussed in detail in the fourth chapter. Schünemann's recordings from World War I were to provide the basis for the later LV volume that appeared on the eve of World War II.

Not only national scholarly institutions produced anthologies representing the different facets of the center in time of war. There were also collections and performance editions produced by those interned in the concentration camps of World War II. Ironically, such songbooks also served the musical activities of an in-gathering defined by their differences and the extent to which the political ideologues of Nazi Germany excluded them as Jewish, Roma, communists, or gays and lesbians, in other words, those placed in concentration camps. The music of these residents of the concentration camps, such as that secretly distributed as a handwritten and illustrated volume in Sachsenhausen, remains unequivocally symbolic of the rhetoric of Central Europe (see Figure 5.4 from *Das Lagerliederbuch* 1980 [1942]). As one canonic repertory, we encounter the best-known songs of the German

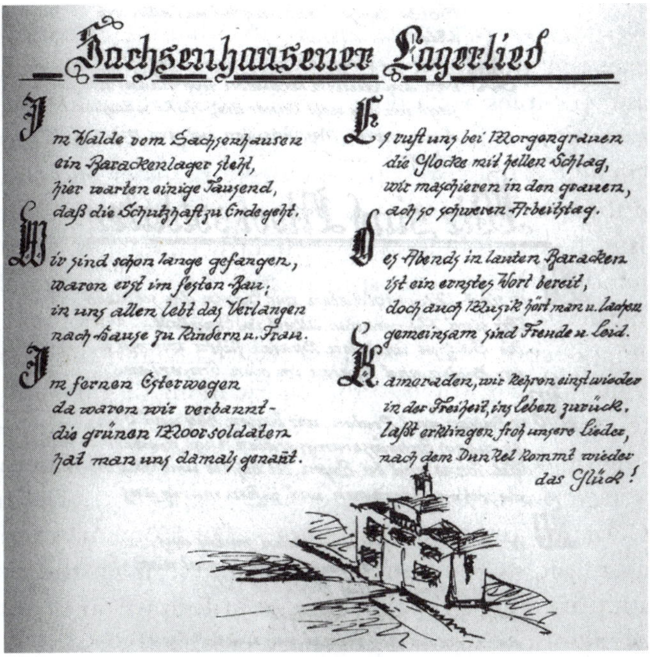
Sachsenhausener Lagerlied

Im Walde vom Sachsenhausen
ein Barackenlager steht,
hier warten einige Tausend,
daß die Schutzhaft zu Ende geht.

Wir sind schon lange gefangen,
waren erst im festen Bau;
in uns allen lebt das Verlangen
nach Hause zu Kindern u. Frau.

Im fernen Esterwegen
da waren wir verbannt -
die grünen Moorsoldaten
hat man uns damals genannt.

Es ruft uns bei Morgengrauen
die Glocke mit hellen Schlag,
wir marschieren in den grauen,
ach so schweren Arbeitstag.

Des Abends in lauten Baracken
ist ein ernstes Wort bereit,
doch auch Musik hört man u. lachen
gemeinsam sind Freude u. Leid.

Kameraden, wir kehren einst wieder
in der Freiheit, ins Leben zurück.
Laßt erklingen froh unsere Lieder,
nach dem Dunkel kommt wieder
das Glück!

*Figure 5.4. Song from the* Lagerliederbuch *for the Sachsenhausen Concentration Camp (reprint in* Das Lagerliederbuch: *1980)*

youth movements. There are workers' songs, popular songs, and folk songs. In short, the *Lagerliederbuch* of Sachsenhausen concentration camp contains the songs Germans collectively chose to represent their own German tradition. Music was placed in an anthology to assert the power of the musical center itself to resist attempts to deprive those who were different of what it meant to them to sing of the nation and musically to celebrate what was also their common identity as residents of Central Europe.

## Most German of All the Arts—Germany

*Now it is obvious that if these two men speak of the diversity of cultures, they actually do not tell the same story, they do not speak on the same level: the German speaks of something essential, the Frenchman about factual but secondary differences.*

***—Dumont 1994: 3***

Core, canon, repertory, genre. The essence that is German. The essential character that music expresses. In the language of German nationalism, music occupies a symbolic position of exceptional importance. In the service of history and of the nation, music has the power to become German and to express the essence, to muster and constitute all that lies at the center. The Germanness of music is not simply a matter of sloganism. It shapes literary and scholarly languages; at certain moments, including those of most aggressive German nationalism, music's Germanness is a matter of open political and ideological debate. Peruse the collections of music from Germany and the journals and secondary literature devoted to that music in any library, and it will be immediately striking just how often the adjective of identity, "deutsch," precedes the object of collection and study—music, folk music, or music history (see, for example, Potter 1998: 342–345). The omnipresence of "German" in discourses about music is not a matter of chance. Identifying music's Germanness is inseparable from the creation of German identity, and German music is, it follows, inseparable from Germany's rhetoric of Central Europe.

Music becomes German in different ways, and it would be impossible to summarize those different ways here. It would also miss the point of why it is important that music becomes German, for music's German identity emerges from a mixture of its essence and its capacity to fulfill the conditions of a collective. These two qualities of Germanness could not differ more from each other, but that should not suggest that they are particularly complicated. On one hand, the essence of Germanness in music might be as simple as language, which is to say, the German language and the ways in which its rhythms and syntax conform to genres that provide the basis for national repertories. On the other, music's collective character means that it does not lend itself to isolation, but rather its power to fit into repertories and genres has the social dimensions of those who maintain those repertories and genres, the music-making collective of the German people. That there is music in Central Europe that does not fulfill these basic conditions of essence and collectivity has never been a matter of debate, but such music is by definition not German. There is no rhetoric of Central Europe that adequately accounts for, say, the music of Germany's Slavic-speaking Serbs; thus it wins no place at the center and forms no canonic repertory.

It is not difficult to identify just when it became important that music be German and that it fit into an identifiably German collective consciousness: in the wake of the **Aufklärung,** or German **Enlighten-ment.** Prior to the nineteenth century there were forms of music that were referred to as German, but there seems to be little in such designations that accounts for German national genres of any kind. We have already seen elsewhere that Johann Gottfried Herder's seminal first collection of folk songs (Herder 1778 and 1779) did not isolate German folk songs, nor did it even give pride of place to songs from German sources. Similarly, in Herder's day, a **deutscher Tanz,** or "German dance," was a general rather than specific designation that demonstrated, in practice, no appreciable difference from the **Ländler.** By no means was the distribution of the *deutscher Tanz* limited to the lands of Germany or to Central Europe.

### Nineteenth-Century Canons of Germanness

> We only grudgingly leave old things behind, and I wager that the Germans turn
> over in bed much less often than the French.
> —*Jean Paul, "On Germanisms" [1809] (Lützler 1982: 230)*

In the early decades of the nineteenth century, however, it rather suddenly became important that folk music be demonstrably German. The passion to collect and anthologize folk music, which first emerged in the initial decades of the century, then accelerated rapidly in the 1820s and 1830s, was virtually driven by the need to label individual pieces and collective repertories as German, willing upon them a national identity even before there was a nation. We witness the growing attention to identity in the shift of the designation "German" from the subtitle of Arnim and Brentano's *Des Knaben Wunderhorn: Alte Deutsche Lieder* ("The Youth's Magic Horn: Old German Songs") (1806 and 1808), the first anthology of folk songs, albeit without melodies, to the main title of Klein and Groos's *Deutsche Lieder für Jung und Alt* ("German Songs for Young and Old") (1818). With these gestures of naming in place, the impulse to draw an increasingly collective repertory into a growing canon was also in place (see Feurzeig 2002).

In the course of the nineteenth century, as collections of folk songs and folk music grew, they insistently included the designation "German." By the end of the century, when Ludwig Erk (posthumously) and Franz Magnus Böhme published the three-volume *Deutscher Lieder-*

*hort* ("German Song Treasury") (1893–1894), which remains until to-day the canonic repertory of German song, Germanness was indispensable, but also comprehensive. It drew more and more music into the center and thus extended the historical and geographical boundaries of the center. German music had become the record of history, extending the national narrative to an era predating the modern (or even premodern) German nation, for example, in Böhme's other canonic anthology, *Altdeutsches Liederbuch: Volkslieder der Deutschen nach Wort und Weise aus dem 12. bis zum 17. Jahrhundert* ("Old German Songbook: Folk Songs of the Germans from the Twelfth to the Seventeenth Century, According to Text and Melody") (1877). At the beginning of the twentieth century, the foundations of German music as a national cultural heritage were very firm indeed.

Resting on the foundations of German music were both myth and monument. The national structure of music should aspire toward the massiveness of monument, according to publishers and public alike, where it not only firmly asserted a presence on the national landscape but it could also withstand historical and military crisis, two qualities crucial to the functioning of German national myth (cf. Flacke 1998b). Myth lent itself to the ascription of time and temporality, whereas monumentality was a geographical condition of Germanness. Together, they could determine the place and time in which German music contributed to the rhetoric of Central Europe. Myth asserted its presence in German music by establishing prehistorical origins, whereas monumentality sustained the national essence infinitely. The myths and monuments of German music, moreover, were distinctive because they were not restricted to genres and repertories. Folk music and art music engendered myth, and monuments could rise from the collections of all musics demonstrating a sufficient Germanness.


### German Myth

*You, nation of people,*
*Who remain in the blossom of your life;*
*Take heed of what I tell to you!*
*You saw Siegfried and Brünnhilde*
*Consumed by the burning fire;*
*You saw the ring dragged to the deep*
*By the daughters of the Rhine;*

*Look then through the night*
*Toward the north:*
*A sacred glow shines there in the sky,*
*Thus all will know—*
*That you are viewing the end of Walhalla!*
        —*Richard Wagner,* Götterdämmerung, Der Ring des Nibelungen

It is perhaps most surprising that myth should play such a significant role in shaping the music that was least anchored in folk music and folklore. The preceding verse from the closing scene of Wagner's *Götterdämmerung* ("Twilight of the Gods"), which opens his cycle, is but one of many examples of the presence of canonic Germanic myths in the canonic repertories of German art music. Wagner's choice of the "Niebelungen" epic for his own four-opera cycle, *Der Ring des Nibelungen,* amounted to a deliberate attempt to imbue his operatic work with an even deeper level of Germanness than many of his other operas had displayed. The choice of an epic that not only embodied but also evoked the prehistorical landscapes of Central Europe had personal as well as national meaning, for Wagner, as his biography demonstrates, was earning growing amounts of capital by playing off the rejection he had encountered when living and composing outside of Germany, especially in France. By incorporating the most Germanic of myths, he was making a rhetorical move, a shift in the musical and literary languages in his later operas toward German nationalism.

The myths of the Niebelungen empowered Wagner to use music to historicize Central Europe, to retrieve it from the past and shape it into musical works that were intentionally modern and nationalist. Indeed, it was the confluence of modernity and nationalism that myth so powerfully effected. In the rhetoric of music and myth, both created by Wagner for the operas, the name of the nation was barely spoken, but rather it was suspended in the sacred symbols of the Rhine River and Walhalla, where the Germanic gods went to live eternally as heroes. Wagner not only used myth but made myth, particularly myth that would serve German nationalism. He transformed the music of late German Romanticism into a rhetoric of Central Europe that would appeal to later generations of nationalists, among them the aesthetic ideologues of the Nazi era.

Myth sets in motion a series of classicizing processes, even in the national imagination that shapes German folk music. The foundations of the canonic Erk-Böhme *Deutscher Liederhort* (1893–1894) were planted in the same mythological soil as Wagner's Niebelungen cycle, even though a very different path of national music history unfolds through folk song. Erk and Böhme rested their classification of German folk song on a set of fifteen pillars, folk-music genres that stretched from the mythological to the spiritual, forming an historical path from the orality of prehistory to the literate inscription of received texts in the future (Erk and Böhme 1893–94, Vol. 1: vii). Critical for the nationalist functions of the pillars was the designation of the first pillar as "Sagenlieder" ("legend songs"), whereby the editors created an umbrella for twelve more subgenres, ranging from "Echoes of the Gods" (number 1) to "Judgments of the Gods or Punishment in Hell" (number 12). The legend songs and their subgenres might have seemed at first glance to belie any kind of national label, at best reflecting a sort of pan-Germanness. But Erk and Böhme assigned another generic label to the legend songs, namely *Balladen,* or ballads; in so doing, they made one of the most critically important moves in the historiography of German folk music: They established the canon of narrative songs within the canon of German musical nationalism.


## Das Balladenwerk

Ballad repertories make frequent appearances in this book, and it may well not be surprising that they turn up at a central moment in a chapter exploring music and nationalism in Central Europe. For Erk and Böhme the ballads narrated stories of the gods and their interaction with human beings. The ballads pushed at the distinctive differences between mortal and immortal beings, animals and humans. They were not, as we have seen already in previous chapters, just any collection of folk songs, even those with narrative texts: Ballads tell their story with a particular type of language, namely High or Literary German (*Hochdeutsch*). In so doing, they locate themselves and those who sing them, whatever their degree of literacy, at the very musical center of Central Europe. Ballads begin as history, but through transmission and performance they take their place as history. The ways in which they narrate stories of the gods or of magical animals serve as the prototypes for the ways in which other narratives will record history and serve as allegories for real events. By placing the legend songs/ballads in a strategic position at the beginning of the *Deutscher Liederhort,* Erk and

Böhme created a musical template for German geography and history, affixed to Central Europe but mobile as well, capable of accompanying those who brought the canonic folk-song repertory with them when they traveled to North America or, even more importantly, to the speech islands of Eastern Europe.

Ballads have played a crucial role at those moments when there was a particular need for national repertories and canons of German music. Ludwig Erk and Franz Magnus Böhme were completing the editorial work on *Deutscher Liederhort* at one of those moments, the decades following German national unity in 1871. We turn now to another and different type of moment when the Germanness of ballads was elevated to a position of ideological importance, the beginning of the Nazi era. Within a few years, if not months, of Hitler's rise to power at the end of January 1933, numerous musical projects were under way that would lead to the publication of new canons of German music from old repertories. The **Balladenwerk,** organized and edited by John Meier and his colleagues at the German Folk-Song Archive, was one such monument project which, like several of the other monument projects, long survived the era of official national-socialism in Germany. The real title of the monument series I and others call the *Balladenwerk* ("Ballad Works") was actually much more encompassing than a single genre would suggest: *Deutsche Volkslieder mit ihren Melodien* ("German Folk Songs with Their Melodies"). The genre name, *Ballads,* appears only as a subtitle to *German Folk Songs,* which is the name given to individual volumes. As a series, however, *Deutsche Volkslieder* demonstrated far more concern for texts, especially historical texts, than for melodies.

The first volume appeared already in 1935, and two more volumes appeared in 1939. From the outset, the historical and historicist potential of ballads determined the shape and contents of the canon. The first ballad in the 1935 edition, which would subsequently bear the prestigious designation of DVldr 1, was "Das jüngere Hildebrandslied" ("The Younger Hildebrand Song"). The editors analyzed two paths of historical development for this classic song about the struggle between father and son, one with origins in the eighth century CE, the other traceable only to the thirteenth century (Figure 5.5). The documentation of the ballad did not begin in the Middle Ages, but rather in early modern Germany, where its origins were already evident in the earliest printed versions. A hermeneutic journey through the ballads of the

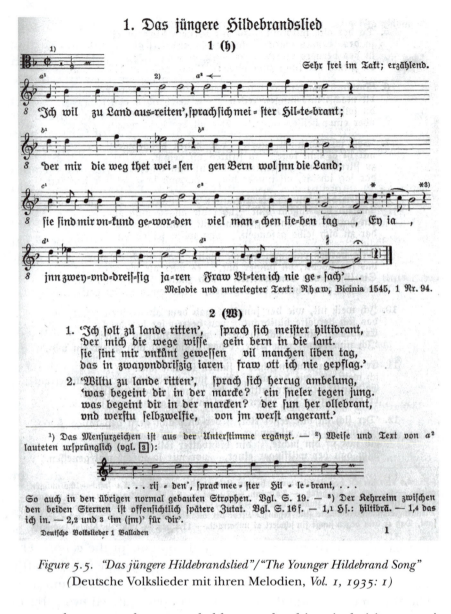

*Figure 5.5. "Das jüngere Hildebrandslied"/"The Younger Hildebrand Song"*
(Deutsche Volkslieder mit ihren Melodien, *Vol. 1, 1935: 1*)

1935 volume reveals a remarkably complex historical vision, one in which folk songs give voice to Germanic myths and chart the journeys of the earliest German heroes (for example, number 15, "Der Tannhäuser"). Europe is sung through the eyes of German poets and singers, and even those songs that chart the historical landscapes at the edges of Europe (such as number 14, "Graf von Rom" ["Count from

Rome"]) are distinctive because of the ways they reimagine those edges as German. Publication of the *Balladenwerk* continued until 1996, when the tenth and final volume appeared, bringing about a type of closure that would seal the relation between myth and history.

The *Balladenwerk* truly functions as a monument to German nationalism, but for whom? Is German history narrated from the bottom up? Or from the top down? If such questions remain rhetorical for the *Balladenwerk,* they unequivocally reveal the rhetoric of Central Europe in the history of another series of musical monuments that began to appear in 1936, *Das Erbe deutscher Musik* ("The Heritage of German Music," hereafter EDM).

## Das Erbe deutscher Musik

From the outset, EDM viewed music from the top, which is to say, as a component of a German history comprising great works by great composers. Unlike the *Balladenwerk,* which was never officially an arm of the National Socialist regime and ceased publication after the beginning of World War II, the EDM wore the politics of its ideological benefactors on its sleeve: The first series bore the additional title, *Reichsdenkmale deutscher Musik* ("Reich Monument of German Music"). Whereas the ballad editors were largely folk-song scholars conducting research at a single institution, the EDM cast its nets widely, gathering as many musicologists as possible, thus providing a type of discursive glue that would bind scholars to the projects of the new regime. Pamela M. Potter has thoroughly traced the links between musicology and German nationalist projects in the Weimar and Nazi periods, particularly those that depended on top-down perspectives (see Potter 1998). It is especially telling that the complicity documented by Potter is no less evident in the projects that aimed to transform folk and non-classical musics into monuments.

Among the projects of the EDM's first year, which included a volume of seven masses by the Renaissance composer Ludwig Senfl and a work of musical theater, *Pimpinone, oder die ungleiche Heirat,* by the Baroque composer Georg Philipp Telemann, there also appeared a volume of works for which the case of belonging to the German canon had to be made more convincingly, namely a volume of *Trumpet Fanfares, Sonatas, and Field Pieces,* edited by Georg Schünemann, a musicologist who had also collected songs from prisoners of war during World War I (cf. Schünemann 1923 and 1936). This EDM volume is of particular interest to us for two reasons. First, its contents, though seemingly innocuous if not boring in their repetitiveness, documents the movement of German armies and administrators across the regions and states of Central Europe and beyond. Some sections contain, for example, works modeled after Pomeranian melodies (ibid.: 41–44), as well as those in which signal trumpets perform "sonatas" as variations of "German folk songs" (ibid.: 44–57). Second, already in the sixteenth and seventeenth centuries, these works, as literate products of "court trumpeters," provide a top-down view of a German musical repertory. The Pomeranian melodies, Italian fanfares and signals, and the German folk songs, therefore, came to form a monument—a "Reich monument"—in 1936 as they never had before. As such they embodied the "Heritage of German Music" in new, even unexpected, ways on the eve of World War II.

Myth-making and monument-making accompanied modern German music history through World War II and its aftermath, the Cold War, when Germany was divided, and into the post-1989 era of the New Europe. Reunification has necessitated new myths about German music, or rather the revival and revitalization of old myths. Some of the monuments that undergird these myths are the same as those that supported the old myths, for example, series such as EDM or, until 1996, the *Balladenwerk*. The rhetoric of Central Europe also underwent a process of revival, partly as a result of a growing interest in the music of Germans in (and from) Eastern Europe. We witness this, for example, in two series of publications, one entitled simply *Musik im Osten* ("Music in the East," vol. 1, 1962), the other more focused in its examination of German music, thus entitled *Deutsche Musik im Osten* ("German Music in the East," vol. 1, 1990). The musical gaze to the East does not attempt to dominate that part of Europe but to locate the boundaries of Central Europe more clearly, which is to say, in ways that are politically appropriate in the New Europe. One of the most recent projects simply bears the title, *Musikgeschichte zwischen Ost- und Westeuropa* ("Music History between East and West Europe," Loos 1997), strategically avoiding references either to "German music" or "Central Europe."

It is not altogether clear where and when the Germanness of music will chart the Central Europe of the New Europe, for several new forms of myth-making are under way. At one extreme is a resurgence of myths advocated by those who see no need to abandon the rhetoric of Central Europe prior to World War II and the Holocaust (see, for example, the arguments emanating from the "Historians' Quarrel" in Augstein et al. 1987). At the other extreme are provocative arguments about Germany's potential to serve as a utopian model, or **Leitkultur,** for integrating the diverse groups of people now living in Central Europe, thus erasing German national identity altogether by rendering it unnecessary (see especially Tibi 1998). But the Germanness of music is unlikely to yield to theoretical models and utopian ideologies, for these fail to tap its essence, those moments suspended between myth and history that so fruitfully yield its monuments.

## The Chorus of Many Voices—Austria

A culture of encyclopedism arose in the Austro-Hungarian Empire as it embarked upon the final decades of its history as the dominant empire of East Central Europe, the era Carl E. Schorske has called fin-de-siècle Vienna (Schorske 1981). Encyclopedic genres and media were capable of gathering and sorting out the abundant cultural differences that filled the lands of the Austro-Hungarian Empire. Necessarily, encyclopedic projects require the apparatus of a central administration, not just for the publication of their many costly volumes, but also as a center from which to control the ways in which scholars, writers, and editors might deal with the vast amount of material that potentially could transform the pages of an encyclopedia into a work projecting the cultural girth of a modern nation.

The production of Austria-Hungary's encyclopedias took place at the center, in Vienna or, less often, in Budapest, where they embodied the very structure of the nation-state, whether monumentally published and distributed by the imperial publishing house, the "kaiserlich-königliche Hof- und Staatsdruckerei" (lit., the "imperial-royal court and state printer"), or conceived in formats that imitated the national editions, but in less costly editions that reproduced the culture of the empire for consumption in every home. Even in the most monumental fin-de-siècle encyclopedias, the tension was tangible between the centralized power of a multivolume cultural artifact and the very cultural differences from the peripheries of Central Europe that its pages, in wildly exotic and strictly scientific discourses, made available as public spectacle and public knowledge. That tension, moreover, was critical to the ways in which Austria-Hungary realized its political control over and fantasies of fin-de-siècle Mitteleuropa.

### Die österreichisch-ungarische Monarchie in Wort und Bild

The most sweeping encyclopedic endeavor of the age was the empire's official encyclopedia, *Die österreichisch-ungarische Monarchie in Wort und Bild* ("The Austro-Hungarian Empire in Word and Picture" and hereafter the ÖUMWB), a massive undertaking that began in the 1880s and concluded only several decades later. Published by the imperial publishing house, the ÖUMWB wore its imperial imprimatur on its sleeves, yet it was an encyclopedia that literally mapped the provinces of the German-speaking center and the multilingual provinces in successive volumes. The contents of each volume followed an organizational scheme that began with geographical and historical sections, which then yielded to sections on folklore and economics, with extensive closing sections devoted to the arts. Volumes from the periphery, such as volume 19, "Galicia," in southeastern Poland and Ukraine (published 1898), documented the diversity of a province with detail and care but without any overt attempt to level cultural differences. The authors of the rather long essays were local—scholars, journalists, or administrators whose expertise came not from Vienna but from the regions represented in the individual volumes.

Music appears throughout the ÖUMWB, and the volumes from the outlying provinces include essays on folklore and folk music, as well as essays that are the equivalent to small music histories (for example, Franz Bylicki's entry on "Music and Folk Music" in the "Galicia" volume; 1898: 539–566). The ÖUMWB employed the format of an encyclopedia to project Central Europe as a region in which difference could and should be celebrated. There was no single way to celebrate difference or to draw upon it to represent the nation-state. A parallel edition of the ÖUMWB in Hungarian, the essays of which were produced separately, appeared in Budapest and projected the distinctive ideology and politics of Hungary's interests in Central Europe, especially those in regions of East Central Europe with Hungarian-speaking communities, such as Transylvania. However, it is not the politics of the ÖUMWB that is most striking, but its willingness to encounter and accommodate cultural difference. Many of the essays in the encyclopedia remain even today among the finest ethnographic studies of linguistic and ethnic minorities in East Central Europe.

As a result of the encyclopedic culture of fin-de-siècle Central Europe, virtually every domain of culture could claim one type of encyclopedic project or another. Those who contributed to one project, moreover, were often drafted to contribute to others, therefore spinning out a web of essays and publications that together lent themselves to interpretation as early versions of an Austrian rhetoric of Central Europe. I turn briefly to two of the projects devoted to quite different kinds of music in the Austro-Hungarian Empire before and after the turn of the century.

### The Österreichisch-ungarische Cantoren-Zeitung

Virtually unknown to historians of Central Europe, the *Österreichisch-ungarische Cantoren-Zeitung* ("Austro-Hungarian Cantors' Magazine" and hereafter the AHCM) was one of the first undertakings to treat music and music professionals as active participants in the creation of Central European culture. Published in eleven volumes, from 1881 to 1891, the AHCM opened its pages to the Jewish musical life of the Austro-Hungarian Empire at a time of growing centralization and professionalization (see Schmidt 2000–2001 and 2003). On one hand, the AHCM provided an historical record for the development of Jewish music in Central Europe during the nineteenth century. Canonic repertories had formed after oral traditions had been recorded and published and as Jewish cantors had acquired the religious, musical, and financial power to embark upon careers as composers. On the other hand, the AHCM's editors recognized the potential of the journal to serve as the basis for experimentation and consolidation. In each issue of the biweekly journal there appeared new works or arrangements of liturgical works, submitted from Jewish music professionals from throughout Central Europe and beyond. The modernity of the Viennese liturgical rite, or *Wiener Ritus,* had been established by the Vienna cantor Salomon Sulzer earlier in the nineteenth century, and the AHCM's editors were motivated to extend the process of centralizing Jewish music that Vienna had already come to symbolize. Jewish music, therefore, would radiate out from the center and beyond the borders to Europe and the world. The editors announced and pursued this goal as unequivocally as possible:

What do we want?

We want to create an organization of brothers, and the *Österreich-isch-ungarische Cantoren-Zeitung* should provide the material to bind that organization together, in order that all our colleagues, both in the Austro-Hungarian Empire and in the rest of the continent and even beyond, on the other side of the ocean, can exchange ideas back and forth without encumbrance. ("Unser erstes Wort!" 1881: 1)

The AHCM is remarkable for the microcosm of Jewish music that it realized in Central Europe in the penultimate decade of the nineteenth century. Even though the journal itself ceased publication after eleven years, a new process of consolidating Jewish music from Vienna and Budapest acquired momentum. Within a decade the activities of Europe's Jewish folklorists and folk-music scholars, organized by Max Grunwald, would move from Switzerland to Vienna, where the *Jahrbuch für jüdische Volkskunde* ("Yearbook for Jewish Folklore") became the major receptacle for publishing collections of Jewish folk traditions. Within a decade of the turn of the century, the Latvian-German cantor and musicologist Abraham Zvi Idelsohn would undertake a fieldwork project in Jerusalem supported with financial and scientific assistance (such as wax cylinder recording machines) from the Imperial Academy of Sciences in Vienna. That project, the ten volumes of the *Thesaurus of Hebrew Oriental Melodies* (Idelsohn 1914–1932), would establish itself as the major encyclopedic collection of Jewish music, a position that is in many ways unassailable even at the turn of another century. These various encyclopedic projects were connected to greater and lesser degrees, and one should not exaggerate the extent to which repertories published in one found their way, directly or indirectly, into another, for the very concept of what constituted Jewish music was still inchoate in fin-de-siècle Central Europe (cf. Bohlman 2002d). All of the projects, nonetheless, formed from the tension between center and periphery, with the result that they came to share the common culture not only of Jewish tradition but of a modern, multicultural Central Europe.

### Das deutsche Volkslied

There were also encyclopedic projects that used music to represent fin-de-siècle Central Europe as an exclusive rather than inclusive region of

Europe. The first volume of *Das deutsche Volkslied* ("German Folk Song") appeared on the very eve of the new century, in 1899, and quickly established itself as the first major journal in Central Europe to devote itself to folk music. *Das deutsche Volkslied* struggled with problems of exclusivity throughout its 46 volumes until its demise in 1944, one year before the end of World War II. Thus it illustrates one of the most sustained rhetorics of Central Europe through the half century during which the Austro-Hungarian Empire collapsed and Austria found its position in Central Europe greatly reduced by defeats in both world wars. The founder and editor of *Das deutsche Volkslied*, Josef Pommer, took authenticity as the subject for his journal and other Austrian folk-music projects. Austrian folk song was to be defined by language, namely German and its dialects, and by authenticity, a conviction that folk song ultimately arose from the folk themselves and thus could never be polluted by other forms of mediation. *Das deutsche Volkslied* was therefore not the product of modernity, and German folk song had to be sought in places that had been spared the influence of cosmopolitanism.

The essential tension for Pommer formed between the **Kernland** ("core land") of the mountains and isolated regions of the empire, and the metropolis, even Vienna, whose culture he decried because it had become multilingual. In German folk song, according to Pommer, one would find the culture of Central Europe writ small rather than large. The eastern regions of the empire did, indeed, exist, especially because it was in the speech islands of the provinces that one could discover German folk songs in some of their purest forms. It was, after all, Vienna that Pommer regarded as most extensively polluted. When the empire came to its end after World War I, Josef Pommer, the nestor of Austrian folk-music scholarship (see Figure 5.6), took his own life rather than face what he regarded as inevitable consequences for the national folk music of Austria (see the various eulogies in *Das deutsche Volkslied*, volume 21, 1919). Claims that the German language should enjoy a privileged national position in Austrian folk music did not diminish, however; instead, they continued to influence encyclopedic musical projects in Austria into World War II and beyond.

If the rhetoric of Central Europe engendered the encyclopedic culture of fin-de-siècle Austria-Hungary, it loosened its grip on major projects dedicated to collecting and controlling national musics for Austria in the century that followed. Austria found itself in a position of having to reconceive its national culture behind greatly reduced borders, a difficult ideological regrouping indeed after it had for some four cen-

*Figure 5.6. Josef Pommer,*
*nestor of Austrian folk music*
*(courtesy of the Österreichisches*
*Volksliedwerk and Almut Pietsch)*

turies located itself at the center of Mitteleuropa. From an imperial standpoint, Central Europe ceased to exist for Austria after World War I, making it necessary to reconfigure the nation's cultural borders and to rewrite its national music history.

Austria succeeded in repositioning its national history by shifting its rhetoric of Central Europe from the tension between center and periphery to a tension between East and West. The makings of an East-West tension had long contributed to the rhetoric of centrality, with the difference being that the culture of the West had previously dominated that of the East. Cultural rivalries between East and West, especially between Vienna and Budapest, had long determined the ways in which the power structures of one part of the empire were copied from those in the other (see Hanák 1998). The opera house in Vienna, for example, served as a direct model for the opera house in Budapest; the opera houses in the imperial and royal capitals, furthermore, eventually became the models for the opera houses that spread to the Habsburg cities of Eastern Europe, such as L'viv and Czernowitz in Ukraine. East and West mirrored each other, and the competition that this produced spread to all areas of cultural life, even to the migrations of minorities from one part of the empire to the other. The Jews in the former eastern provinces, for example, traveled to Budapest and Vienna in greater numbers than ever, bringing with them the culture of Yiddish-speaking Eastern Europe, which would be both integrated and rejected by the cosmopolitan Jewish communities at the cultural center.

Folk music, popular music, and art music at the center all found themselves fertilized by the diversity from an Eastern Europe that now lay outside the modern political borders. Accordingly, many of the shaping influences of musical modernism came from the East, for example, in the aesthetic vocabulary of musical expressionism or in artistic movements such as the **Blaue Reiter** ("Blue Riders"). The aesthetic vocabulary of cabaret in the metropolises of the former Habsburg Monarchy, too, absorbed the tensions between East and West, and then turned them inside-out, recreating an Austrian national culture on the cabaret stage, at which cosmopolitan audiences would laugh (listen to CD examples 13 and 16). The aesthetics of Austrian modernism that dominated the first half of the twentieth century drew extensively upon the loss of the East and the increasing public challenge to multiculturalism. That challenge found its way to journalism and fictional literature (see, for example, the discussion of Joseph Roth's *Radetzky March* in Chapter 4 and anti-utopian novels such as Hugo Bettauer's *The City without Jews,* a portrayal of a Vienna from which all Jews had been expelled [1922]). The transformation of the operetta stage to accommodate modernist themes and forms was made possible by the nostalgic treatment of the exotic cultures that had formerly occupied the eastern regions of the empire (see Czáky 1996). The operetta stage had traditionally been populated with Eastern European "others," such as Romanian Roma in the *Gypsy Baron* and Balkan Slavs in the *Merry Widow.* But after World War I the European "others" provided stereotypic images that mobilized the nostalgia for the past, for the Central Europe that no longer belonged to Austria (ibid.: 226–263). Severed from the multiculturalism of its former provinces in the East, Austria began to generate a nostalgia for a return to Central Europe, thus filling the cultural void to which modernism was calling attention.

Nostalgia is fashionable in Austria at the beginning of the twenty-first century, and one of its most striking images is the 1877 map of the

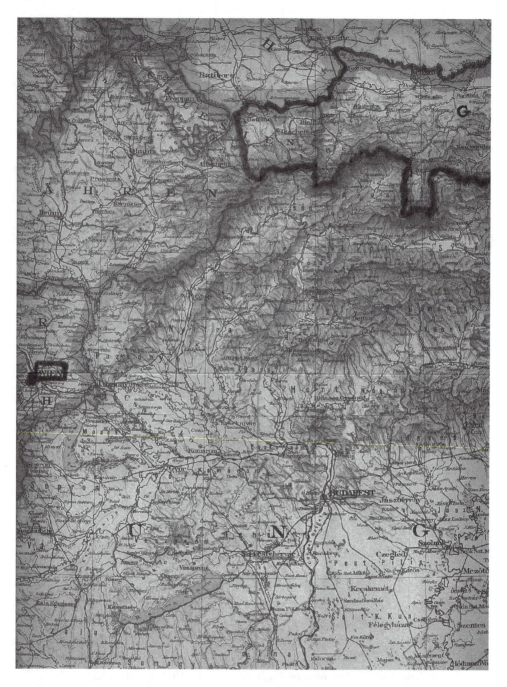

*Figure 5.7.  "Central Europe" as the Austro-Hungarian Empire. Vienna is in the box on the western edge of the map (courtesy of Freytag-Berndt und Artaria K. G.)*

Austro-Hungarian Empire that appears as Figure 5.7. In today's Vienna, one is hard-pressed not to run into this map. It hangs in the windows of bookstores and map shops; it graces the walls of just about any kind of cultural institution devoted to Austrian history, geography, folklore, or folk music; it finds its way into books with many subjects, serving perhaps as the dust cover (e.g., Busek 1997a) or to introduce the series of maps that illustrate the expansion and reduction of the Habsburg Monarchy. Symbolically, Austria employs this 1877 map to retrieve Central Europe from the past and to ponder it again.

In a post–**Velvet Revolution** Europe where East and West have undergone radical reconfiguration, this map poses the question: Does Austria have a chance to reclaim Central Europe? The nostalgia for Central Europe has motivated a remarkable range of musical activities in Austria since 1989. At one extreme is a spate of publishing projects that, like the publication of old maps, connect Central Europe to the Austria of the European Union through historicism. The European music culture in book form that Emperor Franz Joseph I presented to his bride, Elisabeth, on the occasion of their wedding in 1854 has been reprinted (Mraz 1997), replete with all the images of male and female couples from the national cultures of the provinces of Austria and its imperial holdings (see Figure 2.3 and 2.4 in Chapter 2). Complementing the images of national costumes worn by courting couples, the volume includes an extensive section of "Austria's National Melodies," which consist of the "Kaiserhymne" and songs from all regions of Mitteleuropa, many with verses in a regional language and the German-language translations. Even the 1854 edition took considerable pains to account for multiculturalism, for it includes songs from several provinces among "Austria's national melodies." For the region referred to as "Serbia and the Timişoara Banat" (the border area shared by Romania and Serbia, historically a region of extensive multiculturalism), we find at the very end of the volume two songs, both originally Serbian but presented also in a German translation that consciously mixes the cultural borders between the Romanians and the residents of the German speech island of Banat, both of them affording the Empress Elisabeth the chance to mix and match the border region's national character as she paged through the wedding present (see Figure 5.8). The volume, nonetheless, takes an unequivocal stance toward the Central Europe of Austria's past and that of its present: imperial control over multiculturalism. And lest anyone miss that message, the es-

*Figure 5.8. "Austria's National Melody" for "Serbia" and the "Timişoara Banat," German and Serbian texts, in Empress Elisabeth's wedding gift of 1854 (Mraz 1997)*

says that introduce the reprint volume explicitly take "parallels and differences" as their focus (see, e.g., Busek 1997b).

At the turn of the present century, Austria can claim a new rhetoric of Central Europe. It does not so much run parallel to or distinguish itself from the rhetoric of the fin-de-siècle as it seeks to historicize the past. Projects motivated by nostalgia have their scientific components, that is, the participation of historians, musicologists, and folk-music scholars (see, for example, *Musica imperialis* 1998). Similarly, there are scholarly projects that, on one hand, treat sources with utmost concern for their authenticity yet permitting flaws in the fabric that allow for a more cloying nostalgia to penetrate the project. The monument series of Austrian folk music, the *Corpus musicae popularis austriacae* (COMPA), which began appearing in 1993 (see Deutsch 1993), openly fashioned itself after the imperial project "Das Volkslied in Österreich" ("Folk Song in Austria"), launched in 1904 as an encyclopedia that would include canonic repertories collected in all of Austria's regions and in all the provinces in the Empire. Volume by volume, these encyclopedic projects map and remap Austria's presence in Central Europe, in the past and the present. Seen as a whole, their parallels and differences become indistinguishable until past and present blur and until the nation and Central Europe overlap to become one.

### Healing the Fissure through Central Europe— Prospects for a New Europe

*What's left of Central Europe? Countries that follow the ways of the West? West Europeans who stayed behind? The edge of the West? Marginal Europe? Meeting point for the Eastern and the Western? At any rate, the road from West to East leads across Central Europe.*
*—Konrád 1999: 9*

The New Central Europe resonates with the music of its past. Historicism is very serious business and very public business. The revival of music from a period before the Holocaust and the world wars is also relatively new business, which is to say, its importance accompanied many of the other transformations following 1989, the "reunification" of east and west in Germany, and the reconnection of the East and the West by reopening Austria's borders with its neighbors behind the Iron Curtain. In a single gesture, these political acts restored the Central Europe that had been lost through the division of Europe after World War II and through the elimination of much diversity and difference at the center. Not only was there a split through the middle, but there was a cultural vacuum left where once the center had been. Within the few feverish months of the period known as the *Wende* it became vitally important to reimagine Central Europe and to reconstruct it from the dysfunctional political configuration that had replaced it. Given the many ways that music afforded Central Europe its identity, it was hardly surprising that the orchestrators of the *Wende* should turn swiftly and effectively to music as a means not only of retrieving the past but also of suturing the wounds that would need to heal before a New Central Europe could rise phoenix-like from the ashes of twentieth-century European history (cf. von Hallberg 1996 and Ladd 1997).

In the New Central Europe it is impossible not to find Jewish music just about everywhere. No large city dares to ignore the appeal of staging festivals of Jewish music and culture, for they bring political and financial gains, and they publicly announce a city's willingness to engage in *Wiedergutmachung,* or "reparation," with the past. Concert series specialize in Jewish music, and CD labels accommodate every imaginable genre and ensemble. Music publishers do their best to accommodate what are announced as "discoveries" of music by Jewish composers before and during the Holocaust. Initiatives to make Jewish music public come from above and below. Regional and national government officials take on Jewish music as favorite projects, risking little and gaining much by doing so. Recording projects, especially, reveal a proliferation of local initiatives, from the seemingly unchecked spread of folk- and popular-music ensembles willing to perform klezmer music to the establishment of synagogue choruses or community ensembles that muster enough specialists for a representative CD (see Barzilai 1996; *10 Jahre Wiener Jüdischer Chor* 1999; see Chapter 7 below).

Though benefiting from generous coffers in the major metropolitan centers of Germany and Austria, the explosion of Jewish music also finds sufficient public interest and support elsewhere in the New Central Europe. The Jewish quarters of Prague and Budapest are bustling tourist destinations, and public support of Jewish music in both has emphasized that music, too, is one of the draws for the cultural tourism infused by nostalgia. During the mid-1990s there was a major campaign to attract donations for the restoration of the organ in the Dohány Street Synagogue of Budapest, Europe's largest synagogue (Bohlman 2000c). These ghettos and the many synagogues restored as public concert halls during the 1990s provide a network of venues for touring klezmer bands and synagogue choruses alike.

The Jewish music of the New Central Europe fills an absent center. Jewish music cannot replace the communities whose synagogues at-

tract few if any of the remaining Jews for worship. Many Jewish choruses have relatively few Jewish singers; most klezmer bands have no
Jewish instrumentalists. The concert series may play to audiences from
across Central European society, but they do little to integrate even
those Jews living again in the cities. CD manufacturers specializing in
Jewish music most often find their largest markets outside Central Europe, particularly in the United States and other lands to which some
Jews were able to escape before the Holocaust was fully under way (cf.,
e.g., Klotz 1995 and Zemel Choir 1996). The Jewish musicians of the
New Central Europe are keen to make an impact on Israel, but what attention they do win generally takes the form of polite acknowledgment
(cf., e.g., Berke et al. 1996 and Beth Hatefutsoth 1989).

Jewish culture and Jewish music did migrate toward the center of
Europe in the early decades of the twentieth century, reconfiguring
the cosmopolitanism of Central Europe as modernism. The Jewish
populations in the metropolitan centers grew rapidly in the years leading up to World War I, but especially so in the years following the war,
when Eastern Europe was effectively cut off from Central Europe, thus
convincing many Jews in former imperial provinces of the periphery
that the center was now the most attractive political home (see Ladd
1997: 110–115). Even during the politically unstable decades of the interwar Weimar period, the Jewish communities filling the centers of
the metropolis undertook many projects that created new public open-
ings for Jewish music. In the late 1920s, recording projects used modern technologies to represent the music of **Reform Judaism** as a modern, if not modernist, canon (see Beth Hatefutsoth 1997). Even in the
mid- and late 1930s, after the Nazi policy of forcing Jews into the cultural ghettos of the *Jüdischer Kulturbund* implemented another stage of
locating Jewish music at the center, collection, publication, and recording lost little time in representing a Jewish rhetoric of Central European music (see Geisel 1987). Against this historical backdrop of a
Jewish center, the revival of Jewish music since the *Wende* seems all the
more symptomatic of a restoration of an absent center as it connects
the present to the past (cf., CD examples 13 and 16).

The question raised by the prospects of healing upon which the
New Central Europe depends is whether the absent center will now become the surrogate center for the revival of an older nationalism as the
new. The sounds at the center may well help us answer the historical issues implicit in that question, but what about the future of the absent

center? Some answers and even more questions are evident in the cultural space of the ethnographic present with which this chapter began and now closes: street music in the New Central Europe.

## Street Music in the New Central Europe

The street musicians of the New Central Europe read the urban landscapes of the center with remarkable skill. They must compete for the spaces they fill with their music, not just with other musicians who covet the financial advantages of locating themselves near the entrance of a subway or store that attracts the right kind of shoppers-cum-audience; they must also deal with the civil authorities, especially the police, who are uneasy with the ways in which music and musicians disturb the flow of pedestrian traffic at the center of the city. The improvised stages occupied by musicians rarely fit into the original planning that created the new city centers. The pedestrian zones and shopping arcades that now fill the center were, after all, products of a mid-century vision for the future of the Central European city. It called for the modernization of the center, for supplanting the past with an urban architecture that would channel city residents and international tourists to the center again, thus revitalizing those urban areas most devastated by aerial bombing during World War II. Street musicians were not among those the urban architects had hoped or planned to attract. They have taken their places, nonetheless, as some of the most durable monuments to the meaning of the center and the rhetoric of Central Europe.

The music played by the street musicians in Berlin and Vienna—or in Mannheim, Salzburg, Brno, Győr, or Cluj-Napoca, as we follow the path of cultural exchange from West to East—is not the music of the modern nation-state of a reunified Europe; it draws primarily on the music of the historical and cultural peripheries to envoice a more complex nationalism, that symbolized by the absent center. This is a street music that depends on the juxtaposition of time and space that only the urban center provides, but it is a street music that rigorously restrains itself from entering that time and space. Vienna's street musicians perform the folk music of former and current Slavic neighbors; Roma and Andean musicians recirculate a complex mix of foreignness. These are musicians who cross borders—the social borders of the city and the political borders that bound the nation-state. Their ability to perform depends on the ways in which these borders conflict with each other and in which their conflicting displacements constantly skew the relation of the center to the nation itself. Modern shops, with their accompanying display and consumption of goods, depend on globalization and the flow of capital across European Union borders, and those who come to the city center to visit those shops become the audiences for musicians moving musical goods no less globally across European borders.

Whose center do the street musicians occupy? The cultural and historical center of a reunified Germany or an Austria with open borders to the East? The virtual center of a New Europe, forged by urban architects to serve nations struggling for some kind of integration into the European Union? The street musicians surely draw attention to the center of Europe, but they do so by revealing the very ephemeral and transitory nature of the identities forming there, above all, the identities of the nation-states that have in the twenty-first century again taken up the nationalist banner, with which they brandish their competing claims to the very center of Europe.

## REFERENCES

*10 Jahre Wiener Jüdischer Chor: Jiddische, sephardische und hebräische Lieder.* 1999. CSM 9911-F1.

Arnim, Achim von, and Clemens Brentano. 1957 [1806 and 1808]. *Des Knaben Wunderhorn: Alte deutsche Lieder.* Munich: Windler.

Augstein, Rudolf, et al. 1987. *"Historikerstreit": Die Dokumentation der Kontroverse um die Einzigartigkeit der nationalsozialistischen Judenvernichtung.* Munich: Piper.

Barzilai, Shmuel. 1996. *Schir Zion: Kompositionen der Wiener Kantoren.* ORF CD 62.

Berke, Steven C., Elizabeth S. Berke, and the Madrigalchor of the Hochschule für Musik in München. 1996. *Jewish Masterworks of the Synagogue Liturgy: A Concert in Honor of the Re-Establishment of Liberal Judaism in Germany.* Deutsche harmonia mundi 05472 7738 2.

Beth Hatefutsoth. 1989. *Masoret kehillit Danzig* ("The Danzig Tradition"). Beth Hatefutsoth BTR 8901.

Bohlman, Philip V. 1999b. "Ontologies of Music." In Nicholas Cook and Mark Everist, eds., *Rethinking Music,* pp. 19–34. Oxford: Oxford University Press.

_____. 2000c. "To Hear the Voices Still Heard: On Synagogue Restoration in Eastern Europe." In Daphne Berdahl, Matti Bunzl, and Martha Lampland, eds., *Altering States: Ethnographies of Transition in Eastern Europe and the Former Soviet Union,* pp. 40–69. Ann Arbor: University of Michigan Press.

_____. 2002d. "World Music at the 'End of History'." *Ethnomusicology* 46 (1): 1–32.

Böhme, Franz Magnus. 1877. *Altdeutsches Liederbuch: Volkslieder der Deutschen nach Wort und Weise aus dem 12. bis zum 17. Jahrhundert.* Leipzig: Breitkopf und Härtel.

Busek, Erhard. 1997a. *Mitteuropa: Eine Spurensicherung.* Vienna: Kremayr & Scheriau.

_____. 1997b. "Aufbrüche und Aufbruch: Ein Essay über Parallelen und Unterschiede." In Gerda Mraz, ed., *Österreich Ungarn in Lied und Bild,* pp. 9–13. Vienna and Munich: Christian Brandstätter.

Csáky, Moritz. 1996. *Ideologie der Operette und Wiener Moderne: Ein kulturhistorischer Essay zur österreichischen Identität.* Vienna: Böhlau.

Deutsch, Walter. 1993. *Volksmusik in Niederösterreich: St. Pölten und Umgebung.* Vienna: Böhlau.

Doegen, Wilhelm, ed. 1925. *Unter fremden Völkern—Eine neue Völkerkunde.* Berlin: Otto Stollberg, Verlag für Politik und Wirtschaft.

Dor, Milo. 1996. *Mitteleuropa: Mythos oder Wirklichkeit—Auf der Suche nach der größeren Heimat.* Salzburg and Vienna: Otto Müller.

Dumont, Louis. 1994. *German Ideology: From France to Germany and Back.* Chicago: University of Chicago Press.

Erk, Ludwig, with Franz Magnus Böhme. 1893–1894. *Deutscher Liederhort.* 3 vols. Leipzig: Breitkopf und Härtel.

Flacke, Monika. 1998b. "Deutschland: Die Begründung der Nation aus der Krise." In idem, ed., *Mythen der Nationen: Ein europäisches Panorama,* pp. 101–128. Munich and Berlin: Koehler & Amelang.

Geisel, Eike, et al. 1987. *Wegweiser durch das jüdische Berlin: Geschichte und Gegenwart.* Berlin: Nicolai.

Goehr, Lydia. 1992. *The Imaginary Museum of Musical Works: An Essay in the Philosophy of Music.* Oxford: Oxford University Press.

Grimmelshausen, Hans Jakob Christoffel von. 1975 [1669]. *Der abenteuerliche Simplicissimus Teutsch.* Munich: Deutscher Taschenbuch Verlag.

Hanák, Péter. 1998. *The Garden and the Workshop: Essays on the Cultural History of Vienna and Budapest.* Princeton, N.J.: Princeton University Press.

Herder, Johann Gottfried. 1975 [1778–1779]. *"Stimmen der Völker in Liedern"* and *Volkslieder.* 2 vols. published in one. Stuttgart: Reclam.

Holzapfel, Otto. 2001. *Die Germanen: Mythos und Wirklichkeit.* Freiburg im Breisgau: Herder.

————. 2002. *Mündliche Überlieferung und Literaturwissenschaft: Der Mythos von Volkslied und Volksballade*. Münster: Aschendorff.

Idelsohn, A. Z. 1914–1932. *Hebräisch-orientalischer Melodienschatz*. 10 vols. Berlin et al.: Benjamin Harz et al.

Johnson, Lonnie R. 1996. *Central Europe: Enemies, Neighbors, Friends*. New York and Oxford: Oxford University Press.

Kittler, Friedrich A. 1987. *Aufschreibesysteme 1800/1900*. 2d ed. Munich: Wilhelm Fink.

Klein, Bernhard, and Karl August Groos. 1818. *Deutsche Lieder fur Jung und Alt*. Berlin: Realschulbuchhandlung.

Klotz, Helmut, and the Leipziger Synagogalchor. 1995. *Jewish Chants and Songs*. Berlin Classics 0090762 BC.

Konrád, György. 1999. *Die Erweiterung der Mitte Europa und Osteuropa am Ende des 20. Jahrhunderts*. Vienna: Picus.

Ladd, Brian. 1997. *The Ghosts of Berlin: Confronting German History in the Urban Landscape*. Chicago: University of Chicago Press.

*Lagerliederbuch, Das: Lieder, gesungen, gesammelt und geschrieben im Konzentrationslager Sachsenhausen bei Berlin 1942*. 1980 [1942]. Dortmund: Verlag "pläne."

Loos, Helmut, ed. 1997. *Musikgeschichte zwischen Ost- und Westeuropa: Symphonik, Musiksammlungen*. Sankt Augustin: Academia.

Lützler, Paul Michael, ed. 1982. *Europa: Analysen und Visionen der Romantiker*. Frankfurt am Main: Insel Verlag.

Mautner, Konrad. 1910. *Das steyerische Rasplwerk: Vierzeiler, Lieder, und Gasslreime aus Gößl am Grundlsee*. Vienna: Stählein & Lauenstein.

Mraz, Gerda, ed. 1997. *Österreich-Ungarn in Lied und Bild: Ein Hochzeitsgeschenk an Kaiserin Elisabeth 1854*. Vienna: Christian Brandstätter.

*Musica imperialis: 500 Jahre Hofmusikkapelle in Wien, 1498–1998*. Tutzing: Hans Schneider.

Potter, Pamela M. 1998. *Most German of the Arts: Musicology and Society from the Weimar Republic to the End of Hitler's Reich*. New Haven, Conn.: Yale University Press.

Rupp-Eisenreich, Britta, and Justin Stagl, eds. 1995. *Kulturwissenschaft im Vielvölkerstaat: Zur Geschichte der Ethnologie und verwandter Gebiete in Österreich, ca. 1780–1918*. Vienna: Böhlau.

Schmidt, Esther. 2000–2001. "Nationalism and the Creation of Jewish Music: The Politicization of Music and Language in the German-Jewish Press Prior to the Second World War." *Musica Judaica* 15: 1–31.

————. 2003. "From the Ghetto to the Conservatoire: The Professionalisation of Jewish Cantors in the Austro-Hungarian Empire (1826–1918)." Ph.D. dissertation, University of Oxford.

Schönfellinger, Nora, ed. 1999. *"Conrad Mautner, Großes Talent": Ein Wiener*

*Volkskundler aus dem Ausseer Land.* Grundlsee: Kulturelle Arbeitsgemeinschaft Grundlsee.

Schorske, Carl E. 1981. *Fin-de-siècle Vienna: Politics and Culture.* New York: Vintage.

Schünemann, Georg. 1923. *Das Lied der deutschen Kolonisten in Russland.* Munich: Drei Masken Verlag.

———, ed. 1936. *Trompeterfanfaren, Sonaten, und Feldstücke, nach Aufzeichnungen deutscher Hoftrompeter des 16./17. Jahrhunderts.* Cassel: Bärenreiter.

Tibi, Bassam. 2001. *Europa ohne Identität? Leitkultur oder Wertebeliebigkeit.* 2d ed. Munich: Siedler.

von Hallberg, Robert, ed. 1996. *Literary Intellectuals and the Dissolution of the State.* Chicago: University of Chicago Press.

Zemel Choir, The. 1996. *Louis Lewandowski (1821–1894): Choral and Cantorial Works.* Olympia OCD 347.

## Chapter Six

# Europeans without Nations

## *Music at and beyond the Borders of the Nation-State*

*It was hardly worth further discussion that we encountered each other here, in an Albanian mountain village of Calabria in southern Italy, both of us Austrians, albeit one of us from a Danube Swabian refugee family from Voivodina border region of Serbia, the other a real Serb who had grown up in the Hungarian village next door. The people of Europe had always been moving across the continent like this. There was nothing special about it whatsoever.*

*—Gauß 2001: 123*

### At the Borderlands: Burgenland and Its Nationless Traditions

27 June 1989, northern Burgenland. The Hungarian border guards permitted the small fleet of East German travelers to exit Hungary, while moments later the Austrian border guards permitted the same East Germans to enter Austria. The border between East and West had been officially and legally breached. The Old Europe could give way to the New. With the opening of one border, the radical realignment and reorganization of Europe's nation-states was under way.

For most observers the site of the 1989 border crossing could not have been more unlikely. Burgenland is a rural border area, part of Hungary until 1921 and thereafter divided between Austria and Hungary. Hungary would receive the former regional capital, or **Komitat-stadt,** the cosmopolitan city of Sopron, which as Ödenburg (one of the *Burgen,* or "fortress cities," of Burgenland), had fashioned itself after Vienna. The East Germans chose, however, to cross at one of the most remote points along the border, which, for the most part, stretched across one of the most fertile regions of East-Central Europe, the Trans-Danubian Plain. (The Romans called it **Pannonia** when they crossed the border of the Alps and integrated it into the Europe they were attempting to unify through empire.) For the East Germans to reach the Burgenland border crossing, they first had to drive eastward, through Czechoslovakia, Poland, and Hungary, before swinging back toward the West. It was a circuitous route and a seemingly indirect way of reconnecting East and West. The journey that would unleash a radical reformulation of European nationalism, however, was successful beyond anyone's hopes. Not to be overlooked, but in fact very often overlooked, is that crossing at the Burgenland borderlands in neutral Austria could not have provided a more symbolic and efficacious means of dismembering and re-membering a European nationalism predicated on a fissure between East and West.

In June 1989, I was engaged in fieldwork in Burgenland as the momentous events were unfolding. I had come to Burgenland to study the region as one of the most multicultural of all Europe. Historically, Burgenland had attracted ethnic, religious, and racial minorities for centuries, quite intensively throughout the half millennium that records of their settlement were kept. The culture of Burgenland not only tolerates differences but it embraces them, so much so that it is only possible to speak about minorities in a syntax imposed by later conditions of nationalism. The cultural differences that have defined Burgenland's history resulted in large part from the ways it formed geographic borders by opening the space between national cultures in the remote rural region of Pannonia. My own research was—and continues to be until the present—focused on the music of Burgenland's Jewish communities, especially the **Sheva Kehillot,** or "Seven Holy Communities," the most intensive settlements of Jews in rural East-Central Europe from the Middle Ages to the Holocaust (see, e.g., Bohlman 1997). It is impossible to study Burgenland's Jews without also studying other ethnic groups; it was my research into Jewish music that led me to begin work on Burgenland Roma, who combined musical forces with the Jews on many occasions, especially those in public spaces—at festivals, in taverns, and at dances. Most crucially, Jewish and Rom music in Burgenland, though they were distinctive, often combined to constitute the same history.

The music of other ethnic and religious groups also constituted that history. Many areas of what is today Austrian Burgenland contain villages or areas in which Hungarian is spoken, and likewise German enjoys wide currency in the villages of Hungarian Burgenland. Many villages and small cities have two (or more) names. Even the current provincial capital, Eisenstadt, bore the names "Kiss-Marton" (Hungarian) and "Asch" (Hebrew). Into this multicultural mix it is necessary to introduce the substantial and important Burgenland population of Croatians and Protestant Saxon Germans, who on religious and musical grounds differ from German-speaking Austrians elsewhere in overwhelmingly Catholic Austria. With the Burgenland Hungarians, Croatians, and Protestants it is also not appropriate to parse groups into minority and majority categories, for Hungarian and Croatian are official languages in Burgenland, and there is fairly generous funding available for the support of activities that further the cultural distinctiveness of these groups. From any national perspective Burgenland is multicultural, and its history has persistently configured multiculturalism to define a border culture that figuratively, if not politically, occupies a landscape between national borders (cf. Ernst 1987; Baumgartner, Müllner, and Münz 1989; Hemetek 2001; and CD example 14).

The music of Burgenland could not be a better reflection of the multiculturalism of a border culture. It includes many repertories of folk music, defined by ethnic and religious differences but mixed and remixed because of the extensive musical exchange between cultural groups. Although Burgenland is remote and rural, the contact between ethnic and religious groups is extensive, and the diverse repertories of the region are distinctive because of their cosmopolitan character (see, e.g., CDs Bruji, *Burgenländische Volksmusik 1991;* Heanzenquartett 1996; and Gmasz, Haid, and Pietsch 1993). Preservation, revival, and hybridization thrive and are woven into the fabric of active and public support of Burgenland music (cf. Dreo, Burian, and Gmasz 1988; Dreo and Gmasz 1997). The distinctiveness of Burgenland music is not lost upon public policy makers beyond Burgenland's borders, and it is hardly surprising that European Union–sponsored musical festivals take place on both sides of Burgenland's border, which Austria shares not only with Hungary but also with Slovakia and Slovenia (CD example 15).

The European music history engendered by Burgenland reflects its own multicultural character, and it does so by extending across and leveling national borders. The careers of composers from Burgenland move between one nation and another, and more often than not are enriched by a cosmopolitanism that defies nationalism. Franz Joseph Haydn (1732–1809) becomes Austrian, though he was a composer at the Hungarian court in Burgenland. Franz Liszt (1911–1886) is regarded as Hungarian when he has any national label at all, though he was born in Raiding on the Austrian side of the border (Hooker 2002). Carl Goldmark (1830–1915), the son of a Jewish cantor in one of the Seven Holy Cities, might be Austrian, Hungarian, or Jewish, depending on the context in which his music is performed. Interpreted as a collective history of musicians and composers in the European mainstream, Burgenland's music history is notable for the very ways national labels and boundaries are negated.

The question of musical nationalism's absence strikes even deeper into the very heart of Burgenland's role as a cultural landscape between and beyond national boundaries. The reader will remember, for instance, the history of perhaps the most nationalist of all European songs, the "Deutschlandlied" (see Chapter 2), which began as a Croatian folk song that Haydn set as a movement of a string quartet, the first stage on its route to becoming the Austrian and then the German national anthem (listen to CD examples 33 and 34). The nationalist history of the "Deutschlandlied" is inseparable from the nationless multiculturalism of Burgenland. The first book-length study of European musical cosmopolitanism, Franz Liszt's *The Gipsy in Music* (1859), issued from the pen of a Burgenlander. Considered together, the "Deutschlandlied" and *The Gipsy in Music* contrast in the ways they heightened and denied nationalism. Most significantly, they demonstrate the ways in which nationalism in music issues from regions that are multicultural, where cultural and music history follow paths that are nationless.

Throughout its history Burgenland has gathered Europe's borders, minorities, and peripheries into a concentrated region and musical landscape, and that history helps to account for the complex reasons that it was chosen as the border region that would be breached in summer 1989. Those complex reasons also explain why its music history juxtaposes differences so extensively that we begin to understand its nationless parameters. As a region whose music history is often nationless, however, Burgenland is neither unique nor isolated in Europe. There are many other regions, many of them forming borderlands of their own, that lie outside the history of European nationalism, or at least defy that history, successfully or unsuccessfully.

It is to the music of the nationless peoples who live in these borderlands that we turn in the present chapter. Many of these peoples and

areas form old and contested European borderlands, such as those of
the Carpathian Mountains, the Balkans, or the coastal peripheries of
the West and the North. Other nationless peoples never gained a national foothold in Europe but moved across national borders throughout their histories. As we examine the regions in which nationless peoples live or through which they have passed, we also trace the
alternative historical paths articulated by their music, which are no less
political and crucial to the history of European nationalism if indeed
they lie beyond the borders fixed by those with the political power and
nationalist motivation to do so.

## Music and the Imagination of Europe's Others

> From the depths of their graves
> Our noble fathers called out:
> A heavy curse falls on all
> Who no longer speak our mother tongue.
> He who loses his own language
> Will be chased by a firestorm.
> —*The unofficial national anthem of the Aromyn*
> (*Gauß 2001: 206*)

Few who read this book will ever have heard of the Aromunians, who
call themselves the Aromyn in their dialect of Romanian; fewer still will
have heard the Aromunians' national anthem. More of the book's readers, perhaps, will have heard of Burgenland, though it is still very proba-
ble that for many readers the excursion with which I opened this chapter was their first encounter; it is unlikely that any readers remembered
the place where the Iron Curtain was first breached in summer 1989. It
is not particularly difficult to make lists of nationless peoples in Europe
that most of us would not recognize. We might focus on the geographical center of Europe, for example, an area in the Carpathian Mountains
just on the Slovak side of the border between Slovakia and Ukraine, an
area that also serves as the epicenter for the Rusyn people, who, like the
Aromunians, have a language, history, and music of their own, but
never had a nation of their own (see Metil 2000). The list of Europe's
nationless people would also contain the Huzuls (neighbors of the
Rusyns), the Arbëreshë of southern Italy, the Sorbs of Germany, the

Kashubians of Poland, and the Saami of circumpolar Scandinavia and Russia (listen, e.g., to the Arbëreshë songs on CD examples 31 and 32).

Though these peoples may be relatively unknown to us at the beginning of the twenty-first century, there are other nationless peoples whose names and history are more familiar—the Jews and the Roma, for example, whom I examine in greater detail in this chapter. What we may not know, however, is that the reasons that Jews and Roma were historically forced into a nationless status are related to the reasons that Europeans continue to use nationalism to impose a nationless status on many Europeans today. Remarkably, we still only occasionally know the names of these peoples, and all too often we take notice of them, for example, of Chechnyans, only when the borders of nationlessness itself have been breached.

Lest any reader worry that I am taking the moral high road, I must confess that I had never heard of the Aromunians until I began the final stages of researching the present chapter. My own failure to take note of them and the very fact that they fail to be worthy of even a brief reference or a footnote in the standard literature on the Balkans and Balkan nationalism are symptomatic of the plight of Europe's nationless peoples (see, e.g., Glenny 1999 and Mazower 2000). The music of the Aromunians, even a few token examples, appears on no anthology of Balkan music. The Aromunians live today largely in Macedonia and in diaspora. There is no census to account for the numbers of Aromunians, either at the Macedonian center or at the global periphery, but even the most generous estimates suggest that there might be as many as 100,000 Aromunians in Skopje, the capital of Macedonia. The cultural events designed to mark moments of special "national" meaning for the Aromunians, however, rarely attract more than a few hundred souls (Gauß 2001: 197).

### The Aromunians

The culture brokers of the Aromunians—the historians, folklorists, linguists, and political activists—have generated an extensive historical narrative that is remarkable for its consistent portrayal of the Aromunians as one of the oldest—if not the oldest—national cultures in Europe. The narrative begins at least with Alexander the Great, who was, according to Aromunian myth and history, Aromunian. The national narrative is one of survival, not only of retaining cultural integrity and a national language from Ancient Greece through the Roman, Byzantine, and Ottoman Empires, but also of sustaining self-identity against the fragmentation of virtually ceaseless war in the Balkans. The Aromunians have survived by achieving what some other Balkan peoples and nations could not. They negotiated trade between enemies, they managed the exchange of goods between Europe and the Middle East, and they moved across religious and national boundaries that thwarted many others, except for other nationless peoples of the Balkans, such as the Sephardic Jews of Bosnia-Herzegovina. Ironically, Aromunian culture was distinctive also because it knew no national borders. That special role would effectively condemn Aromunians to the status of a people without a nation.

The Aromunian nation takes shape, if always transiently, through performance, and music is always a crucial component of that performance. The Aromunians organize their communities through an extensive network of social and cultural organizations. Political events alternate speeches, with their consistent call for holding on to cultural identity, with performances of youthful dance troupes and young singers. The ensembles themselves symbolize the vitality of the national collective. Considerable investment goes into keeping such performing ensembles alive, not only by endowing the groups with richly ornamented costumes and the instrumental ensembles and choreographic expertise to ensure semiprofessionalism, but also by organizing a seemingly nonstop calendar of competitions and social events throughout Macedonia and the neighboring Balkan nations. The music and dance themselves are distinctive not because of their authenticity—in other words, the ways they are distinct from Albanian, Macedonian, or Greek styles and genres—but because of their malleability, that is, their capacity to absorb neighboring ethnic and national styles, and popular, rock, and **turbo-folk** styles and to make them Aromunian. Contemporary musical performance continues to display the very cosmopolitanism that has formed the historical core of Aromunian identity (Gauß 2001: 185–230).

The places where Europe's nationless peoples meet, where their histories unfold, and where they perform their own musics to create their own identities are strangely anonymous. We do not know the names of the places where they live, we do not know the names of the people who inhabit them, and we do not hear the songs they sing about themselves and their histories. In the discourse of European nationalism, nationless peoples are often invisible and inaudible. Their presence is noticeable because of the silence imposed upon it.

## Displacement and the Identities of Europe's Nationless Peoples

If the place of Europe's nationless peoples is not the nation, then where is it? Is the absence of nation simply a non-experience? Does it encumber the processes of ascribing and expressing identity, or might there be something common, something commonly European, that nationless peoples share? To answer these questions I should like briefly to discuss the concept of **displacement,** for which I draw, on one hand, from theories of African American history and African diaspora (cf. Du Bois 1903 and Gilroy 1993) and, on the other, from more recent attempts to interpret geography and identity as extensions of history and memory (cf. Bammer 1994, Lavie and Swedenburg 1996, and Sebald 2001). Displacement allows individuals and communities to express their connection to a particular place even when they are not residents of the places from which they draw their identity. In one of the most fundamental ways of understanding the concept, displacement characterizes **diaspora,** in which a people interprets its history as a journey that has the potential of leading them back to a homeland they have not been able to occupy, usually because they were violently expelled or because survival in the homeland was no longer possible for various reasons. Diaspora represents a certain type of historical journey, in which the point of departure in the past and return in the present are not usually the same. As the categories that I examine below reveal, however, displacement can assume many different forms, which in turn bear witness to many different forms of nationalism. Displacement, therefore, serves as a corollary to nationalism, providing an alternative, an escape, and even a means of survival when nationalism closes its borders and internal spaces to those without a nation.

The many distinctive forms we examine below notwithstanding, displacement is a condition experienced by all of Europe's nationless peoples. The forms of displacement, moreover, have multiplied to parallel the spread of nationalism, thus making it appropriate to claim that displacement is also a condition of modernity and its shaping of post-Enlightenment Europe. Whereas nationalism arises from notions of fix-

[Guest workers] are the downtrodden in society,
They are society's scapegoats during crisis,
While the real problem, the one totally ignored,
Will be swept under the carpet without notice.
Not recognized, foreign in one's own country,
Not a foreigner, and yet a stranger.
— *"Fremd im eignen Land"/"Foreign in One's Own Land,"*
   *The black German hip-hop group Advanced Chemistry*

Xenophobia's on the rise,
Victims get dehumanized,
Procedures standardized
As the land's Germanized.
Names become numbers
While death is trivialized.
— *"Adriano [letzte Warnung]"/"Adriano [Last Warning],"*
   *The black German hip-hop group Brother's Keeper*

I've travelled, travelled long roads
Meeting with happy Roma.
Roma, where have you come from
With tents on fortune's road?
Roma, oh fellow Roma.
Once I had a great family.
The Black Legion murdered them.
Come with me, all the world's Roma,
For the Romani roads have opened.
Now's the time, rise up Roma,
We shall now rise high.
Roma, oh fellow Roma.
   *—Jarko Jovanović, "Djelem, Djelem,"*
*unofficial Roma anthem from the 1970s; Broughton 1999: 147;*
   *Hemetek 2001: CD 1, tr. 1*

ity and ownership—the very geography and history that belong to the nation—nationlessness results from the inability to claim land as one's own. The nationless group is thought, both correctly and incorrectly, to be forever in motion, to be wanderers. In contrast to common assumptions, however, displaced groups may fail to settle for long periods of time or to claim land as their own because they are legally prohibited from doing so. Jews, for example, could not purchase land as their own in most areas of Europe until the mid-nineteenth century. In the popular imagination there are positive and negative conditions associated with displacement, ranging from romantic portrayals of a culture untrammeled by the burden of living in the limited spaces of modernity to the stigmas placed on refugees and the dispossessed.

Europe is also notable for the ways its historical narratives have been responsible for creating nationless peoples. Racism and ethnic prejudice have prevented Jews, Roma, and other minorities from being able to have their own state or from receiving protection from any state. The new nationalisms reimagined from the old, for example in Serbia, Albania, and Macedonia, also rely on history as a justification for placing geographical restrictions on peoples without lands of their own. Like its counterpart, nationalism, displacement has the power to generate memory and history, and in this sense, because it forms a counterhistory to nationalism, displacement has powerful historical dimensions that are distinctively European.

Many are denied a place in European history because they do not fit in the nation and its history, perhaps because they speak the wrong language (or fail to speak the right one in a certain way), or because they are marked as racial "others." Displaced peoples often bear their history with them, in the stories and songs they employ to express selfness and, above all, in the music that allows them both to transmit their narratives of selfness and perform these as expressions of group identity (cf. Narayan 1996). The music of nationless peoples is well suited to the processes of displacement. Music that maps history as change and adaptation, an expression of the individual and the collective body, rather than as repertory rooted in the soil, is the music that distinguishes Europe's nationless people. It is perhaps for this reason that the nationless people of Europe have been recognized publicly as peoples whose cultures are marked by music—Roma and Jews, Travellers in the United Kingdom and Ireland, and minorities of all kinds. Nationless peoples are singled out as if their specialties in music were the fragments of the nation they were allowed to occupy, enough to sustain the journey of displacement but insufficient to make any nation their own.

What are the conditions that produce nationless peoples? In the paragraphs that follow I sketch the most important conditions of displacement. It will be clear from the outset that these conditions not only differ one from another but that, in part because of their differences, they overlap. The conditions not only act as causes for displacement, but they also provide contexts for the ways in which nationless peoples respond to displacement. They are conditions that produce active processes; as such they rely on human responses to set them in motion. In modern Europe, music provides some of the most important and effective means of mobilizing displacement as a response to nationalism.

*Space and Lack Thereof*
Throughout European history, displacement has resulted when certain groups of people have been denied the ability to occupy and own land. With the emergence of the nation-state after the **Enlightenment,** ownership of property became particularly important because of the ways it establishes legal relations with the state, thus drawing the citizen into the nation's sphere. Those owning land have legal obligations to the state, and the nation relies on them to expand its own control over the lands within and, in times of military expansion, outside its borders. Just as there are musical repertories that connect people to the land locally, regionally, and nationally, there are also those that reflect the mobility of displaced peoples. The folk-song repertoires of the Sephardic Jews of the Balkans, for example narrative **romancero,** contain references to the lands in southeastern Europe where the singers are living or have lived, but they also contain the linguistic and stylistic structure of Andalusia in southwestern Europe. Saami and Traveller repertories express the seasonal movement of the groups who cultivate them. For those lacking land of their own, music ascribes identity by not depending on the institutions and processes of collection and inscription that turn music itself into national property.

*Occupying Cultural and National Borderlands*
The music of many nationless peoples in Europe reflects the necessity of negotiating borderlands. Displacement, therefore, becomes a process of juxtaposing diverse styles, repertories, functions, and languages. Music becomes nationless by opening cultural domains between the nations that exclude those who occupy no other place. Several border regions of Europe are notable for the ways in which repertories expand because of the capacity to absorb the music of the displaced peoples living in those regions. It is almost futile to divide into national styles the folk-music repertoires along the arch of the **Carpathian Mountains** that stretches from western Slovakia along the

borders of Poland, Ukraine, and Romania before terminating in central Romania. The national borders that run along the Carpathians do little to prevent extensive ethnic mixture and the generation of hybrid styles, for example, in the Rusyn repertories that span and ignore the border between Slovakia and Ukraine (Metil 2000). As a border region and a national crossroads at the center of Europe, the Carpathians have nurtured musicians whose repertories are enriched from the contributions of fellow travelers. Roma and Jewish repertories in the Carpathians not only overlap at times, but even form variants that result from folk-song texts with several languages (see especially Krekovičová 1998).

*Religion*
The fear and rejection of religious difference is one of the most widespread conditions of displacement. Civic and national geographies reflect the centrality of a dominant religion—in Europe, Christianity in its several historical and denominational forms. Prior to the modern era, those who did not adhere to the dominant religion had little access to public positions, which usually led to their displacement from the center of power. Jews in medieval and early modern Burgenland, which we visited at the beginning of this chapter, were forced into small villages at some distance from Ödenburg/Sopron, the center of political and religious power, not in small measure because it contained a cathedral. In modern Europe—indeed, in post-Holocaust Europe at the beginning of the twenty-first century—religion remains one of the primary reasons for denying national status to groups and communities, especially in the Balkans, where religious nationalism is inseparable from ethnic nationalism, and where Muslim peoples such as the Kosovars and many Bosnians have engaged in long struggles to resolve the religious conditions of their national displacement. The European fear of Islam—be it in the Balkans, the Central European nations so dependent on Turkish guest workers, or the United Kingdom with growing post-colonial populations of Muslim South Asians—remains one of the primary causes for displacement in Europe.

*Race*
Prior to the Holocaust, the displacement of Europe's nationless peoples almost always had racial dimensions. The ghettoization and genocide of the Holocaust were themselves forms of displacement for entire peoples. Jews and Roma, in particular, were thought to be anath-

ema to racial nationalism with its emphasis on *Blut und Boden* and were deprived of the spaces in which they lived, assembled in concentration camps, and murdered. The vocabulary of race permeated the songs Europeans sang about its nationless peoples, for example, the English-language ballad repertories in which Roma were always dark-skinned and Jews always lived outside of society, thus exaggerating the danger they presumably posed. In the nationalisms taking shape in the wake of the Holocaust, race has asserted itself in ways that are sometimes oblique, at other times direct. Some social scientific literature, for example, has tended to claim that difference in Europe, unlike that in the United States, is ethnic and not racial, though more recently the racial dimensions of ethnicity have been undeniable (see, e.g., Gilroy 1993 and Stokes 1994). The recognition, moreover, that "ethnic cleansing" in Southeastern Europe was at base racially motivated has intensified concern about the persistence of race as a condition for displacement in Europe today.

*Historical Myths*
In the myths that define European nations, place has historically also narrated a geography of displacement. Ironically, those groups who occupy mythical geographies of displacement are given place by being denied place. One of the persistent myths, disseminated in countless variants throughout Europe, is that of the "Wandering Jew," who, having failed to save Christ on his way to the crucifixion, is condemned to an eternity in which it is impossible to live in any single place (see Anderson 1966, and Dundes and Hasan-Rokem 1986). The wandering Jew, who may bear the name Ahasver, from the biblical story of Purim, appears in both Jewish and non-Jewish myth, anti-Semitic and allegorical genres, always in search of a means of ending his journeys. In Early Modern ballads, the wandering Jew often enters a story only to be accused of some heinous deed, which quickly necessitates that he flee and continue the mythical journey. Displacement assumes different forms when the wandering Jew enters Jewish morality plays, for example the morality plays so magically transformed by the single decade of the 1930s during which Yiddish film musicals in which the biblical and modern myths are conflated (e.g., the 1937 *Der Purimshpiler* ["The Purim Actor"]) flourished in Poland.

Wandering as a condition of displacement is also the most persistent myth assigned to Europe's Roma and their music. So persistent is the myth, that historical facts about the centuries-long residence of Roma in many areas, such as Burgenland, are virtually unknown. The journey of European Roma has, instead, become the central theme in many of their own musical repertories and in the ways an entire constellation of European myths represents their placelessness. Travellers' songs, even when not transmitted among Roma, locate the Roma of the British Isles in a world of constant movement. Documentary and popular films about Roma, including the very successful *Latcho drom,* follow Rom musicians across a landscape of ceaseless displacement, from Rajasthan to Spain, clearly suggesting that Europe would never truly yield a place, much less a nation, to its Roma residents (cf. *Latcho drom* 1993, and listen to CD examples 9 and 10).

*Non-Europeanness and Foreignness*
Throughout European history, those regarded as non-European have been denied place. The displacement generated by foreignness has deep historical roots, so deep, in fact, that they were firmly implanted long before the rise of the nation-state and modern nationalism. Even until the present, the legal restrictions placed on Europe's foreigners have extended primarily to the denial of place. Turkish guest workers in Germany and Algerian laborers in France are pushed to the extremes of the industrial landscape, where they struggle, usually in vain, to acquire the legal status of a citizen, which would make it possible for them to cast off the stigma of foreignness. Struggles over the building of mosques or the transformation of existing buildings into mosques rage in hundreds of large and small German cities, often focusing on the ways in which the foreigner's music, the call-to-prayer or **adhān,** would fill and thus take over the urban spaces of Germany. The most pervasive mark of foreignness is that of Asian origins, however long a family's ancestors may have lived in Europe. Modern attempts to displace Europe's Jews, Roma, Muslims, and even Saami, therefore, construct models of non-Europeanness based on myths of land and culture being taken from Europeans by historical foreigners who had left their own land and culture, those of Asia. The race sciences appropriated by European scholarship, not least the musicology, ethnomusicology, and folk-music scholarship of Germany and Austria during the 1930s and 1940s, were quick to seize on the putative traces of Asianness in the music of those groups they wished to racialize as foreign and thus incapable of occupying space in the European nation. Music

that confirmed foreignness, therefore, also confirmed placelessness (see Potter 1998; Bohlman 2000b; Longinović 2000).

*History*

In the history of Western music place is explicit. Place gives geographical meaning to the musical canons that constitute European history. The earliest music to enter the canon, that of Greek Antiquity, did so with place affixed to the names of its modes. Music enters the Middle Ages through monasteries, cathedrals, and courts, to which power and centrality accrue as European history moves through the Early Modern era and toward the Enlightenment. By the late eighteenth and nineteenth century, the place of music is virtually inseparable from the nation and the political and cultural centers that give the nation power. The music of nationless peoples rarely finds only grudging place in European history. Europe's cathedrals and courts, its urban centers and institutions of public music-making were traditionally inhospitable to the displaced. When the nationless are given place in European history, it is often because musicians have found their way beyond their own cultures and communities. The Early Modern Italian composer Salamone Rossi (ca. 1570–ca. 1628) has been one of the rare Jewish composers to find a place in European music history, partly because his fame was secured by active presence at the Gonzaga court of Mantua (Harrán 1999). His compositions for the Jewish ghetto of Mantua survive in vastly fewer numbers than his non-Jewish works. When pogroms forced Rossi to retreat into the ghetto in the 1620s, he disappeared from history without a trace, even though he was one of the finest composers of his age.

In the nineteenth century, folk music found its way into European history almost entirely as national music. Folk-music collectors and arrangers contributed to the building of national musics by identifying national traditions, not by concerning themselves with the musics of ethnic minorities. The folk musics of nationless peoples were present, but in places where they offered little to the culture and power brokers in the metropolis, places where scholars did not go to listen. The writers of music history argue with amazing frequency that the music of placeless people simply does not belong to their history, which means that their history does not include music from urban ghettos, the suburban industrial zones where guest workers establish their traditions, or the border cultures where national traditions overlap, generating a sense of place in history to which no one bears witness. Ultimately, it might disrupt European music to open its places to the music of, say, concentration camps in the twentieth century or **subaltern** groups engaged in resistance in the twenty-first century.

*Language*

Nationless peoples hold on to their languages with extreme tenacity. They take pains to retain it as a vernacular, keeping it alive in oral tradition. They foster literary practices and forms of print culture that formalize it through inscription, keeping it alive in written tradition. And they sing in it. They sing old songs, and they compose new songs; they cultivate religious songs that sacralize the language, and they encourage social practices in which popular song secularizes the language. In the culture of displacement, song anchors language to the places remembered and monumentalized in the music of nationless people.

Linguists and scholars have long recognized that song has powerful mnemonic functions. Displaced peoples of various kinds continue to sing in a language long after its currency as a spoken language has diminished. The Albanian-speaking Arbëreshë of southern Italy, for example, continue to speak Albanian, albeit a form that is at once archaic and classicized, after almost five and one-half centuries of displacement from Albania, during most of which, the centuries of Ottoman rule in Albania, there was relatively little contact between the Arbëreshë and Albania (Gauß 2001: 97–142, and listen to CD examples 31 and 32).

What linguists have documented statistically is often common sense for Europe's nationless peoples. Particularly in those areas where the pressure to assimilate into a regional or national culture is unusually strong, such as in the German speech islands of Eastern Europe or in the Gaelic-speaking areas of Europe's Celtic Fringe, considerable effort is invested in creating and maintaining schools and cultural institutions that support language retention. Festivals and competitions of Celtic choral groups from Europe's Atlantic littoral—one would have to say "Gaelic-singing" not "Gaelic-speaking" groups—combine their insistence on Gaelic repertories with special workshops, or schools attached to festivals, in which language is taught (Chapman 1994). Language provides a place for the displaced, not only through survival and retention. Revival and the invention of new musical traditions to reimagine the linguistic continuity between past and present are common, all the more so as modern aspirations toward achieving a nation-state become more pressing.

*Body of National Discourse*

To elevate a language to the status and functions of a national discourse—the language shared by a national collective and polity—requires considerable effort and the investment in institutional resources. Literature, poetry, and folk song, published and disseminated so that they can be shared by all, serve as only the foundations for the national imaginary of displaced peoples. Museums, dictionaries, and song anthologies lend added strength to the superstructure; schools, music academies, and even universities buttress the edifice of national discourse. The sustenance of a national discourse requires a number of distinctive steps. Publication of a dictionary, for example, requires teams of specialists who distill discrete meanings from words circulating in oral traditions and map the place of the displaced by discerning as many meaningful variants as possible (see Heinschink 1994 for a discussion of Rom languages and dictionaries).

A song anthology, too, is possible only because of the chain of musicians, collectors, and editors that stretches from the cultural core to the virtual metropolis of the nationless people. Songs pass along this human chain, alternatively moving between oral and written traditions, and strengthening the links in the national discourse through the process of transmission itself (see Holzapfel 2002). The Russian Jewish collectors Shaul Ginsburg and Pesach Marek instituted this type of human chain of transmission at the turn of the twentieth century, gathering the most significant anthology of Yiddish songs prior to World War I (Ginsburg and Marek 1901) and making them available to St. Petersburg School of Jewish Music for transformation into compositions that would ensure the survival of Yiddish in Russia, if even in museumized repertories of chamber music and operetta (cf. Zemtsovsky 2000, and *The St. Petersburg School* 1998). The paradox of creating a national discourse lies in the very ways it relies on—and often generates—processes of displacement, whereby music is removed from folk practices and relocated in art or sacred practices, thus elevating the nation but also straining the very sinews that connect it to some of its most vital sources.

*National Genres of Music*

Europe's nationless peoples never want for musical genres they can claim as their own. Alsatian choruses sing from modern editions of Alsatian music, the editors of which turn to earlier publications and collections, such as Rohr (n.d.). Book and music shops in Bolzano, the largest city in the Tyrolean part of northern Italy, offer the people of the historical region of Südtirol a vast array of popular and scholarly folk-music anthologies, historical reprints of sacred song, and recent CD-releases of German-language **Schlager** by local bands (see, e.g., Sulz et al. 1986). Corsican and Catalan repertories are well documented and available in modern editions. Yiddish songs and klezmer recordings have found their ways into collections of all genres and formats throughout the second half of the twentieth century, engendering what have been called "revivals."

Does music afford place to the displaced? Does it provide a surrogate nation for the nationless? To answer in the affirmative would surely be to impute to music a power that it does not have. Its power to create boundaries for the landscapes occupied by Europe's nationless does not function in such ways. Genres of national music create alternative repertories for the nationless, but they do not create alternative realities or alternative nation-states. Instead, they call attention to the conditions of displacement, marking them and even accentuating them, and therein lies a peculiar if also particular power. It is the power that transforms music into one of the most complex and widespread ways of understanding how Europe's nationless peoples perceive their own nationalism.

## European Peoples before the Nation-State

*I was forced to stick my fingers in my ears. It's unbelievable but true that the nomadic Saami do not have any concept of harmony whatsoever, and that they are completely incapable of enjoying music in the same ways nature has endowed other peoples and nations.*
  *—Giuseppe Acerbi, "On Yoiking" [1798] (Schneider 1999: 148)*

When Europeans first encountered the culture of the **Saami,** one of Europe's own indigenous peoples who inhabit the circumpolar region stretching across the northern coast of Scandinavia into Russia, they marveled at Saami music.

**Yoiking,** a vocal style halfway between speaking and singing, but making very spare use of words, was and is the cultural sign of the Saami (formerly called Laplanders), but it is a sign that defies easy classification, meaning, and identity. Although some styles do include words, yoiking presents Europeans with a sign of a music empty of verbal signification; yoiking is the sign of a European music without an historically signifying narrative; yoiking predates history, radically so, in fact, for it has not even acquired the epic narrative qualities of other Scandinavian styles and traditions, such as the Finnish **Kalevala,** the literary and musical product of Finland's emerging nationalism in the nineteenth century. So distinctive is yoiking in the absence of its verbal, narrative, and historical significance that even modern ethnomusicologists vary widely in the interpretive approaches they employ—from melodic analysis to sacred semiotics—to explain what yoiking means (cf. Ling 1997 and Arnberg et al. 1969).

Yoiking does have meaning, but it comes to meaning in ways that have remained different for centuries from those that served to integrate the musics of Europe into European historical narratives. Above all, the meaning of yoiking depends on historical, cultural, and religious traditions among the Saami; these traditions depend upon a way of life that denies and defies European nationalism. The economic mainstay of the Saami is reindeer-herding and the related mobility necessary to respond to the changing seasons of Scandinavia's northern coasts. In the course of the year, Saami herders move their reindeer across vast spaces and, accordingly, across national borders. Family members move to different degrees, with entire families likely to be mobile in the summer months and relatively sedentary during the winter months. During many months of the year men are actively involved in herding, and women remain in settlements to care for the extended family. Saami expressive culture relates closely to the demands placed on families and communities by reindeer herding. The repertories of men and women reflect gender differences. Men use yoiking while moving their herds, and some repertories acquire significance because of the ways in which it facilitates communication with animals, especially dogs assisting in the herding. Women's repertories express much about the life of the Saami family north of the Arctic Circle. Significantly, yoiking has felt the musical influences of the various Scandinavian and Russian cultures with which the Saami have interacted for centuries. Accordingly, we witness a paradox at several different levels. Yoiking is not isolated, and its stylistic diversity provides evidence for change over time, despite the usual predilection of scholars to make claims for lack of change and extraordinary stylistic stasis. Yoiking, too, is European music, just as the Saami are an indigenous people within Europe. At many levels, the Saami are remarkable because they have adapted to the European nation-state and nationalism by not adapting to it.

The history of Europe as the First World has created little space for indigenous peoples. There were Europeans before there was Europe, but their presence has complicated many narratives of European history, especially those that depend on the telos, the movement, that is, toward a political structure resting on the foundations of the nation-state. Just who are the indigenous peoples of Europe? If one uses standard definitions of indigenous peoples, they are those whose cultures occupied a particular land before encounter, often before they were forcibly displaced through colonialism. Whereas it is not customary to describe European history as a process of colonial expansion, settlement, and displacement, a recognition of indigenous peoples might well arise from a counterhistory of colonialism that is not so different from post-colonial histories spawned by the Age of Discovery that began in the fifteenth century. During the spread of the Roman Empire, many European peoples, for example, those north of the Alps and the Danube River, pushed to the continent's peripheries. Others survived in areas that were relatively inaccessible, particularly in mountainous or heavily forested regions. The identity of indigenous peoples rarely went unchallenged by the major cultural changes and political realignments that mark European history. The spread of Christianity, for example, had the power to neutralize much of the distinctiveness of indigenous peoples. The internal expansion of European empires—the Austro-Hungarian, the German, the Russian, and the Ottoman—also became significant threats to indigenous peoples.

Hardly surprising, the greatest threat of all to indigenous peoples has been nationalism, which makes no place for indigenous peoples. Nationalism is accompanied by attempts to write indigenous peoples into national histories. We recognize this in the ways indigenous peoples lose the power embedded in bearing their own names: The Saami, for example, were called Laplanders for centuries, and as such they were made more European as residents of a place called Lapland. Naming and classifying have fueled a long tradition of erasing the differences demonstrated by indigenous peoples of various kinds. By and large, the cultures that occupied places in Europe prior to the European nation-state are unknown to most of us, even in an era when the European Union attempts to restore regionalism and establish new criteria of minority and ethnic status. Although they have been residents of specific regions for centuries, the Huzul people of the Carpathians, the Aromunian people of the southern Balkans, the Sorbs of eastern Germany, and the Kashubians of northern Poland have virtually no presence in the cultural histories of the modern nation-state. The Basques, the Rusyns, and the Galicians may have a greater presence— though perhaps also not—in our modern historical consciousness, and perhaps this is because their status as indigenous or simply nationless may be more difficult to establish. Indeed, these various types of nationless peoples are prime examples of what Karl-Markus Gauß calls "dying Europeans" (2001). Together, the nationless Europeans I am calling "indigenous" in this chapter are remarkably different from each other, and their very differences call attention to the complex problem of interpreting what an indigenous culture may or may not be in Europe's historical *longue durée*. What indigenous people share is not so much similar histories, but rather a similar exclusion from history and the accompanying lack of a place in Europe itself.

The absence of place and history could not be more evident than in the structure and function of the yoik and in the discourse about its presence in European music. A schematic outline of yoiking might well employ the following traits to represent its character (cf. Edström 1977, Jones-Bamann 2000, and Ling 1997: 75–78):

1. The yoik is neither speech nor song, but a phenomenon between them.
2. Each individual creates and performs his or her own yoiks.
3. Yoiks distinguish individual rather than communal practice.
4. Yoiks take shape *sui generis,* gradually, that is, as a singer determines the smaller units that will be combined to give a performance overall shape.
5. Yoiking relies on vocables and textless styles but may also employ words from Saami languages that are specially designated for yoiking.
6. Yoik melodies unfold improvisationally before settling into forms that attain structure from small pitch units.
7. Among the differences in regional style, the division between north and south is important, as is the structural distinction between pentatonic and diatonic scales and modes.
8. Yoiking responds to the influences of Christian hymnody, Scandinavian folk music, and popular musics of several kinds, but it does so without extensively compromising traits that allow it to retain its identity as Saami.

By listing such traits, we do not necessarily come closer to pinning down exactly what it is that makes yoiking so distinctively Saami. The difficulty is complicated by the fact that many of these traits are contradictory. The individuality of yoiking style and motivic matter, for example, contradicts the claims by many scholars that yoiking has remained relatively unchanged from early accounts to the present because, as Matts Arnberg has argued, yoiks are passed from one generation to the next (cf. Arnberg et al. 1969: 34). The five-note, or pentatonic, scale found in the northern styles may be used to establish a proto-European presence for yoiking, or alternatively it may support arguments that dislodge the Saami from European history altogether, claiming Asian origins for and circumpolar connections in the present. Accordingly, the Saami acquire identity from yoiking entirely unlike the ways in which other textless styles, such as alpine yodeling, ascribe identity (e.g., Tromholt 1999). Precisely because of the seemingly inherent contradictions, yoiking fails to give the Saami a place in national narratives of authenticity or growing stylistic complexity.

The history of appropriating and manipulating yoiking as the musical symbol of the Saami as a nationless people is at least as old as modern European nationalism. Travelers, traders, and missionaries encountered the Saami in much the same way they did non-Europeans from the Age of Discovery through the Enlightenment (see, e.g., Acerbi 1999 [1798]). The first Swedish and Finnish folk-song collectors marveled at yoiking, because it differed so radically from the folk songs and song texts they were gathering to fill their own national collections (e.g., Geijer and Avzelius 1814–1817). When yoiks appeared in transcription, the very wonder of their melodic difference was emphasized; the same wonder has inflected and influenced the practice of transcribing yoiking until the present (see Figure 6.1). The discourse of encounter fixed on yoiking, not for what it communicated but for what it did not communicate. Yoiking was distinctive for not allowing itself to be dislodged from nature and for not being "cultural song," as the twentieth-century Saami writer Per Hætta noted. Though Saami music connected the Saami people to nature, in particular the shifting landscapes of Europe's arctic periphery, it did not lay claim to a nation-state, which transformed land in the immutable forms that were anathema to Saami existence.

The representation of nature through yoiking led observers to focus on the hand-held frame drum as a primary or even, as some scholars

The Saami entry in the Eurovision did have considerable significance in Scandinavia, where Saami music was quickly becoming the central symbol in the popular-music revival beginning to dismantle national borders with styles that allied themselves with "Scandinavian roots," the "new Nordic roots," or the "Nordic roots revival." Relying on the technologies of sampling and mixing, the musicians and recording companies fueling the Scandinavian revival turned to historical recordings of yoiking and made an entire palette of sounds available to a new generation of musicians. The most famous and widely influential Saami musician, Wimme Saari (known on his recordings simply as "Wimme"), did not learn to yoik from his family or from other Saami musicians in the Kelottijärvi region in Finland where he grew up. Instead, he studied contemporary and historical recordings. Wimme's songs extensively sample yoiking from across the arctic periphery. He then mixes and remixes his own compositions to reimagine older myths as modern narratives of a European north still anchored in nature (see, e.g., Wimme 2000, and the song "Oainnáhus," track 11 on *The Rough Guide to the Music of Scandinavia* 2000).

Non-Saami musicians in the Scandinavian revival have increasingly embraced the opportunity to mix yoiking into their concerts and CDs. Notable among such groups have been Hedningara, which uses yoiking to move "Scandinavian roots music" to an ahistorical, if not prehistorical, medieval postmodernism (e.g., Hedningara 1998). In post–Velvet Revolution Russia, a revival drawing on indigenous Saami and Karelian music gained impetus around the turn of the present century, with ensembles such as the Russian Karelian Folk Music Ensemble creating hybrid styles from indigenous and folk styles that cross international borders as if to engender new nationalisms, such as that narrated by the *Kalevala* (see Karelian Folk Music Ensemble 2001).

The musical revivals of the late twentieth century have made it possible to imagine the presence of the Saami and other indigenous peoples in ways that at once rely on their historical and geographical position at Europe's periphery and begin to draw that periphery toward the center. Saami music at the beginning of the twenty-first century continues to represent a nationless people, but it does so by increasingly envoicing responses to nationalism itself. It is not a question that yoiking might restore Saami narratives to European history, but rather that, through revival and integration into the popular-music narratives of postmodernism, a new potential to signify may accrue to Saami music, in fact, to signify the national spaces between and across national borders.

## Into the Silence: Rom and Jewish Music in Europe's Borderlands

*The moment you enter ROMANIA, you notice it. On the other side of Gyula it be-comes pitch black. No light, no heating. The johns are filthy. You'll find nothing clean at all. I'm telling you: Europe stops in Budapest.*
      —*Wagner 1999: 171*

February 1996. The winter had been hard, the snow abundant. The Carpathian Mountains promised to be impenetrable to a small Renault minivan overloaded with recording equipment and perhaps also to its five-person recording team. We had chosen February to follow the arch of the Carpathians along the Romanian-Ukrainian border be-cause it should have been a time of rather intensive and public music-making for the Jewish and Rom musicians there. We entered the Carpathians several weeks before Purim and Carnaval, Jewish and Christian mid-winter holidays that employ music to fire the celebra-tions and weave together the many threads of sacred and secular prac-tice. We were attempting to gather the traces and piece together the puzzle of an historical tradition determined, in the popular imagina-tion, by the extensive cooperation of two nationless peoples.

The research team, we imagined, entered the borderlands of the Carpathians prepared for just about any possibility. Along with Profes-sor Rudolf Pietsch of the University for Music and Performing Arts in Vienna, I had invited Roland Mahr, a first-year ethnomusicology and folklore student from the University of Vienna who would run the tape recorders and cameras, film events happening along the sidelines, and, as we increasingly learned, interact with those who came to observe the observers. In Hungary, we picked up Tamás Repiszky, an archeologist and folk-music entrepreneur, who, as a child in the Jewish-Hungarian city of Košice in eastern Slovakia, frequently traveled to Transylvania, where he was well acquainted with the Jewish-Hungarian intellectual community of Cluj Napoca. In Cluj we were joined by Harry Maiorovici, a Jewish composer and concentration camp survivor who had made his career by creating scores and soundtracks for Romanian radio and tele-vision during the Ceauşescu era and writing occasional music for the Romanian Yiddish stage. Maiorovici had spent his childhood years in

Sighetu-Marmaţiei, in the very heart of one of the most intensively Jewish and Roma areas of the Carpathians, a multicultural border city.

The team prepared itself to be comprehensive. We covered as many languages as possible—Romanian and Hungarian were crucial, Yiddish and German proved to be indispensable. We brought different musical skills to the field—Rudi Pietsch and Roland Mahr were semi-professional folk musicians, well known as a violinist and button-box player. We were a mixture of insiders and outsiders, and we came from the Eastern European borderlands and the metropolis beyond the borders. During our preparations we envisioned ourselves collecting and recording anything and everything, a research goal that was based on not knowing quite where to start in a region so remote even in the closing decade of the twentieth century. That goal proved to be critical, even in its naïveté, for it allowed us to detach ourselves from the approaches that had pervaded the Eastern European discourse throughout the Cold War, which were forged largely to sustain nationalism. As we entered Transylvania that winter, we also entered the borderlands of Europe's nationless peoples (see Pietsch 1999).

Transylvania symbolized the East. It was the land of much that remained mysterious and inexplicable to Central and Western Europeans, the obvious home for Dracula in the European imagination. It was also the land of the exotic and the uncivilized "other," a place of **orientalist** fantasy, where the darkness of mysterious mountain peoples could be ironically eclipsed by the symbolic brightness of the sun rising in the East. In Europe's historical imagination, Transylvania was the land where nationless peoples turned borders inside-out. (Listen to Béla Bartók's realization of Transylvania in CD examples 18–26.)

At the turn of the past century, ". . . Nach Großwardein!" (". . . To Oradea!") was one of the hit songs of the popular Jewish stage in Central and East Central Europe (CD example 16). With a text by Anton Groiss and a musical arrangement by Hermann Rosenzweig the song was published in a striking sheet-music version (see Figures 6.2 and 6.3), that announced the successes it had enjoyed in performances by the best known troupes of the Jewish popular stage. The Großwardein of the song is a land where the traveler experiences Eastern Jewry at its most extreme but also at its most humorous. The songwriters and the publishers (the Zipser and König firm of Budapest) portrayed the Jewish world of Großwardein in orientalist excess. The Jewish world across the border and at the cultural gates of Transylvania was both real and unreal. It was real insofar as it recognized, if through stereotype, the

*Figure 6.2. Hermann Rosenzweig's ". . . Nach Großwardein!"/
". . . To Großwardein!" title page (from the author's collection)*

*Figure 6.3. Hermann Rosenzweig's ". . . Nach Großwardein!"/*
*". . . To Großwardein!" first page of music (from the author's collection)*

*". . . To Großwardein!"*

*Text by Anton Groiss*

A city in the Land of the Hungarians—doi deridi ridi ridi roidoi,
Is for a certain reason well known—doi deridi . . .
Because the most beautiful girls live there—
And all of them can dance a *csárdás,*
    God, how nice—
[doi dideridi . . .]
We'll go there full of joy—
Men from far and wide—


TRIO
Aron Hirsch and Isaac Veitel—doi dideridi . . .
Moishe Baer and Natsi Teitel—
And the whole "Beggars'" Society—
Take a trip—to Großwardein.


Kobi Gigerl in his finery—
Wants to go along on the trip—
Because a new surcharge has been placed on that stretch—
So, the trip is the best way to show off these days—
[doi . . .]
One sees a fancy carriage—
And our folks are sitting in it—

diversity that characterized the Jewish life of Großwardein, a Habsburg
border city that, according to some estimates, was 70 percent Jewish at
the end of the nineteenth century. As a border city with cosmopolitan
flair and extensive railroad connections, Großwardein flourished because of its cultural diversity and became one of the metropolises in
which Jews from both East and West encountered each other. ". . . Nach
Großwardein!" was only one of numerous fin-de-siècle Jewish popular
songs that portrayed the city in this way (cf., e.g., "The Jewish Conductor's Song," in Bohlman and Holzapfel 2001: 120–121).

    Traces of a different symbolism of the East also assert themselves in
this popular song, for its characters—in the song text, on its cover, and

---

*". . . To Großwardein!"* (*continued*)

---

TRIO
There's a little city here in Hungary—
Where all the prettiest girls live—
All the men are young and handsome—
Take a trip—to Großwardein.

When it's market day in Großwardein—
One sees the Jews, tall and short—
Merchants, beggars, and hawkers with their goods—
Little thieves and all sorts of ruffians—
[doi . . .]
All of them look forward—
To making some profit on the train—

TRIO
Kobi Giberl, who's totally broke—
Wants to see all the young brides—
And he thinks he can manage it—
Take a trip—to Großwardein.

(Listen to CD example 16)

---

through its extensive potpourri of melodies marking Jewishness—all take their place on a stage. It is on that stage that hassidic Jews dance, but they do so against the backdrop of the East—not the literal East of the Carpathians, but rather the East of Jerusalem with its minarets and **levantine** landscape. The footlights and the curtains of the proscenium make it clear this is a popular stage, but the unequivocal ways in which the stage "orients" the audience would be lost on few at the time: This was also the East of **mizrakh,** literally the "East" toward which Jews in the synagogue prayed when facing the altar and Torah scrolls at the front of the synagogue. Großwardein/Oradea/Nagyvarad, Transylvania, the Land of Israel. The musical images of these Jewish places of the East blur together, on one hand because of the craftsmanship of the song-writers, on the other because of the juxtaposition of self and "other" that made sense only when one crossed the border "to Oradea."

### Border Crossings

Crossing national borders into the borderlands of the nationless presented us with an almost insurmountable hurdle. In 1996 passing through the checkpoints at the Hungarian-Romanian border near Oradea should not have been difficult, even though there was one Hungarian passport-holder among us. We traveled the main route, E 60 (European route 60), between Bucharest and Budapest (and for all intents and purposes farther into western Europe through Vienna, Munich, and Stuttgart to Paris), a so-called "European highway," conceived to move traffic as efficiently as possible, therefore also a designated route for large trucks conveying freight of all kinds. The official Europeanness of our route notwithstanding, we attracted the attention of the border guards and customs officials, first on the Hungarian side, then on the Romanian side. To the border officials the problem we presented was simple: We were entering Romania to study music, the music of Roma and Jews.

The four-and-one-half hours of interrogation and bureaucracy started simply enough. For the border officials we posed an ideological and political threat: After living and working among Roma and Jews, we would return to the West, report their grievances, and describe how Romanians mistreated them. Music was just the obvious excuse, a cover-up using the icons anyone would expect. None of the border officials doubted that we should find Roma, at least, where there was music. In this case, Jews were not the issue because none of the border officials really believed there were Jews to find.

The confrontation intensified once we began emptying the cargo area of the minivan. For our fieldwork we had brought enough recording and film equipment to make high-quality, potentially even professional level, recordings on the spot, for we knew only too well that there was no chance to bring the musicians we would encounter back to Vienna. Electronic equipment of such quality made its way across this border with some frequency, we imagined and then were assured by the border officials. If we wanted to sell it on the black market in Romania, that was our problem, they informed us. They looked right past the array of tape recorders and video cameras, quickly spotting some-thing else, which proved to be the core problem: two violins and a but-ton-box accordion.

For many years, Romania had been a staging area for the interna-tional transport and trade of musical instruments, especially violins. In the racial profile of the instrument trade to which Romanian border officials subscribed, Roma were the primary perpetrators; the pattern was simple. Instruments were built by Roma, usually in Romania, Bul-garia, and Turkey, and then they were traded back and forth across in-ternational borders, on one hand, commanding very high prices, on the other hand, accompanying the sale of other types of illegal goods and large sums of money. Violins were particularly suspicious and valu-able, all the more so because Roma travelers were never without them. Our story about traveling to Roma and Jewish musicians in the Carpathians seemed increasingly implausible, and it was beginning to seem as if the Romanian border officials would prevent us from enter-ing the country.

If the high value of the instruments was the problem, we began to re-alize, it might also be the solution, and we decided to risk striking a deal. We suggested that our exit papers include descriptions of precisely these instruments and their value, and that we use as a type of collateral the official paperwork of our institutions in the West, the University of Music and Performing Arts and the University of Vienna, where, more-over, I had further official American connections, namely to the Ful-bright Commission, which was sponsoring one semester of my guest professorship. All this seemed so improbable that the border officials decided finally to let us pass, after countless signatures and mountains of paperwork did not succeed in turning us back. In the end, they had done their job, wasting enough time on a team of musicians and schol-ars crazy enough to want to play music with Roma and Jews.

### The Buried Music of Oradea

"Our liturgy and music is borrowed from many different traditions. Our prayer- and songbooks were published in Budapest and Vienna, of course, but also in New York and Jerusalem. We did not have that many from Romania, but there are some from Koloszvár."

The representative of the Oradea Jewish community spoke with pride as she guided us through the several buildings of the community's main compound, with its block of offices, its handsome though somewhat dilapidated performance hall, its kosher cafeteria, and its conservative synagogue. There were more than a few signs of life around the compound, particularly at the cafeteria, which was visited at lunchtime by several small groups of girls studying at the Oradea Jewish school. Our guide spoke of upcoming concerts and events, including a Purim celebration.

"Today, there are not too manypeople around, because a member of the community died this morning. There are many preparations to be made."

The loss of a community member sent a wave of sadness and concern through the offices in the compound, where various officials were responsible for keeping track of Oradea's Jews. The reason for the concern is simple: Each death reminds the community that it is dwindling, that another piece of its past has passed away. Oradea was once a thriving Jewish community, estimated by today's officials at 70,000 on the eve of the Holocaust. In 1996, they estimated that perhaps 700 Jews lived in Oradea, which had trebled in size since World War II. The demographics could not weigh more heavily on community officials: The community of 70,000 had to be measured against a total of about 100,000, as opposed to 700 against a total of around 300,000. Once a center of Jewish culture and cosmopolitanism as well as Jewish learning and pietism, Oradea, by the end of the twentieth century, barely took notice of its Jewish population. The community itself assumed all responsibility for the burial of its elderly member and for the recording of another statistic of pastness.

### The Neolog Synagogue

"The Neolog Synagogue isn't used anymore. We try to keep it in some repair because it is so beautiful. For us it's a monument from the late nineteenth century."

Sandwiched between the river and one of the main arteries that had served as Oradea's version of Vienna's Ringstraße, the **Neolog,** or Reform, Synagogue was indeed beautiful. Sun streamed through the windows and through the cracks in the walls and ceiling, some of them gaping. The Neolog Synagogue fitted the imperial architecture of the city magnificently, connecting the culture of Jewish cosmopolitanism to the West, which is to say, the centers in Budapest and Vienna, and to the East, with its subdued Moorish style and the blue of the eastern sky realized by the interior paint color. In the space between the seats for the congregation and the *bima,* a piano stood, a stalwart upright, not so much out-of-tune as in a condition of resolutely refusing to give up its tuning to the elements it had to battle. Scattered about were a few songbooks and **siddurim,** or prayerbooks, from Hungarian, Austrian, and German printers. Their imprints revealed that they had been published at the turn of the last century. They, like everything around them, survived as proud monuments. The monuments had much to say, but who was present to listen?

### The Conservative Synagogue

"We have just buried our books behind the synagogue. We did not know what to do with them, and in our tradition we can't just get rid of them. Burning them would have been unacceptable. Now we know where they are: Packed carefully in boxes to minimize water damage, they are here waiting for a future generation to use them. The music is buried too. Maybe there'll come a day when someone wants to hear it."

Our guide was about to leave us in the conservative synagogue at Oradea's Jewish compound, allowing us a little time to study the main religious and social center of the community on our own. She had withheld her explanation about the synagogue's liturgical and musical holdings until the moment she was about to take her leave from us. She knew we might find it difficult to comprehend that the Jewish community, with few people left to perform from the books of a once-proud local tradition, had decided to preserve it by burying it on the synagogue grounds. On a day when the community was mourning a new death, the fate of Oradea's Jewish music seemed also to mourn death. Or was it to postpone death? The liturgy and music were buried without ceremony; nor was there an attempt to mark the soil where the music lay buried. Tradition and the desire to grasp memory as tightly as possible had given them a sense of what not to do—getting rid of the music was not acceptable—but it had been less specific about what the alternatives were.

"At least, we know where our liturgy and music are when we need it again."

Our guide turned the key in the massive lock that secured the synagogue door and bade farewell.

### Traces of Nations and Nationlessness

"Siebenbürgen"/"Transylvania"

*M. Moltke (text), I. Hedwig (melody)*

1. Transylvania, land of blessing,
land of plenty, and of strength!
With the Carpathian belt,
encompassing the green dress of fertility,
||: Land of gold and of grape nectar. :||

2. Transylvania, soil left by the sea
of a flood long departed!
Now a sea gently gleaned,
Whose shores, forest-lined,
||: touch on the sky's breast. :||

3. Transylvania, land of ruins
of a bygone age strong and powerful!
Traces from a thousand years
still reveal themselves in your open fields,
||: The lap of your fields weakened not at all. :||

4. Transylvania, green cradle
of a colorful humanity!
With the climate of all earth's zones,
with the wreath of all the nations
||: at the altar of the fatherland. :||

5. Transylvania, green temple,
The mountains as the high chorus!
Where paying homage
rises in so many tongues
||: to the one and only God. :||

6. Transylvania, land of tolerance,
all beliefs find certain solace!
May you remain until distant days
a solace for freedom
||: and as a buttress for freedom of speech! :||

## 154  SUS ÎN POARTA RAIULUI

COLINDA
### At the Gates of Paradise
Carol

1 Sus  în  poar - ta  rai - u - lui,  Flo - ri - le  dal - be

sunt  de  mă - ru,  Flo - ri - le  dal - be  sunt  de  măr,

| | |
|---|---|
| 1 Sus în poarta raiului<br>   Florile dalbe sunt de măru,<br>   Florile dalbe sunt de măr, | 1 At the gates of Paradise,<br>   Apple trees bearing blossoms white,<br>   Apple trees bearing blossoms white, |
| 2 Şade Maica Domnului. | 2 There does sit the mother of Christ |
| 3 C-un fiuţ micuţ în braţe. | 3 With her infant in her arms. |
| 4 Fiul plînge, stare n-are. | 4 He does cry and will not sleep. |
| 5 -Taci, fiule, nu mai plînge, | 5 Hush, my child, and do not cry. |
| 6 Că m-oi duce, ţi-oi aduce | 6 I will go and bring to you |
| 7 Două mere, două pere, | 7 Two fine apples, two fine pears; |
| 8 Toate patru aurele, | 8 All the four of them in gold; |
| 9 Şi cheiţa de la rai, | 9 And the key of Paradise. |
| 10 Să te faci mai mare crai. | 10 A great King you will become. |

M. K.

*Figure 6.4.* "*Sus în poarta raiului*"/"*At the Gates of Paradise,*"
*Romanian* **colinda**

7. Transylvania, sweet homeland,
our dear fatherland!
We greet you in your beauty,
and around all your sons
||: draw the bonds of harmony. :||
    (Brandsch and Schullern 1932:3–4)

Although it has long been home to one of Europe's largest populations of nationless peoples, Transylvania has also been a region in
which nationalism has been most contested. Nationlessness and nation
coexist in a complex counterpoint in which there is little harmony and
considerable dissonance resulting from national voices that fit not at
all together. The irony of this coexistence is the historical fact that the
nationless peoples who have made Transylvania their home are not the
ones who have struggled to impose one nation or another on that
home (see Kürti 2001).

Nor were the German-speaking residents of Transylvania engaged in
that struggle, the "**Siebenbürgen** Sachsen," for whom the song "Siebenbürgen" (lit., "Seven Fortresses," or "Fortified Cities") was published
emblematically as a national anthem in 1932 by the German folk-music project, *Landschaftliche Volkslieder* (see Chapter 5). Opening the volume devoted to "Transylvanian folk song" (Brandsch and Schullern
1932), "Siebenbürgen" evokes a land shaped by many different ethnic
and national peoples, "where paying homage rises in so many tongues
to the one and only God" (verse 5). Mottoes about tolerance, freedom
of speech, and harmony punctuate the song, hinting that Transylvania
should rise above the mundane pull of nationalism. But such a sugges-
tion rings emptier and emptier in the course of the song, and by the final verse, with its juxtaposition of homeland and fatherland (**Heimat**
and **Vaterland**), the deeper and darker specter of a German nation in
Transylvania clearly reveals itself. The irony in "Siebenbürgen" is all
the more striking because of what we might call a practice of nameless-
ness. The possibility that peoples of "all beliefs" might "find solace" in
Transylvania does not lend itself to exceptions as long as none of those
peoples has a name.

The motivation of "Siebenbürgen," however, is not difficult to identify. The only two names that do occur among the volume's forty-two
songs are those of the composer and lyricist—hence it is the only case
of a song situated in the modern history of German-speaking Saxons in

*Figure 6.5. Scene from Transylvanian Schäßburg/Sighişoara
(Brandsch and Schullerns 1932)*

Romania rather than in the mixture of myth and past history projected by the folk songs. The songbook's iconography, too, blurs the borders between myth and history in the name of the nation. The cross-stitching of the folk art at the top of the page on which "Siebenbürgen" opens the volume has entirely different temporal and cultural functions from the etching of "Schäßburg" (Sighişoara) four pages later (Figure 6.5).

The nationalist teleology of the "Siebenbürgen," however, remained inchoate. Even during World War II, Transylvania moved back and forth between Axis and Allied powers, a victim not of Germany's nationalist drive to recover speech islands such as the Siebenbürgen Germans—or the Banat Germans and the Danube Swabian Germans, two other German speech islands in western Romanian—but of the historical struggle between Hungary and Romania. In the "green cradle of a colorful humanity" celebrated by this modern hymn to Transylvania, Jews and Roma would quickly fall victim to the rise of new nationalisms.

### At Home with Rom Musicians

We were not alone when we arrived on a Friday night at Cioata's home in Vadu Izei. Streams of people converged on the tiny house in this small village in Maramureş, the northernmost region in the central region of the Carpathians. Undaunted by the necessity of trudging through the streets blanketed during a snowstorm that showed no signs of quitting, the Romanian Roma were arriving at Cioata's home on the off-chance they would hear him play, but also in the very real chance they would see Cioata's visitors, rumored to be a television crew from Hungary. In Vadu Izei, a village of several hundred souls, Cioata was a celebrity, partly because he had played such a prominent role in a family tradition of entertainment music, which he was handing down to his own son, just as he had given him his own real name, Gheorghe Covaci (see Figure 6.6). Two generations earlier Cioata, a violinist, had learned from his father, a **primás** in a band that was reputed to have played with Jewish musicians—*klezmorim* so the tales reported—even to have gone from door to door in the Jewish villages playing at **Purim** celebrations (Frigyesi in Muzsikás 1993: liner notes, p. 2). It is for these reasons that Cioata had attracted attention from outsiders, who thought he might lead them to the traces of a Jewish music that had once flourished in the area. It was no accident that we had arrived for several days of intensive fieldwork just prior to Purim 1996.

Only the family members entered the two-room house with us, though the family's numbers changed from one moment to the next. We managed, without any particular effort, to fit twenty to twenty-five people, many of them children, into the living room at most times. Cioata's family in the area was large, and they regularly came to hear

*Figure 6.6. Gheorghe Covaci, Sr., and Gheorghe Covaci, Jr., "Cioata" (right) (courtesy of Roland Mahr)*

him play and to watch and wonder at the outsiders who came to record him. We quickly dispensed with business: After brief discussions about fees, we settled on $50 for two hours, an enormous amount of money in Vadu Izei but less than Cioata would have required from a real Hungarian television crew. He regarded us sympathetically for two reasons. First, we did not insist that he perform primarily from his Jewish repertory; second, we had a violinist among us, with whom he could swap trade secrets.

Cioata played for two hours, more or less without a break. Joined throughout by his son, who played percussively on a three-string guitar, perched vertically in his lap, Cioata followed a musical journey through several repertories, Rom and Romanian, but also with abundant and polished examples of Jewish songs and dances, and some dance tunes that, for lack of a better term, were pan-Carpathian (listen to CD example 9). The Jewish, or **hassidic** (as he called them after being prodded to do so by Harry Maiorovici), songs and dances were highly stylized, so much so that our recordings fitted the arrangements by the Hungarian band, Muzsikás, remarkably closely, even to some of the smallest melodic and metric nuances. Cioata knew the names of a few songs, classic Yiddish songs such as "Ani Maamin" (CD example 17) and "Belz," and he was willing to accept Harry Maiorovici's titles for others. Cioata knew that giving names to songs was expected. The Jewish tradition was being slavishly reproduced to fit many different expectations, few of them ours; we were not, after all, a Hungarian television crew.

It was when we opened up the session to the gathered family that Cioata departed from the expected path charted by previous outsiders from the metropolis. "What do you play here?" we wanted to know. "What do you like to hear your grandfather play?" we asked of the children tumbling on the divan wrapped along three sides of the room. Cioata began to follow a different route, and his son now began to contribute substantially to a performance style that was driven by the excitement of the dance floor. Family members invested the playing with excitement, clapping and exclaiming their approval, all in all behaving in the ways that the "Hungarian television crew" had asked them not to behave.

In due course but from a different direction, we returned to the central question of Roma and Jews in Transylvania. Cioata's musical responses moved from the margins—Jewish music that Roma presumably played fifty or sixty years earlier—to the center, to the common ground occupied by Jewish, Rom, Romanian, Ukrainian, Hungarian, Catholic, and Orthodox traditions. This was rich musical territory. Though local, it was unencumbered by national and ethnic boundaries, and even religious boundaries. By no means was it utopian territory, for it was realized briefly, even ephemerally, through musical performance. It was, nonetheless, the territory where the nationless peoples of a region often torn asunder by national borders chose to meet.

### Wedding Dance

Encounters with Rom wedding musicians have long been the stuff of travel accounts from Romania.

> At a Gypsy wedding neither wine nor food is stinted. . . . The Gypsy fiddler and his accompanists had been freely supplied with drinks and could hardly stand up, but they went on playing one dance after another. In a corner two men were jumping up and down as though possessed by a kind of malignant St. Vitus's dance. As for the young bride, she was a pitiful little figure in a corner. (Starkie 1933: 253)

On 23–24 February 1996 it would be no different. It would be the last opportunity for a wedding and wedding dance before Lent, so it was hardly surprising that everyone in Vadu Izei excitedly told us that we simply had to come. Gheorghe Covaci, Jr., was particularly insistent, because it was his band that would provide the music. The music, he said, both apologizing and enticing, would be different from what he and his father had played (lislten to CD example 10).

"It's wedding music, Rom wedding music. The mass in the church takes place at 5:00 P.M., and then we take the bride and groom and their families to the community center. The dance will last a long time."

Descriptions of Rom wedding dances fill travelers' accounts and ethnographies of all kinds. The weddings of nationless peoples, however, do not serve as metaphors for reproducing the people who make up the nation, as we have seen elsewhere in this book. However, they do provide moments of intense music-making and celebration at which entire communities gather. They also generate discourses about musical professionalism. Jewish klezmer musicians, for example, often claim self-identity, using a sort of professional shorthand, as "wedding musicians." It is no different for Rom musicians in Romania. They frequently play at weddings, which provide one of their most dependable sources of income. Historically, Jewish and Rom musicians played together at weddings, a custom that had, according to Rom musicians like Gheorghe Covaci, provided opportunities to swap repertories. In Burgenland, too, Jewish and Rom musicians shared the wedding circuit along the Austrian-Hungarian borderlands (Bohlman 1997). For the folk and popular music of Europe's nationless peoples, the wedding was a moment of considerable musical fecundity.

The other theme that is rarely absent from accounts of East European Rom wedding dances is that of unbridled celebration, excessive consumption of alcohol, and public display of sexuality. The word "orgy" does, in fact, appear frequently as a metaphor for the Rom wedding dance itself (Starkie 1933: 250–256; cf. Franz Liszt's ascription of "orgy" to Rom music-making in Russia in Liszt 1926: 152–155). The reputation of the Rom wedding dance preceded the wedding in Vadu Izei, and we knew we should heed the forewarnings. We were, after all, entering the liminal season of Mardi Gras, and the *carnevalesque* would soon be upon us, indeed, in the guise of the wedding dance.

The wedding dance at Vadu Izei was not the least bit orgiastic, in any literal or figurative sense, but the social world of the rural Carpathians was turned upside-down. The Rom musicians orchestrated the evening,

*Figure 6.7. Gheorghe Covaci, Jr.*
*(guitar), and his band,*
*23 February 1996*
*(courtesy of Rudolf Pietsch)*

though they also stood outside the several social and family circles that intersected in the course of the wedding. The wedding was not, in fact, a "Gypsy wedding," but rather a Romanian Orthodox wedding, at which virtually everyone from the surrounding villages was present, along with visitors from far away, especially Bucharest. The lines between Rom and Romanian were blurred, and one of the tasks of the musicians was to make those lines clear at various moments during the dance. The dance music was Rom and Christian, local and regional, Romanian and transnational, folk and popular, sacred and secular. Musical borders were everywhere, and the dancers were constantly called upon to negotiate them, but also to realize their cultural meanings.

Gheorghe Covaci, Jr., and his band (see Figures 6.7 and 6.8) did draw from several core repertories to orchestrate the evening. There were repertories of Romanian dance music, for the most part performed in a style that favored line or ring dancing and drew the diverse ethnic community together. In contrast, the band displayed a virtuosic knowledge of Serbian popular music, some of it versions of well-known turbo-folk, a repertory of folklike music realized in the Balkan rock style of the 1980s and 1990s. The popular repertory favored couple dances, and it attracted a younger crowd to the dance floor, particularly those interested in displaying their more cosmopolitan tastes.

*Figure 6.8.  Gheorghe Covaci, Jr., and his band return to the everyday, 8:00 a.m.,
24 February 1996 (courtesy of Rudolf Pietsch)*

Punctuating the evening were various rituals in which entirely different repertories were employed, sometimes seeming entirely out of place and culturally incongruous (listen to CD example 10).

When the wedding party arrived at the wedding table for the banquet, roughly between midnight and 1:00 A.M., the Rom band played them into the hall, performing a suite that illustrated all the traits of a cakewalk: The wedding party followed the cake, baked over the course of many days by village women, into the hall. The cakewalk and the half hour of toasting and roasting the couple that followed comprised a potpourri of music that was, at the time, foreign, even "exotic" in an inverted sense. In reality, the music was almost entirely German, symbolic of the culture that was imagined to be the European metropolis. Toasts were inevitably followed by the German "Hoch soll er leben!" ("He should live well"). As the wedding party negotiated the spaces separating the wedding table from the banquet guests, every manner of German dance stereotype unfolded in succession, with hoots of laughter when couples gyrated to the standard of international kitsch, the "Chicken Dance."

The music pulsed through the night, usually amplified to ear-splitting decibel levels by the band's unsophisticated sound system. Dance after dance drew and redrew the map of the Carpathians and the Balkans. History and geography, ethnicity and race, were at once subtly mapped and aggressively performed. Alcohol and food were consumed non-stop, clearly in part to fuel the musicians and the dancers. Non-dancers, not least our own documentation team, had to monitor alcohol consumption more cautiously, something we managed to various degrees. The musical energy demanded and expressed was impressive, and it became a bit easier to understand why those who would witness it from the outside might impute the qualities of an orgy to the wedding dance. When dawn arrived between 7:00 and 8:00 A.M., the dancers and the band, very ceremoniously, which is to say, fully and intensely aware of the rite of passage that would lead them back into the everyday world of the Carpathians, exited the community hall and performed the music that would send the wedding party and the guests to their homes. Freshly falling snow covered the tracks left by the musicians and the dancers as they disappeared into the Lenten season.

### Final Station of a Sacred Journey

German music had flourished in the Saxon cities of Transylvania, and we wondered whether traces of it might ring out, if briefly, on a Sunday morning. The German, actually the German-language and cultural heritage of Transylvania, or "Siebenbürgen," had been the subject of much speculation since the opening of Romania in the early 1990s. In some communities, such as the church congregations resettled by the German government during the Cold War, there was real hope, not so much in following the path of return as in connecting the present to the past in a diasporic culture. Music, church music, would be crucial to chronicling that journey, and the repertories of German sacred music from Transylvania were rich indeed.

Germans began to settle in Transylvania as early as the thirteenth century, already relieving pressure on overpopulated areas of Central Europe and forming a bastion of Christian civilization against the potential spread of Islam across southeastern Europe. The first north German Saxon settlements established a pattern that later immigrants—**"Danube Swabians"** from southern Germany and the **"Ländler"** from

*Figure 6.9. The Way to Church in Transylvanian Kleinscheuern*
*(Brandsch and Schullern 1932: between 28 and 29)*

Austria—would sustain through half a millennium and more, until World War II. They enjoyed remarkable agricultural success, which they converted into a cosmopolitan life that flourished within and contributed substantially to the multiculturalism of Transylvania. In their farming villages and small cities they founded the institutions that would sustain a distinctive cultural life: printing presses, church organizations, symphonies and choruses, and schools, seminaries, and university faculties. The surviving musical records—publications, manuscripts, cathedral records, and biographies of notable musicians—reveal a musical life that was woven into the Romanian Catholic and Orthodox traditions, Hungarian Calvinist traditions, and Jewish Reform traditions (cf. Metz 1996 and Teutsch 1997).

At the beginning of the twentieth century, the musical life of Transylvania, enriched by German sacred traditions and undergirded by its institutions, was as spectacular as anywhere in the world. When we arrived at the end of the twentieth century, we found barely a trace of a once proud German musical life. The churches were quiet, the printing presses largely still, the communities displaced yet again, this time back to Germany, not only a foreign country but the source of the nationalism that had accelerated the final stage of an historical journey among and with other nationless peoples in Transylvania (listen to CD example 4). In 1996, most Romanians had no memories of the German musical life of their land, but they were ironically aware that there were memories to have. They knew of the "seven fortress cities" that had given Transylvania its German name, Siebenbürgen; they could direct us to German churches; and they were quick to point out that the used bookstores would have shelves containing German literature and abundant scores and editions of music.

This music, Romanian colleagues and friends noted, would sound the past of a displaced people only silently.

### *Rom Musicians on the Road in Transylvania*

Street music is different in Transylvania. Even in the dead of winter, in the midst of a period of insistent heavy snowfall, street music has an everyday quality. Rather than being a site of otherness, it is a site where otherness and selfness mingle to stage Romania's modern multiculturalism. When musicians take to the street, they take it over, if temporarily. They arrest the attention of those passing by and interrupt the everyday.

In Transylvania, few musicians know how to use the street as a stage more efficaciously than the Roma. In cities such as Cluj Napoca, Rom musicians ply the marketplaces as musicians and instrument hawkers. The culture of daily exchange belongs to them, and they orchestrate the public spaces at the urban center and periphery. Musically, they transform the open markets, the old shopping arcades next to train stations, and the inner squares from the Habsburg past into liminal public spaces. If one wants to pay for a tune or buy an instrument, it does not take long to find the right Rom musicians. Musicians ensure that the street overflows its boundaries, detouring through a coffee shop or closet-sized bar, the doors of which are open and inviting no less in February than in August.

In the country and in the villages, it is the same and different. Entering a small town on the main road, it is not unusual, especially at certain moments during the day and the week, to find a crowd of people encumbering the way. They do not so much block traffic, which for the time being does not really interest them, as they turn their attention to musicians, perhaps as they escort a wedding party, which indeed they do with frequency during the closing of the wedding season before Lent. Not all the musicians of the street are Roma, but the street is theirs for music-making. With music they claim a sort of ownership and a place in modern Romania. Music affords a special form of temporary citizenship in a public sphere whose ethnic and racial boundaries are very fluid.

As musicians on the street and on the road, the Roma of Transylvania also join an historical and transnational network that runs parallel to the discourses that identify Roma as displaced and nationless. The "adventures of Gypsy musicians" inevitably read like travelogues that take the reader farther and farther along the streets from the time-bounded world of the metropolis—from Europe—to the timeless paths stretching toward the periphery—beyond Europe's horizons (cf. Brown 1929 and Starkie 1932, both musical travelogues among European Roma). Franz Liszt's collected encounters with Rom musicians, one of the most remarkable works of mid-nineteenth-century musical ethnography, is no less a product of experiences on his own journeys and musical pilgrimages, woven into a single fabric of European racialism charted by a "wandering race" (Liszt 1926).

The streets and roads of Transylvania stand out, even in the tropes and stereotypes reproduced in musical travelogues. Rom music channels pedestrian, automobile, and commercial traffic alike. Music gives alternative meaning to the space of the street, which is also the space of Romania. Music allows the Roma to divert the flow of traffic, commanding attention to the place of the placeless in a modern Romania struggling to find the path along which the ethnic, religious, and racial diversity of Transylvania can travel toward a national future.

### The Last Jewish Farmer of the Carpathians

> "Czikszereda—Miercurea Ciuc"
> *22 Sept. 1978*
> Just behind living quarters #1, allotted to
> Klára and István, the cornfield
> begins, where the sheep bleat
> during the day, while the dogs bark at night
> or next door the water faucet in the kitchen
> crows, there's a security chain
> on the front door—it would appear
> as if human beings also live here.
> this land is your land
> this land is my land
> from california
> to staten island
> —Anemone Latzina (Aescht 1999: 167)

Exactly why we should seek out the "last Jewish farmer of the Carpathians" was never clear to us. As the twentieth century in the Carpathians reached its end, he had become a hero of sorts. He had survived the Holocaust, not by joining the Soviet Army or slipping across the border into Ukraine or farther east before the Germans and their Hungarian allies could take full control of the land of their sometimes-allies, the Romanians. The last Jewish farmer, so the growing epic of his fame proclaimed, survived by doing what he had always done, tending his herds in the high Carpathians along the Romanian-Ukrainian border. So World War II and the Holocaust, many were led to believe, never reached him. The last Jewish farmer is a living link to the past, an icon of authenticity.

To reach the farm—actually a modest cabin surrounded by some remnants of a building that might house livestock—we turned northeast from Valea Vişeului toward Mt. Farcau, at 1,561 meters the highest peak in this section of the Carpathians. Were we to reach it, we would have crossed into Ukraine.

*Figure 6.10.    The last Jewish farmer of the Carpathians and Philip V. Bohlman
(courtesy of Rudolf Pietsch)*

The elderly Jewish residents of the Carpathians had been willing to share their pasts with us, welcoming interviews and inviting community members who knew some songs. They worried that the pasts they bore with them in song would be uninteresting to us. Those with a relatively large store of songs, such as Josef Tenebaum of Sighetu-Marmaţiei, were at once proud to be tradition bearers and embarrassed that they had mixed hit songs from the Soviet era and secular songs from Romanian, Hungarian, and German sources. Tenebaum, for example, moved effortlessly from Hebrew children's songs to Ukrainian pop tunes to Russian and Romanian songs with military tunes. A former language teacher who insisted on speaking in English "just to practice" a language he claimed not to know, Tenebaum commanded a repertory that narrated the stages of his life. At each stage of recreating that vocal memoir, however, he apologized for the absence of what he perceived we wanted to hear, "authentic Jewish music" (listen to CD examples 28, 29, and 30).

We entered the farmyard of the last Jewish farmer of the Carpathians only after several ferocious dogs were secured behind the fences. Visitors, it became apparent, rarely reached this point. Initially, Tamás Repiszky spoke Romanian and Hungarian, the preferred language of many Jews in Valea Vişeului, but to no avail. I then tentatively attempted to communicate in Yiddish, and the last Jewish farmer responded in Yiddish. I failed to understand much of anything beyond the fact that this was a Yiddish dialect that was far removed from anything I had heard; it was a Yiddish that had not found its way to written form. The two of us exchanged phrases. Nothing. We were going nowhere. I made small talk, trying to interest him in telling me about his dogs, who were his sole companions. Perhaps he might say a few words about his experience with the national borders that literally cut through the lands on which his livestock had once grazed. The borders, I managed to understand, were not important to the livestock, so what's to tell? The conversation strained to move in a coherent direction but achieved no more than a few faltering steps. I raised the subject of music and songs. What did he sing as a Jewish farmer along the Romanian-Ukrainian border? *He didn't.* Did the Jewish farmers sing in Yiddish, Romanian, or Ukrainian? *They didn't.* Did Jewish music mix with Romanian music? *What do you mean?* What about music of the synagogue? *What synagogue?*

Photographs survive as testaments to this journey to the most remote part and person of the Jewish Carpathians. The last Jewish farmer and an American ethnomusicologist. Icons of authenticity and the futile search to recover it (see Figure 6.10).

### *Of Yiddish and Rom Musical Theater*

"I only speak Yiddish, Hebrew, Romanian, Russian, Ukrainian, English, and French. And, since I'm speaking to you in German, I have to say also that I know some German."

Yitzchak Schwarz was quick to apologize for his linguistic limitations. At almost 90, he had needed to know many languages throughout his long life. A resident of Iaşi in northeastern Romania, Schwarz had spent his life plying the borders between Romania and the Soviet Union, and then later between Romania, Ukraine, and Moldavia. Growing up in the cosmopolitan culture of a border city, which claimed Romania's first university, an urban infrastructure established by the Habsburg Monarchy, and flourishing sacred and secular Jewish cultures, Schwarz was a living monument to all that was triumphant and tragic about Jewish culture in twentieth-century Romania. He apologized for his linguistic skills not because he knew too few languages, but rather because he knew how much he could intensify, by speaking with us in German, his contributions to memorializing the past that survived because he and his wife embodied it for the dwindling Jewish community of Iași.

"Iași once had many Yiddish theaters. In the decades after the Holocaust we could claim two surviving Yiddish theaters, while Bucharest really had only one. It has only been a few years since we no longer could support a Yiddish theater."

Schwarz had become an icon of Yiddish theater in Romania and the borderlands shared by the Carpathians and the Ukrainian plain. One made a pilgrimage to his minuscule apartment in Iași to hear his tales of the past and to share a bit in his hopefulness about better times, not so much about survival as about revival as a path into the future. Our own pilgrimage was somewhat different, for Harry Maiorovici and Itzchak Schwarz were old friends and colleagues. Maiorovici had written interludes and orchestral parts for some of Schwarz's productions, and lists of these were held in records Schwarz kept in his bookshelves. The two of them reminisced with gales of laughter as they mentioned one production after another. Some of the collaborations were in productions for Yiddish stages in Iași and Bucharest. Harry Maiorovici was proudest of those that had made it to Romanian state television in its earliest years.

"That was long ago, but we could do it again. Maybe. It would be interesting to try."

By the end of the nineteenth century, Yiddish musical theater had seized the stage of much of East Central and Eastern Europe. Yiddish actors, singers, and complete troupes were resident in the cities of Romania, Poland, Galicia, Bukovina, Ukraine, and Russia, and traveling companies moved from the East to the West, sinking roots into the theatrical soil of Budapest, Vienna, and New York (cf. Sandrow 1977 and Dalinger 1998). Yiddish theater took as its primary theme the conflict of Jewish tradition with European modernity. It was a theater of self-representation: on one hand, a theater trading almost entirely in stereotypes; on the other, a theater conscious of traditional narrative forms and genres. Music, from biblical cantillation (the chanting of biblical texts) to early **klezmer** styles, provided fertile soil for the nurturing of these stereotypes. Yiddish theater set images of the self on the stage: Jews as selfness against the theatrical backdrop of Europe as otherness. Yiddish theater thrived because of an act of metaphoric inversion that acting itself makes powerfully possible.

"There still is Yiddish theater in Romania today, in Bucharest. It's different, however, because they only produce the old plays and musicals as if they belonged in a museum."

Rom theater, too, thrived along the borders between self and other in modern Eastern Europe, and its stock-in-trade depended on the ways music inverted and subverted that relation. Rom theater, according to Alaina Lemon (2000), performed memory, but to do so it juxtaposed reality and representation. The Romani theater that Lemon encountered in late twentieth-century Moscow may not have been so different from the self-representations that Franz Liszt encountered in mid-nineteenth-century Moscow (Liszt 1926: 149–155). The state support that Romani theater received in the Soviet Union and the New Russia drew it into the cultural orbit of the nation, but the footlights themselves still marked the difference between nation and nationless, and they defined that difference as crucial. Crossing the footlights by confusing stereotypes with reality—truly joining the nation—would be a fatal mistake.

"I don't really sing Yiddish songs, but if you want me to do so, I'll do it. Remember, I don't sing Yiddish songs."

Cilla Schwarz dismissed her musical prowess no less quickly than her husband had dismissed his knowledge of languages. But like her husband, she knew the Yiddish theater and had learned repertories of song for the stage. Apologies made, she sang six songs in quick succession. Her voice was true to the tradition, her feeling for the language secure and seasoned. If we wanted more, she'd need some prompting, and Cilla quickly received it from Itzchak, who had turned understudy in the course of the interview. As soon as he reminded her that she remembered a song, she smiled and then sang. When we knew it would be counterproductive and impolite to push her for more songs, we thanked her, and she closed with a smile and a final comment.

"They are beautiful songs, but they're old and from another time. I don't know why anyone wants to hear them."

**Out of the Borderlands, from Border to Border**

"Jacob's Song from Romania" (Jewish Folk Song)

The Lord spoke to Jacob . . .
Oy, Father.
You really did speak to me:
Don't be afraid, my servant, Jacob.
Oy vey, Father.
Why did you strike me, Father?
Why do you cause me so much trouble, Father?
When will it come to an end, oy, when?

## 3.  JAKOBS-LIED AUS RUMÄNIEN

*Figure 6.11.  "Jakobs-Lied aus Rumänien"/"Jacob's Song from Romania,"
Yiddish folk song from the early twentieth century (Kaufmann 1920)*

"Elmënyëk"/"Long the Road I Travel"

1. I am going, going,
Long the road I travel,
Long and dusty roadside,
Cloak of dust around me.

2. Sorrow, grief and sadness
Bound like a braid around me,
And my coat is buttoned
With my countless tear-drops.
   —Hungarian song from Romania (Karpeles 1956: 230)

## 158   ELMËNYËK

'Long the road I travel

*Figure 6.12.   Hungarian song from Transylvania (Karpeles 1956: 230)*

A specter had followed us through Romania, but it was in Iaşi that we knew it had caught up with us. As we were loading the recording equipment and the musical instruments in the back of the Renault Espace minivan, the routine inspection of the undercarriage turned up the nail wedged underneath one of the back tires, placed in such a way that it would puncture the tire the moment the car moved. The nail was no more than a small symbolic gesture, an act of vandalism perhaps, but nonetheless a gesture that drew our attention to the welter of small gestures that had come to our attention. Together they were gestures that accumulated as traces of the specter of violence in Romania. Considered alone, most were senseless, but it was, in fact, because they were senseless that they projected a lingering sense of violence that found its way into the borderlands of the nationless.

The many songs that celebrate Romania's natural and cultural riches notwithstanding, there are also many songs that chronicle the tragedy that has accompanied a history struggling with and against the nation's cultural diversity. The tales of survival and the moments of interethnic and cross-cultural performance that this ethnographic journey during the pre-Lenten and Purim seasons draws together yield a musical portrait of Romania that many, if not most, Romanians would not welcome. Not only do many wish the insistent details of klezmer musicians and Roma wedding bands erased from the picture once and for all, but they would be willing to endorse measures to encourage the erasure.

The musical competition for national space was palpable from the moment we crossed the border, and each stage of the journey magnified it. In Transylvania especially, the struggle for a present carved from Hungarian or Romanian nationalism asserted itself in every village. We encountered almost no one who did not argue strongly for or against a Romanian or Hungarian view of the musical present (cf. Bălaşa forthcoming and Trumpener 2000). The historical battle over the national present was part even of the everyday fabric of making decisions about whom we would record and how we would listen to the voices of the nationless. To take just the most obvious case, our Romanian colleague, Harry Maiorovici, aligned himself with the Romanian-speaking nationalists in Transylvania, even though the Jewish community was overwhelmingly Hungarian-speaking. Maiorovici had thriven as a state-sponsored composer throughout the communist era, and his position was therefore shaped not in small part by his own decades-long successful competition for scarce cultural resources. His dislike of the Hungarians meant that one stream of discourse during the journey quite relentlessly attacked the music of Hungarian-speaking Romanians as culturally bankrupt. The music of the Hungarian population was simply bad, not worthy of our attention.

The nationalist struggle between Hungarians and Romanians spilled over into the public and private attitudes toward the multitudes of nationless peoples. Hatred and cultural violence leave little room to cultivate a true understanding or appreciation of Rom music and musicians. Religious minorities, even in a secular state, were seen as threatening, and their music, Greek or Roman Catholic, Jewish or Calvinist, or even Pentecostalist, entered the public imagination as evidence of secret languages that empowered believers to compete successfully for Romania's future. The musics of such peoples were to be avoided. They posed a danger by their very existence, which in turn was a form of resistance against what modern Romania was striving to be: a nation of Romanians.

Crossing Romania from east to west, both following the arch of the Carpathians and cutting across the mountains to the extent that side roads in winter permitted, we became increasingly attuned to the extent to which national borders failed to contain the hatred of and sundry acts of violence against the music of Romania's nationless peoples. In the national discourse, the music of Romanian Roma was constantly likened to the music of American blacks, from jazz to hip hop. The comparison was entirely critical, which is to say, the "dreadful nonmusic" of the Roma was equated with the presumably negative impact of African American music on American culture. Why presumably? Romanians repeatedly asked me about African American music, not merely because I was an American ethnomusicologist, but because I was white. They were giving vent to a deep-seated, globalized racism they presumed white Americans naturally shared. Romania's race problem was akin to the race problem of any nation-state.

28 February 1996. The Romanian-Hungarian border. A bootlegged Michael Jackson video, a compilation of greatest hits, plays in the electronics store in the duty-free zone of the border-crossing. Clips from *Dangerous* are playing out as we engage in the type of feeding frenzy common in such zones of untrammeled capitalism between nations. There are the *lei* (the standard Romanian currency) we need to dump, and the dollars that seem worth millions. The shop is paradise after a long journey, and it allows us to replenish film and tape supplies, and to buy unlimited supplies of electronic cables for the computers and recording equipment of our dreams. The Romanian clerks have their eyes glued to the screen on which Michael Jackson moves with one of the street-gang-type dances that had become his trademark since *Thriller.* They know little about the merchandise, which, for the most part, has little use-value for Romanians, who, moreover, do not have the same quantities of *lei* to dump. But the clerks have the sliding scales of the prices in their heads, for their job is one of moving the goods. Customers do not come back if this or that cable does not fit, or if recording tape does not deliver the advertised fidelity. Michael Jackson has the shop spellbound. From the video he commands the culture of the border crossing. Only a few kilometers from the toll station where it had taken hours to explain why we were bringing musical instruments into Romania, I place my pile of cables and tapes on the counter and quickly dispose of cash that was about to become useless.

The young Romanian clerk diverts his eyes from Michael Jackson briefly, glances over the merchandise, and surveys me with disbelief.

Michael is intoning for all to hear, "Remember the Time." The clerk asks, "You're an American. Why would you possibly want to visit Romania?"

Twenty minutes later, we crossed the border into Hungary.

### Points of No Return: National Landscapes of Displacement

*The moment the armed men appeared in their village, each one of them [Bosnian Muslim women] had ceased to be a person. Now they are even less so, they have been reduced to a collection of similar beings of female gender, of the same blood. Blood alone is important, the right blood of the soldiers versus the wrong blood of the women.*

—*Slavenka Drakulić, S. (2000: 73)*

The future of nationless peoples in Europe is anything but bright. As right-wing politics rises at the turn of our own century, with strong election showings in Austria for Jörg Haider in 1999 and in France for Jean-Marie Le Pen in early 2002, nationless peoples have come to occupy—yet again—the cultural arena at the borders of the European nation-state that most endangers them. The political parties of a rising European right stoke the fires that make violence even more attractive. The nationless, argues the political right, take jobs from the real citizens of the nation. The nationless, the diatribes continue, are responsible for diverting national histories. They force a reckoning with the Holocaust, and they are reminders of colonial disgraces in places like Algeria. The nationless are unpleasant symptoms of all that it is wrong with Europe, so much so, that their presence in Europe's nations is cause for terminating membership in the European Union, one of the unifying themes of right-wing parties throughout Europe.

Nationless Europeans live in zones of displacement in which oppression and violence are omnipresent. These zones, lying along national borders or in the temporary housing allotted for refugees or in the detention camps of the Balkan wars, are nothing new. They are entirely European, partly because they are zones created by and for the modern nation-state. In cultural studies and post-colonial studies, these are the spaces that lie "beyond culture" and that open up spaces where difference can thrive. They are the landscapes of hybridity and the postmodern mix (cf. Appadurai 1996 and Slobin 1993). On one hand, we recognize their boundaryless borders in Homi Bhabha's formulation of a "third space," a cultural domain between the structures of the nation-state and the claims of groups to history (Bhabha 1994). The third space exists beyond the reach of the state, whose hegemony fails to offer viable ways of defining the third space. On the other hand—and more crucially—they constitute the zones of wildness identified by Mattijs van de Port, where civilization's discontents live (van de Port 1998). The zone of wildness is a cultural space that threatens nationalism and the nation because those who inhabit it recognize other possibilities for human existence. Even at the end of the twentieth century it was

> an uncharted territory—a space in which the beastlike potential of human beings not only finds a fertile soil in which to grow, but also takes on cultural form, acquires connections, patterns, images and stories. Here, the beastlike potential becomes entangled, in an obscure way, with motives and drives that are embedded in social reality. (van de Port 1998: 15)

Van de Port examines such zones in the taverns and bars along the Serb-Hungarian border, near Novi Sad, to which cosmopolitans and urban Serbs travel to find escape through a type of music-induced abandon. The music of the Roma who perform in the zones of wildness narrates other histories, which by their very existence undermine the nation's claims to history. We enter into such zones of displacement in the conclusion, virtually without passing across its border as we leave Transylvania.

Ironically, many critics who speculate about the nature of zones of displacement have not really examined them ethnographically. The result is a tendency toward romanticizing third spaces, which in turn reveals a tendency to glorify the creative aspects of displacement and to ignore the tragic histories that zones of displacement continue to enforce. For many of Europe's nationless peoples, the newest forms of nationalism generate few reasons to find refuge in the romantic narratives about Europe's third spaces. They are increasingly destabilized in the name of the nation, but also in the name of Europe. Literally and figuratively, they are caught in the middle.

If, however, they are in the middle, zones of displacement are not invisible, though they are often overlooked. It is precisely because they are not invisible that the danger of violence is so immediate. To raise their visibility in a discussion of Europe's nationless peoples I turn schematically to several of the zones of displacement to close the present chapter and make a transition to the final chapter of the book, in which the music of the New Europeans actually serves to mix the cultures of the nationless with the national in a new era.

In his recent study of "dying Europeans" Karl-Markus Gauß charts the landscapes of historical and modern displacement. In each of his case studies a nationless people has survived in a border culture—between nations and empires for the Sorbs of northern Germany, between nations and empires for the Gottschee colonists, and between linguistic and religious worlds for Sarajevo's Sephardic Jews and Italy's Arbëreshë. The distinctive nature of these landscapes has been one of sustaining cultural survival but doing so under only the most fragile of circumstances. Inevitably, the circumstances are most fragile of all when nationalism is on the rise.

Music has been one of the most cherished cultural goods maintained in the zones occupied by dying Europeans. It is cherished above all because it concentrates the many cultural practices that constitute the zone of displacement: language, religion, historical narrative, collective and communal performance, and music's evanescence. The music of the Gottschee colonists, for example, has become the historical model for Europe's German-language speech islands (see, e.g., Brednich, Kumer, and Suppan 1969–1972). Sorbian music has preserved the sound of a pre-Germanic Germany, which by extension has become the exception that proves the rule of Germanness in German folk song (Raupp 1963). These traces may even be steeped in the symbolism of death, for example, the celebration of Jewish **Jahrzeiten** ("year anniversaries") of community members, in some places the primary cause for gathering in Romanian synagogues. We might wonder, moreover, whether Gauß's emphasis falls on the active quality of the present participle he has thoughtfully chosen, the "dying" (*sterbende*) Europeans. They cling to their own history by gathering whatever traces of nationalism they can find in a European history that eludes them.

Acts of preservation motivate the creation of new spaces for Europe's nationless. The open-air museum, for example, not only tolerates cultural difference but provides an arena for its performance. The phenomenon of the **skanzen,** which, as its name suggests, began in Scandinavia, locates clusters of villages in a single space, usually in the expanses available at the edges of the metropolis, for example, in the *skanzen* near Szentendre outside Budapest. Border cultures, too, stage their own cultural survival by building open-air museums and ethnic theme parks. Alsace-Lorraine has afforded itself a rich endowment of such museums, which allow the tourist and the ethnographer alike to witness regularly scheduled performances of Alsatian folk music, dance, and theater. The museum creates a zone of displacement that may seem frozen and appropriated from the past, but in fact it enters the national imaginary as a museum of "living culture." In other words, the open-air museum provides Alsatian, Catalan, or Welsh culture with a space in which it can live through revival. As a phenomenon of the modern European nation-state, such spaces of living culture have become ubiquitous and arresting symbols of the ways displacement is bracketed off, even at moments of extreme nationalism.

Marginalization is a process of surviving through the deployment of zones for the displaced. The culture of the nationless depends extensively on processes of marginalization. Displaced peoples choose the margins of the city, for example, for deliberate reasons. The hip hop and *raï* music of North African immigrants (and multigenerational ethnic groups) in France assert themselves not in the city center but in the suburbs, in the shifting zones of the industrialized, working-class culture that Mediterranean peoples occupy in France. Roma and Rom musicians throughout Europe, moreover, exploit the possibilities of culture on the margins. The Eastern European taverns in which Rom musicians entertain lie on the city's margins, thus extending the margins beyond the cosmopolitan pull of the city. In the United Kingdom and Ireland, the margins are realized through movement, so much so that Roma and other displaced peoples often receive the name "Travellers," who by extension perform "traveller music." The music of the Travellers represents the zones of displacement through the performance of mobility, making the margins dynamic and fluid, and ideally safe in a climate where the specter of violence is never far behind.

Fueled by nationalism, the specter of violence all too frequently turns into a violation of the zones of displacement. It was displacement, historically determined and politically manipulated, that created the conditions for ethnic cleansing in the Balkans, especially in Yugoslavia and its successor states. The fragmentation of greater nations into lesser nations generates increased competition for the nation, and the historically displaced do not find safe haven even along the borders or in the third spaces. In the displacement of new zones for the nationless, racism of the most violent and deadly kind quickly identifies victims. Ethnic cleansing, we might say, depended on the ways in which Bosnian

Muslims or Kosovar Albanians had occupied zones for the displaced that were too easily identified. At earlier moments of contested nationalism it was fundamentally little different, for example, when the ghettos and **shtetls** of East European Jews were cultural centers for nationless peoples on the eve of the Holocaust. The zones of displacement can slip very quickly into sites of racism and destruction.

We wonder, then, what is left after the romanticized enthusiasm for third spaces is stripped away to reveal their fragility and the peril that nationalism forces them to withstand. In the final chapter I turn to that question by addressing the various ways in which Europeans are returning to Europe and its nationalisms. The New Europeanness that serves as the focus for reflections on the aesthetics of European music today is also a domain of European nationalism, albeit in a New Europe. As an aesthetics of music that leads to the ascription of national identities, New Europeanness by no means eliminates the specter of violence that so closely follows nationalism; it reveals that violence, and it attempts to repair the damage left in its path. The New Europeanness opens its spaces for both Europeans with nations and those without, and it locates music in historical processes that show considerable evidence of empowering music to make the modern Europe of today in decisively new ways.

## REFERENCES

Acerbi, Giuseppe. 1999 [1798]. "Über den Joik." In Lothar Schneider, ed., *Europa erlesen: Lappland*, p. 148. Klagenfurt: Wieser Verlag. (Europa erlesen). Orig. publ.: Giuseppe Acerbi. 1802. *Travels through Sweden, Finland and Lapland to the North-Cape in the Years 1798 and 1799*. London: J. Mawman.

Aescht, Georg, ed. 1999. *Siebenbürgen: Europa erlesen*. Klagenfurt: Wieser Verlag.

Anderson, George K. 1966. *The Legend of the Wandering Jew*. Hanover, N.H.: University Press of New England.

Appadurai, Arjun. 1996. *Modernity at Large: Cultural Dimensions of Globalization*. Minneapolis: University of Minnesota Press.

Arnberg, Matts, and Pål-Nils Nilsson. 1965–1966. *Jojk: Da, när var mannen pa Oulavuoli*. Stockholm: Swedish Broadcasting.

Bălaşa, Marin Marian. Forthcoming. "Music on Money: State Legitimation and Cultural Representation." In Bruno B. Reuer, ed., *Vereintes*

*Europa–Vereinte Musik? Vielfalt und soziale Dimensionen in Mittel- und Südosteuropa.* Berlin: Weidler Verlag.

Bammer, Angelika, ed. 1994. *Displacements: Cultural Identities in Question.* Bloomington: Indiana University Press.

Baumgartner, Gerhard, Eva Müllner, and Rainer Münz, eds. 1989. *Identität und Lebenswelt: Ethnische, religiöse und kulturelle Vielfalt im Burgenland.* Eisenstadt: Prugg Verlag.

Bhabha, Homi. 1994. *The Location of Culture.* London and New York: Routledge.

Bohlman, Philip V. 1997. "Fieldwork in the Ethnomusicological Past." In Gregory F. Barz and Timothy Cooley, eds., *Shadows in the Field: New Directions in Ethnomusicological Fieldwork,* pp. 139–162. New York: Oxford University Press.

_____. 2000b. "The Remembrance of Things Past: Music, Race, and the End of History in Modern Europe." In Ronald Radano and Philip V. Bohlman, eds., *Music and the Racial Imagination,* pp. 644–676. Chicago: University of Chicago Press.

_____, and Otto Holzapfel. 2001. *The Folk Songs of Ashkenaz.* Middleton, Wisc.: A-R Editions.

Brandsch, Gottlieb, and Adolf Schullerns, ed. 1932. *Siebenbürgische Volkslieder.* Berlin and Leipzig: Walter de Gruyter.

Brednich, Rolf Wilhelm, Zmaga Kumer, and Wolfgang Suppan, eds. 1969–1984. *Gottscheer Volkslieder.* Mainz: B. Schott's Söhne.

Broughton, Simon, Mark Ellingham, and Richard Trillo, eds. 1999. *The Rough Guide to World Music.* Vol. 1: *Africa, Europe and the Middle East.* 2d ed. London: The Rough Guides.

Brown, Irving. 1929. *Deep Song: Adventures with Gypsy Songs and Singers in Andalusia and Other Lands, with Original Translations.* New York: Harper and Brothers Publishing.

Bruji. N.d. *Kein Wort Deutsch.* Extraplatte EX 341–2.

*Burgenländische Volksmusik.* 1991. *Burgenländische Volksmusik.* SSM-Records CD 020 124–2.

Chapman, Malcolm. 1994. "Thoughts on Celtic Music." In Martin Stokes, ed., *Ethnicity, Identity and Music: The Musical Construction of Place,* pp. 29–44. Oxford: Berg.

Crowe, David M. 1994. *A History of the Gypsies of Eastern Europe and Russia.* New York: St. Martin's.

Dalinger, Brigitte. 1998. *Verloschene Sterne: Geschichte des jüdischen Theaters in Wien.* Vienna: Picus.

Drakulić, Slavenka. 2000. *S.: A Novel about the Balkans.* Trans. by Marko Ivić. New York: Penguin.

Dreo, Harald, Walter Burian, and Sepp Gmasz. 1988. *Ein burgenländisches Volksliederbuch.* Eisenstadt: Verlag Nentwich-Lattner.

_____, and Sepp Gmasz. 1997. *Volksmusik im Burgenland: Burgenländische Volksballaden*. Vienna: Böhlau.

Du Bois, W. E. B. 1989 [1903]. *The Souls of Black Folk*. Repr. ed. by Henry Louis Gates, Jr. New York: Bantam.

Dundes, Alan, and Galit Hasan-Rokem, eds. 1986. *The Wandering Jew: Essays in the Interpretation of a Christian Legend*. Bloomington: Indiana University Press.

Edström, Karl-Olof. 1977. *Den samiska musikkulturen: En källkritisk översikt*. Göteborg: Skrifter från Musikvetenskapliga institutionen.

Ernst, August. 1987. *Geschichte des Burgenlandes*. Vienna: Verlag für Geschichte und Politik.

Gauß, Karl-Markus. 2001. *Die sterbenden Europäer: Unterwegs zu den Sepharden von Sarajevo, Gottscheer Deutschen, Arbëreshe, Sorben und Aromunen*. Vienna: Paul Zsolnay.

Geijer, Erik Gustaf, and Arvid August Afzelius. 1814–1817. *Svenska folk-visor från forntiden*. Stockholm: Z. Haggstrom.

Gilroy, Paul. 1993. *The Black Atlantic: Modernity and Double Consciousness*. Cambridge, Mass.: Harvard University Press.

Ginsburg, Shaul M., and Pesach S. Marek. 1901. *Evreiskie narodnye pesni v Rossii* ["Jewish Folk Songs in Russia"]. St. Petersburg: Voskhod. Reprinted 1991: Ramat Gan: Bar-Ilan University Press.

Glenny, Misha. 1999. *The Balkans: Nationalism, War, and the Great Powers, 1804–1999*. New York: Viking.

Gmasz, Sepp, Gerlinde Haid, and Rudolf Pietsch, eds. 1993. *Tondokumente zur Volksmusik in Österreich*. Vol. 1: *Burgenland*. Vienna: Institut für Volksmusikforschung. RST-91557–2.

Harrán, Don. 1999. *Salamone Rossi: Jewish Musician in Late Renaissance Mantua*. New York: Oxford University Press.

Heanzenquartett. 1996. *20 Jahre Heanzenquartett*. RST Records 91619–2.

Hedningarna. 1998. *Trä*. Northside NSD6008.

Heinschink, Mozes F. 1994. "E Romani čhib—Die Sprache der Roma. In idem and Ursula Hemetek, eds., *Roma, das unbekannte Volk: Schicksal und Kultur*, pp. 110–129. Vienna: Böhlau.

Hemetek, Ursula. 1992. *Romane gila: Lieder und Tänze der Roma in Österreich*. Vienna: Österreichische Dialektautoren and Institut für Volksmusikforschung.

_____. 2001. *Mosaik der Klänge: Musik der ethnischen und religiösen Minderheiten in Österreich*. Vienna: Böhlau.

Holzapfel, Otto. 2002. *Mündliche Überlieferung und Literaturwissenschaft: Der Mythos von Volkslied und Volksballade*. Münster: Aschendorff.

Hooker, Lynn. 2002. "'Liszt Is Ours': The Hungarian Commemoration of the Liszt Centennial." Paper delivered at the conference, "Festivals and Festivalization in a Globalizing World," University of Chicago, 11 May.

Jones-Bamman, Richard. 2000. "Saami Music." In Timothy Rice, James Porter, and Chris Goertzen, eds., *Europe*. Vol. 8: *The Garland Encyclopedia of World Music,* pp. 299–308. New York: Garland.

Karelian Folk Music Ensemble. 2001. *From the Land of the Kalevala.* Gadfly 511.

Karpeles, Maud. 1956. *Folk Songs of Europe.* London: Novello.

Kaufmann, Fritz Mordechai, ed. 1920. *Die Schönsten Lieder der Ostjuden.* Berlin: Jüdischer Verlag.

Krekovičová, Eva. 1998. *Zwischen Toleranz und Barrieren: Das Bild der Zigeuner und Juden in der slowakischen Folklore.* Frankfurt am Main: Peter Lang.

Kürti, László. 2001. *The Remote Borderland: Transylvania in the Hungarian Imagination.* Albany: State University of New York Press.

*Latcho drom.* 1993. *Latcho drom: La musique des Tsiganes du monde de l'Inde a l'Espagne.* Caroline Carol 1776–2.

Lavie, Smadar, and Ted Swedenburg, eds. 1996. *Displacement, Diaspora, and Geographies of Identity.* Durham, N.C.: Duke University Press.

Lemon, Alaina. 2000. *Between Two Fires: Gypsy Performance and Romani Memory from Pushkin to Postsocialism.* Durham, N.C.: Duke University Press.

Ling, Jan. 1997. *A History of European Folk Music.* Rochester, N.Y.: University of Rochester Press.

Liszt, Franz. 1926 [1859]. *The Gipsy in Music.* Trans. by Edwin Evans. London: William Reeves.

Longinović, Tomislav. 2000. "Music Wars: Blood and Song at the End of Yugoslavia." In Ronald Radano and Philip V. Bohlman, eds., *Music and the Racial Imagination,* pp. 622–643. Chicago: University of Chicago Press.

Mazower, Mark. 2001. *The Balkans: A Short History.* New York: Modern Library.

Metil, Robert Carl. 2000. "Post–Velvet Revolutionary Cultural Activism and Rusyn Song in the Prešov Region of Eastern Slovakia, 1989–2000." Ph.D. dissertation, University of Pittsburgh.

Metz, Franz. 1996. *Die Kirchenmusik der Donauschwaben.* Sankt Augustin: Academia Verlag.

Müller, Herta. 1984. *Niederungen.* Berlin: Rotbuch Verlag.

Muzsikás. 1993. *The Lost Jewish Music of Transylvania.* Hannibal HNCD 1373.

Narayan, Kirin. 1996. "Songs Lodged in Some Hearts: Displacements of Women's Knowledge in Kangra." In Smadar Lavie and Ted Swedenburg, eds., *Displacement, Diaspora, and Geographies of Identity,* pp. 181–214. Durham, N.C.: Duke University Press.

Pekić, Borislav. 2001. "Spieler aus Goldener Zeit." In Jörg Schulte, *Europa erlesen: Belgrad,* pp. 37–44. Klagenfurt: Wieser.

Pietsch, Rudolf. 1999. "Between Romas and Jews: An Ethnomusicological Field Expedition to Romania." *East European Meetings in Ethnomusicology* 6: 3–10.

Potter, Pamela M. 1998. *Most German of the Arts: Musicology and Society from the*

*Weimar Republic to the End of Hitler's Reich.* New Haven, Conn.: Yale University Press.

*Purimshpiler, Der.* 1937. Directed by Joseph Green. Available as video. Teaneck, N.J.: Ergo Films.

Raupp, Jan. 1963. *Sorbische Volksmusikanten und Musikinstrumente.* Bautzen: VEB Domowina-Verlag.

Rough Guide, The, ed. 2000. *The Rough Guide to the Music of Scandinavia.* The Rough Guide RGNET 1051 CD.

Sandrow, Nahma. 1977. *Vagabond Stars: A World History of Yiddish Theater.* New York: Harper & Row.

Schneider, Lothar, ed. 1999. *Europa erlesen: Lappland.* Klagenfurt: Wieser.

Sebald, W. G. 2001. *Austerlitz.* Trans. by Anthea Bell. New York: Random House.

Slobin, Mark. 1993. *Subcultural Sounds: Micromusics of the West.* Hanover, N.H.: University Press of New England.

Starkie, Walter. 1933. *Raggle-Taggle: Adventures with a Fiddle in Hungary and Roumania.* London: John Murray.

Stokes, Martin. 1992. *The Arabesk Debate: Music and Musicians in Modern Turkey.* Oxford: Oxford University Press.

St. Petersburg School. 1998. *The St. Petersburg School: Music for Cello and Piano.* Beth Hatefutsoth BTR 9801.

Sulz, Josef, Johanna Blum, Gretl Brugger, and Stefan Demetz. 1986. *Kommt zum Singen: Liederbuch aus Südtirol.* 2d ed. Bolzano: Verlagsanstalt Athesia.

Teutsch, Karl, ed. 1997. *Siebenbürgen und das Banat: Zentren deutschen Musiklebens im Südosten Europas.* Sankt Augustin: Academia Verlag.

Tromholt, Sophus. 1999 [1885]. "Das Jodeln der Lappen." In Lothar Schneider, ed., *Europa erlesen: Lappland,* pp. 149–150. Klagenfurt: Wieser.

Trumpener, Katie. 1995. "The Time of the Gypsies: A 'People without History' in the Narratives of the West." In Kwame Anthony Appiah and Henry Louis Gates, Jr., eds., *Identities.* Chicago: University of Chicago Press.

van de Port, Mattijs. 1998. *Gypsies, Wars and Other Instances of the Wild: Civilisation and Its Malcontents in a Serbian Town.* Amsterdam: Amsterdam University Press.

Wagner, Richard. 1999. "Auf ungarisch." In Georg Aescht, ed., *Siebenbürgen: Europa erlesen,* pp. 171–172. Klagenfurt: Wieser Verlag.

Wimme. 2000. *Cugu.* Northside NSD6048.

Zagajewski, Adam. 2002. *Without End: New and Selected Poems.* Trans. by Clare Cavanagh, Renata Gorczynski, Benjamin Ivry, and C. K. Williams. New York: Farrar, Straus and Giroux.

Zemtsovsky, Izaly. 2000. "'Jiddischismus' in der Music: Bewegung und Phänomen." In *Jüdische Musik in Sowjetrußland: Die "jüdische Nationale Schule" der zwanziger Jahre,* pp. 1–21. Berlin: Ernst Kuhn.

*Chapter Seven*

# The New Europeanness

## *New Musics and New Nationalisms*

### Encountering New Europeanness

It was 1991, in Budapest, when I had my first encounter with **New Europeanness** in music. While spending the year as a Humboldt Fellow in Germany, I took advantage of the sudden liberalization of travel and research restrictions to work intensively in Budapest, splitting my time between the archives of the Rabbinical Academy and field studies of music in several synagogues. But it was on the streets of downtown Pest that I encountered New Europeanness for the first time. There, for most of the afternoon in the heady days of Hungary in the summer of 1991, a marimba player wheeled out his instrument and held forth for several hours in the public space where Károly Körút opens into Deák Square. The marimba player wore a knitted *kipa,* a traditional head-covering made fashionable and modern through the use of bright fabrics, thus publicly asserting his Jewishness and consequently a foreignness that was either Israeli or American, but unquestionably not European.

He was in fact an American, which was evident from the way he displayed his religious orthodoxy and from the repertory he played with considerable virtuosity. To me, the repertory unquestionably expressed a fairly standard American klezmer sound, but it was new for the crowds of Hungarians who gathered to listen and even occasionally to drop forints nervously into the small suitcase in front of the marimba player. For these Hungarians in 1991, klezmer was quite exotic, because it both belonged and did not belong in the public spaces of Budapest. The marimba, too, was exotic because of its familiarity and strangeness. It reminded them of their own **tsimbalom,** yet it was distinct from the portable metal- or glass-slab xylophones played by Rom women on the narrow streets leading into and out of downtown Pest.

More than anything, it was the Jewishness of the experience that was for the Hungarians both exotic and strangely familiar. It was theirs, but it wasn't, which is to say, they persisted in telling me that klezmer was also Hungarian, but that it had been repressed during Hungary's fascist and communist periods during the twentieth century. And here it was again: their own Hungarian-Jewish music. Not surprisingly, I was often asked what I thought about the return of klezmer and revival of Hungarianness. I was always polite. I preferred not to tell them that this style of klezmer was distinctively American and that it bore scarcely any relation to the Jewish instrumental music that, for all the historical evidence we possessed, had thriven in Hungary prior to World War II (cf. Ottens and Rubin 1999).

In the wake of the Velvet Revolution of 1989 an aesthetic of "New Europeanness" became palpable in such experiences with growing frequency. The New Europeanness of the American marimba player was rife with paradox and contradictions. It did not belong to the space in which it was being performed, but it was embraced by those who heard it as their own. It seemed pregnant with the potential to revive, but it was unclear what it was reviving, or for whom it was reviving. It was also striking that the musics that were filling the vacuum left by implosion of the Old Europe were ephemeral and transitory, that they contributed to a culture in transition and of transition.

Klezmer, so new and yet so very traditional in the Europe of the past decade and a half, has provided me with an opening excursion for the present chapter, and it will lurk at the margins as the chapter unfolds (see Gruber 2002). Theoretically at least, I might have chosen a different ethnographic moment to symbolize the entry into the New Europe, perhaps the Rom xylophone players who were more often located along Budapest's side streets. There are also many repertories that might serve me, say the aesthetic and political debates surrounding the creation of a European anthem, both real, such as the series of decisions leading to the choice of the Beethoven/Schiller "Ode to Joy," and fictional, as in Krzysztof Kieslowski's film, *Blue* (see Chapter 1, and Paulus 1999).

All these choices would be possible, but none would suffice in and of itself. The New Europeanness has emerged from a new metaphysics of place and region, and music participates in the evocation of that metaphysics and the social construction of that place in new ways. The New Europeanness also arises from a conscious turn toward the making of history, or rather the remaking of history that results from taking the past and situating it in the present. Is there, we might ask in all fairness, anything new about the New Europeanness? It is that question, which is so bound to the overabundance of the word "new" in the chapter title above, that I answer in the conclusion of this book, with which I draw us ever closer to Europe today, to the New Europe, with its musical landscapes of paradox and contradiction.

### The New Europeanness as a New Aesthetics of Place

The New Europeanness is an aesthetics of connection and connectedness. At its core, it is an aesthetics that connects music to place and to time, and by extension it empowers music to connect place to time. The New Europeanness therefore possesses both historical and geographical qualities. These qualities make it possible for music to give meaning to place and to time through its power to effect the connections that have become necessary as Europeans seek wholeness after a half-century of Cold War in which East and West were politically held apart, and North and South were economically divided. As attempts emerge, locally, regionally, nationally, and internationally, to suture the fragments and parts of a modern history driven by the politics and culture of divisiveness, the New Europeanness charts not only an alternative model of cultural cooperation, but it also assumes specific forms that aim to repair the historical schisms and fissures wrought by modernity. Accordingly, it is an aesthetics that counters placelessness and displacement, insisting on the necessity of affording place to those who have been denied it through the long and protracted history of European nationalism.

We witness the aesthetics of New Europeanness at the places and moments charted by connection. The public spaces of the metropolis, as Budapest's klezmer musicians symbolize, serve as a cultural arena that fosters connections between the city's Jewish past and the uncertain world of minority culture and politics in post-socialist Hungary. The pattern of Budapest's public squares and transportation routes makes it possible for musicians to connect through performance. The borders that separated musical traditions in the Old Europe now function in entirely new ways, encouraging the free flow of musical traditions across them, for example, between the Finnish and Russian regions of

Karelia (see Ramnarine 2003; CD example 7). Connection between past and present is equally as crucial to the functions of New Europeanness, and it is hardly surprising that the temporal vocabulary of the aesthetics describes processes that endeavor to close historical gaps: monument and memory, historicism and revival (cf. Kertész 2003).

The healing powers of its connective potential notwithstanding, the New Europeanness was forged through revolution, specifically the revolutions that undermined and toppled the walls separating the nations of Eastern and Western Europe in 1989 and thereafter in the 1990s. Like the political revolutions, there are aesthetic revolutions, which produce new contexts and meanings of music. Music, both autonomous and yet fundamentally evocative of the identity of place, has become European again, which is to say, its meanings since 1989 increasingly connect it to place.

Conscious efforts to express the Europeanness of music have been implemented throughout the continent. Some of these originate in the cultural institutions that increasingly attend to European cultural policy, be they public programs sponsored by the European Union or private undertakings funded by the European Broadcasting Union (EBU). One marker of the transformation of both types of programs since 1989 is that they are no longer restricted to member states. Festivals celebrating European borders or cities have, since the mid-1990s, regularly taken place in Eastern Europe, for example, in Kraków or along Slovakia's borders. The EBU's annual Eurovision Song Contest regularly includes entries from non-member nations, unabashedly with the goal of drawing them into the orbit of European popular song and politics, and it is hardly by chance that the most recent Eurovision winners, Estonia (2001), Latvia (2002), and Turkey (2003), represent the New Europe.

The aesthetics of New Europeanness signals a new interest in and attention to the presence of Europe in a modern ontology of music. The emergence of the New Europe, with its radical departure from modernity and yet its postmodern turn back toward modernity, raises new aesthetic questions about modernity. Music, as the dozen years since the revolutions that produced the New Europe have proved, can do powerful cultural work. Europe-wide cultural policy turns to music precisely because of music's potential to make connections and effect connectedness across historical and political borders.

The New Europeanness also assumes subaltern forms, permitting the nationless to give voice to their connections to Europe. One of the most dramatic of these has been the connections among Rom musicians throughout Europe. If music had been manipulated as a sign and enforcement of the lack of connection in European Rom music and culture, since 1989 it has increasingly laid the groundwork for a new presence, surely a history of the present for Europe's considerable Rom populations. Through a dramatic historicism, Roma and Rom musicians have achieved enormous visibility and audibility in European history. Whether in Russia (Lemon 2000) or Spain (Gay y Blasco 1999), Serbia (van de Port 1998) or Austria (Hemetek 2001), Roma now appear in ethnographies of European expressive culture as if they are constituent citizens of a national culture. The cultural connections made possible by a European Rom music culture, even when mediated by films such as *Latcho Drom* (1993), may not have dismantled all stereotypes about and prejudices against the Roma, but they have fundamentally altered the ways in which they project a history of nationlessness through performance. In the aesthetic discourse of the New Europeanness, Roma are no longer a people without place and history: One need but listen to the music of Roma, to the genres folk, popular, and sacred music (Lange 2003) performed by Roma today, to recognize that music has carved out a place for them, however contested, in the New Europe (listen to CD examples 9, 10, and 27).

The connections of the New Europeanness to the nation are manifold and complex. New Europeanness is, it follows, also a musical aesthetics of a new nationalism. Whether that new nationalism is more generally an aesthetic condition of the New Europe, or whether it assumes forms that contribute to the positive and negative effects of the "new nationalisms" that have sustained political instability in the Balkans and fed tensions in the Basque region of Spain or in Northern Ireland, frame the questions that I pose in this chapter. Beyond question, though, is that the New Europeanness exposes rather than obscures the issues of nationalism today. Experiencing the New Europeanness in contemporary musical activities forces one to confront the very struggle to make and sustain the connections that ultimately will determine how Europe enters the future as a community of nations.

### What the New Europeanness Is *Not*

The music of the New Europe exists in a state of flux, characterized by instability and what we might call "open-ended transition." We know where the point of departure for the transition lies—in the colonial structures of late capitalism, in the institutionalized folklore crucial to socialism, in the juncture of Romanticism and nationalism—but it remains an open question just where the transitions are leading (see, e.g., Verdery 1996 and Lampland 2000). Further augmenting the instability of transition is the prevalence of competition for space on what Martha Lampland has called the "landscapes of transition" in the New Europe (ibid.: 6–9). On such landscapes of transition, New Europeanness is not one condition, but many. It resists being pinned down; it belies attempts to bound it with definitions.

In the course of this book definitions have been employed only sparingly and tentatively, usually as a means of avoiding the essentialism that has historically led to an equation of European music with elite repertories and practices, so the transitory nature of the New Europeanness in music might well seem to provide me with a convenient opportunity to avoid definitions almost entirely. There is, however, something too convenient about that opportunity. In all fairness it is important to speculate about what New Europeanness is or could be. However, the tentative gestures toward definition that follow do not move teleologically, but rather more circuitously. What follows is a brief disquisition about what the New Europeanness in music is *not*.

First of all, the New Europeanness is neither a process nor a product of centralization or canon formation. It is in no sense of a definition singular, and it shows no signs of being refracted into core repertories. The resistance to centralization and canons of all kinds means that the musical landscape of New Europeanness is one of borders rather than of centers. This is not, I argue, the musical geography of Europeanness as it unfolded from the Late Middle Ages until the mid-twentieth century, which was dominated by centers, be they cities and courts in the fourteenth century or nations and empires in the nineteenth (see Kaufmann 1995).

The New Europeanness is not a process of sustaining change and maintaining or establishing tradition. Tradition is up for grabs. It goes to the highest bidder, who then can do with it what she or he wants. The bidder might be local or national, say, a revivalist movement, or the bidder might be regional or international, say, a transnational record company in search of global pop. Aesthetically and economically, these bidders are more often than not in competition. What this also means is that the New Europeanness is not necessarily connected by tradition—severed or otherwise—to an earlier Europeanness. It might be, but usually only when an old Europeanness offers some kind of advantage for establishing the new.

Similarly, New Europeanness is not distinguished by progress, in other words creative or performative strategies that privilege the present and the future. Instead, it draws wantonly from the past. There is no sense that the sounds or the ideas are new, even though the adjective "new" is consciously applied to them. Gone is any sense that today's music must distinguish and distance itself from an earlier music. Drawing from the past, however selectively, enriches the ways in which the present is given new meaning.

Lest the reader think this chapter simply substitutes one teleology for another, let me state very clearly that New Europeanness does not lend itself to reduction to a mere condition of postmodernism, nor is it yet another form of or excuse for globalization. Whereas there can be no denial that the historicism implicit in New Europeanness depends on the decline and passing of modernism, it is no less consequent to the dissipation of postmodernism. Similarly, though New Europeanness exists within and is not independent from globalization, it is not a product of globalization. Its tendencies are, if anything, anti-global, indeed in a paradoxical way, because New Europeanness has an undeniable connection to the West and its hegemony in modern history and modern music history. That means, for example, that New European musics draw upon the technologies that undergird globalization, but they resist being manipulated by those technologies. As a response to and a critique of globalization New Europeanness unleashes a complex, alternative aesthetics for interpreting the history of the present, and it places that aesthetics in the hands of musicians and audiences, and in the acts of performance that connect them.

In sum, New Europeanness cannot be reduced to a set of stable practices or styles, even in those cases where nationalist labels are slapped on it. New Europeanness is distinctive because of the mobility and adaptability of those drawing upon it, of those who make it their own. New Europeanness reflects larger processes of transition, albeit transition that has been stripped of its teleology of progress and of its ability to narrate distinctively Western processes of history. What is left—or, rather, what emerges from the landscapes of transition—is a different set of musical ontologies altogether. And it is to these that we now turn.

### Musical Ontologies of New Europeanness

In the midst of non-definitions running through the previous section, there lurked more than a few definitions. Such lurking definitions suggest that New Europeanness accrues to quite different and distinctive ontologies, in other words, the philosophical and aesthetic ways in which music conveys its in-the-world meanings. The musical ontologies that have taken shape since 1989 have come to yield a different landscape and soundscape for the New Europe.

Crucial to the musical ontologies of New Europeanness is that music and musicians are mobile. Performance does not so much ascribe a sense of place as derive from a crisis of placelessness. The same musicians who play street music in Berlin and Paris shuttle from EU-sponsored youth and cultural festivals on alternative weekends. There are some musicians, in fact, whose performances follow officially sanctioned and commercially viable circuits so extensively that they rarely perform for audiences at home. The displacement that characterized the musical practices of the nationless peoples examined in Chapter 6 assumes myriad forms in the ontologies of New Europeanness.

Art-music composers, too, wantonly claim their identity from many places, picking, choosing, and reshuffling their claims to place as best suits their needs. Such mobility has characterized the career, for example, of the Estonian composer, Arvo Pärt, who lived largely in Germany before and after Estonian independence from the Soviet Union and composes with a vocabulary in which Estonianness is only one of several aesthetic components. Pärt often weaves sacred themes and forms into his music, which paradoxically has meant to signal a liberation from the silenced sacred qualities in much Soviet contemporary music, but in fact relies on the aesthetic and theological meanings of icons in Russian Orthodox Christianity, historically still another presence in Catholic and Lutheran Estonia. These paradoxes notwithstanding, Pärt, who only rarely visits Estonia, has become the paradigmatic composer—one might say, the musical icon—for the New Estonia.

Music of all kinds, therefore, can be freighted across European borders, both drawing attention to those borders and denying their power to enclose and imprison. It follows that such mobility spawns fundamentally different types of landscapes, which in turn constitute new ontologies. Rather than centripetalizing as national styles, the spatial ontologies of New Europeanness centrifugalize to form diasporas. They undergo patterns of seasonal flux as workers from the South— the Mediterranean and the Middle East—fuel the industries of the North. Dominating the new landscapes are its border regions— Kosovo, Northern Ireland, Saamimaa, Basque country. Even the centers have been recharted, as musicians move along the transportation arteries of the street and subway lines (see, e.g., Bohlman 1994).

Performance spaces and spectatorship also respond to radically different ontologies. Performances no longer depend upon and not infrequently are excluded from segregated spaces, but they must compete for and within space in very real senses. Music is often transformed into a commodity that is always accessible, and the new performance spaces enhance that accessibility. Paradoxically, just as some ontologies of performance are made more accessible to some, they may be closed to others. This has become the case for the now ubiquitous performance of Rom musicians from Slovakia or Romania in concert halls throughout Western Europe, which few Roma themselves, or Romanians for that matter, could ever afford to attend. Rom musicians such as Taraf de Haïdouks may have built substantial public careers, but they do so largely by not performing for Roma (see, e.g., Taraf de Haïdouks 1991, 1994, and 2001).

The transitions and migrations that determine the musical landscape of the New Europe necessitate intense forms of competition for musical place. Competition, it follows, is constitutive of the ontologies of music itself. Musicians literally and figuratively compete for musical space within the nation. The musical landscape of the nation becomes a scaffolding of competitive levels from top to bottom. National, regional, and local; urban, suburban, and rural; racially central and ethnically peripheral. Just as such levels of musical place and identity reveal, the rules of competition vary, suggesting a sort of quantum physics of musical space. In Scotland, the pride and bulwark of national competition may be Celtic music in the regional dialect of **pibroch** and pipebands. Inaudible on the regional level is, in contrast, **Hindustani** music, which thrives in an alternative musical universe. Ironically, those living in that musical universe, Urdu speakers of Pakistani heritage, now outnumber those living in the dominant universe, Gaelic speakers.

Competition for scarce media resources is another ontological reality. Folk music in Eastern Europe, long ago appropriated from the folk, falters under the weight of new forms of competition since 1989. In Hungary, for example, government resources are poured into the well-known ensemble Muzsikás, while all other groups must scramble for the scraps. The reliance on competitions in Eastern Europe and Hungary is not unique. It is, for example, during the annual cycle of the "Grand Prix der Volksmusik" in German-speaking Central Europe—Germany, Austria, and Switzerland, and Südtirol, Luxembourg, and Alsace-Lorraine—that bands playing electronically enhanced and aesthetically popularized folk repertories win the rights (and contracts) that allow them to represent their regions and nations (Mahr 2002).

The ontologies of identity in the New European musics depend on double, if not multiple consciousness, to borrow from W. E. B. Du Bois (1903) and Paul Gilroy (1993). In the New Europe, moreover, race enters into the calculus of musical identity with ethnicity and nationalism (see Bohlman 2000b), a calculus that creates processes of hybridity that have previously not characterized European music, for example, the increased presence of blackness in European popular music (see below). It follows then that new hybridities emerge from the ontologies of multiple consciousness. New Europeanness provides an aesthetics for identifying the new spaces—geographical, performative, and ontological—that accommodate such hybridity. Several of the landscapes in the following section reveal a different sort of space between the sacred and secular. Because music has multiple functions, it hybridizes these spaces in many different ways. The ontological spaces of musical hybridity are, to some degree, related to Homi Bhabha's concept of a "third space" (1994), which depends on the opposition of binary spaces and then forms an alternative to them, perhaps in the regions and regionalism that form along national borders, or in the urban neighborhoods that accommodate the growing populations of New Europeans.

New Europeanness provides a way to account for a new ontology of hybridity that is European. It becomes more and more discomfiting to find comfort in the axioms that take European hegemony for granted. Even hegemony, as the enemy of hybridity, has been destabilized in the past decade. How might we recognize and reckon the new ontologies of hybridity? We must begin by identifying the new spaces—geographical, performative, and ontological—that accommodate such hybridity. The ontologies of hybridity insinuate themselves within and between the spaces constituting the historical musical landscape of Europe.

Rather than offering a theoretical alternative to Europe and its music history, they make their presence known as European, indeed more to the point of this chapter, as insistently New European.

## Five Landscapes of New Europeanness

*In this world [of the tavern] there's none of that craziness about nationalities and race. The national is entirely subconscious.*
                                                        —*Schulhoff 1924: 84*

New Europeanness has remapped the place of the nation since 1989, carving out new spaces for nationalism. The new places of the nation resemble the old cultural geography of nationalism, not least because the new historically depends on the old. New Europeanness has, nonetheless, transformed the aesthetics of place, not least because it has become quite impossible to reduce the aesthetics of place to bounded categories of place. Although I borrow terms and concepts from previous aesthetics of place, they apply only to places formed within and without shifting boundaries. Indeed, placelessness itself, as we witnessed in Chapter 6, is one of the aesthetic conditions charted by New Europeanness.

To draw us more specifically into an understanding of the aesthetics of place in the New Europe, I employ at the most general level a concept that has been crucial to nineteenth- and twentieth-century interpretations of the relation of music to place, the musical landscape. The concept of landscape bears witness to an historiographic tradition of ascribing musical meaning to place, for example, in the German notion of *Volksliedlandschaft,* or "folk-song landscape" (see, e.g., Farwick 1986 and Bohlman 2002b). Since the formation of the European Union and then again since the revolutions of 1989 the musical landscape has acquired a new set of meanings, however, particularly those connecting landscape to the new regionalism in Europe. The new regionalism seeks ways to find alternatives to nationalism, or at least to accommodate the slippage that occurs when nationalism is insufficient or extreme. The music of the region forms at the spaces between nations, often using languages or dialects that are not central to the official music culture of the nation, such as Welsh in the United Kingdom, Basque along the French-Spanish border, or Finnish dialects in the music of Russian Karelia. The music of the new regionalism may have survived the rise of modernity, or it may be the product of recent revival, especially in music. Whatever its origin and tradition, the music of the new regionalism takes shape across the landscape that receives some official recognition from the political and cultural institutions of the New Europe itself, such as the European Regional Development Fund (ERDF) of the European Union (Pinder 2001: 84–86).

The musical landscapes shaped by New Europeanness are significant because they are sites of movement, on which music and music-makers are mobile. Whereas earlier, historical musical landscapes emphasized rootedness—the connection of music to place—the new landscapes are the products of rootlessness and disconnectedness. The landscapes of New Europeanness overlap and intersect, and in so doing they give a new musical shape to Europe itself. In the section that follows I begin with a larger concept of landscape and then move to a phenomenon of New Europeanness that moves across it and locates itself on it. A set of interrelations between music and place in the New Europe thus emerges. New choralism, to take one example, is an almost Europe-wide phenomenon, and within the new choralism synagogue choruses form a landscape both unique to them—the destroyed Jewish urban culture of Eastern Europe—and shared by other choruses, say, EU-sponsored choral festivals. Baltic choruses, too, enjoy a significant and visual presence in the new choralism while still fulfilling nationalist agendas in their own nations. The landscapes of New Europeanness provide a place in which musicians representing different linguistic, regional, religious, and national traditions join together, and they do so at the places their boundaries intersect. The boundaries of New Europeanness do not exist so much to contain tradition and protect it from external influences as to facilitate exchange that utilizes music to redefine the identity of place in the New Europe. I now turn to five landscapes where New Europeanness has been particularly sweeping in its capacity to rechart the meanings of nation and nationalism in the New Europe.

## The International Media Competition—*The Eurovision Song Contest*

The Eurovision Song Contest responded immediately to the political events of 1989 and their aftermath. The Eurovision Song Contest, which claims to be the single largest musical competition of its kind in the world, had for decades pushed and tugged at the boundaries of Europe. From the first Eurovision Song Contest in Lugano, Switzerland, in 1956, until the competitions that took place during the writing of this book, in Stockholm (2000), Copenhagen (2001), Tallinn (2002), and Riga (2003), the organizers of the Eurovision have mixed a political concern for European unity with the financial interests of the member networks of the European Broadcasting Union (EBU). As the Eurovision grew in popularity and in importance for the EBU, it included a growing number of European states. By the time I began following the Song Contest in 1979 during fieldwork in Israel—the Israeli entry, "Halleluja," performed by Gali Atari and Milk and Honey, won that year—nations not geographically a part of Europe were beginning to participate in the contest with some regularity, especially Morocco, Malta, Cyprus, and Turkey (see the annual charts of competing nations in Gambaccini et al. 1999).

By the mid-1980s, Eastern European nations had begun competing, though only those that would have been considered "more liberal" by the West because of economic reform and encroaching capitalism, notably Hungary and Yugoslavia. The political importance of the entries outside of Central and Western Europe was seldom overlooked, and it remains emblematic of Eurovision's engagement with the role of popular music as a means of representing European unity that Yugoslavia— in the parlance of the 1990s, the "former" Yugoslavia—won the Eurovision in 1989. The message of Europeanness in the winning entry, Riva's "Rock Me," had both musical and ideological resonance in the very paradox of a song that was deliberately conservative. Indeed, 1989 was the first and last time a nation from the Balkans would win the Eurovision in the Cold War era.

Throughout the 1990s, a growing number of countries from Eastern Europe sent national entries, and their successes on the evening of the final Eurovision of the century were followed closely by audiences across the continent. Even though Estonia, Bosnia, Croatia, or Poland did not win during the 1990s, their entries were given vocal support, and the regional biases of the contest itself shifted, at least symbolically, to Eastern Europe. With the new millennium and the new concern in Europe about drawing the nation-states of Eastern Europe into the continent as a whole, the Eurovision has provided a distinctive and very public forum for cultural and musical integration. In the 2001 Eurovision Song Contest in Copenhagen, the open shift toward Eastern Europe was complete, for Estonia's entry, performed by Tanel Padar and Dave Benton, won first place. Again, ideological questions of European unity—the song's title was "Everybody"—seem at first hearing out of place against the musical choice to employ an amalgam of dancehall and gospel styles. As with the Yugoslav winner in 1989, it was the amalgam itself that established both the newness and the Europeanness of the Estonian winner in 2001.

This brief sketch of the political agenda implicit in the colonization by the Eurovision Song Contest of national popular music institutions in an expanding Europe might strike some readers as a bit odd. Stylistically, it is the exception rather than the rule that an Eastern European entry chooses to draw attention to a song's easternness. The leveling of musical style in the winning entries that we examined in Chapter 1 holds no less for the recent spate of entries from Eastern Europe, those that compete well, as well as those that are less successful. It is still the case that, in order to win, a song must be unobtrusive, musically and ideologically, and this was indeed the stylistic path chosen by Latvia in 2002 with its winning entry, "I Wanna." The rare *cause célèbre* that does produce a winning entry, such as transsexual Dana International in 1998, must perform at her or his most stylistically homogeneous (see Swedenburg 1997). Watching the May television extravaganza, one can only wonder how such a spectacle of bread and circus could possibly signal political issues of any real significance. Everything from national costume to national musical nuance is remade for television and transformed to sound more similar than different. Ofra Haza's "Chai" in 1983 and Céline Dion's "Ne partez pas sans moi" (the 1988 entry for Switzerland) were among the most innocuous songs the two singers ever recorded, even though it was the Eurovision Song Contest in both cases that launched their international careers. We might even ask whether there is not a palpable attempt to introduce the political, say, by introducing new national entries, only to depoliticize and level their differences. Even non-entries, such as Michael Flatley and one of the first international broadcasts of *Riverdance*, staged only as a seven-minute interlude at the 1994 Eurovision, may use the song contest as a breakthrough from innocuous to distinctive (for a video performance see McColgan 1995).

As a domain of New Europeanness the Eurovision Song Contest exposes a remarkable degree of paradox. ESC entries accommodate the

*Figure 7.1.*
*Cover of Eurovision CD anthology*
*of Israeli Eurovision entries*

local, the national, and the international, or European, but they can only do this within the strictures of national committees and national broadcasting networks. Winning is very important, as the careers of previous winners and near-winners, such as ABBA and the late Ofra Haza, demonstrate. Clearly, there are nations that invest a great deal in the production of winning entries, foremost among them Ireland and Israel (see Figure 7.1, the cover of a CD-compilation of Israel's Eurovision entries).

National entries may also contrast with and contradict a traditional aesthetics of nationalism. France's entries in the 1990s have come several times from colonial *départements,* Guadaloupe and Martinique, for instance, as if to suggest that the national sound is really Caribbean. Austria's entries since the mid-1990s (such as "The Rounder Girls" in 2000) have included musicians of African descent, indeed, African-Americans, flagrantly snubbing both the nationalist politics of Austria's right-wing Freedom Party and its call for restrictions on the entry of foreigners into Austria. These entries openly disregard the Austrian musical establishment's claims for a nationalist musical aesthetics that links classical, folk, and popular music in a long historical tradition canonized by the geographic centrality of Austria in Europe itself. Consciously choosing black musicians and sanctioning a song in the girl-band Motown style of the Supremes, as in the case of the Rounder Girls, flagrantly violates the nationalist canon and embraces New Europeanness.

The Eurovision has, on occasion, been an opportunity to give voice to the voiceless, for example, in 1980, when the Saami musician Mattis Hætta was the Norwegian entry in the European Song Contest (see also

Chapter 6). Together with Sverre Kjelsberg, Hætta performed the Norwegian entry, "Saamiid Aednan," a juxtaposition of Norwegian folk song and Saami yoiking. If Hætta's entry made a particularly bad showing for Norway (placing sixteenth out of nineteen entries), it nonetheless drew attention to larger questions of nationalist politics. For Norway and the other Scandinavian nations in which Saami lived, Hætta made it clear that the music of a nationless people could represent the nation. "Saamiid Aednan" stood in for the nation at a moment when Saami were making particularly strong claims for self-representation and the limited autonomy of regional legislative bodies. The performance itself, on the political and musical stage of the Eurovision, contributed substantially to political gains for the Saami in subsequent years.

In contrast, there are national entries that flaunt their own abnegation of a more serious nationalist voice. Israel's 2000 entry, the band Ping Pong's "Sameach" ("Happy"), ridiculed peace discussions with Syria, suggesting instead a sort of a national political ennui.

| | |
|---|---|
| Kol hayom ba-televizia milhamot | All day long wars on television |
| Uve-ostralia shuv hithilu shitfonot. | And in Australia floods have begun again. |
| Hine ba hadika'on shel yom rishon | Here comes Sunday's depression |
| Ani rotza ani rotza melafefon. | I want, I want a cucumber. |
| Oh oh sameah . . . | Oh oh happy . . . |

On the eve of the intifada that began in September 2000, "Sameach" seems at first glance to minimize the political presence of the nation in song. Historically, however, "Sameach" reveals connections to the tradition of "pioneer songs" (**shireh chalutzim**) from the 1920s and 1930s, in which nation-building itself was focused on the labors invested in transforming the desert to a fertile landscape capable of feeding a still nascent nation (see Nathan 1994). The song does not, therefore, espouse an apolitical ennui, but rather draws the listener's attention to the very danger that it signals.

The paradoxes of the Eurovision Song Contest combine to illustrate the ways in which New Europeanness enters the public spheres of the constituent members of the European Broadcasting Union. At one level—the commercial level that determines EBU interests—the Eurovision furthers a type of European unity, however superficial it may be, however driven by recording companies and broadcasting authorities it may be. At another series of levels, the Eurovision has provided a public space for the emergence of alternative voices and politics. Questions of winning, media ratings, and star careers do dominate the first level. Accordingly, that level represents the publicity of music at the center. The questions dominating the other levels are of a different order altogether. Accordingly, they represent a shifting publicity of music at the periphery. The space of New Europeanness forms at these various levels, drawing attention to their intersections but enforcing their separateness at the same time.

To determine how we might begin to investigate and understand the spaces in which the New Europeanness is manifest in the European Song Contest, let us turn briefly to the German entry for 1999, Sürpriz's "Kudüs'e seyahat/Reise nach Jerusalem/Journey to Jerusalem" (see Figure 7.2). The song itself frames the spaces of New Europeanness, calling attention to where they are, without itself actually occupying the spaces. Since that may sound a bit abstract, let me suggest that we sift through some of the issues of multiple consciousness. "Journey to Jerusalem" exemplifies the ways in which peripheries and centers have collapsed in the public sphere of the New Europe. Sürpriz was Germany's first Turkish entry, and as such she symbolized a politicization of Germany's traditionally dispassionate involvement. Sürpriz had been one of the first singers to rise from the class of **Gastarbeiter** and cross the nationalist border barring Turkish workers, even those born in Germany, from citizenship. At a national level, Sürpriz symbolized a distinct ideological shift, an admission of Germany's Turkish residents into the public sphere of musical nationalism (cf. Özdogan 2000). Known to Germans as a children's game, played like musical chairs, the "Journey to Jerusalem" was both familiar and defamiliarizing. The paradox of pilgrimage to Jerusalem, an experience of profound multiple consciousness for Europeans, is resituated in the present by the song, written specifically for the 1999 Eurovision competition in Jerusalem

*Figure 7.2. CD containing cover versions of Sürpriz's 1999 Eurovision entry for Germany, "Journey to Jerusalem"*

(Dana International, singing "Diva," had won for Israel the year be-fore). The symbolic journeys of the song explicitly inscribe the journeys of transition onto the song itself, where it remaps the journeys of so many *Gastarbeiter* returning again and again in search of a place between Germany's industries and Turkey with signposts of New Europeanness.

"Kudüs'e seyahat" ("Journey to Jerusalem") refrain

> Turn, turn, here we go again,
> "Journey to Jerusalem" . . .
> Life is a long, long journey
> into Tomorrowland.

## The New Choralism

In April 1997, a chorus with massed singers from various parishes and different Christian traditions in the area around Split, Croatia, em-barked on a German tour. The tour took the Croatian chorus to major German cities, where various organizations hosted it and provided con-cert facilities. By and large, the concerts took place in religious facili-ties, either in churches or in the large halls available for conferences and other gatherings that religious and charitable organizations lo-cated in the urban center. On 20 April 1997, the Croatian chorus per-formed in the social hall of one such church-sponsored charitable or-ganization in the center of Berlin, or rather, in the area of massive construction along the former border, the zone earlier occupied by the Berlin Wall—in this case within ten-minutes walk from the various mass-transit stops at the Potsdamer Platz. That the concert took place at the very epicenter of the events that had divided Europe into West and East, Christian and non-Christian regions, was lost on no one (see Chapter 5). Symbolically, the concert occupied the epicenter of at-tempts to heal the political and religious schisms of the Cold War, most specifically the wounds of the successor lands of the former Yugoslavia, which resolutely refused to heal (cf. Ladd 1997).

Announced as a concert celebrating a new era of religious and polit-ical freedom in Croatia, the performance drew an overflow crowd, the majority of whom were able to hear only through the windows that opened onto the parking lot and street next to the hall itself. The repertory was intentionally diverse, which is to say, programmed in such a way that performers and audiences alike would discover something of their own. The program began with Croatian sacred works from earlier style periods, stretching from early works in Latin through Early Modern repertories representing the growing presence of Croatia and finally culminating in nineteenth- and twentieth-century sacred works utilizing larger forms. After establishing the legitimacy of a Croatian music history, the program shifted to vernacular music, for the most part consisting of choral arrangements of folk and folklike music, all of it showing the vibrancy of Croatian folk Catholicism. Finally, the program took a turn toward the Austro-German chorales and motets, intentionally mixing the Catholic works from the high-church Croatian context and the Lutheran works of J. S. Bach that were historically more suited to their North German host city of Berlin.

All who experienced the Croatian concert found it enormously moving. Packed into the space of some three hours—there was no attempt to observe the temporal economy of the standard concert—were so many symbols of New Europeanness that it hardly becomes possible to separate one set from another. History and religion, politics and aesthetics intersected and blurred into a single experience. It was impossible not to recognize that it was the Croatian chorus that made such conscious unity possible. The chorus was, at one level, an artifice of an active attempt to freight unity about Europe, highlighting it by performing it at the sites where the return to unity was most publicly pursued. The performance itself fused several communities: new and old Croatian communities in Berlin, the committed and the curious, Germans eager to repair their city, and tourists relieved that there was still time to recognize the scars left by the past. It was an ethnographic moment of intense New Europeanness, and it was a musical moment that only a chorus, imbued with that New Europeanness, could bring into being.

The Croatian choral concert also serves as a concentrated moment of the "new choralism," a domain of New Europeanness to which I now turn. Choralism, as I examine it in this section, was hardly new in the 1990s, but rather was a phenomenon with nineteenth-century, nationalist origins, for example, in the Baltic states, Germany, and in Wales (for a study of choralism in Switzerland see Bolle-Zemp 1992). The importance of the chorus for the consolidation of the national in music has repeatedly appeared in this book. In the 1990s, however, the phenomenon spread across Europe with an especially renewed vigor and, in some cases, ideological agenda, inspired in the East by the "Singing

Revolutions" in Estonia, Latvia, and Lithuania, and in the West by the proliferation of choral competitions along the Celtic fringe. The symbolism of the new choralism was overt, that is, intentionally rendered as obvious as possible. The chorus embodies a community or the people of a region or nation and expresses their unity through song. The new choralism also responded to an historical irony, in other words, to the political fissures that would otherwise prevent unity. Both irony and symbolism are abundantly evident in the case study to which I should now like to turn: The rise of the synagogue chorus in the New Europe.

## The Rise of the Synagogue Chorus

The synagogue chorus accompanied the Jewish community as it adapted to modern Europe in the nineteenth century, and the synagogue chorus again accompanied the struggles of many Jewish communities attempting to find a place in the New Europe at the end of the twentieth century. Choruses are not historically traditional in the synagogue, for the polyphonic choral sound they foster, especially when women take their place in the chorus, violates a sacred aesthetics that privileges the text in both cantillation and liturgical practices. The synagogue chorus has served as a marker of Europeanness, and, whether in late Renaissance Italy or early nineteenth-century Germany, it has ushered in change and progress into European Jewish communities (see, e.g., Harrán 1999). With remarkably few exceptions synagogue choruses are found only in Europe, above all in Ashkenazic regions, and in the United States, where they confirm the musical transitions that characterized religious communities with European roots, in recent decades through the massing of choral festivals regionally and nationally. As a marker of Europeanness, however, the synagogue chorus historically stirred up controversy and became the focus of debates that had both religious and abstractly aesthetic dimensions.

In the 1990s, the rise of the synagogue chorus quickly became a marker of New Europeanness, with debates about religious propriety and aesthetic dimensions not unlike those of the Modern era. It might seem as if I am suggesting that the New Europeanness marked by the rise of the synagogue chorus is a reflection of the past, if not a revival in the narrow sense. It is not, nor could it be. One of the most fundamental differences between past and present is the way the chorus represents the synagogue and its liturgy. Even when sponsored by the synagogue, the synagogue chorus of the 1990s does not serve the synagogue or its liturgy. Temporally and historically, the New European synagogue chorus calibrates its own relation to tradition. The New European synagogue chorus is mobile in several ways. It moves geographically across Europe, as if to symbolize the return of European Jewry for the first time since the Holocaust. Stylistically and historically, the synagogue chorus moves into and out of diverse repertories, wantonly circumventing any semblance of authenticity.

New European synagogue choruses fall into three categories whose functions are fluid, but which reflect New Europeanness in different ways. First, there are choruses in Eastern Europe that have remarkably retained an unbroken tradition during the Holocaust and then through the Communist era. The best examples of such choruses have been those of the Dohány Street Synagogue and the Rabbinical Academy of Budapest, both of which managed to survive because the Nazi-imposed ghetto in Budapest was never entirely liquidated during World War II. Immediately after the war, the synagogal tradition was circulated in manuscripts, which continue to serve the cantorial chorus even today (see Figure 7.3; see also Figure 7.4, the cover of a recent CD released by the Dohány Street Synagogue). The CD accompanying this book also contains an example of new choralism from the Budapest Jewish tradition.

The second kind of synagogue chorus was formed in the wake of the 1989 revolution as a means of instantiating a Jewish community that had chosen to remain relatively invisible during the post-Holocaust/Cold War era. This was particularly the case in Germany, Austria, and the Soviet Union, obviously because of the long histories of anti-Semitism. Not surprisingly, Americans and Israelis actively participated in the reestablishment of these post-1989 choruses (see Figures 7.5 and 7.6).

Finally, there are synagogue choruses whose primary function is to historicize past traditions. Many of these choruses maintain, at best, loose affiliations with synagogues or with Jewish communities. Their primary activities center around concertizing and recording, and not surprisingly they tend to record on the larger European and transnational labels (see Figures 7.7 and 7.8).

The repertories of the New European synagogue choruses vary considerably, one might even say, wildly. They lay claim to the past, but with rare exceptions they make no attempt to recuperate local community

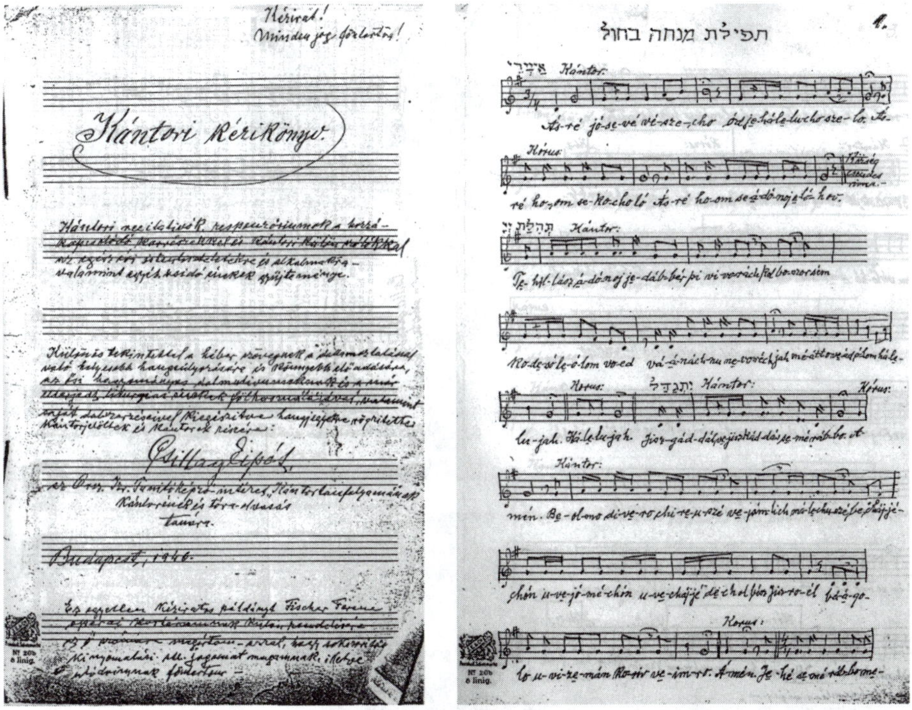

*Figure 7.3.   Post–World War II liturgical tradition of the Budapest Jewish community, cover and page 1 (Eipós 1946)*

*Figure 7.4.*
*Cover of CD,* Liturgy of Dohány Street Synagogue *(1994)*

*Figure 7.5.*
*CD cover of* Sacred Chants
of the Contemporary
Synagogue *(1998)*

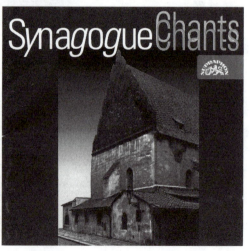

*Figure 7.6.*
*Cassette cover of JOINT-*
*sponsored Male Choir of*
*the Moscow Academia of*
*Cantorial Art (mid-1990s)*

*Figure 7.7.*
Synagogue Chants *(1990)*

*Figure 7.8.*
Jewish Masterworks of the
Synagogue Liturgy *on deutsche
harmonia mundi (BMG)*

traditions—that is, they do not demonstrate a concern for a community's **minhag** (musical custom and convention) or **nusach** (musical and liturgical style). What most choruses do share, nonetheless, is a concern for an expansive Ashkenazic tradition that includes diverse styles but common European historical referents, a *bricolage,* albeit one that does not spill over carefully realized boundaries. Yiddish folk songs arranged for chorus, for instance, have become a staple for the synagogue chorus. When Russian choruses such as the Moscow Male Choir of the Cantor Art Academy (see Figure 7.6) tour Central European synagogues, they devote as much as the entire second half of their concert to Yiddish songs, **niggunim** and **hassidic** "hit songs" consciously trying to evoke a feeling that these musical practices are what all European Jewish communities have in common.

There is yet another repertory that serves many synagogue choruses, which for lack of a better term might be described as "New Age." One is tempted to imagine that these repertories have benefited from the fascination with Gregorian chant as a repertory of religious musical revival, and perhaps that fascination has spurred a willingness to render liturgical works with the accompaniment of slowly shifting harmonies played by organs and even by synthesizers. The more visible recordings dipping into these styles, however, predate 1989—the Old-New Synagogue recording from Prague illustrated on Figure 7.7, for example, was first made in 1956—at which time they signified an Eastern exoticism.

The New Age versions of synagogal music, with the evocation of exotic otherness, are the most extreme case of a more generalized disembodiment of congregations from religion. In the New Europe, synagogue choruses largely do not serve synagogues. They no longer serve as a simulacrum for the corporate presence of a vital Jewish community, but rather they are surrogates for the absence of voice. Might not their proliferation after 1989 be a paradox? Such a question generates contradictory answers. Yes, if we attempt to see in the synagogue chorus a bridge between the New Europe and previous Europes with substantial Jewish communities. No, if we realize that the jumble of Jewish synagogal repertories now unleashed by increased mobility, non-European funding, and a market for CDs that sample the past have the power to jerrybuild tradition in the historical rupture between the Holocaust and the present.

The synagogue chorus does not revive the past, for there is no context in the New Europe suitable for its revival, as there is for, say, klezmer music (cf. Gruber 2002). In no sense does the synagogue chorus sing music for worship. The synagogue chorus, nonetheless, rescues the past by mobilizing its performance and preventing it from slipping from memory. The very mobility and paradox of the New Europe have created a field in flux, where the Jewishness of a music that was once European insists that it still has a presence in the New Europe. The new choralism of that New Europe has made it possible to reach across the historical distance of the Cold War and the Holocaust to an earlier era of modernity.

## Religion and Religious Revival

Religion and religious revival have acted as two of the most sweeping forces for the mobilization of New Europeanness, and they have provided crucial templates for New Europeanness in music. It should not surprise us that religion has provided conduits for the return to Europeanness in music, for the identity of Europe in music has historically owed a special debt to religion. Here, I am not referring primarily to the complex role religion and religious institutions have played in the history of European music, though I should by no means diminish that role. The intellectual histories of music history and musicology, particularly in the style period broadly included under the label "early mu-

sic," largely focus on sacred repertories and rely on establishing the relations between the traditions and institutions of sacred music and European society in general. The Early Music Revival, itself a phenomenon of the outgoing twentieth century, often returned to sacred spaces
(e.g., a cathedral for which a Medieval or Renaissance mass was conceived) in order historically to restore early music's authenticity. The
music history that the Early Music Revival has successfully constructed
and mediated through, say, CDs of Gregorian chant could not confirm
a claim of Europeanness in more singular historical and religious,
which is to say Christian, terms. At the beginning of the twenty-first
century there are more musical reasons than ever to realize that Europe's historical identity is inseparable from the continent's Christianity and its struggle to form a bulwark against the other religions of its
neighbors, and of the vast regions of the world colonized and mission-
ized by Europeans.

The ways in which music confirmed or contested historical patterns
of Europeanness have not been lost upon contemporary composers,
several of whom have introduced or even reintroduced religion into
their compositions. They range from, say, the sacred aesthetics of many
of Estonian Arvo Pärt's compositions to the political ideologies of
American-Israeli Shulamit Ran's "Jewish works," such as her opera *Between Two Worlds,* her setting of Ansky's *The Dybbuk,* which were conceived for a premiere in Germany. Contemporary classical music, in
fact, took a decided turn toward the sacred as the Cold War's assertions
of secularism waned. For example, Henryk Górecki and Krzysztof Penderecki, perhaps Poland's best known composers at the turn of our own
century, devoted themselves largely to restoring a religious content to
their works during the decades framing the break-up of socialist Poland
and the transformation to the New Poland (Engelhardt 2002). In the
present section, however, I treat the revival of the sacred in European
classical music as a symptom rather than as a cause, concerning myself
instead with the everyday intersection of religious and musical practices, and the ways they mobilize the remapping of the New Europe.

Since 1989, the religio-musical intersection has unleashed at least
seven distinct processes of transformation. These have proved to be of
particular importance, though they have not excluded other processes
of transformation. Instead, these processes open spaces within musical
practices for the expansive presence of religious meaning and function, thus contributing together to the recognition that music has

become increasingly available as a set of social practices and social poetics imbued with the power of religious revival.

1. Historicism
2. Political and social resistance
3. Transformation of the public sphere
4. Diaspora
5. Pilgrimage
6. Feminizing the public uses of music
7. Healing the fissures in European society and the ruptures along political borders.

I want to make clear that I employ the term "processes" in order to emphasize that music and religion intersect to become sites for action and thus social activism and transformation. Religion functions both as private practice and public action. The religious revival that has been accelerating since 1989 has brought about new forms of conscious negotiation between the private and public practices of religion, unleashing into the public sphere what had previously been relegated to the private. Simply stated, religious practice has a radically new presence, and music has been crucial to winning that presence for it. The place of religious music has been transformed, and conversely religious music has transformed the sacred landscapes of the New Europe, landscapes that may or may not resonate with political landscapes.

The negotiation and mobilization to which I refer is writ large in the revival of pilgrimage in the New Europe. By the end of the 1990s some 125 million Europeans were undertaking a pilgrimage of one kind or another each year—a foot pilgrimage to a local shrine, one of the millennial journeys that accompanied the arrival of the year 2000, an organized trip to the destroyed centers of Jewish Europe (e.g., Frank 1996), or a *haj* from one of Europe's many growing Muslim communities. The statistics are, quite frankly, staggering, when we imagine that perhaps one out of every six Europeans goes on a pilgrimage each year.

Equally staggering is the sheer volume of music that accompanies these pilgrims as they ply their ways across Europe and negotiate shifting patterns of identity as they cross borders and form new communities around pilgrimage sites. The musical repertories that mobilize the New European pilgrimages are expanding rapidly, and they draw upon every possible medium. The new repertories have benefited on one

*Figure 7.9.*
*German-language cassette from the*
*pilgrimage site at Medjugorje,*
*Bosnia-Herzegovina (mid-1990s)*

level from what Peter Manuel has called "cassette culture" (1993), the production, distribution, and consumption of very inexpensive audio-cassettes (see Figure 7.9). At this level, pilgrimage music mixes with traditional forms of colportage, the public sale of religious artifacts, such as votive cards and song pamphlets (see Figure 7.10).

At a very different level, the sacred musics of the New European pilgrimage benefit from the mediating technologies of the internet, which transform traditional modes of colportage into postmodern forms (see Bohlman 2000e). New songs from European pilgrimage sites can be quickly downloaded from one of myriad pilgrimage home-pages. Those homepages rely on the virtual replication of iconic images—not infrequently, icons themselves—which mediate the sounds and symbols of the sacred journey at the far reaches of cyberspace. Clicking on masses available in real-time through the webpages of pilgrimage sites allows one to join the pilgrimage, mobilized on a global level (see Figure 7.11).

The mass mediation of music emanating from a pilgrimage site does not make a case for sacred music in the New Europe as just another manifestation of globalization. Quite the contrary, the mediation of pilgrimage musics has the power to localize and to make the religious experience a matter of intensely personal devotion and meaning. I wish to suggest, moreover, that this is the reason that sacred music has so powerfully given voice to issues central to New Europeanness. To examine a pilgrimage center whose history parallels that of the New Europe

*Bozóki:* **Énekeskönyv (1797)**

1. Má-ri - át dí - csér - ni,    Hí -vek, jöj-je - tek,
2. Ha ér-tünk Má-ri - a    Fi - át kér-le - li,

Mert ő fog-ja kér - ni    Fi - át ér-te - tek.
Ké - ré- sét szent Fi - a    Meg nem vet-he - ti.

Üd-vöz-légy,    Má-ri - a!    Mond-ja minden    hív, .

Ál - dott légy,Má- ri - a!    Mond-ja nyelv és    szív.

3. Istentől csodával néki adatott, — Hogy anyaságá-
val Szűz maradhatott. — Üdvözlégy, stb.

4. Teljes áldásokkal, mint ·világgal tűz, — És szent
malasztokkal e dicsőült Szűz. — Üdvözlégy, stb.

5. Fogantatásában Ő vétkes nem volt, — Sem élte
folytában, sem midőn megholt. — Üdvözlégy, stb.

6. Ó Szűz, életfája a jámboroknak, — És főpátrónája
hív magyaroknak. — Üdvözlégy, stb.

*Figure 7.10. Marian song from Hungarian pilgrimage song
pamphlet (mid-1990s)*

and its troubled presence in the Balkans, we can look briefly at the pilgrimages to Medjugorje, located in Bosnia-Herzegovina in the mountainous region of its southwestern border with Croatia and some thirty
kilometers from Mostar and 100 kilometers from Sarajevo.

### The Medjugorje Pilgrimage

Medjugorje is a new pilgrimage site, and it emblematizes the response
of religion and revival to the complex conditions of the New Europe.
Pilgrims to Medjugorje come to worship the "Gospa," the Virgin Mary,
who first appeared in 1981, but who has continued to appear on
Thursdays, particularly on the third Thursday of every month. By the
mid-1980s, Medjugorje had come to form a response to the deteriorat-
ing political situation in the former Yugoslavia, and by 1990, on the eve
of Yugoslavia's breakup, 18 million pilgrims had visited Medjugorje.

**Medjugorje &
Our Lady Queen of Peace**

The apparitions at Medjugorje

*Hvaljen Isus I Marija!!!*                                                    *Praised be Jesus and Mary!!!*

*Statement of intent:* This Medjugorje Web Page was first put on line in the Fall of 1994. The sole intent of this page is to make the events of this phenomenon known to the world, and to share the messages that have touched the hearts of millions. It was my own personal experience at this place that *converted* me from a spectator Catholic Christian to a true believer in Christ and the truth that His blessed mother continues to echo from the gospels. She spreads this message through 6 human vessels in the heart of what was a Communist country in 1981. I invite you to read her messages with an open mind and an open heart, for her messages have such great love, as she sees each one of us as her children who are in so much need of her care and guidance to help us to know her son and to return to God. As she repeatedly points out - we need to pray, pray, pray!

**Click here for the latest message - Direct from Medjugorje**

**What's New**

A movie about St. Therese of Lisiux (the Little Flower) is depending on web site visits to get released in theaters. Please visit http://www.theresemovie.com, sign up and add to the numbers. We need to let Hollywood know that we WANT movies like this!

**Have questions regarding Medjugorje? Apparitions? The Catholic Faith?**
**Check out the FAQ Page!**

**Medjugorje Pilgrimage - 15th Anniversary**

Here are some links relating to our pilgrimage in June 1996:

- Pictures and stories
- Fr. Jozo's homily on the Eve of the 15th anniversary.
- The homily given at the evening Croatian mass on the 15th anniversary.

Since June 25, 1981, Mary the Mother of God is reported to visit daily with several young adults in this Croatian village in Bosnia-Hercegovina, bringing messages on how to achieve peace in our hearts, homes and world.

Medjugorje has become an international center of prayer, devotion and conversion of the heart. Our Lady has told the visionaries that these are her last appearances on earth and it is for this reason her visits are so long and frequent. She has come to tell us "God exists". Before her last appearance she has promised to leave a visible sign on the mountain where the first apparition occurred so that all will believe.

While the Catholic Church has yet to approve any of the modern day apparitions, in 1986, The Holy Father said, "Let the people go to Medjugorje if they convert, pray, confess, do penance and fast." Some 30 million laity and clergy have visited and returned home spiritually renewed.

Despite the recent war in Bosnia, Medjugorje remains a center of peace and of profound spirituality.

*Figure 7.11. A homepage for the Medjugorje pilgrimage
in Bosnia-Herzegovina (2004)*

At each stage in the ethnic and national struggles during the 1990s, Medjugorje has provided a foundation for subaltern response (cf. D. Manuel 1992 and Bax 1995). During the struggle for Bosnian independence, the messages of Medjugorje apparitions voiced an intense engagement with healing. Following the outbreak of war between Serbia and Kosovo in February 1999, the human tragedy in Kosovo became central to the pilgrimage and ritual at Medjugorje. At each stage, moreover, new musics have given voice to the meaning of Medjugorje's symbolic presence in the Balkans and the ways it has assumed the forms and functions of sacred icon in the public sphere of Balkan conflict. Audio cassettes with Medjugorje songs, sermons, and ritual performances circulated quickly and widely (CD example 5, a choral performance of "The Medjugorje Song"). Today, not least because so many different linguistic and national groups come as pilgrims, song repertories in most European languages and several non-European languages are most readily accessible through the internet.

Without putting too fine a point on it, I do not wish to claim that the songs of Medjugorje pilgrims can undo what ethnic cleansing, NATO military incursions, and unceasing civil war have done. The songs of the pilgrims, nonetheless, bear a message that continues to resonate long after the military struggle for different regions in the Balkans. They resonate as an alternative vision for those regions, indeed an alternative vision to which millions respond each year. The alternative they seek is a constituent part of their vision for a New Europe, and it is to bring about this end that they raise their voices in song. The music of revival provides a medium for connecting response and resistance in the Balkans to the rest of Europe and for transforming religion into a subaltern text for the history of the New Europe.

## The New Folk Musics

New Europeanness won its position on the stage of world music—of worldbeat or global pop (Taylor 1997)—through folk music. If one plows one's way through the Europe sections of *The Rough Guide to World Music* (Broughton et al. 1999) or sifts through the European national and regional bins of CDs at Borders Books and Music, the music that one most often encounters announces itself as folk music. And not just as folk music, but usually in some configuration of "new folk music." First encounters with new folk music may suggest that such overt attempts to make folk music at once local and global can only founder in naïve paradox, but in fact those who map Europeanness on world music are fully aware of what is at stake in mustering folk music, with its cultural baggage of nationalism and parochialism, to lay claim to new aesthetic and ideological turf for Europeans. It is for this reason, among others, that the label "new folk music" appears as an icon of New Europeanness on folk music at the turn of our own century.

The "new folk music" must be both old and new, traditional and avant-garde, national and international. These are the juxtapositions that invest it with New Europeanness. Whereas, at first glance, it might seem that such juxtapositions are merely superficial, they empower new folk music to do many different types of cultural work. New folk music develops along an historical path that negotiates several landscapes of New Europeanness. "New folk music," while cultivated in certain nations already in the wake of the international folk-music revival of the 1950s and 1960s, spread during the 1980s. By the 1990s few European nations were spared from the growth of repertories that publicly claimed connections between traditional and contemporary styles, national and international elements.

By the turn of our own century, the "new folk musics" had come to wear national characteristics on their sleeves, so much so that it was virtually impossible to separate them from the nation itself. The texts and styles of the new repertories used explicit references to past nationalism to critique and, not infrequently, to advocate a nationalism of the present. The "new folk music" of Austrian Hubert von Goisern, for example, has relied on traditional alpine folk dances—*Ländler* and yodeling, for instance—from the area around von Goisern's home region, Bad Aussee, the same region that had provided the font for Konrad Mautner's seminal collection, *Das steyerische Rasplwerk* (1910), which Austrian folk-music scholarship had elevated to the position of a regional and national canon (see Chapter 5 and Figures 5.2 and 5.3). Von Goisern, however, rearranges the alpine folk repertory for his rock band, the Alpinkatzen ("The Alpine Cats"), and alters traditional texts wantonly, and many would claim irreverently (see, e.g., von Goisern 1995; cf. 1999).

The new Austrian folk music poses complex questions about regional and national tradition, not least among them, Whose representation of the tradition, Mautner's or von Goisern's, is more authentic? Mautner relied on the imagination and romanticism of an outsider in a folk culture that was not his own; his *Rasplwerk* reproduced not his own traditions but those of rural Styrians among whom he lived only during the summer. Von Goisern, in contrast, performs as an insider, transforming a tradition he acquired through traditional means, including oral tradition. The new Austrian folk music sounds new, but it is arguably more traditional than the old. It both challenges our notions of folk music and reinforces the validity of identifying folk music and ascribing historical process to it. And, of course, it raises the question, Whose nationalism is this?

When the label "new" first begins to accompany the transformations of national folk musics in the New Europe, it asserts connections to the traditions that initially define a type of authenticity. In the new folk music, unlike historically earlier canons of folk music, say, national folk music in the nineteenth century, authenticity is not an end but a beginning. New folk music consciously encourages its practitioners to create a pastiche, in which the authentic is only one part. In Finnish new folk music (**uusikansanmusiikki**), for example, there is an undeniable presence of the Finnish national epic, the *Kalevala,* but it plays an entirely different role from its first appearance in the nationalist efforts of Elias Lönnrot and other folklorists/collectors in the early and mid-ninteenth century (see Ramnarine 2003). Rather than creating a narrative and geographical space of northernness between Finland and Russia, the *Kalevala* and other traces of the authentically Finnish, especially instruments such as the **kantele,** chart an international position of negotiation between East and West in Finnish new folk music. Indeed, relatively little importance may be attached by the proponents of *uusikansanmusiikki* to what has long been recognized as a mixture of authentic and invented nineteenth-century imaginations that invested the *Kalevala* with its symbolic nationalism (listen to CD examples 2, 3, and 7).

The new folk music also differs from the old because of the ways in which it comes into being. Whereas it would have been unthinkable to admit to the hand of an individual creator or composer in earlier folk music, the New Europeanness often enters and shapes a repertory through conscious acts of creativity, even reroutings of the tradition itself. In some cases, notably the **"newly composed folk music"** that emerged in Yugoslavia in the 1980s and in its successor states in the 1990s, the act of composition is openly admitted. The point is not merely that much new folk music is composed. New melodies and arrangements accrue to the tradition to endow it with an ideological mobility that it could not otherwise display. Composition introduces difference to a musical template that previously emphasized sameness. It expands the landscape across which new folk music can move by asserting that the present no longer constrains folk music, and it does so by drawing attention to the nation at the same time it poses questions about the cultural and historical meanings of the nation's borders (see Rasmussen 1996 and 2002).

Finnish new folk music, though one of the first movements of its kind, seeks to mix the Karelian song traditions from Finnish-Russian border regions with the emblems of the *Kalevala,* and then remix all of these with Saami yoiking and electronically generated soundscapes from the Nordic roots movement. Newly composed folk music in Yugoslavia might unfold across a Balkan landscape already crisscrossed with Serb turbo folk, Bosnian *illahiya,* a Muslim sacred popular music, or, for that matter, Medjugorje pilgrims. In my own fieldwork I encountered the influences of newly composed folk music most directly in the central range of the Carpathian Mountains along the Ukraine-

Romanian border, where Rom wedding musicians had adopted it in order to ameliorate the surfeit of local styles in one of the most ethnically
mixed regions of Eastern Europe (see Chapter 6).

The new folk musics also open a musical and ideological landscape
for nationless peoples. In some cases, those landscapes support a nationless people or an imaginary nation, primarily through revival, for
example, by breathing life into Sephardic music in the Balkans during
the 1990s, at a time coeval with the final egress, in some cases expulsion, of Jews from the cosmopolitan centers of Sarajevo, Dubrovnic,
and elsewhere. In contrast, many of the new Celtic folk musics have increasingly made the case for a process of returning to and reclaiming
the Celtic fringe, Europe's Atlantic littoral (see Bohlman 2000a: 79).
Music, in fact, provides a crucial form of evidence for Celticism, sup-
plying it with a central store of common artifacts—especially bagpipes
and harps—and what should be a single language with common linguistic roots (listen, e.g., to CD example 11).

The new Celtic folk music lays claim to a remarkably deep store of
New Europeanness. There have been attempts to transform earlier
forms of choralism, notably in Wales, into a culture of choral festivals
along the entire fringe. Celtic religion, which draws selectively from
several distinctive mythologies, from pagan through New Age, is undergoing a mediated revival, which nonetheless finds its way increasingly into the production and dissemination of Celtic music. Celtic religion provides only one route for revival, and it is perhaps more
critical for an understanding of New Europeanness to turn to the revival of pilgrimage in the Celtic fringe, which embraced the pilgrimage
to Santiago de Compostela in northwestern Spain, that is, in Celtic
Galicia, as its own (see, e.g., the CD *Santiago,* which won a Grammy for
the Chieftains in 1997). The question raised by the New Europeanness
of Celtic folk music becomes: Does it rip the Celtic Fringe from Europe
or suture it back to Europe? The answer is, of course, both (see Stokes
and Bohlman 2003).

## The New European Popular Music

The New Europeanness does not make popular music in Europe more
nationalist. It does raise new questions about what the nation is. As the
present chapter shifts its focus from folk music to popular music, I admit from the outset that, seen from certain perspectives, the differ-

ences between the two may seem to be fewer. Folk musicians, traditional and "new," aspire to a more international scene; popular music increasingly searches for ways to attach itself to certain conditions that are local. The tension between new folk musics and new popular musics also recontextualizes the genres and styles in-between, for example, Central European *volkstümliche Musik,* or "folklike music." Fundamental to my understanding of the new European popular music, nonetheless, are the ways in which it bears witness to influences—musical, national, and ideological—that are international and global. Indeed, it is because the new popular music has become transnational that it also competes for national markets, thereby finding its way into the nationalist marketplace. In some ways, the New Europeanness of the new popular music is not difficult to detect: It is the voice of the New Europeans. Understanding that voice as a component of the New Europeanness, however, is anything but easy, and it is toward the process of understanding that I now turn.

The term New Europeans designates individuals, communities, and groups whose cultures and musics have historically lain outside the strictures of nationalism. These may be racial and ethnic minorities; they may be religious outsiders; they may be social and cultural others; increasingly, they are the "new immigrants," former colonial subjects, such as South Asians in the United Kingdom or North Africans in Spain and France, or the descendants of guest workers in Central Europe. There are also Europeans who have lived for centuries in Europe (e.g., the Basques) but who have, in the late twentieth century, come to enter the history of the present in new ways, not least because of their reengagement with Europe through the new nationalism. The New Europeans, quite obviously, are by no means an insignificant presence in Europe; quite the contrary, their presence is more and more significant all the time. With this in mind, the crucial point in the present section is really very simple: It is to the new European popular music that the New Europeans have turned to find a voice.

The new popular music takes as its point of departure questions of regional and national significance for individual groups. Bands such as the new Viennese "Tschuschenkapelle" or "Bruji" in Austria, for example, transform traditional Croat songs into a rock-influenced repertory that draws explicit attention to the conditions of Croat and Balkan minorities in Austria (see, e.g., Bruji's *Kein Wort Deutsch* and Tschuschenkapelle's *G'rebelt*). The style called Rom-pop broadly consolidates themes and styles from Roma repertories from across East-Central Europe, reworking them musically for performance in a transnational public sphere entirely new to Rom musicians. Instead of traces gathered to mark the exotic margins of European music, Rom-pop, performed by groups such as Veřa Bílá and Kale, moves questions of the presence of Roma in modern Europe to the center in a mainstream popular style (see, e.g., Veřa Bílá and Kale 1997). The musical redefinition of the center may sometimes be fleeting, at other times may persist over longer stretches of time, for example, in the case of Tarkan's hit song, "Şimarik," which, though in Turkish, stayed near the top of the pop charts in Germany and Austria from 1999 until 2003. Tarkan, whose songs also contain an Islamist message, uses this song to address the very centrality of modern Turkish experience itself, both within and outside European modernity.

The New European popular music opens aesthetic landscapes for New Europeanness in ways both expected and unexpected. Not surprisingly, one of the most unexpected and historically radical transformations of the aesthetic landscapes is the introduction of blackness into the aesthetic whiteness of European traditional music. The aesthetic blackness of the new popular musics, significantly, extends far beyond the global influences of African, African American, and Afro-Caribbean musics, influences that are, of course, undeniable. The blackness to which I refer has been sampled and mixed for specific reasons, many of which consciously draw ideological attention to musical and political change as a force of nationalism. The black aesthetics of new popular musics draws our attention to the increasing presence of black musicians living in Europe who are performing in contexts that are European. It is in those contexts that the landscapes of New Europeanness are dramatically shifting.

### Blackness on a Landscape of Whiteness

The points of entry for blackness into New Europeanness are both at the peripheries and at the center. In the December 2001 issue of *Nordic Sounds* the cover article (Aidt 2001) and a series of articles moving across Scandinavia are devoted to the new mix of sounds that has come to occupy center stage in Scandinavian popular music (cf. Wellner 2002). Sweden's 2002 Eurovision entry, a three-member girl group of African and South Americans, even dubbed themselves "Afro-dite," exploiting the presence of blackness in Swedish popular music. That mix, of course, is figuratively and literally the presence of African and African American musicians in Scandinavia, in the metropolises but also in more regional music making. Black music is present at the canonic center of European popular music; or, perhaps, it would be better to realize the center as the intersection of multiple canons, as in the case of the songs of Xavier Naidoo, now a superstar on the German pop scene. Naidoo mixes a variety of African American popular styles in his songs, particularly soul and hip-hop, but not infrequently a European-inflected gospel and rhythm 'n' blues (see, e.g., Naidoo 1998).

Some African and African American popular styles are marketed by emphasizing their otherness and hence their non-Europeanness—the title of the *Nordic Sounds* special edition is *Music of Another World,* and one of Naidoo's most popular CDs bears the title *Nicht von dieser Welt* ("Not from This World"). Other styles recognize and historicize the longer presence of specific African American musics, especially jazz, and more recently, hip-hop. Europe and Europeans have long welcomed American jazz and jazz musicians, at least since James Reese Europe's military band during and after World War I and the émigré tradition that began in the 1920s and 1930s and then returned after World War II, before and then after the American Civil Rights legislation of the early 1960s. European colonialism, too, provided a conduit between African and Afro-Caribbean musicians and the European history of jazz. Some jazz musicians from the European colonial world, notably Manu Dibango (see Dibango 1994), have enjoyed international prominence, largely playing jazz in Paris, London, and Vienna.

In both historical and modern practices (e.g., jazz and hip-hop), African American music has been appropriated to symbolize a broad range of resistive strategies. These strategies reveal the ways in which issues of nationalism, old and new, accrue to the European aesthetics of blackness. At various points in the twentieth century, jazz was the music of the exile, providing an aesthetic haven removed from American and post-colonial nationalism. Black musicians joined black writers and intellectuals, such as Richard Wright, in Europe, where blackness in the arts could survive. It was from this tradition of jazz exiles that national European styles also developed. The resistive potential of jazz was recognized by Czech and Russian musicians and forged into local and national movements during the Cold War. Joe Zawinul, the dean of Austrian jazz, has expanded on the specifically national potential of jazz, for example, to create large-scale works that use jazz to renarrate and interrogate the ways in which Austrian racism played itself out in extreme form during the Holocaust (see, e.g., Zawinul's CD, *Mauthausen* [2000]).

During the late twentieth and early twenty-first centuries, rap and hip-hop spread across the landscapes occupied by New Europeanness. Black and Asian communities in the UK along with North African and Middle Eastern communities in France and Italy all adopted and adapted hip-hop to narrate their contemporary historical struggles and to move the voice of resistance to the public sphere. As with jazz, European hip-hop styles used the historical struggles of Africans and African Americans against racism to shape a language for the political struggles of disenfranchised and nationless Europeans. The Basque hip-hop group Negu Norriak used African American music as a template for Basque nationalism. Jacqueline Urla has argued that it was necessary for the group to emphasize and amplify one set of nationalist messages with another, on one hand singing in Basque to support the Basque language revival, and on the other drawing "upon the visual codes and musical forms of nation-conscious rappers in African American hip-hop, as well as punk, ska, reggae, and raï music" (Urla 2001: 171). The African American, therefore, became a code for specific forms of European nationalism.

To chart the full range of the new blackness in European popular music, it is helpful to turn again to the Eurovision Song Contest. Throughout the 1990s, as we have seen elsewhere in this book, the number of black musicians representing the national entries has grown. But it was in 2000 that a palpable reconfiguration of the center was dramatically evident. Entry after entry represented the nations competing in the Eurovision by juxtaposing the national and a different, often distinctive, black musical style. The gamut stretched from gospel to motown to hip-hop, but the stylistic impact on the Eurovision was clear: Black voices were now present on the European popular music scene. The very aesthetic core of the competition—the locus of its Europeanness—had shifted. Indeed, the winner of the 2001 Eurovision was the Estonian entry, Tanel Padar and Dave Benton's "Everybody," the dancehall framework of which was entirely familiar to Dave Benton, who had emigrated from Aruba. The question raised by the outcome of the 2001 Eurovision, therefore, might be whether the blackness of the song's style represented the nation of emigration (Aruba) or the nation of immigration (Estonia). The question is not rhetorical, nor is it meant to represent a play on sociological terminology. By explicitly borrowing from the Caribbean dancehall but appropriating it for Estonia's national entry, Padar and Benton were also expressing an aesthetics of New Europeanness, which we realize as the presence of the New European, Dave Benton, in the national song culture of the New European nation-state, Estonia.

### Who Owns the Europe of the New Europeanness?

In each of the five landscapes I have explored in this chapter, questions of ownership are extremely difficult to sort out. If the place signified by New Europeanness is constantly in flux, if transition characterizes its contradictory ontologies, the music itself does not lend itself to possession and ownership. The multiple consciousness of spaces in transition reveals even a resistance to ownership. It is not entirely clear who owns the Europe of the New Europeanness, or if, indeed, ownership is a property that accrues to the musics of Europe since 1989. The difficulty in determining or ascribing ownership confronts us with the question of nationalism, indeed, what we increasingly recognize as a "new nationalism," in which altogether different forms of ownership lay claim to the nation-state. Does the New Europeanness undergird the new nationalism, or does it undermine the girders supporting it?

I raise the question of ownership as I begin my own transition toward the end of this chapter and book, because that question has become increasingly critical in discussions about place and musical identity. At one level, ownership of music is important if music is to serve as a vehicle and symbol for the construction of place (see the essays in Stokes 1994). To construct place—the region or nation, the "imagined community" (Anderson 1991) or the "third space" (Bhabha 1994)—music itself must undergo a transformation so that it serves as a tool, malleable yet palpable. Music makes place one's own because it is possessed as one's own. Throughout this book we have seen that one does not borrow music from someone else to create nationalism. The story is different, however, if another nation's music just happens to slip across the borders and then to close them, as in the case of Germany's "Deutschlandlied," which came from the Austrian-Hungarian border as a melody but picked up Germany's borders with the addition of Hoff-mann von Fallersleben's text (see Chapter 2 and CD examples 33–35).

At another level, the problems of ownership are inherent in the eco-nomic realities of music in the public sphere. The discussions of music emanating from cultural studies—whether they focus on the inscrip-tion of style (Hebdige 1979) or the globalization of the culture indus-try (Appadurai 1996)—concern themselves with musics produced and distributed in a market economy. Just who controls that market and the means of production has become a fundamental question in popu-lar-music studies. The market-value of nationalist music can mean that the recording industry is able to make a certain type of financial claim to ownership of the musical object once it is reduced to CDs and other commodities of exchange. Ownership of commodities, however, is vastly different from ownership of symbolic meanings.

The questions of ownership did accompany the research, ranging from spectatorship and web-surfing to intensive ethnographic field-work, which led to my discussions of the landscapes of New European-ness in the present chapter. It is not only a question of who really owns the copyrights of the tunes one can download from Eurovision websites, but also who owns the synagogues or the property in the former Jewish communities of Central and Eastern Europe. These are questions of ownership writ large across the musical landscapes of the New Europe.

It is important to make what might appear to be a fine distinction but is in fact a distinction critical to understanding the ways in which New Europeanness expresses new forms of nationalism at the turn of our own century. I do not want to say that New Europeanness in music belies ownership. Claims to ownership are made wherever one turns. The songs of the Eurovision Song Contest have virtually countless own-ers: recording companies and copyright agencies in the European Broadcasting Union; transnational labels, especially BMG, which re-leases Eurovision entries on CD compilations within weeks of the con-test (see *Eurovision Song Contest Stockholm 2000, Eurovision Song Contest Kopenhagen 2001,* and *Eurovision Song Contest Tallinn 2002*); bootleg-gers who release the entries on websites and CDs even faster; the singers themselves and the national broadcasting companies that fur-ther their careers; both national- and special-interest groups wanting to cash in on the financial packages that accompany the festival itself.

The synagogue choruses navigate a world in which court cases about the European past of Jewish culture—and music—rage. To restore a synagogue abandoned or partially destroyed in the Holocaust so that it might become a site for Jewish music again confronts Central and East Europeans with a dilemma of enormous proportions. Theoretically, Jewish communities own these spaces, but where are the Jewish communities? And what is the Jewish community? Is it the religious polity of a European city or region, whose concerns are religious and not political? Or does it consist of national and international Jewish agencies, whose interests lie in protecting properties illegally taken from Europe's Jews during the Holocaust? In response to such perplexingly rhetorical questions, voices are raised in song, giving voice to those no longer capable of ownership (Bohlman 2000c).

For the pilgrim to Medjugorje, too, questions of ownership are faced at every step taken on the journey. For the pilgrim herself it is not a question of personal ownership, but of the phenomenon of ownership and the ways it has fractured the Balkans. The pilgrim's song is transitory to the extreme. It accrues to place only as a means of accomplishing transit through and beyond that place. The pilgrim's song reminds the singer that others have passed this way before, and that previous pilgrims had not claimed ownership of the sacred journey. Embedded with questions of place and identity, the pilgrim's song celebrates a repertory beyond ownership, because place and identity are no longer products of an older nationalism but processes of a new nationalism.

### Three Processes of New Nationalism

Europe's new nationalism appears in various places and guises on the landscape of the New Europe. It does not merely, nor even primarily, comprise processes that characterize the center. The new nationalism forms along both historical and geographical axes, usually intersecting both in several places. Depending on where we examine it, the new nationalism may exhibit explicit forms that draw attention to the political and geographical claims of the present, or it may more subtly weave the past into the present. The question that arises is: How do we recognize the new nationalism? The three processes that follow suggest three possible responses to that question and, at the same time, remind us that there are many more possible responses, which together further remind us of the ways in which the new nationalism reuses many of the structures of the old nationalism.

## The New Regionalism

In the New Europe the concern for national culture has shifted from maintaining the center to the peripheries. Concomitantly, there has been a shift from locating musical and cultural activities in institutions that express national unity to those programs and activities that represent the nation as an amalgam of border cultures, border identities, and regions. The old regionalism was used to justify the nation and the extension of its power in Europe. This was the regionalism that the Austro-Hungarian Empire represented. The new regionalism draws attention to Europeanness that forms at the overlapping areas of borders. The hybridity and multiculturalism that form at borders lend themselves to celebration in the New Europe, whereas in the Old Europe it served as a symptom of disintegration at the fringes.

The old regionalism imposed nationless status on European minorities; the new regionalism attempts, albeit not always successfully, to integrate minorities into the nation. It is in European border provinces, for example, that multilingualism is officially tolerated, even supported by the admission of programs of language instruction into the schools or the use of several languages in official state business. In the case of Austria, it is in the border provinces of Carinthia and Burgenland that multilingualism—Slovenian in the former, Croatian and Hungarian in the latter—has been recognized through provincial and national legislation. Regional culture also thrives along the borders of the United Kingdom, Finland, and Italy. Even in nations that have most fervently sought to centralize the national culture, such as France and Romania, there are new tendencies toward regionalism. The three languages and cultures (Alsatian, French, and German) supported in Alsace-Lorraine enjoy open recognition, not least because Strasbourg, the cultural center of the region, is also the seat of the European Parliament.

The music that provided repertories for the old regionalism was more often than not that of nationless peoples. Several of the most characteristic repertories of Ashkenazic Jewish folk song, for example, formed along old national borders where cultural conditions fostered their commonality. Already by the emergence of European Jewish modernity in the late eighteenth century there were Ashkenazic musical areas around the regions formed at the French, Swiss, and German borders, the Austrian, Hungarian, and Slovak borders, and the Romanian, Polish, and Ukrainian borders (see Bohlman and Holzapfel

2001). Similarly, European Sephardic Jewish musical areas formed in Balkan regional cultures, notably that of Bosnia-Herzegovina.

The new regionalism creates a space of accommodating difference, often in the name of tolerating difference. The regional culture, therefore, is a surrogate for the nation, receiving much of the same support but by no means acquiring the status of the nation. Since 1989, the border region of Karelia between Finland and Russia, historically a site of struggle between the two nations, has undergone a transformation into an area of permeable boundaries that musicians regularly cross. Though they may share repertories, styles, and instruments that were central to earlier nationalist repertories, for example, the symbolic weight of the national epic, the *Kalevala,* musical activity emphasizes the region and its connections through music. It is the function of regional music to effect such connections, emphasizing areas of overlapping nationalism and musical commonality rather than marking differences as cultural boundaries between one nation and its neighbors.

### The New Cosmopolitanism

The metropolis has always been central to European modernity. In the New Europe, the metropolis is even more crucial to the formation of New Europeanness. In the past decade, a new discourse about the city and its culture has swept across Europe, generating a literature and an in-gathering of musical forces explicitly dedicated to processes of ameliorating, if not healing, cultural differences in the metropolis. The term "discourse" in this case is particularly apt, for the new cosmopolitanism is not so much a phenomenon of European cities as they really are at the turn of our century, but rather as we should wish them to be in the New Europe. The New European metropolis is the virtual image of its historical predecessors. Multiculturalism was present already at the moment of mythical origins, when today's cities had different names—Pressburg for Bratislava, Christiania for Oslo, Agram for Zagreb, Lemberg for L'viv and Lvov. Book series and CD series together gathered the traces of city history and city culture, appropriating such traces to juxtapose them on the new cosmopolitanism that would emerge as the history of the present.

Few critics of the New Europe have captured the essence of the new cosmopolitanism more brilliantly than Slavenka Drakulić in her volume of essays, *Café Europa* (1996), the title of which refers to the proliferation of coffee houses with the same name throughout the Europe of the 1990s. Most striking for Drakulić was the recognition that the similarities of the microcultures in the Café Europa outweighed the differences, and that the similarities arose from the imagination of what a European coffee house really should be. The cosmopolitanism of the Café Europa extends in all directions in today's Europe: to the music festival and competition, to the ethnomusicology division of the academy of science, to the revival of sacred music, to the clubs where techno and lounge music continue into the wee hours night after night, and to the belief that the urban center is the site for the culture of a multicultural First World. These are the conditions to which the new cosmopolitanism dedicates itself.

The discourse of the new cosmopolitanism openly acknowledges its historical debt to the earlier culture of the metropolis, which we might, in retrospect, call the old cosmopolitanism. In its earlier manifestation, the culture of the European city formed a series of networks between centers, but also from the centers to the peripheries. The old cosmopolitanism became increasingly important during the rise of modernity, providing a means of implanting urban musical culture at Europe's center in the modern cities of the peripheries. It was a product of the internal colonialism and the expansion of empire from the late eighteenth through the nineteenth century, and it was within the internal European empires—the Russian, Austro-Hungarian, German, and Ottoman—that the cities of the old cosmopolitanism came to display a common Europeanness. Triest and Czernowitz looked like Vienna, partly because they served the Habsburg Monarchy at its southern and eastern frontiers. The cities of trade and business networks also provided a geographical-historical grid for the old cosmopolitanism, which in turn formed the template for districts where cultures were common, for example, the harbor districts of the Hanseatic cities stretching from Bergen to Hamburg to Königsberg.

We might turn to Czernowitz as a city that has spawned a considerable quantity of new cosmopolitanism. The modern history of Czernowitz parallels that of the imperial-colonial struggles between East and West over the multiculturalism in the center of Europe. We know virtually nothing of significance of the city of Czernowitz/Cernăuţi/Černivci, today in Ukraine, in the region of Bukovina north of the Romanian and Moldavan borders. When the Habsburg Monarchy absorbed the city at the time of the Napoleonic wars, it quickly established cultural institutions that would draw the Jews, Ukrainians,

*Figure 7.12. Historical postcard of Czernowitz (ca. late nineteenth century)*

Huzuls, Poles, Romanians, Russians, and Germans in the area into a common cultural center. The Habsburgs built a university, an opera house, concert halls, museums, and many more grand, monumental edifices in its own urban and multicultural culture (see Figure 7.12). Czernowitz did not so much become a mirror image of Vienna and Budapest as it did a reflection that refracted the Danube metropolis in such ways that true spaces for the culture of East European nationless peoples were opened. Jewish culture—modern, Jewish cosmopolitanism—flourished in Czernowitz, transforming the city. Culturally, Czernowitz was the entrepôt between East and West, a gathering place for intellectuals and political extremists, writers and artists, and for a music culture that placed no limits on the European (see Corbea-Hoisie 1998, and Brusatti and Lingg 1999). Czernowitz especially opened its doors to modern European Jewish culture, providing an urban home to the Jewish Enlightenment, the flowering of Yiddish literature, cultural Zionism, and, in the twentieth century, the Holocaust poet Paul Celan.

In the New Europe, Czernowitz is home to none of this. The largely Ukrainian- and Romanian-speaking residents use any means at their disposal to erase the immediate past, the years of Soviet control, as well as the not-so-distant past, the Czernowitz ghetto during the Holocaust. It would seem an unlikely site for the new cosmopolitanism. Yet Czernowitz has become the focus for intense cultural activism, not from Ukraine, but rather from the outside—from the old Habsburg metropolis and the Jewish revivalists in Central Europe. Czernowitz has found a secure place in museum exhibits, restoration projects, and cultural tourism. The trade networks at the turn of the last century (e.g., Austrian brewery and grocery chains such as Gösser and Julius Meinl) have quickly turned toeholds into financial footholds. No Jewish music revival project neglects Czernowitz and the surrounding region of the Bukovina. Institutions dedicated to the rediscovery of "deutsche Musik im Osten" ("German music in the East") give Czernowitz pride of place. All this to restore the greatness of a cosmopolitan city that has fallen victim to the nationalist struggles of modern Europe.

## Revivalism and the New Nationalisms

The old and the new coexist through revival. Though on its surface a paradox, the omnipresence of revival in the New Europe is crucial to the new nationalism in its many forms. Wherever one searches for recent cultural and musical activities, the formation of new musical genres and the rebuilding of national music institutions, one is confronted by revival and revivalism. The past is very, very new in the New Europe, and its culture brokers are clamoring to tap into it.

There are various motivations for the explosion of musical revivalism in the New Europe, but it is the belief that music has the power to restore the past and to recover something lost that embodies almost all motivations. By extension, it is the belief that music contains some aspects of the nation prior to the divisive wars and ideologies of the twentieth century that transforms revivalism into such a widespread process of the new nationalism. Revivalism, moreover, often assumes dual forms, and in this sense it adapts itself well to the multiple forms of the "two Europes" that we explored in Chapter 1.

First of all, revivalism in its most widespread forms is both sacred and secular. There is a revival of pilgrimage music, for example, which is notable for the ways it intersects and crosses national boundaries (Bohlman 1996b). Similarly, folk music has undergone extensive revival, usually with considerable support from central national institutions (see the essays in Fujie 1996). Second, some revivalists may strive to recover authentic sources, whereas others may wantonly experiment with hybridity and fusion. Max Peter Baumann refers to these dialectically opposed ways of recuperating musical materials from the past and present as the two conflicting models of "purism" and "syncretism" (Baumann 1996). Revival that is syncretic, according to Baumann, consciously attempts to fuse the old and the new. Third, there are forms of revival that identify authenticity within restrictive national borders, whereas other forms recognize that the authenticity of certain styles, genres, and repertories has always been capacious, in other words, open to mixing the national and the international (Livingston 1999). Authenticity becomes important in new ways, but it does so by tolerating its own hybridity. Finally, revivalism comes from both below as a subaltern movement and from the top, that is from the institutions of the nation itself. When it comes from below, its aesthetic content is mobilized by those who want nationalism to serve them locally rather than globally. When it comes from above, it is the nation itself, in its most strictly historical forms, that takes center stage.

Revivalism has extended the new nationalism to the old and the new nations, as well as to the nationless and the New Europeans. Folk-music revivals have gained considerable importance in centralized nations, such as Hungary and Finland, but they have been no less important in the musical formulation of Celticism through revival or in the imagination of a place for Jewish klezmer music throughout Europe (see Gruber 2002). The musics of the Celtic and klezmer revivals have become truly European musics, for it would be almost impossible to find an urban center, music festival, or street-music scene anywhere in Europe where Celtic music and klezmer music were not thriving. New Finnish folk music may have been revived largely for the Finnish nation, together with its international nationalist imaginary (Ramnarine 2003), but Celtic music serves the web of nationalisms that stretch along Europe's Celtic fringe, and the klezmer revival monumentalizes a nationless European past to which Jews can never return. Return remains perhaps the most powerful motivation for remapping the new nationalisms with music.

## Re-Encountering New Europeanness, Returning to Europe

"Ejne klejne waiße Taibel"/"A Little White Dove"

| Ejne klejne | A little |
| Waiße Taibel | White dove |

| | |
|---|---|
| Fihrte mich | Took me |
| In Ejngeland. | To England. |
| Is zugeschlossen, | It was locked up, |
| Un die Schlissel | And the key |
| Is opgebrochen. | Is broken off. |
| Eins, zwej, drai— | One, two, three— |
| Pejlen is vorbai; | Poland is gone; |
| Ruß is gelofen | Russia has run away |
| Mit alle Harmaten, | With all its cannons, |
| Pejlen is gebliben | Poland is left |
| Ohn Soldaten. | Without soldiers. |

*(Eliasberg 1918: 140–41, and Ginsburg and Marek 1901: 78;*
*cf. Bohlman and Holzapfel 2001: 167)*

A children's song and game, known widely across Europe in Yiddish and German dialects, "A Little White Dove" concentrates complex issues of nationalism. At one level, the song illustrates the fate of nationalist ambitions at the time of its appearance in Europe, probably during the Napoleonic wars. At another level, the variant of the song above marks a number of historical borders, for it appeared in anthologies of Jewish folk song published on the eve of and during the collapse of European empires, those of Russia and Germany. At still another level, the song returns to Europe at a time of revival, the Yiddish song revival and the revival that provides aesthetic energy for New Europeanness. Simple as its textual and melodic variants may be (see Bohlman and Holzapfel 2001: 167–169), the song speaks to issues of European nationalism that are anything but simple.

The symbolism of the "white dove" as the messenger of peace was lost on none of the editors who pulled it from oral tradition; among the generations of European Jews, self-identity with the white dove was no less obvious. A song circulating largely among children, "A Little White Dove" might seem also to accompany child's play, say, the games that require toy soldiers. In modern Europe, nonetheless, the song has come to signify the folly and futility of war. The nation fails to welcome the dove of peace, or the Jews and other nationless people who wander in search of a nation willing to accept them. There is no finality. The nation has failed to sustain itself and to sustain Europe in time of war. What survives is the dove, which like the song, returns, through revival and through its capacity to historicize the past. Through its journeys and the very peregrinations of a folk song in European history, we arrive again at the borders of European nationalism, where Europe itself, as a whole made of many nations, waits to return.

For rhetorical balance it might seem appropriate to close this chapter with another encounter with New Europeanness. Throughout this book, the ethnographic present has served to draw attention to the persistence of nationalism in European music and to remind us that we can and do encounter it at all levels of modern European society. I turn therefore to an ethnograpic moment at the junctures of numerous fieldwork experiences to underscore my gesture of rhetorical closure by commenting upon one of my most recent encounters with New Europeanness. The ethnographic experience grows from various interactions and collaboration with some Hungarian colleagues, an ensemble that has just this year adopted the name "Odessa Klezmer Band." The Odessa Klezmer Band, with its lead singer, Katalin Szvorák, who in 2001 received Hungary's "Franz Liszt Prize" for artistic achievement, has for several years provided a sort of community ensemble in Budapest's Jewish community. It draws its repertories from standard collections, from recordings gathered during fieldwork in Romania (and followed in detail in Chapter 6), and in the new anthology of Ashkenazic folk songs from which "A Little White Dove" is taken (Bohlman and Holzapfel 2001). The edition contains Jewish songs, all with variants in German and Yiddish, and we use this edition to enlarge the basis for Jewish vernacular music in the European diaspora, a pan-Ashkenazic if not pan-European tradition.

In my ethnographic encounter with this band in Budapest in 2000, I have come full circle, ten years after my first encounter with New Europeanness in the guise of klezmer music on the streets of Budapest. Things have changed. Klezmer bands in Eastern Europe are hardly anything unusual these days (see Ottens and Rubin 1999, and Gruber 2002). Old klezmer musicians are being discovered, and new klezmer bands are inventing themselves. Even as I turn to performance in the ethnographic present, that is, as artistic director of my own Jewish cabaret troupe in Chicago, the "New Budapest Orpheum Society," I struggle to sort out the strands of a welter of new nationalisms (listen, e.g., to CD examples 13 and 16).

Sorting out the new nationalisms is also striking in the case of Kati Szvorák and the Odessa Klezmer Band. Kati comes from an Hungarian-speaking village in central Slovakia, but she received her primary music education in the folk ensembles of the Hungarian army in the early 1980s. She is known for singing in a wide range of styles and repertories, but her most distinguished and distinctive work has always been Hungarian repertories from Romania and Catholic devotional song.

When Kati Szvorák sings "Kárpáti menyasszony" ("The Fiancée from the Carpathians") with the Odessa Klezmer Band (listen to CD example 8), she draws together a remarkable number of historical themes that locate the song in an aesthetics of New Europeanness. The song survived in the border culture of Transylvania, and its narrative is about the survival and reproduction of a European Jewish community. Throughout this book the wedding and wedding music have drawn our attention again and again to the nation and its music, and this song is no exception. Stylistically it is a hybrid, with Hungarian, Ukrainian, Romanian, and Jewish threads impossible to separate from each other. The destruction of the Jewish past in one of the heartlands of European Jewish culture serves as a point of departure for a historicism that revival makes possible. The Jewish community is given another chance in Budapest, where twenty-seven synagogues, in one form or another, especially the Dohány Street Synagogue, Europe's largest, survived the Holocaust. The narrative of return is simple but compelling.

So many strands of New Europeanness converge in the modern collection, publication, and performance of "The Fiancée from the Carpathians" that it has become almost impossible to sort them out. Through fieldwork and scholarship we have cobbled together a repertory from fragments to evoke a sense of destroyed Europeanness. As performers and scholars, we attempt to use music to remember even more than to revive. With the goal of remembering we have chosen not to privilege one style or Jewish folk-song tradition over another, in order to let a past Europeanness speak somehow more clearly, though there are no strict editorial rules about how to make this happen. None of us engaged in this project of mobilizing a return to the ethnographic present—ethnomusicologist, singer, klezmer band—would claim ownership of this music.

All these are the fragments of New Europeanness. Their paradoxes notwithstanding, they also somehow cohere. It is surely very difficult to pin down the individual fragments and to extract meaning from them. It is surely difficult to seize them for more than a moment as they undergo vertiginous change on the landscapes of transition. What is sure, however, is that these fragments have been welling up around us as the history of the New Europe becomes our own history. Whatever else we learn about the New Europeanness of this history, we increasingly confront the reality that we can no longer extricate ourselves from it.

## Coda—Nationalism's Still, Small Voice

When we imagine the music of nationalism and nationalistic music, we usually expect the mustered voices of many or the bombastic salvos of, perhaps, a military ensemble. Nationalism is the nation writ large, and it follows that its music often becomes the nation sounded in full volume. In the present book, with its accounts of operas and choruses, marches and competitions, the volume of the nation's music has been more often pitched at a *forte*, occasionally a strident *fortissimo*, than at a *piano*, much less a *pianissimo*. National epics stretch across centuries, and national anthems rally the country in rituals of unity. The leaders and institutions of national governments turn to music as an instrument of power, power so crucial to maintaining the nation that it must be experienced at full strength. The music of nationalism asserts itself upon listeners across a vast public sphere, too often leaving little chance for contemplation. Sounding the nation, ironically and sometimes tragically, leaves no chance for anything but "unisonality" and "uniaurality."

In this brief coda, the final gesture of formal conclusion in a large-scale musical work, it might seem as if we had arrived at the moment to allow the full force of nationalist music to ring forth in a closing chord of assertiveness. I have chosen, however, to move the book toward its end more quietly, choosing not grandiose examples in the preceding section, but two folk songs, peaceful in character but disturbing in the nationalist narratives they convey. These songs, because their own narratives are so tied to the survival of an historically nationless European people in the face of nationalism, have competed against the full force of nationalist music rather weakly. But competed they have, for they are songs about survival and ultimately about the possibility of return. Aesthetically, they would likely wilt when placed before the overpowering volume of a massed ensemble, yet in their fragility they also make the most resolute case for the fragility of the nation and its people. Their voice is arresting because we hear it with great difficulty, and it has been heeded with even greater difficulty. Theirs, too, is a voice of European nationalism.

In Europe, music also functions as nationalism's still, small voice. When it is still and small, music reminds us that the nation and nationalism have many forms and make many appearances, not only those writ large across the landscape of modernity. The questions raised by the solo voice in a folk song are more pointedly and poignantly about place than the most stirring march; the ritual enacted in the homes of a nationless or minority group expresses the needs of the collective no less powerfully than the ritualized performance of a national ballet or orchestra. At the beginning of the twenty-first century, it is music's quietest voice in a new nationalism that requires most critically that we listen carefully and attend to the historical narrative that the most vocal forces of nationalism have yet to silence. In the stillness of the small voice, the message remains the loudest. In the twenty-first century, nationalism continues to be one of the most powerful forces in the making of modern Europe. Its historical paradox, in other words, its tendency to build up the nation for some Europeans while dismantling it for others, has diminished not in the least. All these tendencies of European nationalism demand our attention, and many demand our diligence. As we seek to separate the strident voices from those searching for compromise and peace, the destructive uses of nationalism from the constructive, music will be there, expressing those voices in all their variety. The challenge we face is to listen as closely as possible.

### REFERENCES

Aidt, Mik. 2001. "Music of Another World." *Nordic Sounds* 4: 3–13.

Anderson, Benedict. 1991. *Imagined Communities: Reflections on the Origins and Spread of Nationalism*. 2d ed. London: Verso.

Appadurai, Arjun. 1996. *Modernity at Large: Cultural Dimensions of Globalization*. Minneapolis: University of Minnesota Press.

Baumann, Max Peter. 1976. *Musikfolklore und Musikfolklorismus: Eine ethnomusikologische Untersuchung zum Funktionswandel des Jodels*. Winterthur: Amadeus Verlag.

Bax, Mart. 1995. *Medjugorje: Religion, Politics, and Violence in Rural Bosnia*. Amsterdam: VU Uitgeverij.

Bhabha, Homi. 1994. *The Location of Culture*. London and New York: Routledge.

Bohlman, Philip V. 1994. "Music, Modernity, and the Foreign in the New Germany." *Modernism/Modernity* 1 (1): 121–152.

_____. 1996b. "The Final Borderpost." *The Journal of Musicology* 14 (4): 427–452.

_____. 2000a. "Jewish Music in Europe." In Timothy Rice, James Porter, and Chris Goertzen, eds., *Europe*. Vol. 8: *The Garland Encyclopedia of World Music*, pp. 248–269. New York: Garland.

_____. 2000b. "The Remembrance of Things Past: Music, Race, and the End of History in Modern Europe." In Ronald Radano and Philip V. Bohlman, eds., *Music and the Racial Imagination*, pp. 644–676. Chicago: University of Chicago Press.

_____. 2000c. "To Hear the Voices Still Heard: On Synagogue Restoration in Eastern Europe." In Daphne Berdahl, Matti Bunzl, and Martha Lampland, eds., *Altering States: Ethnographies of Transition in Eastern Europe and the Former Soviet Union*, pp. 40–69. Ann Arbor: University of Michigan Press.

_____. 2000e. "Auf dem Weg zur Wallfahrt: Musikalische Kolportage an den Grenzen der Volksfrömmigkeit." In Gerlinde Haid, Ursula Hemetek, and Rudolf Pietsch, eds., *Volksmusik — Wandel und Deutung: Festschrift Walter Deutsch zum 75. Geburtstag*, pp. 505–522. Vienna: Böhlau.

_____. 2002b. "Landscape–Region–Nation–Reich: German Folk Song in the Nexus of National Identity." In Celia Applegate and Pamela M. Potter, eds., *Music and German Nationalism*, pp. 105–127. Chicago: University of Chicago Press.

_____, and Otto Holzapfel. 2001. *The Folk Songs of Ashkenaz*. Middleton, Wisc.: A-R Editions.

Bolle-Zemp, Sylvie. 1992. *Le réenchantement de la montaigne: Aspects du folklore musical en Haute-Gruyère*. Geneva: Georg Éditeur.

Broughton, Simon, Mark Ellingham, and Richard Trillo, eds. 1999. *The Rough Guide to World Music*. Vol. 1: *Africa, Europe and the Middle East*. 2d ed. London: The Rough Guides.

Bruji. *Kein Wort Deutsch*. Extraplatte EX 341–2.

Brusatti, Otto, and Christoph Lingg. 1999. *Apropos Czernowitz*. Vienna: Böhlau.

Chieftains, The. 1996. *Santiago*. RCA BMG 09026 68602.

Corbea-Hoisie, Andrei, ed. 1998. *Czernowitz: Jüdisches Städtebild*. Frankfurt am Main: Jüdischer Verlag.

Dibango, Manu. 1994. *Three Kilos of Coffee: An Autobiography*. Trans. by Beth G. Raps. Chicago: University of Chicago Press.

Drakulić, Slavenka. 1999. *Café Europa: Life after Communism*. New York: W. W. Norton.

Du Bois, W. E. B. 1989 [1903]. *The Souls of Black Folk*. Repr. ed. by Henry Louis Gates, Jr. New York: Bantam.

Engelhardt, Jeffers L. 2002. "Asceticism and the Nation: Henryk Gorécki,

Krzysztof Penderecki, and Late Twentieth-Century Poland." *European Meetings in Ethnomusicology* 9:197–207.

*Eurovision Song Contest Kopenhagen 2001.* 2001. BMG 74321 78583 2.

*Eurovision Song Contest Stockholm 2000.* 2000. BMG 74321 76587 2.

*Eurovision Song Contest Tallinn 2002.* 2002. BMG 74321 [] 2.

Farwick, Petra. 1986. *Deutsche Volksliedlandschaften: Landschaftliches Register der Aufzeichnungen im Deutschen Volksliedarchiv.* Berne: Peter Lang.

Frank, Ben G. 1996. *A Travel Guide to Jewish Europe.* 2d ed. Gretna, La.: Pelican Publishing Company.

Gambaccini, Paul, Tim Rice, Jonathan Rice, and Tony Brown. 1999. *The Complete Eurovision Song Contest Companion 1999.* London: Pavillion.

Gay y Blasco, Paloma. 1999. *Gypsies in Madrid: Sex, Gender and the Performance of Identity.* Oxford: Berg.

Gilroy, Paul. 1993. *The Black Atlantic: Modernity and Double Consciousness.* Cambridge, Mass.: Harvard University Press.

Gruber, Ruth Ellen. 2002. *Virtually Jewish: Reinventing Jewish Culture in Europe.* Berkeley: University of California Press.

Harrán, Don. 1999. *Salamone Rossi: Jewish Musician in Late Renaissance Mantua.* New York: Oxford University Press.

Hebdige, Dick. 1979. *Subculture: The Meaning of Style.* London: Methuen.

Hemetek, Ursula. 2001. *Mosaik der Klänge: Musik der ethnischen und religiösen Minderheiten in Österreich.* Vienna: Böhlau.

Kaufmann, Thomas DaCosta. 1995. *Court, Cloister and City: The Art and Culture of Central Europe 1450–1800.* Chicago: University of Chicago Press.

Kertész, Imre. 2003. *Die exilierte Sprache: Essays und Reden.* Frankfurt am Main: Suhrkamp.

Ladd, Brian. 1997. *The Ghosts of Berlin: Confronting German History in the Urban Landscape.* Chicago: University of Chicago Press.

Lampland, Martha. 2000. "An Anthropology of Postsocialism." In Daphne Berdahl, Matti Bunzl, and Martha Lampland, eds., *Altering States: Ethnographies of Transition in Eastern Europe and the Former Soviet Union,* pp. 1–13. Ann Arbor: University of Michigan Press.

Lange, Barbara Rose. 2003. *Holy Brotherhood: Romani Music in a Hungarian Pentecostal Church.* New York: Oxford University Press.

*Latcho drom.* 1993. *Latcho drom: La musique des Tsiganes du monde de l'Inde a l'Espagne.* Caroline Carol 1776–2.

Lemon, Alaina, and Midori Nakamura. 1996. *T'an Bakhtale! (Good Fortune to You!): Roma (Gypsies) in Russia.* New York: Documentary Educational Resources.

Livingston, Tamara E. 1999. "Music Revivals: Towards a General Theory." *Ethnomusicology* 43 (1): 66–85.

Mahr, Roland. 2002. "Von der Aufwärmrunde bis ins Ziel—Der 'Grand Prix der Volksmusik': Eine musikwissenschaftliche Untersuchung des Wettbewerbs als Schlüsselstelle zum Karrieresprung in der volkstümlichen Unterhaltungsbranche." Master's thesis, University of Vienna.

Manuel, David. 1992. *Medjugorje under Siege*. Orleans, Mass.: Paraclete Press.

Manuel, Peter. 1989. "Andalusian, Gypsy, and Class Identity in the Contemporary Flamenco Complex." *Ethnomusicology* 33 (1): 47–65.

Mautner, Konrad. 1910. *Das steyerische Rasplwerk: Vierzeiler, Lieder, und Gasslreime aus Gößl am Grundlsee*. Vienna: Stählein & Lauenstein.

McColgan, John. 1994. *Riverdance: The Show*. Tyrone/RTE Video.

Naidoo, Xavier. 1998. *Nicht von dieser Welt*. Pelham Power Productions 3P 489869 6.

Nathan, Hans, ed. 1994. *Israeli Folk Music: Songs of the Pioneers*. Madison, Wisc.: A-R Editions.

Ottens, Rita, and Joel Rubin. 1999. *Klezmer-Musik*. Cassel: Bärenreiter.

Özdogan, Selim. 2000. *Im Juli*. Hamburg and Vienna: Europa Verlag.

Paulus, Irena. 1999. "Music in Krzysztof Kieslowski's Film *Three Colors: Blue*. A Rhapsody in Shades of Blue: The Reflections of a Musician." *International Review of the Aesthetics and Sociology of Music* 30 (1): 65–91.

Pinder, John. 2001. *The European Union: A Very Short Introduction*. Oxford: Oxford University Press.

Ramnarine, Tina K. 2003. *Ilmatar's Inspirations: Nationalism, Globalization, and the Changing Soundscapes of Finnish Folk Music*. Chicago: University of Chicago Press.

Rasmussen, Ljerka. 1996. "The Southern Wind of Change: Style and the Politics of Identity in Prewar Yugoslavia." In Mark Slobin, ed., *Retuning Culture: Musical Changes in Central and Eastern Europe*, pp. 99–116. Durham, N.C.: Duke University Press.

_____. 2002. *Newly Composed Folk Music of Yugoslavia*. New York: Routledge.

Schulhoff, Erwin. 1995. *Erwin Schulhoff: Schriften*. Ed. by Tobias Widmaier. Hamburg: Von Bockel.

Stokes, Martin. 1992. *The Arabesk Debate: Music and Musicians in Modern Turkey*. Oxford: Oxford University Press.

_____, and Philip V. Bohlman, eds. 2003. *Celtic Modern: Music at the Global Fringe*. Lanham, Md.: Scarecrow Press. (Europea: Ethnomusicologies and Modernities, 1.)

Swedenburg, Ted. 1997. "Saida Sultan/Danna International: Transgender Pop and the Polysemiotics of Sex, Nation, and Ethnicity on the Israeli-Egyptian Border." *The Musical Quarterly* 81 (1): 81–108.

Taraf de Haïdouks. 1991. *Musique des Tziganes de Roumanie*. Crammed Discs CRAW 2 CD.

_____. 1994. *Honourable Brigands, Magic Horses and Evil Eye*. Cram World CRAW 13.

_____. 2001. *Band of Gypsies*. Nonesuch 79641–2.

Taylor, Timothy D. 1997. *Global Pop: World Music, World Markets*. New York: Routledge.

Urla, Jacqueline. 2001. "'We Are All Malcolm X!': Negu Gorriak, Hip-Hop, and the Basque Political Imaginary." In Tony Mitchell, ed., *Global Noise: Rap and Hip-Hop outside the USA*, pp. 171–193. Middletown, Conn.: Wesleyan University Press.

van de Port, Mattijs. 1998. *Gypsies, Wars and Other Instances of the Wild: Civilisation and Its Malcontents in a Serbian Town*. Amsterdam: Amsterdam University Press.

Veřa Bílá and Kale. 1997. *Rom-Pop*. RCA Victor 74321–27910–2.

Verdery, Katherine. 1983. *Transylvania Villagers*. Berkeley and Los Angeles: University of California Press.

von Goisern, Hubert, und die Alpinkatzen. 1995. *Wia die Zeit vergeht.* . . . 2 CDs. BMG 74321 263 262.

Wellner, Christoph. 2002. "Pluralismus in Nordeuropa." *Österreichische Musikzeitschrift* 57 (3/4): 33–40.

Wiener Tschuschenkapelle. 1994. *G'rebelt: Live*. Extraplatte EX 205–2.

Zawinul, Joe. 2000. *Mauthausen: . . . vom großen Sterben hören—Chronicles from the Ashes*. ESC Records EFA 03666–2.

# Epilogue

## *The New as the Old, the Old as the New*

This book steadfastly resists finality. It struggles against the numerous moments I have been calling "ethnographic presents." As I turn toward the epilogue to effect closure, none is in sight. The year that stretches from the Eurovision Song Contest that opens the book to the Eurovision that now closes the book has been one of the most divisive in Europe's modern history. The New Europe, formed from union, threatened to collapse into fragments yet again. European nationalism had clearly entered the twenty-first century, and the only certain claim that one can make about it is that it had begun struggling under the weight of its present and future even more than of its past.

The political events that undermined the formation of a New Europe did not unfold entirely in Europe itself, rather in the Middle East, specifically in conjunction with the Iraq War. The primary perpetrator of that war was the United States, but it was because the United States needed to claim a European, hence an international, alliance that it employed a strategy of driving a wedge into the processes of European unity. Politically, the European Union became the enemy, the international force most staunchly opposed to the American invasion. Though it was able to muster a few European allies for its anti-Iraq coalition, most vocally the United Kingdom, Spain, and Denmark, the United States succeeded primarily in turning public and political opinion in Europe's most powerful nations, Germany and France, against the war, and they were joined, both in European politics and at the United Nations, by Russia. As deadline after deadline for an imaginary Iraqi disarmament came and passed, the chasm widened between Europe and the United States, with its least-European European partner, the United Kingdom.

The Old World was failing to follow the lead of the New World against the Third World and the Islamic World—until a new New Europe was rallied to the cause of the New World Order. By early 2003,

the countries of Eastern Europe, above all those seeking membership
in the European Union, were openly declaring support for the American policy of preemptive invasion of Iraq. Poland, Romania, the Baltic
States, the Czech Republic, Slovakia—indeed, a majority of nations
sandwiched in the space between the former imperial powers of Russia
and Central Europe—announced their new alliances, in some cases
even their willingness to send a handful of troops to the Middle East.
Recognizing the growing schism in European politics, President
George W. Bush and U.S. Secretary of Defense Donald Rumsfeld
cheered the alliance they had formed with their European partners:
The nations of Eastern Europe quickly ascended to the status of the
"New Europe," emerging with fresh ideas and clear international vi-
sion from the historical anachronism of an "Old Europe" comprising
Germany, Russia, and especially France.

The paradox could not be more striking: In their desire to join the
European Union and profit from European unity, the nations of the
New Europe declared by American-led global political rhetoric were
willing to turn their backs on the most powerful nations of the European Union itself. Fractionalism seemed more politically advantageous
than unification. And perhaps it was, for by early April 2003, as American troops were entering Baghdad, ten new Eastern European nations—Cyprus, the Czech Republic, Estonia, Hungary, Latvia, Lithuania, Malta, Poland, Slovakia, and Slovenia—had been tentatively
approved for admission to the EU on 1 May 2004. The American prog-
nostications about the New Europe were coming true.

But expanding the European Union to rally support for American
global politics that pitted the new New Europe against the Old Europe
was not that simple. From an historical standpoint the most obvious
new member of the EU was Turkey, a NATO ally since 1952 and a nation with a sustained economic presence in Europe. Turkey's interest
in joining the EU was a matter of historical record and of longstanding
military service to Europe itself: Occupying its position at the international border between Europe and Asia, Turkey maintains an army
larger than any member of the European Union. In the closing
months of 2002, during which time the United States was attempting
to muster its European coalition, it was well aware of the value of
adding Turkey to the European Union, that is, adding a friend to a political entity with potential as a political and economic nemesis in the
new global order of the twenty-first century. And so, as the EU Copen-

hagen summit in mid-December 2002 drew closer, growing importance accrued to the decision about Turkey's membership in the European Union.

On 13 December 2003, the EU decided to postpone further discussions of Turkish membership for another two years, and it voted to extend invitations to the ten applicant nations from Eastern Europe and
the Eastern Mediterranean. Officially, the reasons for rebuffing Turkey
were that it had failed to meet the necessary criteria for human rights
and economic stability. Whether the ten nations invited to join the EU
had met those same criteria—several had disastrous economies, and
the treatment of Roma in several were the subjects of international
condemnation—was not open to question. It was apparent that the
new questions about European unity and the EU retained all the earmarks of the old questions. Economically, the new members would extend EU economic control over Europe beyond the frontline of former communist Eastern Europe. The Baltic States, former Soviet
republics, extended the imperial reach of the EU to the very doorstep
of Russia by erasing the final traces of the northwestern frontier of the
Soviet Union. Malta and Cyprus extended the EU borders in different
geographical directions, that is, to North Africa and the Middle East.
The EU had reestablished the position of Europe along the threshold
between the Christian and Muslim worlds, in the case of a Cyprus divided along Christian-Muslim (or Greek and Turkish) lines, quite literally so. Here, the criteria to which Turkey had been held both were and
were not relevant. It depended on how one viewed Europe.

In 2002–2003, the question of how one viewed Europe turned
around Turkey. National parliaments and EU commissions alike
dredged up historical prejudices and exposed deep convictions that
even a united Europe must accept the fissures creating fragments that
could never adhere to a common whole. Turkish admission to the EU
unleashed virulent debate in the German parliament, the Bundestag,
threatening the prospects of a unified government. After Chancellor
Gerhard Schröder's declaration of support for Turkish membership,
the opposition Christian Democrats (CDU) and Christian Socialists
(CSU) clarified their belief that Turkey's 67 million residents, overwhelmingly Muslim, were not really European. Former French president Valéry Giscard d'Estaing, given the responsibility of drafting a
constitution for the European Union, weighed in on the debate by declaring that Turkey simply was "not a European country," and that
inviting it to join the EU would mean "the end of Europe" (quoted in

Sciolino 2002). But the doors were not entirely closed and locked in the wake of the December 2002 Copenhagen summit on European Union expansion. When the discussions resume again in late 2004, a new deadline for admission will be tentatively put in place: If it lived up to the requisite membership criteria, Turkey might expect admission as early as 2012.

As I write the epilogue of this book, the ethnographic present displays the startling appearance of the historical past. Europe, recognizing the need for unity, insists that its wholeness be postponed until sense can be made of its fragments. The fragments are not just the products of nationalist political agendas that refuse to disappear; they are often the very simulacra of European nations. Borne by a desire to eliminate empire from European soil, the European Union has instead remixed the conditions necessary for empire. It measures the expansion of its borders against the expansion of Islamic nations, Muslim guest workers, and Islamist politicians in North Africa and the Middle East—and, of course, in Turkey. Another imperial era piles upon those that came before, setting the EU in opposition to NATO and both of them in opposition to the anti-Iraq coalition.

No single Europe can survive such competition, and no single nation is freed of the need to choose sides. Unity in one political or regional sector leads to fragmentation elsewhere. The music of European nationalism depends on, even feeds on, such fragmentation, for it forms along the fissures and effects connections otherwise vetoed by politicians and cultural ideologues. In 2002, music has drawn attention to the problems of wholeness in European history as the music of Europe's most feared historical Other, the Muslim cultures and countries to the south and southeast, asserted their Europeanness. Ineluctably, the closure of the book is made possible only by listening to the musics that coalesce as fragments around Europe's Muslim peripheries, peripheries that are collapsing into Europe's center.

## Europe 2003—The Counterpoint of Empires and Fragments

The music of empire runs through this book, shaping the voices of an historical fugue. Nationalism waits in the wings, aware that the spaces claimed by empire will also yield themselves to the spoils of competing national histories. Throughout European history, empire and nation have been locked in an embrace, sometimes for the common good,

*Figure E.1.* *"Kaiserwalzer"/"Empire Waltz," op. 437, first waltz, opening theme,
Johann Strauss, Jr.*

*Figure E.2.* *"Kaiserwalzer"/"Empire Waltz," op. 437, third waltz, trio section,
Johann Strauss, Jr.*

often not. No other musical announcement of empire has surfaced as
repeatedly in the course of the book as Haydn's "Kaiserhymne," whose
very imperial ambiguity afforded it the power to symbolize the Austro-
Hungarian Empire in the nineteenth century and the German imperial impulse in the twentieth century. The musical realization of the
imperial imaginary depends on the capacity of music to muster frag-

ments and to redeploy them in the texture of grand compositions (CD examples 33–35). Even Beethoven, first recognizing and then rejecting the power of empire in his third symphony, the "Eroica," famously dedicated to Napoleon and his imperial claims on Europe before they had exceeded the boundaries of nations and human rights, thus leading Beethoven to remove the dedication, located the musical emblem of empire in the final movement of his ninth symphony. In the grand choral expression, the "Ode to Joy," that today, without the voice of its choristers, has become the "European Anthem," it is the sound of another empire, the Ottoman Empire, that interrupts the final movement, in a trio section that unequivocally opens the parade grounds of Turkey, the Balkans, and modern Eastern Europe for the Janissary troops of the Ottoman Empire (see Figure 1.2). In the heart of what has become the most officially "European" of all musical works, the sound of the Islamic East arrests our attention.

The music of empires at the center and the peripheries of Europe grows from fragments, and it is the music itself that sutures the fragments into a whole that bears witness to the nationalist struggles that ceaselessly form the counterpoint of modern European history. The epigraph for this penultimate section of the book, Johann Strauss, Jr.'s "Empire Waltz," one of the Waltz King's numerous peons to empire, exposes the ways in which fragments are loosely gathered to forge the musical representation of European political unity (listen also to CD example 37). The introduction sets the dance of empire in motion not as a waltz, but as a march, indeed, an extended march that exploits the sounds and textures of a military band. Before it reaches the four distinctive waltzes that form the core of the composition, the "Empire Waltz" sets out for war. Strauss arrives at the first waltz (see Figure E.1) only after 75 measures, in which the martial meters and rhythms obscure melody, or at least relegate it as a voice of mere secondary importance.

The texture changes the moment the waltzes domesticate the texture of "Empire Waltz." The string voices of the first waltz, for many the best known of the waltzes in the composition, hence *the* "Empire Waltz," move largely in parallel lines, layering additional voices in the comforting consonance of C Major. The rigidity and impatience of the Central European waltz are delayed just a bit longer, with the second theme's chords, borrowed from the opening march, underlying the melody. The "Empire Waltz" weaves its way through a welter of textures and melodies, some familiar and cloying in their insistent reference to the traditions that formed a canon of European popular music at the end of the nineteenth century and at the height of European empire. At other moments the "Empire Waltz" enters unfamiliar ground and foreign territory.

The fragments of empire evoke meanings of both Self and Other. We should not be surprised, because the Strauss repertory persistently stretches over national boundaries and plays with the sounds of empire. "Vienna Blood" ("Wiener Blut," Op. 354; see Figure 3.3) may flow deeply, but "Tausend und eine Nacht" ("A Thousand and One Nights," Op. 346) conjures up the Muslim Ottoman Empire that borders the Christian Austro-Hungarian Empire. Fragment upon fragment enters the "Empire Waltz," and the map of empire unfolds before us. The other familiar melody from the "Empire Waltz" does not make an appearance until the trio, or middle, section of the third waltz (see Figure E.2 above), where the unison strings comprising the melodic line compete with the accompaniment that coarsely supports the whole. The empire and the lands it claims as its subjects openly compete again, for Strauss feels compelled to mark this section "sempre ben marcato," "always very march-like"). At its very core the "Empire Waltz" stays its martial course (CD example 37, in fact, is performed by the orchestra of the Austrian army).

At the beginning of the twenty-first century, fragments increasingly provide the material substance of national memory work in Europe. Museums provide homes to fragments from the past, so it is hardly surprising that museums multiply. Monuments, too, do powerful memory work by gathering fragments into them, reconstructing them as traces to form the surfaces that charge the viewer to remember through the construction of monumental time (Herzfeld 1991). Nostalgia, moreover, intensifies feeling for the past because it concentrates expression into the limited space of the fragment. Fragments, finally, allow for selective memory work, and accordingly they are ideally suited for the rhetoric of nationalism, which necessarily privileges some layers of fragmentary evidence and excises others. It is amazingly uncomplicated, therefore, to fit fragments to the musical vocabularies that help us remember inchoate nations and to use fragments to construct the rhetoric requisite for imagining new nationalisms from the old.

When the music of European nationalism assumes the forms and functions of fragments, it also expresses moments in time and history that are incomplete. We have witnessed such moments of incompleteness throughout this book, and their surfeit explains why the book itself resists closure. The nationless peoples and the nations at the fringes, in particular, have shaped musical meaning and national repertories from fragments. But the fragments with which they have shaped and performed national and nationalist musics have not been devoid of meaning, even of power. Musical fragments have not only afforded new sets of musical tools to Europeans at the fringes. The movements to bring about reunification in Central Europe, especially Germany, after the fall of communism were most effective and eloquent when they built upon the mobility and enhanced signification that are immanent in fragments. The musical rebuilding of a single Germany exhumes fragments from the destruction of the twentieth century, recognizing that compositional and performative attempts to assemble a modern Germany from them figuratively undergo transformation to national acts of healing, in which the nation torn asunder by its own misguided imperial aspirations in the twentieth century can suture a new well-being from the remainders of the past (cf. Bohlman and Currid 2001).

Festivals, choral movements, folk-music collecting projects, the mixing and remixing of Europop repertories. These are the musical sites at which fragments are gathered and new processes of reconciliation converge. The voices of indigenous Europeans. The struggles of nationless Europeans. The revival of repertories by the most repressed of Europe's Others. The sounds of a New Europe thrive because they are fragmentary and because they belie the hegemony of empires and new world orders alike. The Arabic, Turkish, and Urdu songs of the European metropolis, the public and private expression of new religious musics, the push of the Eurovision Song Contest into Eastern Europe and beyond. It is as fragments that all these musics cohere in 2003 as the music of European nationalism.

## Eurovision 2003—Beyond Old and New Europes

*I know whatcha thinkin', uh-huh good*
*Now, the rest of the world is overruled.*
*—Sertab Erener, "Every Way That I Can"*
*2003 Eurovision Song Contest Winner for Turkey*

24 May 2003. The Eurovision Song Contest 2003 in Riga, Latvia. The groove opening Turkey's 2003 entry was at once familiar and exotic. It

was European and it wasn't. It conformed to Eurovision aesthetic expectations but it also defied them. Early predictions indicated that the Russian entry would win, completing the move into Eastern Europe that had characterized the early Eurovision contests of the twenty-first century. The musical and political questions raised by the year since the Tallinn Eurovision that opened this book, however, had not been predicted at the time. The real question that the Riga contest would—or would not—address was just how this year's contest would speak to the various parsings of Europe into Old and New, relevant or irrelevant to the new global order.

The groove that songwriter Sertab Erener chose to open "Every Way That I Can" did not equivocate: It announced that this would be a song from Turkey, and that Turkey is no less rooted in Europe than Asia. It is a Turkey whose Ottoman past spread across the eastern Mediterranean and across southeastern Europe. That same Turkey had supplied workers to drive the engines of Central European factories for generations and had offered military bases to shore up Europe against the East, be it the Soviet Union during the Cold War or Iraq thereafter. The Turkey of "Every Way That I Can" claimed a nationalist voice borne of an historical and modern position between East and West.

The unison strings, both acoustic and synthesized, that enunciated the groove were driven from the start by a bass guitar. The bass line was brief but clear, and it announced itself as Turkish and Muslim through the inflection of a **darbucca,** the characteristically Middle Eastern goblet-shaped drum. For the Eurovision listener, this was the sound of Islam that entries from the Muslim countries of southeastern Europe and the Mediterranean had been employing for a decade, declaring the presence of their Islamic history in a modern Europe. The unison strings of a Middle Eastern orchestra had never produced a winning sound. They situated any entry at the edge of Europe, not in the center, and thus symbolized political and ideological dissonance. They referred too obliquely to the sounds essential for Europop, even at its most global extremes.

In the collaboration this time, however, lyricist Demir Demirkan and songwriter and singer Sertab Erener were all too aware of the risk and potential of where the clearly Turkish sound of "Every Way That I Can" would locate Turkey on the contemporary European landscape. Sertab Erener was, in fact, a well-known musical **Gastarbeiterin.** Istanbul-born Sertab Erener had been a star in Turkey for over a decade, and she had released a relatively steady stream of albums since her first in 1992. Those albums, not to mention the videos that accompanied many of the tracks, circulated perhaps just as extensively in Europe as in Turkey. Erener's songs circulated widely in Vienna and Berlin, and she had established herself as a star in Europe's guest-worker heartland (see Stokes 2003). By the late 1990s she had managed to cross over into several other global pop scenes as well, most famously by singing with Ricky Martin in his 1999 hit "Private Emotion," but also significantly by joining tenor José Carreras in the popularization of his operatic repertory. In 2000, Erener began releasing albums in a Turkish and "European" counterpoint, first one in Turkish, followed then by one intended for the mainstream European popular market. As a singer, she was perfectly poised for the Turkish Europop sound of "Every Way That I Can."

The 2003 Eurovision entries responded in different ways to the international challenges to European nationalism that the Iraq War had unleashed (cf. the compilation of all twenty-six entries on *Eurovision Song Contest Riga 2003*). As different as the responses were, they also fell largely at the two extremes of a continuum, and that continuum, in turn, represented a set of complex figurations of the Old and the New Europes that the new global order was foisting upon the continent. A rather large number of entries determined simply to avoid the political crisis that was afflicting the world. The United Kingdom, despite—or because of—its military coalition with the United States in the Iraq War, sidestepped politics entirely, musically exchanging any pretense of its anointing as a partner from the New Europe for the self-consciously innocuous song "Cry Baby." Both Old and New European voters, nonetheless, took the UK musical gesture very seriously, placing it ignominiously not only in last place (and thus ineligible to compete in 2004) but in the extraordinary position of receiving "nul points," no votes whatsoever. The entries looking to avoid the present by recuperating a past Eurovision sound, such as Estonia's Ruffus with "Eighties Coming Back," also fared poorly.

Eurovision voters were taking the 2003 contest very seriously (see Hong 2003). A rather large number of entries also took European national and international politics very seriously. National politics surfaced in many songs, even when they did not necessarily overflow into the larger debates about Old and New Europes. Mija Martina Barbarić's entry from Bosnia-Herzegovina, "Could It Be," espoused an

Orthodox Christian, hence Serb, counterpole to Nino's "Hana" from 2001, but in so doing sustained the Bosnian national practice of alternating Muslim, Catholic, and Orthodox entries. The epitome of the Old Europe, Austria, which had been faring dreadfully for many years, despite its self-proclaimed reputation as Europe's most musical nation, broke with its own Eurovision tradition by returning to national tradition, submitting Alf Poier's "Weil der Mensch zählt" ("Because Human Beings Count"), a song with an environmentalist theme, but performed in a Viennese dialect that effectively took it out of the competitive running as it highlighted Austria's political neutrality at the center of Europe.

There was a surfeit of European nationalisms at Eurovision 2003, some local, others international. The Belgian entry, Urban Trad's "Sanomi," employed an artificial language and thus departed from the practice of alternating French and Flemish songs, and for this it received second place. France, the pillar of the *chanson* style that had proved remarkably durable since the first Eurovision in 1956, followed an entirely different route, to its post-colonial periphery in the Parisian suburbs, where Algerian *raï* had thrived for a generation. In 2003, Hovine Hallaf's "Monts et merveilles" ("[The Promise] of the Whole World") sensitively integrated the aesthetic of France's own Muslim present into the entry from the Old European nation that took the most aggressively critical stance toward the Iraq War. Poland, afforded the role of poster child in America's New Europe, entered the Eurovision for the first time, a significant political gesture only two weeks before the June 7–8 referendum to decide on European Union membership. Just as the Polish entry, a duet between German- and Polish-speaking singers, called for "No Borders"—"Keine Grenzen/ Żadnych Granic"—Polish voters overwhelming approved their government's solicitation for EU membership.

Against the backdrop of Europe's most important display of music and nationalism, however, the day belonged to Turkey. And the Turkish entry made its case for Europe eloquently. After a year of political fractionalism, "Every Way That I Can" laid claim to Turkey's European presence because it was old and new. Sertab Erener seized the political moment to remix a groove Sezen Aksu had previously used in Tarkan's "Şimarik," which had hit the top of the charts—in Germany and Austria—in 1999 and remained a hit through 2003 (see cuts 1 and 14 on Tarkan 1998; cf. Chapter 7). "Every Way That I Can" played on the immediacy of the Turkish-European sound that Sertab Erener had embedded in Tarkan's sound, which European audiences had embraced despite the popular singer's growing Islamist associations. In the "middle-eight" section of "Every Way That I Can" Sertab Erener turned the Turkish sound outward, making an international claim by rapping over a groove that was now stripped of its orientalist stereotypes. Her proclamation that "now, the rest of the world is overruled" had implications that few could or did miss.

> *Nothing in the world*
> *That could stop me, no sir,*
> *No, no, no!*
> —Sertab Erener, "Every Way That I Can"

Whether for the New Europe or for the Old, "Every Way That I Can" seized the power of popular song to make the case for nationalism, even to advance the cause of a new European nationalism. This was a European nationalism that included rather than excluded Europe's historical Others, and that opened national spaces at the very center of the continent for those forced to its historical and global fringes. The music of European nationalism had again proved to be powerfully trenchant at the historical juncture of our own present, when the very essence of the European nation is undergoing dramatic change on an increasingly global level.

## REFERENCES

Bohlman, Philip V., and Brian Currid. 2001. "Suturing History, Healing Europe: German National Temporality in *Wolokolamsk Highway*." *The Musical Quarterly* 85 (4): 681–717.

*Eurovision Song Contest Riga 2003*. 2003. EMI CMC 5843942.

Herzfeld, Michael. 1982. *Ours Once More: Folklore, Ideology and the Making of Modern Greece*. Austin: University of Texas Press.

Hong, Y. Euny. 2003. "Rise of the New Europe in Euro Pop." *The New York Times* (on-line). 26 May.

Stokes, Martin. 2003. "Globalization and the Politics of World Music." In Martin Clayton, Trevor Herbert, and Richard Middleton, eds., *The Cultural Study of Music: A Critical Introduction*, pp. 297–308. New York: Routledge.

Tarkan. 1998. *Tarkan*. Polygram 559 981–2.

# CD Notes and Commentary

Music inscribes history on the nation. Music also inscribes the nation on history. While realizing and narrating nationalism, music acquires the potential to exhibit both mediation and agency, not just representing the nation but also giving voice to those who wish to claim the nation and its history. In the examples gathered for the CD accompanying *The Music of European Nationalism,* music reveals itself to be powerfully historical, possessing the potential to locate the nation in history and thus to historicize nationalism. The power to historicize may well be the most resonant characteristic that all examples on the CD share. In their different ways, they narrate a nation's past in order to give meaning to its present and future.

The nation's historical narrative may reside in musical genres (e.g., in the folk music of the first section) that negotiate the borders between myth and history, thus setting the *longue durée* in motion. The historical narrative may aggressively tackle the most pressing social issues of the present, thereby opening spaces that nationalism might previously have denied. The CD contains examples that celebrate the imperial reach of the nation (e.g., in the final group), but resisting these are the examples that speak powerfully for Europeans otherwise denied voice (e.g., the numerous tracks containing the music of Roma and other "Europeans without Nations"). The historical narratives of the nation may symbolize imperial expansion or celebrate military action (e.g., in the final section), or they may accompany the sacred journeys that mobilize Europeans to cross national borders in search of peace and reconciliation (e.g., the music for pilgrimage in the second section). Musicians may sing of local heroes and regional events, but they may also draw their repertories from diaspora and the globalized modernity of the nation-state in the twenty-first century (cf. the third and fourth sections). The histories whose fabric is constituted by the music of European nationalism are stunning when we witness the full range of their variety and complexity.

There is, clearly, no single form of history that we find in the music of European nationalism. Some histories are local, others regional, and still others national (cf. the Central European and Carpathian examples on the CD). In some genres historical facts may be preeminent, thus presented in minute detail or peopled with real biographies, of aristocrats in the "Kosovo Cycle" (Track 1) or of Austrian generals remembered with each performance of the march named in their honor (Track 36). In contrast, others trade in the imagery of the imagination, relying on a modern willingness to accept invented traditions as real and as different as an Irish "Trip Jig" (Track 11) or the rags-to-riches life journey of a Viennese coachman to the cosmopolitan center of empire (Track 13).

The musical examples on the accompanying CD were not chosen because their historical narratives were linked to individual nations but rather because together they bear witness to the ways music is crucial to the agency necessary for the historicizing of nationalism. No example comes simply from a single place and time, rather each example joins the others on the CD to locate music in the making of modern Europe. Individual examples, therefore, derive meaning from their own narrative histories, the movement between oral and written traditions, or processes of transmission spurred on by censorship or contrafact. A Croatian Austrian folk song (Track 33) becomes the theme in a set of variations for string quartet (Track 34) en route to one of the most contested national anthems in modern history, the German national anthem. Many of the tracks contain examples whose wholeness—whose narrative of the nation-state—is the result of fragments juxtaposed musically. The epics of the *longue durée* result from the collection of Saami runes or the musical tales of battles against the Ottoman Empire (cf. Tracks 1–3). Polkas vie with waltzes in the songs of the metropolis (Track 13) or the choreography of diaspora (Track 11). Waltzes, marches, Ländlers, and wedding dances compete for the same collective and multiply the options for the public performance of history (e.g., in the section "Wedding Music and Dance Music").

The place of the nation may seem to be fixed in the landscapes described by the songs and dances, but more often than not it is contested by the movement of people and the crossing of fragile borders (cf. Tracks 14–15). The Europeans that we encounter in the songs and instrumental pieces are on the move, both because of and in spite of nationalism. I have chosen the examples for the CD, it follows, because they illustrate the contested and multifaceted conditions of European nationalism. The tracks from the Carpathian Mountains are Jewish, German, Romanian, Hungarian, and Romani, hence they all belong to the Carpathians. Pilgrims carry the memory of past places in their songs as they set out on new sacred journeys across a New Europe. Traditional folk songs travel across style and genre, from the rural wedding scene of the *Kalevala* to the globalized sound of Värttinä (Track 7). Rather than original versions that might give undue authority to a notion of the authentic, I have preferred to choose examples with multiple versions and variants. Rather than songs about places and identities that no one questions, I have included pieces that illustrate the ways in which any place and identity may be up for grabs when nationalism is being negotiated (e.g., in the Bartók *Violin Duos* in Tracks 18–26).

The sources for the examples on the CD are themselves very different one from another, and they therefore reflect the many ways that I as an ethnomusicologist approach European nationalism. There is documentary evidence, from my own fieldwork (e.g., Tracks 9, 10, 17, and 28–30, ethnographic recordings from Romania that illustrate the ethnographic journey in the second part of Chapter 6), but also from earlier historical projects, especially my studies of European Jewish music and the five foot pilgrimages I undertook myself in the mid-1990s (Track 4). The studio and live recordings with which I was involved in one way or another—my children perform here, as does the New Budapest Orpheum Society, of which I am the Artistic Director—come from both Europe and from the communities of Europeans in diaspora (Track 1), revealing the extent to which European nationalism has never been confined to Europe. I am indebted to the fieldwork of numerous colleagues and friends, whose research and published audio anthologies allow this CD to document places I have not yet visited. The vitality of these recordings is all the greater because they capture moments of a more distant past and of the multiple ethnographic presents necessary for understanding European nationalism today.

Performances of living performers, some generously contributing to this CD project, mix with performances created for mass dissemination and consumption. I have the great privilege to know and work closely with many outstanding musicians, who contributed willingly to the contents of the CD. Some I can only admire for their consummate artistry; others are among my closest friends; still others are members of my own immediate family. The historical narratives on the CD provide several kinds of counterpoint with the book it accompanies. Several examples illustrate crucial arguments in individual sections and chapters. Others, however, draw our attention to ideas that cut through all the chapters.

The modern history of European nationalism unfolds at a number of different levels in the narrative counterpoint shared by the book and the CD. There are individual and collective voices; there are musicians who conservatively revive and those who radically politicize; there are voices amplified by power and those mobilizing the powerless. Moving from voice to voice in the rhetorical counterpoint shared by the book and the CD of *The Music of European Nationalism* allows the reader/listener to draw closer to the many historical moments at which music participated actively in the making of modern European nationalism.

### Epic, Myth, and the Historical *Longue Durée*

**Track 1.** Boro Roganović (Montenegro/Balkan). Epic song from the "Kosovo Cycle." "Tzarina Milica and Duke Vladeta," recorded 6 August 2003, in Chicago, Illinois.

**Track 2.** "Kantele." Song from the *Kalevala* about the fashioning of the *kantele* from Väinämöinen's boat. Sung by Anni Kiriloff (1922), archival recording on *The Kalevala Heritage* (1995: Track 1).

**Track 3.** "Maailman synty" ("The Birth of the World") from the beginning of the Finnish national epic, *Kalevala*. Sung by Iivana Onoila (1905), archival recording on *The Kalevala Heritage* (1995: Track 5)

Three examples from epic traditions of southern and northern Europe, from historical field recordings at the beginning of the twentieth century and from the diaspora at the beginning of the twenty-first century. As a living *guslar*—a *gusle* player and epic singer—Boro Roganović maintains a family tradition, albeit in the large diaspora community from Southeastern Europe, which has for several generations lived in Chicago and its suburbs. Roganović performs extensively from historical repertories (e.g., Track 1), but he also creates his own songs. Music and creation are common subjects in the two Finnish examples, both pieces that have been woven into the Finnish national epic, the *Kalevala*. Epic singing styles bear witness to certain stylistic similarities—not least the narrow melodic range and line-by-line form of the first three tracks—even as the nations whose myths they narrate must have distinctive histories.

## Sacred Music

**Track 4.** "Radnalied" ("Radna Song"). Banat-German Romanian pilgrims. Field recording from September 1993 pilgrimage near St. Peter, southwestern Germany.

**Track 5.** "Medjugorje Song." Composed by Leander Prinz. Pilgrimage song for Medjugorje (ca. 1990) from *Maria, Königin der Apostel* (Augustinus Verlag, n.d., Track 3). Cf. Haid, Hemetek, and Pietsch (2000: CD, Track 18).

**Track 6.** Tambores del Bajo Aragón: "Desperadoes y toque procesional." From the field recordings of Goffredo Plastino (2001), CD with book (Track 4).

Music mobilizes religious communities in the three examples of this section, transforming the local into the European, with far-reaching political significance. The two pilgrimage songs (Track 4 and 5) are modern in every sense. Sung by a resettled community of German-speaking Romanians, the "Radnalied" memorializes the symbolic importance of the community's church in the small city of Radna in the Banat region of Romania, where a massive fire spared the image of the Virgin Mary around which the community gathers on pilgrimages, allowing them to cohere as Romanians. The "Medjugorje Song" has fully entered the "new choralism" that we witness on Track 5, even though the miracle at Medjugorje in Bosnia-Herzegovina occurred only two decades ago. In his fieldwork among brotherhoods in Spanish Aragón, Goffredo Plastino (2001) documented an astonishing array of musical practices, made audible through the processions fostered by highly specialized percussion ensembles.

### Wedding Music and Dance Music

**Track 7.** Värttinä: "Kylä vuotti uutta kuuta" ("The Village Awaits the New Moon"). Karelian wedding song on *Värttinä, Live in Helsinki* (2001: Track 7).

**Track 8.** Kati Szvorák: "Kárpáti menyasszony" ("The Fiancée from the Carpathians"). Odessa Klezmer Band, *Isaac's Dry Rice* (2000: Track 7), arranged by Ferenc Kiss.

**Track 9.** Gheorghe Covaci, Sr. ("Cioata") and Gheorghe Covaci, Jr.: "Khused" (Hassidic wedding dance), recorded 23 February 1996, Vadu Izei, Romania.

**Track 10.** Rom Band of Gheorghe Covaci, Jr.: Village Wedding Dance, recorded 24 February 1996, Vadu Izei, Romania.

**Track 11.** Anish: "Trip Jig," arranged by Anish and Aibhlín Dillane, from the CD *Anish* (2001: Track 9).

In most musical genres and national music histories, wedding and dance serve as metaphors for the formation and reproduction of the national collective through music. The music that we experience in this section displays remarkable variation and style, and the narrative of the nation follows many different historical trajectories. The Karelian wedding song performed by the Finnish all-woman ensemble, Värttinä, takes the listener to one of the most contested border areas from Finnish-Russian history, but it does so by transforming a source symbolic of the *Kalevala* into a modern emblem of "new" Finnish folk song. The journey of the Jewish fiancée across Transylvania is deceptively simple in style, for it raises the possibility of multiculturalism—it opens in Hungarian, closes in Yiddish—as well as the displacement that is historically normative in the Carpathians. The Rom musicians who perform on Tracks 9 and 10 also draw attention to the displacement and complex national fabric of Transylvania. On the first track, a father and son play a Hassidic wedding dance from the past, while on the next track, the son's modern band performs live for an Orthodox Christian wedding dance. Juxtaposition continues to underlie the dance styles in the Irish diaspora band, Anish, in "Trip Jig," actually a combination of three jigs and a polka, traditional music provided with the commentary of electronic accompaniment.

### Central Europe

**Track 12.** Die Tanzgeiger: "Bläserweise" and "Ländler" from the CD *Die Tanzgeiger* (1994: Track 4).

**Track 13.** Gustav Pick: "Wiener Fiakerlied" ("Viennese Coachman's Song") from *Dancing on the Edge of a Volcano* (Cedille Records CDR 90000 065), performed by the New Budapest Orpheum Society (Stewart Figa, baritone), used by permission of Cedille Records, available at www.cedillerecords.org.

**Track 14.** Laxblech: "Jedlička" from the CD *Laxblech* (2001: Track 17).

**Track 15.** Skaličan: "Ve Skalici na rínečku sekajú sa o d'ívečku" from the CD *L'udová hudba* (1999: Track 1).

Center and periphery compete with each other in these examples from Central Europe, complicating the very notion of "central" itself. The section begins with an example that would seem on its surface to be traditional. The brass open with a recitative quality, revealing the vocal character of alpine Austrian music, and then a *Ländler* follows and unfolds from a slow courting dance toward a more urban style. The bounds of authenticity could not be more beautifully articulated by Die Tanzgeiger, one of the finest ensembles in Central Europe, but the members do not leave the piece without commentary about style, offering a musical exclamation mark that reminds us that we live in a modern world. Gustav Pick's "Viennese Coachman's Song" was the hit song of Central Europe from the 1880s until World War I. The traditional and the modern are paired in the cosmopolitan, musically so when the duple meter in the verse gives way to the urban waltz in triple meter for the refrain. The final two tracks in the section (Tracks 14 and 15) come from the "same" border region, where Austria, Hungary, and Slovakia (with Moravia and the Czech Republic only a few kilometers to the northwest) run up against each other. One might expect the styles to be deliberately contrastive along national lines, but the musicians of Laxblech and Skaličan are in fact frequent collaborators. Modernity may be very difficult to hear, but it is in fact modernity that effects the synthesis of two examples representing the same border region.

### Carpathian Mountains

**Track 16.** Hermann Rosenzweig and Anton Groiss: ". . . Nach Großwardein" (". . . To Großwardein") from *Dancing on the Edge of a Volcano* (Cedille Records CDR 90000 065), performed by the New Budapest Orpheum Society (Deborah Bard, soprano), used by permission of Cedille Records, available at www.cedillerecords.org.

**Track 17.** Gheorghe Covaci, Sr. ("Cioata") and Gheorghe Covaci, Jr.: Jewish and Rom music, Yiddish folk song, "Ani maamin" ("I Believe") recorded 23 February 1996, Vadu Izei, Romania.

**Tracks 18–26.** Béla Bartók: 9 Duos from the *44 Violin Duos* (Andrea F. Bohlman and Benjamin H. Bohlman), recorded 13 August 2003, Chicago, Illinois.
    18. "Máramosi Tánc" ("Dance from Máramoros")
    19. "Oláh Nóta" ("Walachian Song")
    20. "Ujévköszöntő" ("New Year's Song")
    21. "Párnás Tánc" ("Pillow Dance")
    22. "Rutén Nóta" ("Ruthenian Song")
    23. "Tót Nóta" ("Slovak Song")
    24. "Gyermekrengetéskor" ("Lullaby")
    25. "Magyar Nóta" ("Hungarian Song")
    26. "Menetelő Nóta" ("Hungarian March")

The music of the Carpathian Mountains contains seemingly countless historical narratives, and it can hardly be surprising that nationalism has been and remains contested in an area geographically at the center of Europe. The examples in this section begin with a cosmopolitan style, a song about Jewish residents of a Hungarian city in Romania, circulating at the turn of the past century as a popular song in Budapest and Vienna. The singer visiting Großwardein (modern Oradea) is surprised and amused by the human mixture she encounters as she reaches the city in which she expects to find traditional Jewish culture. The two Rom musicians from the Romanian-Ukrainian border region have retained the Jewish past of their region in a different way, weaving the Hassidic tradition of the past into their own modern Transylvanian village tradition. In a region of displaced people, however, the Yiddish character of "Ani maamin" remains fully intact. Béla Bartók's *44 Duos for Violin* is one of the most complex collections of national and ethnic fragments to come from the workshop of a Hungarian composer who questioned identities in Transylvania throughout his life. As specific as the titles and styles are— Máramoros on Track 18 is the Romanian designation of Transylvania, for instance—each came into being as a musical translation of place and genre. When we hear the *Duos* as a group, as in this recording by my children, we also witness a stunning diversity of styles, each a transformation of the past into a present that has not ceased to survive through transition.

### Europeans without Nations

**Track 27.** Rom song of mourning: Ruža Nikolić-Lakatos, "Phurde, bajval, phurde" ("Blow, Wind, Blow"), recorded by Ursula Hemetek, 9 February 1995; traditional Lovara melody, also in Ursula Hemetek's *Mosaik der Klänge* (2001: CD 1, Track 24).

**Tracks 28, 29, 30.** Josef Tenebaum: 3 songs from the Jewish community recorded 24 February 1996, Sighetu-Marmaţiei, Romania.
    28. "Hanukah Song" (sung in Romanian)
    29. "Yesh Lanu Eretz" ("We Have a Land"), Zionist song (sung in Hebrew)
    30. "Love Song," Romanian folk song (sung in Romanian)

**Tracks 31, 32.** Arbëreshë in Italy: 2 sacred songs from Ardian Ahmedaja, in Pettan, Reyes, and Komavec, *Music and Minorities* (2001: Tracks 20 and 21).
    31. "Song from Vespers" (Arbëreshë in Sicily)
    32. "Santa Maria Song" (Arbëreshë in Calabria, southern Italy)

The music of Europeans without nations is at least as vast and diverse as that of Europeans who claim nationalism. The songs in this section give only a brief sense of the ways in which music gives voice to those without a national voice. Ruža Nikolić-Lakatos's lament, "Blow, Wind, Blow," came into being as a direct response to the 1995 murder of four Rom children by a pipe bomb in the mailbox of their home near Oberwart, along the Austrian-Hungarian border. Such violence against the Roma has a history of centuries, and it shows no signs of abating in the twenty-first century, when attempts to move Roma to the peripheries of the European nation continue to threaten their existence. Josef Tenebaum, one of the last surviving members of a once flourishing Jewish community in Sighetu-Marmaţiei, Romania, maintains a musical repertory that embodies the ethnic and religious diversity of the border region in which he made his life as a language teacher. The three songs I have chosen here from my fieldwork provide an ethnic and linguistic mix, but even more striking are the ways in which nationalism acquires such contrastive meanings, from the purely Zionist message of a song in Hebrew ("We have a land, a language, a law") to Romanian translations of Jewish and Ukrainian repertories. The Arbëreshë, Albanian-speaking communities in Italy, constitute one of the oldest European communities without a nation. Their modern struggle is not one of realizing a nation of their own, but rather of holding onto identity through music, as we witness in these field recordings by Ardian Ahmedaja.

### Anthems of Nationalism, Dances of Empire

**Tracks 33, 34, 35.** 3 versions of "Kaiserhymne/Deutschlandlied" ("Emperor's Hymn/Song of Germany").

33. "Jutro rano sam se ja stal" ("I Wake before the Dawn"), original Croatian folk song, field recording from Ursula Hemetek, *Mosaik der Klänge* (2001: CD 1, Track 3)

34. Franz Joseph Haydn: "Kaiser-Quartett," Op. 77, no. 3, Hob. III: 77 (2d mvt.). Theme, plus the first and final variations, recorded for this CD by the Merle Quartet (Andrea F. Bohlman, Nikki Buechler, Jessica Chuang, Hector Moreno)

35. "Emperor's Hymn," sung simultaneously in German, Hungarian, Czech, and Polish. World War I Austro-Hungarian Army "Völkerchor" archival recording on *Soldatenlieder der k.u.k. Armee* (2000: Track 1)

**Track 36.** Joseph Strauss, "Radetzky March," recorded live by Die Tanzgeiger at the ORF-Radiokulturhaus in Vienna, December 2003.

**Track 37.** Johann Strauss, Jr., "Kaiser-Walzer" ("Empire Waltz"), Orchestra of the Austrian Army (Gardemusik des österreichischen Bundesheers) unpublished recording, created for *The Music of European Nationalism*.

National histories are as explicit as they are complex in the final tracks of the CD. Each track represents the nation—specifically, Austria, from the eighteenth century to the present—in a distinctive way, grounding the representation of the nation in a particular moment, even through a specific performance. As a group, however, these closing tracks raise the question, Just how do we experience the nation: as the same or as different, as myth or as history? The set begins with the Croatian folk song whose predecessor in oral tradition was likely the source for the theme in Haydn's *Emperor Quartet*, which in turn became the basis for the "Emperor's Hymn," which remained the national anthem of the Austro-Hungarian Empire until the end of World War I, soon thereafter, however, providing the music for the German national anthem. The transitions necessary for such a history are clearly audible, for example, in the transition of the Croatian folk song form into the typically AAB form in the quartet and the anthem. Meanings are heaped upon meanings as history accumulates the baggage of nationalism: How could this be more evident than in the military version from World War I, with soldiers from the imperial army singing their anthem in four languages at the same time? The military character of anthems, official and unofficial, remains intact on the final two tracks, compositions by two different Strausses. As it always does (e.g., in the New Year's Day concert broadcast around the world), this live performance of "Radetzky March" inspires listeners to rise to their feet and clap, participating in the performative affirmation of the nation. The CD closes with the opening sections of the "Empire Waltz," beginning not with a waltz, but a march, and unfolding as a series of waltzes, each representing the empire in different ways, each documenting the ways national styles struggle to draw upon many parts in order to imagine the whole nation into being.

### ACKNOWLEDGMENTS

The recordings on the CD would have been impossible without the efforts of countless musicians and scholars, who willingly shared their artistry and the fieldwork with me. I owe an enormous debt of gratitude to:

Anish, Ardian Ahmedaja, Andrea F. Bohlman, Benjamin H. Bohlman, Christine W. Bohlman, Nikki Buechler, Jessica Chuang, Gheorghe Covaci, Jr., and Gheorghe Covaci, Sr., Aibhlín Dillane, Thomas DuBois, Jeffers Engelhardt, the Gardemusik of the Austrian Army, James Ginsburg, Ursula Hemetek, Inge and Otto Holzapfel, David Hunter, Jacqueline Jones, Ferenc Kiss, Laxblech, Gerda Lechleitner, Ilya Levinson, Roland Mahr, Marin Marian Bălaşa, Harry Maiorovici, the Merle Quartet, Hector Moreno, Barbara Need, the New Budapest Orpheum Society, Ruža Nikolić-Lakatos, the Odessa Klezmer Band, Nada Petrović, Rudolf Pietsch, Goffredo Plastino, Tamás Repiszky, Boro Roganović, Skalican, Kati Szvorák, Die Tanzgeiger, Josef Tenebaum, and Joseph Toth.

# Glossary

**Absolute music**   Music with no social functions except those expressed through its own form and performance. Sometimes equated with chamber and orchestral work in the late nineteenth and twentieth centuries.

**Adhān**   Muslim call-to-prayer.

**Alemannisch**   The Germanic dialect historically spoken in areas through which the upper Rhine River flows.

**Alsatian**   The Germanic language spoken as a vernacular and literary language in Alsace-Lorraine.

**Aufklärung**   The German Enlightenment (ca. 1770–1810), during which the ideals and ideology of German nationalism took shape.

**Ausgleich**   Established by an 1867 treaty, the official equality among the national groups of the Austro-Hungarian Empire in nineteenth-century Eastern Europe.

**Autonomy** (usually *musical autonomy*)   A property of music that is performed with independence from cultural functions, often claimed as a property toward which modern European art music aspired.

**Ballad**   A narrative genre of folk song that chronicles local and regional events in a nation's history.

**Balladenwerk**   The ten-volume anthology of German folk ballads (1935–1996), which established the narrative ballad in a canonic position in the music history of German-language Europe.

**Banat**   A German *speech island* in southwestern Romania.

**Bänkelsänger**   German street hawker, who performed and sold printed *ballads* in the public sphere.

**Bar-Form**   Common folk-song form in German-language traditions, using the musical pattern AAB. The two "A" lines, however, have different texts.

**Biedermeier Era**   A period of Austrian cultural history during the first half of the nineteenth century, which witnessed the growth of bourgeois culture in the imperial capital of Vienna.

**Bilina**   Russian folk-epic style.

**Blaue Reiter**   Lit., "Blue Riders." Modernist artistic movement, in which Eastern European influences, especially from folklore, came to bear on Western European traditions.

**Blut und Boden**   Lit., "blood and soil." Criteria that serve reactionary forms of German nationalism and justification for German imperial expansion.

**Broadside ballads**   Printed narrative songs, usually sold inexpensively as popular music reporting recent events through song.

**Carpathian Mountains**   One of the largest European mountain ranges, forming an arch along numerous national borders from western Slovakia to central Romania. Extensive ethnic, national, and religious musical differences distinguish the Carpathians.

**Colinda**   Romanian carol. Colinde (pl.) have historically constituted the most prized genre for folk-song collectors in Romania, therefore affording the colinda symbolic national significance.

**Contrafact**   A song created from a preexisting melody, to which a new text is adapted.

**Danube Swabians (Donauschwaben)**   Residents of the speech islands of Transylvania in Romania, most of them immigrants from Swabia in South Germany.

**Darbucca**   Goblet-shaped Middle Eastern drum.

**Denkmal**   Lit., "monument." As used in European music history, a *Denkmal* (pl. *Denkmäler*) is a series of musical editions or published repertories, usually meant to include a nation's most significant and representative works.

**Départements**   Former colonial holdings from the era of extensive French imperialism, today independent but connected to France in a commonwealth relation.

**Deutscher Tanz**   Lit., "German dance." A genre of alpine dance, belonging to the broader category of *Ländler*.

**Diaspora**   Dispersion of a people from an historical homeland, usually motivating an ideology of return in order to establish a modern nation. More specific uses of the concept include the Jewish Diaspora, especially the Ashkenazic and Sephardic presence in Europe, and the African diaspora in the Americas.

**Displacement**   The various processes of adaptation to changing places and identity, especially in New Europe.

**Écossaise**   Lit., "Scottish." Art-music dance form meant to represent Scotland.

**Ecu**   Name and denomination of the first EU currency, replaced in the mid-1990s by the Euro.

**Edda**   Mythological cycles in Scandinavia.

**Enlightenment**   Historical period of intellectual liberalism in the eighteenth century, during which many ideas of European nationalism took shape; see also *Aufklärung*.

**Epic**   A narrative genre of folk song, more common prior to the modern nation-state, in which great leaders and events are celebrated. Still traditional in some areas of northern and southern Europe.

**Eretz Yisrael**  Lit., "Land of Israel." The traditional designation of the historical nation of Israel, used primarily during the centuries of the Jewish Diaspora.

**Ethnonationalism**  Nationalism predicated on the belief that an ethnic group should serve as the basis for a nation.

**Euro**  Common European currency, introduced to twelve nations of the European Union on 1 January 2002 to replace their national currencies.

**European Broadcasting Union** (EBU)  Umbrella organization for coordinating common broadcasts created by and disseminated through national broadcasting agencies (e.g., the BBC). The EBU has organized the Eurovision Song Contest since 1956.

**European Union** (EU)  International organization fostering trade and political cooperation among European nations. Fifteen member states in 2001, with ten new members admitted to the European Union on 1 May 2004.

**Eurovision Song Contest**  The largest popular-music competition in the world, taking place annually during the spring and broadcast by the member stations of the European Broadcasting Union. Nations compete for the grand prize by submitting a national entry chosen after months of competition.

**Fin-de-siècle**  Lit., "end of the century." Refers to the period of rapid cultural change at the beginning of the twentieth century.

**Finno-Ugric**  The largest non-Indo-European language group in Europe, a subfamily of the Uralic family of languages in Asia; the language for several national folk-song traditions, notably Hungarian, Finnish, and Estonian.

**Flugblätter**  Lit., "pages in flight." German *broadside ballads*.

**Folk-song landscape**  The representation of cultural regions through collections of common repertories of folk song.

**Gastarbeiter**  Lit., "guest workers." The extensive workforce of Germany in the second half of the twentieth century and in the early twenty-first century, most often comprising workers of Turkish or Southeastern European ancestry who rarely are permitted to earn German citizenship.

**Germanen**  Lit., "the Germans." A generalized term designating the larger cultural identity of premodern inhabitants of Central Europe, the so-called "Germanic peoples."

**Gottschee colonies**  A German-speaking cluster of communities, or *Sprachinsel,* whose first residents settled in the late Middle Ages. A region in modern Slovenia, the Gottschee colonies have attracted folk-music scholars and linguists from the nineteenth century to the present.

**Hanseatic League**  Trade alliance among the major cities of northern Europe, especially those on the North and Baltic seas.

**Hassidism**    A sect and movement of devout Judaism that emerged first in the eighteenth century as a response to the teachings of the spiritual leader, Baal-Shem Tov. In European Jewish music history, the musical traditions of Hassidic Jews were often counterpoised against those of enlightened or emancipated communities.

**Heimat**    Lit., "homeland." Used extensively in German national and nationalist songs, often serving to embody the genre known as *Heimatlieder,* or "songs of the homeland."

**Hindustani**    North Indian and Pakistani musical traditions.

**Historicism**    Recasting the past to serve as a model for the present.

**Jahrzeit**    Lit., "year's time." The anniversary of an individual's death in Jewish tradition.

**Kalevala**    The Finnish national *epic.*

**Kantele**    Plucked string instrument recognized by many as the Finnish national folk instrument. Not only does the kantele enter Finnish national mythology through the national myth, the *Kalevala,* but it has become an important component in Finnish "new folk music."

**Karelia**    Region encompassing northern Finland and northwestern Russia, which is home to the indigenous Karelian people.

**Kernland**    Lit., "core land." In Austrian folklore and folk-music scholarship a geographical area in which Austrian and German traditions are imagined to be authentic and of central importance.

**Klezmer**    Lit., "vessel of song." Jewish, primarily European and Ashkenazic, instrumental ensemble, which traditionally played at weddings and other Jewish celebrations in East and East-Central Europe. Europeans revived klezmer music in the late twentieth century as a means of recuperating Jewish culture destroyed during the Holocaust.

**Komitatstadt**    Hungarian administrative capital in the Hungarian provinces of the Austro-Hungarian Empire.

**Krakowiak**    Polish dance form from the region around Kraków.

**Ladino**    (1) Spanish-derived language of Sephardic Jews, written with Hebrew characters.
(2) Also used as the name of Latinate languages in the Alps, with no connection to Sephardic *ladino.*

**Lander**    Residents of a speech island in Transylvania, most of them Protestants from Austria.

**Ländler**    Genre of alpine folk dance in triple meter, often specific to certain regions or *Länder.*

**Leitkultur**    Lit., "model or leading culture." A proposed framework for multiculturalism in the new nation-states in the European Union. According to the model, larger nations, notably Germany, would provide ways of accommodating and integrating the differences of their minorities.

**Levantine** The lands of the Eastern Mediterranean, known generally as the Levant.

**Longue durée** A broad stretch of a nation's history, over several epochs.

**Magyar nóta** Hungarian "folk-like music," often representing Roma and other minorities as semiprofessional musicians. Cf. *volkstümliche Musik*.

**Mazurka** Polish dance form from the Mazur region.

**Minhag** Jewish religious and cultural traditions, among them music and liturgy, that are transmitted locally, in a city or region, and come to represent tradition as practiced through history.

**Mitteleuropa** Lit., "Central Europe." The nations and cultures at Europe's center.

**Mizrakh** Lit., "East" in Hebrew. The symbolic representation of the Land of Israel and the sacred geography serving as the ultimate goal of the Jewish Diaspora.

**Modernism** Artistic movement of the early twentieth century, characterized by rapid change and unexpected juxtapositions of images, sounds, and concepts.

**Neolog** The designation for liberal, or Reform, Judaism in East Central and Eastern Europe.

**New Europe** Europe after the fall of communism in Eastern Europe during 1989 and 1990.

**New Europeanness** The aesthetics of place characterizing the musical practices emerging since the political and cultural transformations that accompanied the formation of the New Europe.

**Newly composed folk music** Popular repertories and styles that combined traditional Balkan folk musics with rock techniques and performance practices. Newly composed folk music was a particularly important phenomenon in Yugoslavia on the eve of its dissolution in the early 1990s and during the subsequent Balkan wars.

**Niebelungen** Mythological cycles in Germanic areas, largely of Central Europe. The Niebelungen myths have lent themselves to many versions in German folklore and the arts. Cf. the *Edda* myths of Scandinavia.

**Niggun** (pl. *niggunim*) Lit., "something played." Textless songs central in the folk-song tradition of Eastern European Ashkenazic Jews.

**Nusach** Correct rules and style for local and denominational performance of Jewish liturgical music. Knowledge of nusach comes from oral tradition and learning repertory and style using the correct rules.

**Organology** The scientific study of musical instruments.

**Orientalism** Exaggerated imagery of the "East," used in popular and scientific art, literature, and music from the Enlightenment to the present to evoke, positively and negatively, the world of the European Other (see the classic study of Orientalism, Said 1978).

**Pannonia**   Roman name for the Trans-Danubian Plain of Hungary and the adjacent border regions of its modern neighboring nations.

**Parlando rubato**   A quality of "Old Style" Hungarian folk songs, in which rhythmic flexibility reflects the influence of speech.

**Pibroch**   Bagpipe tradition of Scotland, the authenticity of which is employed to symbolize a national repertory.

**Polka**   Couple dance in duple meter, with origins in the Czech lands, but dispersed in myriad variants throughout Europe and many parts of the world settled by European immigrants.

**Polonaise**   Polish folk dance used extensively for art-music compositions in the nineteenth century.

**Primás**   Lead violinist in the string bands of East and East Central Europe.

**Purim**   Jewish midwinter holiday, celebrating joyously the ways in which Jews overcame the oppression of the Persian king, Haman. The biblical book of Esther provides the traditional text for celebrations, which in pre-Holocaust Europe took the form of community balls and the performance of traditional folk music by bands passing from door to door.

**Quodlibet**   A musical work formed from two or more different pieces with identity and integrity of their own, symbolically uniting distinctive parts into a new work.

**Reform Judaism**   Liberal nineteenth-century movement in Central European Judaism, characterized by the introduction of changes that would modernize Jewish worship and musical practices, for example, by the introduction of musical instruments and vernacular languages into the synagogue.

**Revival** (especially folk-music revival)   Revitalizing and performing earlier repertories of traditional music to connect the present to the past.

**Roma**   The broadest designation used by Gypsies for their own sense of self and the culture to which they belong. Used instead of "Gypsy" throughout this book.

**Romance**   One of the most common genres of Spanish *ballad* traditions.

**Romancero**   The corpus of Spanish-language and Sephardic-ladino *ballad* traditions.

**Romanticism**   Period of European cultural history, roughly the first half of the nineteenth century, when folk music was increasingly connected to national culture.

**Saami**   The indigenous people of circumpolar Scandinavia and Russia, previously called Laplanders.

**Schlager**   A German-language "hit" song, usually employing a popular style that combines folklike music with popular instruments and techniques.

**Schottische**   Lit., "Scottish." Central European folk-dance form.

**Shamanism**   Religious practice in which specialized healing professionals intercede by mediating the entrance of healing spirits into the body of a sick person. Music often enhances the intercession, so much so that shamans are also often musical professionals.

**Sheva kehillot**   Lit., "Seven Communities." The intensively Jewish villages and small cities of Burgenland, along the Austrian and Hungarian border.

**Shireh chalutzim**   Lit., "songs of the pioneers." Repertories of folk, popular, and composed art songs, elevated in Israel's pre-statehood period (i.e., prior to 1948) to the status of a protonational repertory.

**Shtetl**   Lit., "little city." A Jewish village in the Yiddish-speaking regions of Eastern Europe, which often served as an idealized source and context for European Jewish folk song.

**Siddurim**   Jewish prayerbooks, the contents of which comprise the order of daily and weekly services.

**Siebenbürgen**   Lit., "Seven fortresses" or "seven fortress cities." German speech island in Transylvania (western Romania).

**Skanzen**   Open-air museum; often a cluster of different villages from an entire nation or a wider region. The generic name derives from its origins in Scandinavia.

**Slåtter**   Norwegian folk, or "peasant," dances in several forms, played primarily on the folk violin and Hardanger fiddle.

**Socialist-realism**   Aesthetic ideal and ideology of the Soviet Union, especially during the Stalinist era (ca. 1930–1953), according to which works of art, literature, and music should reflect the realism of the people engaged in building the culture of the nation.

**Speech island**   See *Sprachinsel.*

**Sprachinsel**   Lit., "speech island." Region with a large number of German-speaking residents, historically most often in Eastern Europe.

**Subaltern**   The working or powerless class in the nation-state. Subaltern responses result from the mobilization of political and cultural movements with that class.

**Syncretism**   Hybridity resulting from combining elements that are largely compatible, for example, related languages or musical repertories.

**Systematische Musikwissenschaft**   Lit., "systematic musicology." The study of music, especially the musics of different cultures, based on the use of complex technologies that enhance the scientific analysis of sound itself.

**Style russe**   Cosmopolitan Russian style meant to give nationalist flavor to nineteenth-century compositions.

**Tamburitza**   Instrumental folk-music ensembles of the south Slavic ethnic and national groups, especially Croatia and Serbia. Consisting primarily of stringed instruments with different sizes and shapes as well as functions in the hierarchically arranged dance music.

**Tempo giusto**   A quality of "Old Style" Hungarian folk music, shaped by the rapid, metric organization of dance.

**Trachten**   German: Traditional clothing, which localizes folk culture through extensive cultivation of traditional fashion.

**Travellers**   Members of cultural groups in the United Kingdom and Ireland that, historically or currently, live in mobile vehicles, or caravans. Travellers are often Roma, but by no means exclusively. There is, nonetheless, some exchangeability between the designations "Traveller" and "Gypsy."

**Tsimbalom**   The common designation for a hammered dulcimer in Eastern European folk, folklike, and popular music. Sizes range from small, portable instruments to those that are mounted on a substantial frame that may be as large as a small piano.

**Turbo-folk**   Popular music styles used by many musical groups in the Balkans at the end of the twentieth century to connect local vocabularies of national identity to international rock styles.

**Unisonality**   A term coined by Benedict Anderson (1991) to describe the ways in which certain songs (e.g., national anthems) embody the nation when sung together by the nation's citizens.

**Uusikansanmusiikki**   Lit., "new folk music." The general term used to describe the revival of folk music in late twentieth-century Finland, which drew upon national repertories, such as the *Kalevala* epic, while embracing many of the sounds and media of world music.

**Vaterland**   Lit., "fatherland." The more common reference to the cultural embodiment of a German nation.

**Velvet Revolution**   The series of events bringing an end to communist governments in Eastern Europe (ca. 1989–1991).

**Vergleichende Musikwissenschaft**   Lit., "comparative musicology." The largely German and Austrian field of ethnomusicology, in which different cultures were compared in order to determine largely similar concepts of music among different practices.

**Vielvölkerstaat**   Lit., "multicultural state." The Austrian model for recognizing cultural differences in the single political entity of Central Europe.

**Volkslieder**   German for "folk songs." Coined by Johann Gottfried Herder in the *Enlightenment*.

**Volksmusikpflege**   Lit., "care of folk music." The conscious practice of cultivating and reviving historical folk-music practices.

**Volkstümliche Musik**   Lit., "folk-like music." Music of the German-speaking countries, in which folk and popular music are mixed. Cf. *magyar nóta* in Hungarian music.

**Yoiking**   Singing style used by the *Saami* to communicate to the animals of their herding culture, now symbolic of the distinctiveness of Saami culture.

# Bibliography

Acerbi, Giuseppe. 1999 [1798]. "Über joik." In Lothar Schneider, ed., *Europa erlesen: Lappland,* p. 148. Klagenfurt: Wieser Verlag. (Europa erlesen.) Orig. publ.: Giuseppe Acerbi. 1802. *Travels through Sweden, Finland and Lapland to the North-Cape in the Years 1798 and 1799.* London: J. Mawman.

Adler, Guido. 1925. "Internationalism in Music." *The Musical Quarterly* 11: 281–300.

Adriányi, Gabriel. 1997. *Deutsche Musik in Ost- und Südosteuropa.* Cologne: Böhlau Verlag. (Studien zum Deutschtum im Osten, 28.)

Aescht, Georg, ed. 1999. *Siebenbürgen: Europa erlesen.* Klagenfurt: Wieser Verlag. (Europa erlesen.)

Aidt, Mik. 2001. "Music of Another World." *Nordic Sounds* 4: 3–13.

Anderson, Benedict. 1991. *Imagined Communities: Reflections on the Origins and Spread of Nationalism.* 2d ed. London: Verso.

_____. 1998. *The Spectre of Comparisons: Nationalism, Southeast Asia and the World.* London: Verso.

Anderson, George K. 1966. *The Legend of the Wandering Jew.* Hanover, N.H.: University Press of New England.

Andersson, Gregor. 2001. *Musikgeschichte Nordeuropas: Dänemark, Finnland, Island, Norwegen, Schweden.* Stuttgart: Metzler.

Appadurai, Arjun. 1996. *Modernity at Large: Cultural Dimensions of Globalization.* Minneapolis: University of Minnesota Press.

Applebaum, Anne. 1994. *Between East and West: Across the Borderlands of Europe.* New York: Pantheon.

Applegate, Celia. 1992. "What Is German Music? Reflections on the Role of Art in the Creation of the Nation." *German Studies Review* (Winter 1992): 21–32.

_____. 1997–1998. "How German Is It? Nationalism and the Idea of Serious Music in the Early Nineteenth Century." *19th Century Music* 21: 274–296.

_____, and Pamela M. Potter, eds. 2002. *Music and German Nationalism.* Chicago: University of Chicago Press.

Armistead, Samuel G., and Joseph H. Silverman, with Israel J. Katz. 1986. *Judeo-Spanish Ballads from Oral Tradition: Epic Ballads.* Berkeley and Los Angeles: University of California Press. (Folk Literature of the Sephardic Jews, 2.)

Arnberg, Matts, Israel Ruong, and Håkan Unsgaard. 1969. *Yoik.* Stockholm: Sveriges Radio Förlag.

Arnim, Achim von, and Clemens Brentano. 1957 [1806 and 1808]. *Des Knaben Wunderhorn: Alte deutsche Lieder.* Munich: Windler.

Ash, Timothy Garton. 2000. *History of the Present: Essays, Sketches and Despatches from Europe in the 1990s.* Harmondsworth: Penguin.

Askew, Kelly. 2002. *Performing the Nation: Swahili Music and Cultural Politics in Tanzania.* Chicago: University of Chicago Press. (Chicago Studies in Ethnomusicology.)

Asplund, Anneli, and Ulla Lipponen. 1985. *The Birth of the Kalevala.* Trans. by Susan Sinisalo. Helsinki: Finnish Literature Society.

Augstein, Rudolf, et al. 1987. *"Historikerstreit": Die Dokumentation der Kontroverse um die Einzigartigkeit der nationalsozialistischen Judenvernichtung.* Munich: Piper.

Austerlitz, Paul. 2000. "Birch-Bark Horns and Jazz in the National Imagination: The Finnish Folk Music Vogue in Historical Perspective." *Ethnomusicology* 44 (2): 183–213.

Aylmer, Kevin J. 1995. "British Bhangra: The Sound of a New Community." *Rhythm Music Magazine* 4: 14–17.

Baker, Houston A., Jr., Manthia Diawara, and Ruth H. Lindeborg, eds. 1996. *Black British Cultural Studies: A Reader.* Chicago: University of Chicago Press. (Black Literature and Culture.)

Balakrishnan, G., ed. 1996. *Mapping the Nation.* London: Verso.

Bălaşa, Marin Marian. Forthcoming. "An Introduction to the Discussion of Musical References Printed on Banknotes." In Bruno B. Reuer, ed., *Vereintes Europa–Vereinte Musik? Vielfalt und soziale Dimensionen in Mittel- und Südosteuropa.* Berlin: Weidler Verlag.

Ballinger, Pamela. 2003. *History in Exile: Memory and Identity at the Borders of the Balkans.* Princeton, N.J.: Princeton University Press.

Bammer, Angelika, ed. 1994. *Displacements: Cultural Identities in Question.* Bloomington: Indiana University Press. (Theories of Contemporary Culture.)

Banerji, Sabita. 1988. "Ghazals of Bhangra in Great Britain." *Popular Music* 7: 207–213.

Barker, Francis, et al., eds. 1985. *Europe and Its Others.* Vol. 2. Colchester: University of Essex.

Barolsky, Daniel. 2002. "Performing Polishness: The Interpretation of Identity." *European Meetings in Ethnomusicology* 9: 187–196.

Bartlett, Thomas. 1988. "'What Ish Is My Nation?': Themes in Irish History 1550–1850." In Thomas Bartlett et al., eds., *Irish Studies: A General Introduction,* pp. 44–59. Totowa, N.J.: Barnes and Noble.

Bartók, Béla. 1913. *Cântece poporale românesti din comitatul Bihor.* Bucharest: Academi Româna Librariile Socec & Comp. si C. Sfeta.

———. 1923. *Volksmusik der Rumänen von Maramures.* Munich: Drei Masken Verlag.

_____. 1924. *A magyar népdal* ("The Hungarian Folk Song"). Reprint. Albany: State University of New York Press.

_____. [1931] 1976. "Gypsy Music or Hungarian Music?" In Benjamin Suchoff, ed., *Béla Bartók Essays*, pp. 206–233. New York: St. Martin's.

_____. 1934. *Népzenénk és a szomszéd népek népzenéje* ("The Folk Music of the Magyars and Neighboring Peoples"). Budapest: Somló Béla.

_____. 1935. *Melodien der rumänischen Colinde*. Vienna: Universal Edition.

_____. 1954. *Serbo-Croatian Heroic Songs*. Ed. by Albert B. Lord. Cambridge, Mass.: Harvard University Press.

_____. 1959–1970. *Slovenské l'udové piesne* ("Slovakian Folk Songs"). 2 vols. New York: Universal Edition.

_____, and Albert B. Lord. 1951. *Serbo-Croatian Folk Songs*. New York: Columbia University Press.

Bauer, Susan. 1999. *Von der Khupe zum Klezkamp: Klezmer-Musik in New York*. Book and CD. Berlin: Piranha Musik.

Bauerdick, Rolf. 1995. *Lourdes*. Freiburg im Breisgau: Herder.

Baum, Michael J. 2000. *A Wider Europe: The Process and Politics of European Union Enlargement*. Lanham, Md.: Rowman and Littlefield. (Governance in Europe.)

Baumann, Gerd. 1990. "The Re-Invention of Bhangra: Social Change and Aesthetic Shifts in a Punjabi Music in Britain." *The World of Music* 32: 81–98.

Baumann, Max Peter. 1976. *Musikfolklore und Musikfolklorismus: Eine ethnomusikologische Untersuchung zum Funktionswandel des Jodels*. Winterthur: Amadeus Verlag.

_____. 1996. "Folk Music Revival: Concepts between Regression and Emancipation." *The World of Music* 38 (3): 71–86.

_____. 2000. "The Local and the Global: Traditional Musical Instruments and Modernization." *The World of Music* 42 (3): 121–144.

_____, ed. 2000. *Music, Language and Literature of the Roma and Sinti*. Berlin: Verlag für Wissenschaft und Bildung. (Intercultural Music Studies, 11.)

Baumgartner, Gerhard, Eva Müllner, and Rainer Münz, eds. 1989. *Identität und Lebenswelt: Ethnische, religiöse und kulturelle Vielfalt im Burgenland*. Eisenstadt: Prugg Verlag.

Bausinger, Hermann. 1980. *Formen der "Volkspoesie."* Berlin: Erich Schmidt Verlag. (Grundlagen der Germanistik, 6.)

_____, Klaus Beyrer, and Gottfried Korff, eds. 1999. *Reisekultur: Von der Pilgerfahrt zum modernen Tourismus*. Munich: C. H. Beck.

Bax, Mart. 1995. *Medjugorje: Religion, Politics, and Violence in Rural Bosnia*. Amsterdam: VU Uitgeverij.

Beckerman, Michael. 1986–1987. "In Search of Czechness in Music." *19th Century Music* 10: 61–73.

_____. 1992–1993. "Dvořák's New World Largo and *The Song of Hiawatha.*" *19th Century Music* 16: 35–48.

_____. 1993a. "The Master's Little Joke: Antonín Dvořák and the Mask of Nation." In idem, ed., *Dvořák and His World,* pp. 134–154. Princeton, N.J.: Princeton University Press.

_____, ed. 1993b. *Dvořák and His World.* Princeton, N.J.: Princeton University Press.

Beiner, Ronald, ed. 1999. *Theorizing Nationalism.* Albany, N.Y.: State University of New York Press.

Beissinger, Margaret H. 1991. *The Art of the Lăutar: The Epic Tradition of Romania.* New York: Garland. (Harvard Dissertations in Folklore and Oral Traditions.)

_____. 2001. "Occupation and Ethnicity: Constructing Identity among Professional Romani (Gypsy) Musicians in Romania." *Slavic Review* 60 (1): 24–49.

_____, Jane Tylus, and Suzanne Wofford, eds. 1999. *Epic Traditions in the Contemporary World: The Poetics of Community.* Berkeley: University of California Press.

Bellier, Irène, and Thomas M. Wilson, eds. 2000. *An Anthropology of the European Union: Building, Imagining and Experiencing the New Europe.* New York: New York University Press.

Bellman, Jonathan. 1993. *The Style Hongrois in the Music of Western Europe.* Boston: Northeastern University Press.

Belting, Hans. 1992. *Die Deutschen und ihre Kunst.* Munich: C. H. Beck.

Benary, Peter. 1979. "Nationalcharacteristik in der Musik des 19. und 20. Jahrhunderts." In Dieter Rexroth, ed., *Zwischen den Grenzen: Zum Aspekt des Nationalen in der neuen Musik,* pp. 17–25. Mainz: B. Schott's Söhne.

Bendix, Regina. 1997. *In Search of Authenticity: The Formation of Folklore Studies.* Madison: University of Wisconsin Press.

Benjamin, Walter. 1982. *Gesammelte Schriften.* Vol. 5: *Das Passagen-Werk.* In 2 parts. Ed. by Rolf Tiedemann. Frankfurt am Main: Suhrkamp.

Berdahl, Daphne. 1999. *Where the World Ended: Re-unification and Identity in the German Borderland.* Berkeley and Los Angeles: University of California Press.

_____, Matti Bunzl, and Martha Lampland, eds. 2000. *Altering States: Ethnographies of Transition in Eastern Europe and the Former Soviet Union.* Ann Arbor: University of Michigan Press.

Bergeron, Katherine. 1998. *Decadent Enchantments: The Revival of Gregorian Chant at Solesmes.* Berkeley: University of California Press. (California Studies in Nineteenth Century Music, 10.)

Bettauer, Hugo. 1996 [1922]. *Die Stadt ohne Juden: Ein Roman von Übermorgen.* Hamburg and Bremen: Achilla Presse.

Bew, Paul. 1996. "The National Question, Land, and 'Revisionism'." In D. George Boyce and Alan O'Day, eds., *The Making of Modern Irish History: Revisionism and the Revisionist Controversy,* pp. 90–99. London: Routledge.

Bhabha, Homi. 1994. *The Location of Culture*. London and New York: Routledge.

_____, ed. 1990. *Nation and Narration*. London and New York: Routledge.

Blum, Steven. 2000. "Local Knowledge of Musical Genres and Roles." In Timothy Rice, James Porter, and Chris Goertzen, eds., *Europe*. Vol. 8: *The Garland Encyclopedia of World Music*, pp. 112–126. New York: Garland.

Blume, Friedrich. 1939. *Das Rassenproblem in der Musik*. Wolfenbüttel and Berlin: Georg Kallmeyer.

Bohlman, Philip V. 1980. "The Folk Songs of Charles Bannen: The Interaction of Music and History in Southwestern Wisconsin." *Transactions of the Wisconsin Academy of Sciences, Arts and Letters* 68: 167–187.

_____. 1985. "Deutsch-amerikanische Musik in Wisconsin: Überleben im Melting Pot." *Jahrbuch für Volksliedforschung* 30: 99–116.

_____. 1987. "The European Discovery of Music in the Islamic World and the 'Non-Western' in 19th-Century Music History." *The Journal of Musicology* 5 (2): 147–163.

_____. 1988. *The Study of Folk Music in the Modern World*. Bloomington: Indiana University Press.

_____. 1989. *"The Land Where Two Streams Flow": Music in the German-Jewish Community of Israel*. Urbana: University of Illinois Press.

_____. 1992. *The World Centre for Jewish Music in Palestine 1936–1940: Jewish Musical Life on the Eve of World War II*. Oxford: Oxford University Press.

_____. 1994. "Music, Modernity, and the Foreign in the New Germany." *Modernism/Modernity* 1 (1): 121–152.

_____. 1996a. *Central European Folk Music: An Annotated Bibliography of Sources in German*. New York: Garland. (Garland Library of Music Ethnology, 3.)

_____. 1996b. "The Final Borderpost." *The Journal of Musicology* 14 (4): 427–452.

_____. 1996c. "Pilgrimage, Politics, and the Musical Remapping of the New Europe." *Ethnomusicology* 40 (3): 375–412.

_____. 1997. "Fieldwork in the Ethnomusicological Past." In Gregory F. Barz and Timothy Cooley, eds., *Shadows in the Field: New Directions in Ethnomusicological Fieldwork*, pp. 139–162. New York: Oxford University Press.

_____. 1999a. "(Ab)Stimmen der Völker in Liedern: Musik bei der Neubelebung der Frömmigkeit in Südosteuropa." In Bruno B. Reuter, ed., *Musik im Umbruch: Kulturelle Identität und gesellschaftlicher Wandel in Südosteuropa*, pp. 25–44. Munich: Verlag Südostdeutsches Kulturwerk.

_____. 1999b. "Ontologies of Music." In Nicholas Cook and Mark Everist, eds., *Rethinking Music*, pp. 19–34. Oxford: Oxford University Press.

_____. 2000a. "Jewish Music in Europe." In Timothy Rice, James Porter, and Chris Goertzen, eds., *Europe*. Vol. 8: *The Garland Encyclopedia of World Music*, pp. 248–269. New York: Garland.

_____. 2000b. "The Remembrance of Things Past: Music, Race, and the End of History in Modern Europe." In Ronald Radano and Philip V. Bohlman, eds., *Music and the Racial Imagination,* pp. 644–676. Chicago: University of Chicago Press.

_____. 2000c. "To Hear the Voices Still Heard: On Synagogue Restoration in Eastern Europe." In Daphne Berdahl, Matti Bunzl, and Martha Lampland, eds., *Altering States: Ethnographies of Transition in Eastern Europe and the Former Soviet Union,* pp. 40–69. Ann Arbor: University of Michigan Press.

_____. 2000d. "Composing the Cantorate: Westernizing Europe's Other Within." In Georgina Born and Dave Hesmondhalgh, eds., *Western Music and Its Others: Difference, Representation, and Appropriation in Music,* pp. 187–212. Berkeley: University of California Press.

_____. 2000e. "Auf dem Weg zur Wallfahrt: Musikalische Kolportage an den Grenzen der Volksfrömmigkeit." In Gerlinde Haid, Ursula Hemetek, and Rudolf Pietsch, eds., *Volksmusik — Wandel und Deutung: Festschrift Walter Deutsch zum 75. Geburtstag,* pp. 505–522. Vienna: Böhlau.

_____. 2000f. "East-West: The Ancient Modernity of Jewish Music." *East European Meetings in Ethnomusicology* 7: 67–90.

_____. 2002a. *World Music: A Very Short Introduction.* Oxford: Oxford University Press. (Very Short Introductions, 65.)

_____. 2002b. "Landscape–Region–Nation–Reich: German Folk Song in the Nexus of National Identity." In Celia Applegate and Pamela M. Potter, eds., *Music and German Nationalism,* pp. 105–127. Chicago: University of Chicago Press.

_____. 2002c. "World Music at the 'End of History'." *Ethnomusicology* 46 (1): 1–32.

_____. 2002d. "The Place of Displacement—Polish Musics at Home and Beyond." *European Meetings in Ethnomusicology* 9: 166–178.

_____. 2003. "Before Hebrew Song." In Michael Berkowitz, ed., *Nationalism, Zionism and Ethnic Mobilization of the Jews in 1900 and Beyond,* pp. 25–59. Leiden: E. J. Brill.

_____. 2004a. *"Jüdische Volksmusik": Eine mitteleuropäische Geistesgeschichte.* Vienna: Böhlau. (Schriften zur Volksmusik, 21.)

_____. 2004b. "Popular Music on the Stage of a United Europe— Southeastern Europe in the 'Eurovision Song Contest'." In Bruno B. Reuer, ed., *Vereintes Europa–Vereinte Musik? Vielfalt und soziale Dimensionen in Mittel- und Südosteuropa,* pp. 27–45. Berlin: Weidler Verlag.

_____. Forthcoming a. *Music Drama of the Holocaust: Opera and Performance in Theresienstadt.* Cambridge: Cambridge University Press.

_____. Forthcoming b. *Herder on Music and Nationalism.* Berkeley: University of California Press.

_____, ed. 2002. *Poland: Music, Lyric, Nation.* Special section of *European Meetings in Ethnomusicology* 9.

_____, and Brian Currid. 2001. "Suturing History, Healing Europe: German National Temporality in *Wolokolamsk Highway*." *The Musical Quarterly* 85 (4): 681–717.

_____, and Otto Holzapfel. 2001. *The Folk Songs of Ashkenaz*. Middleton, Wisc.: A-R Editions. (Recent Researches in the Oral Traditions of Music, 6.)

Böhme, Franz Magnus. 1877. *Altdeutsches Liederbuch: Volkslieder der Deutschen nach Wort und Weise aus dem 12. bis zum 17. Jahrhundert*. Leipzig: Breitkopf und Härtel.

Boiagi, Mihail G. 1988. *Gramaticâ Aromânâ icâ Macedonovlahâ: Kommentierter Nachdruck*. Freiburg im Breisgau.

_____, and Pericle N. Papahegi-Wurduna. 1915. *Gramatica româna, sau, macedo-româna*. Bucharest: F. Göbl fii.

Boiko, Martin. 1995. "Volksmusikbewegung im Baltikum in den 70er und 80er Jarhren: Kontexte, Werte, Konflikte." In Joachim Braun, Vladimir Karbusický, and Heidi Tamar-Hoffmann, eds., *Verfemte Musik: Komponisten in den Diktaturen unseres Jahrhunderts*, pp. 349–358. Frankfurt am Main: Peter Lang.

Boisits, Barbara. 2002. "Austria's *Neue Volxmusik:* The Sound of the Global Village?" In Susan Ingram, Markus Reisenleitner, and Cornelia Szabó-Knotik, eds., *Reverberations: Representations of Modernity, Tradition and Cultural Value in-between Central Europe and North America*, pp. 105–112. Frankfurt am Main: Peter Lang.

Bolle-Zemp, Sylvie. 1992. *Le réenchantement de la montaigne: Aspects du folklore musical en Haute-Gruyère*. Geneva: Georg Éditeur. (Mémoires de la Société Suisse des Traditions Populaires, 74.)

Born, Georgina, and David Hesmondhalgh, eds. 2000. *Western Music and Its Others: Difference, Representation, and Appropriation in Music*. Berkeley: University of California Press.

Borneman, John. 1991. *After the Wall: East Meets West in the New Berlin*. New York: Basic Books.

_____. 1992. *Belonging in the Two Berlins: Kin, State, Nation*. Cambridge: Cambridge University Press.

_____. 1998. "*Grenzregime* (Border Regime): The Wall and Its Aftermath." In Thomas M. Wilson and Hastings Donnan, eds., *Border Identities: Nation and State at International Frontiers*, pp. 162–190. Cambridge: Cambridge University Press.

Boswell, David, and Jessica Evans. 1999. *Representing the Nation, a Reader: Histories, Heritage, and Museums*. New York: Routledge.

Boyd, Malcolm. 2001. "National Anthems." In Stanley Sadie, ed., *The New Grove Dictionary of Music and Musicians*. 2d ed. Vol. 17: 654–687. London: Macmillan.

Brăiloiu, Constantin. 1960. *Vie musicale d'un village: Recherches sur le répertoire de*

*Dragus (Roumanie), 1929–1932*. Paris: Institut Universitaire Roumain Charles 1er.

———. 1984. *Problems of Ethnomusicology*. Ed. and trans. by A. L. Lloyd. Cambridge: Cambridge University Press.

Brandsch, Gottlieb, and Adolf Schullerns, eds. 1932. *Siebenbürgische Volkslieder*. Berlin and Leipzig: Walter de Gruyter. (Landschaftliche Volkslieder, 21.)

Brass, Paul. 1991. *Ethnicity and Nationalism*. London: Sage.

Braun, Joachim, Vladimir Karbusický, and Heidi Tamar-Hoffmann, eds. 1995. *Verfemte Musik: Komponisten in den Diktaturen unseres Jahrhunderts*. Frankfurt am Main: Peter Lang.

Brednich, Rolf Wilhelm, Zmaga Kumer, and Wolfgang Suppan, eds. 1969–1984. *Gottscheer Volkslieder*. Mainz: B. Schott's Söhne.

Brednich, Rolf Wilhelm, Lutz Röhrich, and Wolfgang Suppan, eds. 1973. *Handbuch des Volksliedes*. Vol. 1: *Die Gattungen des Volksliedes*. Munich: Wilhelm Fink.

———. 1975. *Handbuch des Volksliedes*. Vol. 2: *Historisches und Systematisches—Interethnische Beziehungen—Musikethnologie*. Munich: Wilhelm Fink.

Bresgen, Cesar. 1970. *Der Komponist und die Volksmusik*. Vienna: Universal Edition.

Breuer, János. 1995. "Verfemte Musik in Ungarn." In Joachim Braun, Vladimir Karbusický, and Heidi Tamar-Hoffmann, eds., *Verfemte Musik: Komponisten in den Diktaturen unseres Jahrhunderts*, pp. 263–272. Frankfurt am Main: Peter Lang.

Bronson, Bertrand Harris. 1959–1972. *The Traditional Tunes of the Child Ballads*. 4 vols. Princeton, N.J.: Princeton University Press.

Broughton, Simon. 1999. "Gypsy Music: Kings and Queens of the Road." In idem, Mark Ellingham, and Richard Trillo, eds., *The Rough Guide to World Music*. Vol. 1, 2d ed.: 146–158. London: The Rough Guides.

Broughton, Simon, Mark Ellingham, and Richard Trillo, eds. 1999. *The Rough Guide to World Music*. Vol. 1: *Africa, Europe and the Middle East*. 2d ed. London: The Rough Guides.

Brown, Irving. 1929. *Deep Song: Adventures with Gypsy Songs and Singers in Andalusia and Other Lands, with Original Translations*. New York: Harper and Brothers Publishing.

Brown, Julie. 2000. "Bartók, the Gypsies, and Hybridity in Music." In Georgina Born and David Hesmondhalgh, eds., *Western Music and Its Others: Difference, Representation, and Appropriation in Music*, pp. 119–142. Berkeley: University of California Press.

Brown, Keith. 2003. *The Past in Question: Modern Macedonia and the Uncertainties of Nation*. Princeton, N.J.: Princeton University Press.

Brubaker, Rogers. 1996. *Nationalism Reframed: Nationhood and the National Question in the New Europe*. Cambridge: Cambridge University Press.

Brusatti, Otto. 1978. *Nationalismus und Ideologie in der Musik*. Tutzing: Hans Schneider.

_____, and Christoph Lingg. 1999. *Apropos Czernowitz*. Vienna: Böhlau.

Buch, Esteban. 2003. *Beethoven's Ninth: A Political History*. Trans. by Richard Miller. Chicago: University of Chicago Press.

Buchan, David. 1972. *The Ballad and the Folk*. London: Routledge and Kegan Paul.

Buchanan, Donna A. 1995. "Metaphors of Power, Metaphors of Truth: The Politics of Music Professionalism in Bulgarian Folk Orchestras." *Ethnomusicology* 39 (3): 381–416.

_____. 1997. "Bulgaria's Magical *Mystère* Tour: Postmodernism, World Music Marketing, and Political Change in Eastern Europe." *Ethnomusicology* 41 (1): 131–157.

_____. Forthcoming. *Performing Democracy: Bulgarian Music and Musicians in Transition*. Chicago: University of Chicago Press. (Chicago Studies in Ethnomusicology.)

Bujic, Bojan. 1988. *Music in European Thought 1851–1912*. Cambridge: Cambridge University Press.

Bukofzer, Manfred. 1946. "The New Nationalism." *Modern Music* 23: 243–247.

Buraway, Michael, and Katherine Verdery, eds. 1999. *Uncertain Transition: Ethnographies of Change in the Postsocialist World*. Lanham, Md.: Rowman and Littlefield.

Burleigh, Michael, and Wolfgang Wippermann. 1991. *The Racial State: Germany 1933–1945*. Cambridge: Cambridge University Press.

Burton, Antoinette, ed. 2003. *After the Imperial Turn: Thinking with and through the Nation*. Durham, N.C.: Duke University Press.

Busek, Erhard. 1997a. *Mitteuropa: Eine Spurensicherung*. Vienna: Kremayr & Scheriau.

_____. 1997b. "Aufbrüche und Aufbruch: Ein Essay über Parallelen und Unterschiede." In Gerda Mraz, ed., *Österreich-Ungarn in Lied und Bild*, pp. 9–13. Vienna and Munich: Christian Brandstätter.

_____. 1999. *Österreich und der Balkan: Vom Umgang mit dem Pulverfaß Europas*. Vienna: Molden Verlag.

Cadden, Jerry A. 2003. "Policing Tradition: Scottish Pipeband Competition and the Role of the Composer." In Martin Stokes and Philip V. Bohlman, eds., *Celtic Modern: Music at the Global Fringe*, pp. 119–143. Lanham, Md.: Scarecrow Press.

Calhoun, Craig. 1997. *Nationalism*. Minneapolis: University of Minnesota Press. (Concepts in Social Thought.)

Campbell, Stuart, ed. 1994. *Russians on Russian Music 1830–1880: An Anthology*. Cambridge: Cambridge University Press.

Caplan, Richard, and John Feffer, eds. 1996. *Europe's New Nationalism: States and Minorities in Conflict.* New York and Oxford: Oxford University Press.

Carolan, Nicholas. 1997. *A Harvest Saved: Francis O'Neill and Irish Music in Chicago.* Cork: Ossian Publications.

Carr, Edward. 1945. *Nationalism and After.* London: Oxford University Press.

Case, Sue Ellen, Philip Brett, and Susan Leigh Foster, eds. 1995. *Cruising the Performative: Interventions into the Representation of Ethnicity, Nationality, and Sexuality.* Bloomington: Indiana University Press.

Chakrabarty, Dipesh. 2000. *Provincializing Europe: Postcolonial Thought and Historical Difference.* Princeton, N.J.: Princeton University Press.

Chapman, Malcolm. 1992. *The Celts: The Construction of a Myth.* London: Macmillan.

――――. 1994. "Thoughts on Celtic Music." In Martin Stokes, ed., *Ethnicity, Identity and Music: The Musical Construction of Place,* pp. 29–44. Oxford: Berg.

Chatterjee, Partha. 1993a [1986]. *Nationalist Thought and the Colonial World: A Derivative Discourse.* Minneapolis: University of Minnesota Press.

――――. 1993b. *The Nation and Its Fragments.* Cambridge: Cambridge University Press.

*Chicago's World's Fair Song Book: A Collection of Authentic International Songs of Every Large Country.* N.d. Chicago: M. M. Cole.

Christie, Clive J. 1998. *Race and Nation: A Reader.* London: I. B. Tauris.

Clark, Caryl. 1997. "Forging Identity: Beethoven's 'Ode' as European Anthem." *Critical Inquiry* 23 (4): 789–807.

Cohen, Alan. 2001. *On European Ground.* Chicago: University of Chicago Press.

Cohler, Anne M. 1970. *Rousseau and Nationalism.* New York: Basic Books.

Cole, Jeffrey. 1998. *The New Racism in Europe.* Cambridge: Cambridge University Press.

Connor, Walker. 1984. *The National Question in Marxist-Leninist Theory and Strategy.* Princeton, N.J.: Princeton University Press.

――――. 1994. *Ethno-Nationalism: The Quest for Understanding.* Princeton, N.J.: Princeton University Press.

Conversi, Daniele. 1998. *The Basques, the Catalans, and Spain: Alternative Routes to Nationalist Mobilisation.* London: C. Hurst & Co.

Cooley, Timothy. 2002. "Migration, Tourism, and Globalization of Polish Tatra Mountain Music-Culture." *European Meetings in Ethnomusicology* 9: 208–226.

――――. Forthcoming. *Making Mountain Music: Tourism, Ethnography, and Music in the Polish Tatras.* Bloomington: Indiana University Press.

Corbea-Hoisie, Andrei, ed. 1998. *Czernowitz: Jüdisches Städtebild.* Frankfurt am Main: Jüdischer Verlag. (Jüdisches Städtebild.)

Cronshaw, Andrew. 1999. "Sámiland (Lapland): Joiks of the Tundra." In Simon Broughton, Mark Ellingham, and Richard Trillo, eds., *World Music:*

*The Rough Guide.* Vol. 1: *Africa, Europe and the Middle East,* pp. 255–260. London: The Rough Guides.

Crowe, David M. 1994. *A History of the Gypsies of Eastern Europe and Russia.* New York: St. Martin's.

Csáky, Moritz. 1996. *Ideologie der Operette und Wiener Moderne: Ein kulturhistorischer Essay zur österreichischen Identität.* Vienna: Böhlau.

Currid, Brian. 1998. "The Acoustics of National Publicity: Music in German Mass Culture, 1924–1945." Ph.D. dissertation, University of Chicago.

Cushman, Thomas. 1995. *Notes from the Underground: Rock Music Counterculture in Russia.* Albany: State University of New York Press.

Dahlhaus, Carl. 1980. "Nationalism in Music." In idem, *Between Romanticism and Modernism,* trans. by Mary Whittall, pp. 79–101. Berkeley and Los Angeles: University of California Press.

Dale, Gareth, and Mike Cole, eds. 1999. *The European Union and Migrant Labour.* Oxford: Berg.

Dalinger, Brigitte. 1998. *Verloschene Sterne: Geschichte des jüdischen Theaters in Wien.* Vienna: Picus.

Danckert, Werner. 1939. *Grundriß der Volksliedkunde.* Berlin: Bernhard Hahnefeld Verlag.

_____. 1966. *Das Volkslied im Abendland.* Berne: Franke.

_____. 1970 [1939]. *Das europäische Volkslied.* 2d ed. Bonn: H. Bouvier.

Daughtry, J. Martin. 2003. "Russia's New Anthem and the Negotiation of National Identity." *Ethnomusicology* 47 (1): 42–67.

Davidová, Eva, and Jan Žižka. 1991. *Folk Music of the Sedentary Gypsies of Czechoslovakia.* Budapest: Institute for Musicology of the Hungarian Academy of Sciences.

Davies, Charlotte Aull. 1989. *Welsh Nationalism in the Twentieth Century: The Ethnic Option and the Modern State.* New York: Praeger.

de la Motte-Haber, Helga, ed. 1991. *Nationaler Stil und europäische Dimension in der Musik der Jahrhundertwende.* Darmstadt: Wissenschaftliche Buchgesellschaft.

del Giudice, Louisa, and Gerald Porter, eds. 2001. *Imagined States: Nationalism, Utopia, and Longing in Oral Culture.* Logan, Ut.: Utah State University Press.

Denitch, Bogdan. 1994. *Ethnic Nationalism: The Tragic Death of Yugoslavia.* Rev. ed. Minneapolis: University of Minnesota Press.

Deutsch, Walter. 1993. *Volksmusik in Niederösterreich: St. Pölten und Umgebung.* Vienna: Böhlau. (Corpus musicae popularis austriacae, 1.)

_____. 1995. "90 Jahre Österreichisches Volksliedwerk: Dokumente und Berichte seiner Geschichte 1904–1994." *Jahrbuch des Österreichischen Volksliedwerks* 44: 12–50.

_____, ed. 1981. *Der Bordun in der europäischen Volksmusik.* Vienna: A. Schendl. (Schriften zur Volksmusik.)

_____, and Gerlinde Haid, eds. 1997. *Beiträge zur musikalischen Volkskultur in Südtirol.* Vienna: Böhlau. (Schriften zur Volksmusik, 17.)

*Deutsche Volkslied, Das.* 1899–1944. 46 vols.

*Deutsche Volkslieder und ihren Melodien: Balladen.* 1935–1996. 10 vols. Berlin et al.: Walter de Gruyter et al.

Deutsches Volksliedarchiv. 1938. *Oberschlesische Volkslieder.* Cassel: Bärenreiter. (Landschaftliche Volkslieder, 33.)

Dibango, Manu. 1994. *Three Kilos of Coffee: An Autobiography.* Trans. by Beth G. Raps. Chicago: University of Chicago Press.

Dinges, Georg, ed. 1932. *Wolgadeutsche Volkslieder mit Bildern und Weisen.* Berlin and Leipzig: Walter de Gruyter. (Landschaftliche Volkslieder, 25.)

Doegen, Wilhelm, ed. 1925. *Unter fremden Völkern—Eine neue Völkerkunde.* Berlin: Otto Stollberg, Verlag für Politik und Wirtschaft.

Döge, Klaus. 1991. *Dvořák: Leben, Werke, Dokumente.* Mainz and Munich: Schott and Piper.

_____. 2001. "Dvořák, Antonín (Leopold)." In Stanley Sadie, ed., *The New Grove Dictionary of Music and Musicians.* Rev. ed. Vol. 7: 777–814. London: Macmillan.

Dohrn, Verena. 1994. *Baltische Reise: Vielvölkerlandschaft des alten Europa.* Frankfurt am Main: S. Fischer Verlag.

Donakowski, Conrad L. 1977. *A Muse for the Masses: Ritual and Music in an Age of Democratic Revolution, 1770–1870.* Chicago: University of Chicago Press.

Donnan, Hastings, and Thomas M. Wilson, eds. 1999. *Borders: Frontiers of Identity, Nation and State.* Oxford: Berg.

Dor, Milo. 1996. *Mitteleuropa: Mythos oder Wirklichkeit—Auf der Suche nach der größeren Heimat.* Salzburg and Vienna: Otto Müller.

Drakulić, Slavenka. 1999. *Café Europa: Life after Communism.* New York: W.W. Norton.

_____. 2000. *S.: A Novel about the Balkans.* Trans. by Marko Ivić. New York: Penguin.

Dreo, Harald, Walter Burian, and Sepp Gmasz. 1988. *Ein burgenländisches Volksliederbuch.* Eisenstadt: Verlag Nentwich-Lattner.

Dreo, Harald, and Sepp Gmasz. 1997. *Volksmusik im Burgenland: Burgenländische Volksballaden.* Vienna: Böhlau. (Corpus musicae popularis austriacae, 7.)

Duara, Prasenjit. 1995. *Rescuing History from the Nation: Questioning Narratives of Modern China.* Chicago: University of Chicago Press.

Dubisch, Jill. 1995. *In a Different Place: Pilgrimage, Gender, and Politics at a Greek Island Shrine.* Princeton, N.J.: Princeton University Press. (Princeton Modern Greek Studies.)

DuBois, Thomas A. 1995. *Finnish Folk Poetry and the Kalevala.* New York: Garland. (New Perspectives in Folklore, 1.)

Du Bois, W.E.B. 1989 [1903]. *The Souls of Black Folk.* Repr. ed. by Henry Louis Gates, Jr. New York: Bantam.

Dumont, Louis. 1994. *German Ideology: From France to Germany and Back.* Chicago: University of Chicago Press.

Dundes, Alan, and Galit Hasan-Rokem, eds. 1986. *The Wandering Jew: Essays in the Interpretation of a Christian Legend.* Bloomington: Indiana University Press.

During, Jean. 1993. "Musique, Nation et Territoire en Asie Interieure." *Yearbook for Traditional Music* 25: 29–42.

Edström, Karl-Olof. 1977. *Den samiska musikkulturen: En källkritisk översikt.* Göteborg: Skrifter från Musikvetenskapliga institutionen.

Eggebrecht, Hans Heinrich. 1991. *Musik im Abendland: Prozesse und Stationen vom Mittelalter bis zur Gegenwart.* Munich: Piper.

Eipós, Csillag, ed. 1946. *Kántori rérikönyo.* Budapest. Manuscript in the archives of the Chorus of the Dohány Street Synagogue, Cantorial Academy, Budapest.

Eley, Geoff, and Ronald G. Suny, eds. 1996. *Becoming National: A Reader.* New York: Oxford University Press.

Eliasberg, Alexander. 1918. *Ostjüdische Volkslieder.* Munich: Georg Müller.

Elschek, Oskár. 1991. "Ideas, Principles, Motivations, and Results in Eastern European Folk-Music Research." In Bruno Nettl and Philip V. Bohlman, eds., *Comparative Musicology and Anthropology of Music: Essays on the History of Ethnomusicology,* pp. 91–109. Chicago: University of Chicago Press.

———. 1995. "Musik, Zeitgeist und Persönlichkeit." In Moritz Csáky and Walter Pass, eds., *Europa im Zeitalter Mozarts,* pp. 21–29. Vienna: Böhlau.

———. 1998. "Musikgeschichtliche Prozesse im mitteleuropäischen Raum und ihre musikwissenschaftliche Reflexion." In Elisabeth Theresia Hilscher, ed., *Österreichische Musik—Musik in Österreich: Beiträge zur Musikgeschichte Mitteleuropas,* pp. 11–28. Tutzing: Hans Schneider.

Elscheková, Alica, ed. 1981. *Stratigraphische Probleme der Volksmusik in den Karpaten und auf dem Balkan.* Bratislava: VEDA.

———, and Oskár Elschek. 1996. "Theorie und Praxis der Erforschung der traditionellen Musik von Minderheiten." In Ursula Hemetek, ed., *Echo der Vielfalt/Echoes of Diversity: Traditionelle Musik von Minderheiten/ethnischen Gruppen—Traditional Music of Ethnic Groups/Minorities,* pp. 17–30. Vienna: Böhlau.

Engel, Carl. 1866. *An Introduction to the Study of National Music, Comprising Researches into Popular Songs, Traditions, and Customs.* London: Longmans, Green, Reader, and Dyer.

Engelhardt, Jeffers L. 2002. "Asceticism and the Nation: Henryk Gorécki, Krzysztof Penderecki, and Late Twentieth-Century Poland." *European Meetings in Ethnomusicology* 9: 197–207.

Entwhistle, William J. 1939. *European Balladry.* Oxford: Clarendon Press.

Enzensberger, Hans Magnus. 1987. *Ach Europa! Wahrnehmungen aus sieben Ländern, mit einem Epilog aus dem Jahr 2006.* Frankfurt am Main: Suhrkamp.

Eörsi, István. 1999. "Die nützliche Arbeit." In Georg Aescht, ed., *Siebenbürgen: Europa erlesen,* pp. 167–169. Klagenfurt: Wieser Verlag.

Erben, Karel Jaromír. 1939. *Proóza a divadlo.* Prague: Melantrich.

Erdely, Stephen. 1987. "Folk-Music Research in Hungary until 1950: The Legacy of Zoltán Kodály and Béla Bartók." *Current Musicology* 43: 51–61.

———. 1995. *Music of Southslavic Epics from the Bihać Region of Bosnia.* New York: Garland.

Ergang, Robert Reinhold. 1966 [1931]. *Herder and the Foundations of German Nationalism.* New York: Octagon Books.

Erk, Ludwig, with Franz Magnus Böhme. 1893–1894. *Deutscher Liederhort.* 3 vols. Leipzig: Breitkopf und Härtel.

Erk, Ludwig, and Wilhelm Irmer. 1838–1841. *Die deutschen Volkslieder mit ihren Singweisen.* Leipzig: B. Hermann.

Erlmann, Veit. 1993. "The Politics and Aesthetics of Transnational Music." *The World of Music* 35: 3–15.

———. 1999. *Music, Modernity, and the Global Imagination: South Africa and the West.* New York: Oxford University Press.

Ernst, August. 1987. *Geschichte des Burgenlandes.* Vienna: Verlag für Geschichte und Politik. (Geschichte der österreichischen Bundesländer.)

Ethnographisches Museum, Schloß Kittsee, ed. 1998. *Galizien: Ethnographische Erkundung bei den Bojken und Huzulen in den Karpaten.* Kittsee: Ethnographisches Museum. (Kittseer Schriften zur Volkskunde, 9.)

Eyck, F. Gunther. 1995. *The Voice of Nations: European National Anthems and Their Authors.* Westport, Conn.: Greenwood Press. (Contributions to the Study of Music and Dance, 34.)

Farwick, Petra. 1986. *Deutsche Volksliedlandschaften: Landschaftliches Register der Aufzeichnungen im Deutschen Volksliedarchiv.* Berne: Peter Lang. (Studien zur Volksliedforschung, 1.)

Fennesz-Juhasz, Christiane. 1996. "'Me ka džav ko gurbeti . . .': Klage- und Abschiedslieder mazedonischer Roma-Migranten." In Ursula Hemetek, ed., *Echo der Vielfalt, Echoes of Diversity: Traditional Music of Ethnic Groups,* pp. 255–270. Vienna: Böhlau.

Feurstein, Michaela, and Gerhard Milchram, eds. 2001. *Jüdisches Wien: Stadtspaziergänge.* Vienna: Böhlau.

Feurzeig, Lisa, ed. 2002. *Deutsche Lieder für Jung und Alt.* Middleton, Wisc.: A-R Editions. (Recent Researches in the Oral Traditions of Music, 7.)

Finkelstein, Sidney. 1989. *Composer and Nation: The Folk Heritage in Music.* 2d ed. New York: International Publishers.

Fischer, Gero, and Maria Wölflingseder, eds. 1995. *Biologismus, Rassismus, Nationalismus: Rechte Ideologien im Vormarsch.* Vienna: Promedia.

Fischer, Jens Malte. 2000. *Richard Wagners "Das Judentum in der Musik."* Frankfurt am Main: Insel.

Fischer, Kurt von. 1979. "Zum Begriff *national* in Musikgeschichte und deutscher Musikhistoriographie." In Dieter Rexroth, ed., *Zwischen den Grenzen: Zum Aspekt des Nationalen in der neuen Musik*, pp. 11–16. Mainz: B. Schott's Söhne.

Flacke, Monika, ed. 1998a. *Mythen der Nationen: Ein europäisches Panorama*. Munich and Berlin: Koehler & Amelang.

———. 1998b. "Deutschland: Die Begründung der Nation aus der Krise." In idem, ed., *Mythen der Nationen: Ein europäisches Panorama*, pp. 101–128. Munich and Berlin: Koehler & Amelang.

Flotzinger, Rudolf, and Gernot Gruber, eds. 1995. *Musikgeschichte Österreichs*. 3 vols. 2d, rev. ed. Vienna: Böhlau.

Fonseca, Isabel. 1995. *Bury Me Standing: The Gypsies and Their Journey*. New York: Vintage.

Forry, Mark E. 1986. "The 'Festivalization' of Tradition in Yugoslavia." Paper read at the 31st Annual Meeting of the Society for Ethnomusicology, Rochester, N.Y.

———. 1990. "The Mediation of 'Tradition' and 'Culture' in the Tamburica Music of Vojvodina (Yugoslavia)." Ph.D. dissertation, University of California, Los Angeles.

Forsyth, Cecil. 1911. *Music and Nationalism: A Study of English Opera*. London: Macmillan.

Frank, Ben G. 1996. *A Travel Guide to Jewish Europe*. 2d ed. Gretna, La.: Pelican Publishing Company.

Frieden, Jeffry, Daniel Gros, and Erik Jones, eds. 1998. *The New Political Economy of EMU*. Lanham, Md.: Rowman and Littlefield. (Governance in Europe.)

Friedrichsmeyer, Sara, Sara Lennox, and Susanne Zantop. 1998. *The Imperialist Imagination: German Colonialism and Its Legacy*. Ann Arbor: University of Michigan Press. (Social History, Popular Culture, and Politics in Germany.)

Frigyesi, Judit. 1994. "Béla Bartók and the Concept of Nation and *Volk* in Modern Hungary." *The Musical Quarterly* 78 (2): 255–287.

———. 1998. *Béla Bartók and Turn-of-the-Century Budapest*. Berkeley: University of California Press.

Fritsche, Peter. 1996. *Reading Berlin 1900*. Cambridge, Mass.: Harvard University Press.

Frovola-Walker, Marina. 1998. "'National in Form, Socialist in Content': Musical Nation-Building in the Soviet Republics." *Journal of the American Musicological Society* 51 (2): 331–371.

Fujie, Linda, ed. 1996. *Folk Music Revival in Europe*. Special edition of *The World of Music* 38 (3).

Fulcher, Jane. 1987. *The Nation's Image: French Grand Opera as Politics and Politicized Art*. Cambridge: Cambridge University Press.

———. 1999. *French Cultural Politics and Music: From the Dreyfus Affair to the First World War*. New York: Oxford University Press.

Gal, Susan, and Gail Kligman. 2000. *The Politics of Gender after Socialism.* Princeton, N.J.: Princeton University Press.

Gambaccini, Paul, Tim Rice, Jonathan Rice, and Tony Brown. 1999. *The Complete Eurovision Song Contest Companion 1999.* London: Pavillion.

Garfias, Robert. 1984. "Dance among the Urban Gypsies of Romania." *Yearbook for Traditional Music* 16: 84–96.

Gauß, Karl-Markus. 2001. *Die sterbenden Europäer: Unterwegs zu den Sepharden von Sarajevo, Gottscheer Deutschen, Arbëreshe, Sorben und Aromunen.* Vienna: Paul Zsolnay.

Gay, David E. 1997. "The Creation of the *Kalevala,* 1833–1849." *Jahrbuch für Volksliedforschung* 42: 63–77.

Gay y Blasco, Paloma. 1999. *Gypsies in Madrid: Sex, Gender and the Performance of Identity.* Oxford: Berg. (Mediterranea.)

Geary, Patrick J. 2003. *The Myth of Nations: The Medieval Origins of Europe.* Princeton, N.J.: Princeton University Press.

Geijer, Erik Gustaf, and Arvid August Afzelius. 1814–1817. *Svenska folk-visor från forntiden.* Stockholm: Z. Haggstrom.

Geisel, Eike, et al. 1987. *Wegweiser durch das jüdische Berlin: Geschichte und Gegenwart.* Berlin: Nicolai.

Geiss, Imanuel. 1988. *Geschichte des Rassismus.* Frankfurt am Main: Suhrkamp.

Geistlinger, Michael, ed. 1994. *Dissonanzen in Europa: Der neue Nationalismus und seine Folgen.* Vienna: Wilhelm Braumüller.

Gellner, Ernest. 1983. *Nations and Nationalism.* Oxford: Blackwell.

———. 1994. *Encounters with Nationalism.* Oxford: Blackwell.

———. 1997. *Nationalism.* New York: New York University Press.

———. 1998. *Language and Solitude: Wittgenstein, Malinowski and the Habsburg Dilemma.* Cambridge: Cambridge University Press.

Germer, Stefan. 1998. "Retrovision: Die rückblickende Erfindung der Nationen durch die Kunst." In Monika Flacke, ed., *Mythen der Nationen: Ein europäisches Panorama,* pp. 33–52. Munich and Berlin: Koehler & Amelang.

Gikandi, Simon. 1996. *Maps of Englishness: Writing Identity in the Culture of Colonialism.* New York: Columbia University Press.

Gilliam, Bryan. 1994. "The Annexation of Anton Bruckner: Nazi Revisionism and the Politics of Appropriation." *The Musical Quarterly* 78 (3): 584–604.

Gillis, John, ed. 1994. *Commemorations: The Politics of National Identity.* Princeton, N.J.: Princeton University Press.

Gilroy, Paul. 1993. *The Black Atlantic: Modernity and Double Consciousness.* Cambridge, Mass.: Harvard University Press.

Ginsburg, Shaul M., and Pesach S. Marek. 1901. *Evreiskie narodnye pesni v Rossii* ["Jewish Folk Songs in Russia"]. St. Petersburg: Voskhod. Reprinted 1991: Ramat Gan: Bar-Ilan University Press. (Abram Aisengart Literature Foundation.)

Giurchescu, Anca. 1987. "The National Festival 'Song to Romania':

Manipulation of Symbols in the Political Discourse." In Claes Arvidsson
and Lars Erik Blomqvist, eds., *Symbols of Power: The Esthetics of Political
Legitimation in the Soviet Union and Eastern Europe.* Stockholm: Almqvist &
Wiksell International.

Glenny, Misha. 1999. *The Balkans: Nationalism, War, and the Great Powers,
1804–1999.* New York: Viking.

Goddard, Victoria A., Josep R. Llobera, and Cris Shore, eds. 1996. *The
Anthropology of Europe: Identities and Boundaries in Conflict.* Oxford: Berg.
(Explorations in Anthropology.)

Goehr, Lydia. 1992. *The Imaginary Museum of Musical Works: An Essay in the
Philosophy of Music.* Oxford: Oxford University Press.

Goertzen, Chris. 1997. *Fiddling for Norway: Revival and Identity.* Chicago:
University of Chicago Press. (Chicago Studies in Ethnomusicology.)

Goldmark, Karl. 1922. *Erinnerungen aus meinem Leben.* Vienna: Rikola Verlag.

Gopinath, Gayatri. 1995. "'Bombay, U.K., Yuba City': Bhangra Music and the
Engendering of Diaspora." *Diaspora* 4: 303–321.

Görner, Rüdiger. 2001. "Arme Spielleute: Improvisationen über ein
musikliterarisches Thema." In idem, *Literarische Betrachtungen zur Musik,*
pp. 208–217. Frankfurt am Main: Insel.

Gossett, Philip. 1990. "Becoming a Citizen: The Chorus in Risorgimento
Opera." *Cambridge Opera Journal* 2: 41–64.

Gow, James, and Cathie Carmichael. 2000. *Slovenia and the Slovenes: A Small
State and the New Europe.* Bloomington: Indiana University Press.

Gowan, Peter, and Perry Anderson, eds. 1996. *The Question of Europe.* London:
Verso.

Graubard, Stephen R., ed. 1999. *A New Europe for the Old?* New Brunswick,
N.J.: Transaction Publishers.

Gravitis, Olgert. 1995. "Die Situation der Musik im Baltikum in den 40er bis
60er Jahren." In Joachim Braun, Vladimir Karbusický, and Heidi Tamar-
Hoffmann, eds. 1995. *Verfemte Musik: Komponisten in den Diktaturen unseres
Jahrhunderts,* pp. 229–235. Frankfurt am Main: Peter Lang.

Greenblatt, Stephen. 1991. *Marvelous Possessions: The Wonder of the New World.*
Chicago: University of Chicago Press.

Greenfeld, Liah. 1992. *Nationalism: Five Roads to Modernity.* Cambridge, Mass.:
Harvard University Press.

Grieg, Edvard. N.d. "Norwegische Bauerntänze für die Geige solo (Slåtter)."
Leipzig: C. F. Peters.

Grimmelshausen, Hans Jakob Christoffel von. 1975 [1669]. *Der abenteuerliche
Simplicissimus Teutsch.* Munich: Deutscher Taschenbuch Verlag.

Gronow, Pekka. 1975. "Ethnic Music and Soviet Record Industry."
*Ethnomusicology* 19 (1): 91–100.

Gruber, Ruth Ellen. 2002. *Virtually Jewish: Reinventing Jewish Culture in Europe.*
Berkeley: University of California Press.

Grufik, Franz. 1970. *Turzovka: Das slowakische Lourdes*. Stein am Rhein: Christiana-Verlag.

Grundtvig, Sven. 1881. *Danmarks gamel folkeviser*. Copenhagen: Thieles bogtrykkeri.

Grynberg, Henryk. 2000. *Drohobycz, Drohobycz: Zwölf Lebensbilder*. Vienna: Paul Zsolnay.

Guiberneau, Montserrat. 1996. *Nationalisms: The Nation-State and Nationalism in the Twentieth Century*. Cambridge, England: Polity Press.

Guss, David M. 2000. *The Festive State: Race, Ethnicity and Nationalism as Cultural Performance*. Berkeley: University of California Press.

Guy, Nancy. 1999. "Governing the Arts, Governing the State: Peking Opera and Political Authority in Taiwan." *Ethnomusicology* 43 (3): 508–526.

———. 2002. "'Republic of China National Anthem' on Taiwan: One Anthem, One Performance, Multiple Realities." *Ethnomusicology* 46 (1): 96–119.

Haber, Peter, ed. 1999. *Budapest: Jüdisches Städtebild*. Frankfurt am Main: Jüdischer Verlag. (Jüdisches Städtebild.)

Hætta, Per. 1999. "Joik und 'Kulturlied'." In Lothar Schneider, ed., *Europa erlesen: Lappland*, pp. 150–151. Klagenfurt: Wieser Verlag. (Europa erlesen.)

Hakobian, Levon. 1998. *Music of the Soviet Age 1917–1987*. Stockholm: Melos Music Literature.

Hall, John A., ed. 1998. *The State of the Nation: Ernest Gellner and the Theory of Nationalism*. Cambridge: Cambridge University Press.

Hanák, Péter. 1998. *The Garden and the Workshop: Essays on the Cultural History of Vienna and Budapest*. Princeton, N.J.: Princeton University Press.

Handke, Peter. 1996. *Eine winterliche Reise zu den Flüssen Donau, Save, Morawa und Drina, oder Gerechtigkeit für Serbien*. Frankfurt am Main: Suhrkamp.

Hannerz, Ulf. 1996. *Transnational Connections: Culture, People, Places*. New York: Routledge.

Harker, Dave. 1985. *Fakesong: The Manufacture of British "Folksong" 1700 to the Present Day*. Milton Keynes: Open University Press.

Harrán, Don. 1999. *Salamone Rossi: Jewish Musician in Late Renaissance Mantua*. New York: Oxford University Press.

Haslinger, Josef. 2001. *Klasse, Burschen, Essays*. Frankfurt am Main: S. Fischer.

Hastings, Adrian. 1997. *The Construction of Nationhood: Ethnicity, Religion, and Nationalism*. Cambridge: Cambridge University Press.

Heaton, Vernon. 1979. *The Oberammergau Passion Play*. London: Hale.

Hebdige, Dick. 1979. *Subculture: The Meaning of Style*. London: Methuen.

Hechter, Michael. 1975. *Internal Colonialism: The Celtic Fringe in British National Development, 1536–1966*. Berkeley: University of California Press.

———. 2000. *Containing Nationalism*. Oxford: Oxford University Press.

Heinschink, Mozes F. 1994. "E Romaničhib—Die Sprache der Roma. In idem and Ursula Hemetek, eds., *Roma, das unbekannte Volk: Schicksal und Kultur*, pp. 110–129. Vienna: Böhlau.

_____, and Christiane Juhasz. 1992. "'Koti džal o mulo . . . ': Lieder österreichischer Sinti." *Jahrbuch des österreichischen Volksliedwerkes* 41: 63–86.

Hemetek, Ursula. 1992. *Romane gila: Lieder und Tänze der Roma in Österreich.* Vienna: Österreichische Dialektautoren and Institut für Volksmusikforschung.

_____. 2001. *Mosaik der Klänge: Musik der ethnischen und religiösen Minderheiten in Österreich.* Vienna: Böhlau. (Schriften zur Volksmusik, 20.)

_____, ed. 1996. *Echo der Vielfalt/Echoes of Diversity: Traditionelle Musik von Minderheiten/ethnischen Gruppen — Traditional Music of Ethnic Groups/Minorities.* Vienna: Böhlau. (Schriften zur Volksmusik, 16.)

_____, and Mozes Hainschink, eds. 1994. *Roma, das unbekannte Volk: Schicksal und Kultur.* Vienna: Böhlau.

Henry, Edward O. 1989. "Institutions for the Promotion of Indigenous Music: The Case of Ireland's Comhaltas Ceoltoiri." *Ethnomusicology* 33: 67–95.

Herder, Johann Gottfried. 1770. *Abhandlung über den Ursprung der Sprache.* Leipzig: Christian Friedrich Voß.

_____. 1975 [1778–1779]. *"Stimmen der Völker in Liedern"* and *Volkslieder.* 2 vols. published in one. Stuttgart: Reclam.

Herre, Franz. 1981. *Radetzky: Eine Biographie.* Cologne: Kiepenheuer & Witsch.

Herzfeld, Michael. 1982. *Ours Once More: Folklore, Ideology and the Making of Modern Greece.* Austin: University of Texas Press.

_____. 1991. *A Place in History: Social and Monumental Time in a Cretan Town.* Princeton, N.J.: Princeton University Press.

_____. 1997. *Cultural Intimacy: Social Poetics in the Nation-State.* New York: Routledge.

Herzl, Theodor. 1896. *Der Judenstaat: Versuch einer Lösung der Judenfrage.* Leipzig and Vienna: M. Breitenstein.

Herzog, Todd, and Sander L. Gilman, eds. 2001. *A New Germany in a New Europe.* New York: Routledge.

Heskes, Irene, ed. 1998 [1912]. *The St. Petersburg Society for Jewish Folk Music.* N.p.: Tara Publications.

Hesmondhalgh, Dave. 2000. "International Times: Fusions, Exoticism, and Antiracism in Electronic Dance Music." In Georgina Born and Dave Hesmondhalgh, eds., *Western Music and Its Others: Difference, Representation, and Appropriation in Music,* pp. 280–304. Berkeley: University of California Press.

Hilscher, Elisabeth T., ed. 1998. *Österreichische Music, Musik in Österreich — Beiträge zur Musikgeschichte Mitteleuropas: Theophil Antonicek zum 60. Geburtstag.* Tutzing: Hans Schneider. (Wiener Veröffentlichungen zur Musikwissenschaft, 34.)

Hirschhausen, Ulrike von, and Jörn Leonhard, eds. 2001. *Nationalismen in Europa: West- und Osteuropa im Vergleich.* Göttingen: Wallstein.

Hobsbawm, Eric J. 1990. *Nations and Nationalism since 1780: Programme, Myth, Reality.* 2d ed. Cambridge: Cambridge University Press.

———, and Terence Ranger, eds. 1983. *The Invention of Tradition.* Cambridge: Cambridge University Press.

Hoffman, Eva. 1993. *Exit into History: A Journey through the New Eastern Europe.* New York: Viking.

Holý, Dušan, and Ctibor Nečas. 1993. *Žalujíci píseň: O osudu Romú v nacistických koncentračních táborech* ("Lamenting Song: The Fate of Rom in Nazi Concentration Camps"). Strážnice: Spisy Univerzity J. E. Purkyné v Brné.

Holzapfel, Otto. 1993. *Das deutsche Gespenst: Wie Dänen die Deutschen und sich selbst sehen.* Kiel: Wolfgang Butt.

———. 1998. "Soldatenlieder und Antikriegslieder: Eine Skizze." *Jahrbuch für Volksliedforschung* 43: 63–78.

———. 2001. *Die Germanen: Mythos und Wirklichkeit.* Freiburg im Breisgau: Herder. (Spektrum.)

———. 2002. *Mündliche Überlieferung und Literaturwissenschaft: Der Mythos von Volkslied und Volksballade.* Münster: Aschendorff. (Literaturwissenschaft: Theorie und Beispiele, 2.)

———, Eva Bruckner, and Ernst Schusser, eds. 1991. *Pfarrer Louis Pinck (1873–1940): Leben und Werk.* Freiburg im Breisgau and Munich: Deutsches Volksliedarchiv and Volksmusikarchiv des Bezirks Oberbayern.

Holzmeister, Johannes, ed. 1965. *Carmina historica: Geschichten im Lied.* Boppard: Fidula.

Hong, Y. Euny. 2003. "Rise of the New Europe in Euro Pop." *The New York Times* (on-line). 26 May.

Hooker, Lynn. 2002. "'Liszt Is Ours': The Hungarian Commemoration of the Liszt Centennial." Paper delivered at the conference, "Festivals and Festivalization in a Globalizing World," University of Chicago, 11 May.

Hopkins, Pandora. 1986. *Aural Thinking in Norway: Performance and Communication with the Hardingfele.* New York: Human Sciences Press.

Hosking, Geoffrey, and George Schöpflin, eds. 1997. *Myths and Nationhood.* London: Routledge.

Huebner, Steven. 1999. *French Opera at the Fin de Siècle: Wagnerism, Nationalism, and Style.* New York: Oxford University Press.

Hutchinson, John. 1987. *The Dynamics of Cultural Nationalism: The Gaelic Revival and the Creation of the Irish Nation State.* London: Allen and Unwin.

———. 1996. "Irish Nationalism." In D. George Boyce and Alan O'Day, eds., *The Making of Modern Irish History: Revisionism and the Revisionist Controversy,* pp. 100–119. London: Routledge.

———, and Anthony D. Smith, eds. 1994. *Nationalism.* Oxford: Oxford University Press. (Oxford Readers.)

Idelsohn, A.Z. 1914–1932. *Hebräisch-orientalischer Melodienschatz.* 10 vols. Berlin et al.: Benjamin Harz et al.

Ignatieff, Michael. 1993. *Blood and Belonging: Journeys into the New Nationalisms*. New York: Farrar, Straus and Giroux.

Imig, Doug, and Sidney Tarrow, eds. 2001. *Contentious Europeans: Protest and Politics in an Emerging Polity*. Lanham, Md.: Rowman and Littlefield. (Governance in Europe.)

Ingram, Susan, Markus Reisenleitner, and Cornelia Szabó-Knotik, eds. 2002. *Reverberations: Representations of Modernity, Tradition and Cultural Value in-between Central Europe and North America*. Frankfurt am Main: Peter Lang.

Initiative Minderheitenjahr. 1994. *Wege zu Minderheiten in Österreich: Ein Handbuch*. Vienna: Verlag der Äpfel.

Jaher, Frederic Cople. 2002. *The Jews and the Nation: Revolution, Emancipation, State Formation, and the Liberal Paradigm in America and France*. Princeton, N.J.: Princeton University Press.

Járdányi, Pál. 1961. *Magyar népdaltípusok* ("Hungarian Folk-Song Types"). Budapest: Editio Musica.

Jarman, Neil. 1997. *Material Conflicts: Parades and Visual Displays in Northern Ireland*. Oxford: Berg.

Johnson, Lonnie R. 1996. *Central Europe: Enemies, Neighbors, Friends*. New York and Oxford: Oxford University Press.

Johnston, Hank. 1992. "The Comparative Study of Nationalism: Six Pivotal Themes from the Baltic States." *Journal of Baltic Studies*, 23 (2): 95–104.

Jones-Bamman, Richard. 2000. "Saami Music." In Timothy Rice, James Porter, and Chris Goertzen, eds., *Europe*. Vol. 8: *The Garland Encyclopedia of World Music*, pp. 299–308. New York: Garland.

Juergensmeyer, Mark. 1993. *The New Cold War: Religious Nationalism Confronts the Secular State*. Berkeley and Los Angeles: University of California Press.

Jusdanis, Gregory. 2001. *The Necessary Nation*. Princeton, N.J.: Princeton University Press.

Kamenka, Eugene, ed. 1976. *Nationalism: The Nature and Evolution of an Idea*. London: Edward Arnold.

Kaplan, Robert D. 1993. *Balkan Ghosts: A Journey through History*. New York: Vintage.

———. 2000. *Eastward to Tartary: Travels in the Balkans, the Middle East, and the Caucasus*. New York: Vintage.

Karady, Victor. 1999. *Gewalterfahrung und Utopie: Juden in der europäischen Moderne*. Trans. by Judith Klein. Frankfurt am Main: Fischer Taschenbuch Verlag. (Europäische Geschichte.)

Karakasidou, Anastasia N. 1993. *Fields of Wheat, Hills of Blood: Passages to Nationhood in Greek Macedonia, 1870–1990*. Chicago: University of Chicago Press.

Karbusický, Vladímir. 1995. "Werte und Wertung in der politischen Totalität." In Joachim Braun, Vladimir Karbusický, and Heidi Tamar-Hoffmann, eds.,

*Verfemte Musik: Komponisten in den Diktaturen unseres Jahrhunderts,* pp. 45–58. Frankfurt am Main: Peter Lang.

Karpeles, Maud. 1956. *Folk Songs of Europe.* London: Novello.

Karsai, László. 1991. "Hungarian Gypsy Songs about the Holocaust." *Cahiers de littérature orale* 30: 37–44.

Kaufmann, Fritz Mordechai, ed. 1920. *Die schönsten Lieder der Ostjuden.* Berlin: Jüdischer Verlag.

Kaufmann, Thomas DaCosta. 1995. *Court, Cloister and City: The Art and Culture of Central Europe 1450–1800.* Chicago: University of Chicago Press.

Kedourie, Elie. 1960. *Nationalism.* London: Hutchinson.

Kemilainen, Aira. 1964. *Nationalism: Problems Concerning the Word, the Concept and Classification.* Yvaskyla, Finland: Kustantajat Publishers.

Kenney, Padraic. 2002. *A Carnival of Revolution: Central Europe 1989.* Princeton, N.J.: Princeton University Press.

Kertész, Imre. 2003. *Die exilierte Sprache: Essays und Reden.* Frankfurt am Main: Suhrkamp.

Khazanov, Anatoly M. 1995. *After the USSR: Ethnicity, Nationalism, and Politics in the Commonwealth of Independent States.* Madison: University of Wisconsin Press.

Kinglake, Alexander William. 1844. *Eothen.* London: J. M. Dent & Sons.

Kircher, Athansius. 1650. *Musurgia universalis, sive ars magna consoni et dissoni.* Rome: Francesco Corbelletti.

Kittler, Friedrich A. 1987. *Aufschreibesysteme 1800/1900.* 2d ed. Munich: Wilhelm Fink.

Klein, Bernhard, and Karl August Groos. 1818. *Deutsche Lieder für Jung und Alt.* Berlin: Realschulbuchhandlung.

Klusen, Ernst. 1969. *Volkslied: Fund und Erfindung.* Cologne: Gerig.

Knopp, Guido, and Ekkehard Kuhn. 1988. *Das Lied der Deutschen: Schicksal einer Hymne.* Frankfurt am Main: Ullstein.

Knudsen, Thorkild, Svend Nielsen, and Nils Schiorring, eds. 1976. *Danmarks gamle folkeviser: Melodier.* Vol. 11. Copenhagen: Akademisk forlag.

Kohn, Hans. 1962. *The Age of Nationalism: The First Era of Global History.* New York: Harper.

_____. 1967 [1944]. *The Idea of Nationalism.* 2d ed. New York: Collier-Macmillan.

Kolberg, Oskar. 1961. *Piesni ludu polskiego.* Kraków: Polskie Wydawnictwo Muzyczne.

_____. 1964a [1889]. *Leczyckie.* Kraków: Polskie Wydawnictwo Muzyczne. (Dziela wszystkie, 22.)

_____. 1964b [1890]. *Chelmskie.* Kraków: Polskie Wydawnictwo Muzyczne. (Dziela wszystkie, 33.)

_____. 1964c [1891]. *Przemyskie.* Kraków: Polskie Wydawnictow Muzyczne. (Dziela wszystkie, 35.)

Kolessa, Filaret. 1910 and 1913. *Melodiia ukrains'kykh narodnikh dum.* 2 vols. L'viv: Naukova Tovarystvo im. Shevchenka. (Materyialy Ukrains'ko-Rus'koi Etnol'ogii, 13 and 14.)

Kommission für das deutsche Volksliederbuch, ed. 1915. *Volksliederbuch für gemischten Chor.* 2 vols. Leipzig: C. F. Peters.

Konrád, György. 1999. *Die Erweiterung der Mitte Europa und Osteuropa am Ende des 20. Jahrhunderts.* Vienna: Picus.

Körte, Mona, and Robert Stockhammer, eds. 1995. *Ahasvers Spur: Dichtungen und Dokumente vom "Ewigen Juden."* Leipzig: Reclam.

Kos, Koraljka. 1972. "New Dimensions in Folk Music: A Contribution to the Study of Musical Tastes in Contemporary Yugsolav Society." *International Review of the Aesthetics and the Sociology of Music* 3: 61–75.

Koshar, Rudy. 1998. *Germany's Transient Pasts: Preservation and National Memory in the Twentieth Century.* Chapel Hill: University of North Carolina Press.

Kovalcsik, Katalin. 1985. *Vlach Gypsy Folk Songs in Slovakia.* Budapest: Institute for Musicology of the Hungarian Academy of Sciences.

———. 1987. "Popular Dance Music Elements in the Folk Music of Gypsies in Hungary." *Popular Music* 6 (1): 45–66.

———. 1992. *Ernö Király Collection of Gypsy Folk Music from Voivodina.* Budapest: Institute for Musicology of the Hungarian Academy of Sciences.

Krader, Barbara. 1990. "Recent Achievements in Soviet Ethnomusicology with Remarks on Russian Terminology." *Yearbook for Traditional Music* 22: 1–16.

Krejci, Yaroslav, and Viteslav Velimsky. 1981. *Ethnic and Political Nations in Europe.* London: Croom Helm.

Krekovičová, Eva. 1998. *Zwischen Toleranz und Barrieren: Das Bild der Zigeuner und Juden in der slowakischen Folklore.* Frankfurt am Main: Peter Lang. (Studien zur Tsiganologie und Folkloristik, 21.)

Kristeva, Julia. 1993. *Nations without Nationalism.* Trans. by Leon S. Roudiez. New York: Columbia University Press.

Krockow, Christian Graf von. 1995. *Von deutschen Mythen.* Stuttgart: Deutsche Verlags-Anstalt.

Kuba, Ludvik. 1884–1888. *Slovanstvo ve svych zpevech.* Nákladem Vydavatelovym: Komissi v Hoblíka v Pardubícich.

Kuhn, Hans. 1998. "Folkevise und Dänentum: Die Re-Popularisierung der dänischen Volksballade im 19. Jahrhundert." *Jahrbuch für Volksliedforschung* 43: 79–92.

Kumer, Zmaga. 1986. *Die Volksmusikinstrumente in Slovenien.* Ljubljana: Slovenska akademija znanosti in umenosti.

Kunz, Ludvik. 1974. *Die Volksmusikinstrumente der Tsechoslowakei.* Vol. 1. Leipzig: Deutscher Verlag für Musik.

Künzig, Johannes. 1935. *Deutsche Volkslieder aus dem rumänischen Banat, mit Bildern und Weisen.* Berlin and Leipzig: Walter de Gruyter. (Landschaftliche Volkslieder, 28.)

Kürti, László. 2001. *The Remote Borderland: Transylvania in the Hungarian Imagination*. Albany: State University of New York Press. (National Identities.)

Kurzke, Hermann. 1990. *Hymnen und Lieder der Deutschen*. Mainz: Dietrich'sche Verlagsbuchhandlung. (Excerpta classica, 5.)

Kuter, Lois. 2000. "Celtic Music." In Timothy Rice, James Porter, and Chris Goertzen, eds., *Europe*. Vol. 8: *The Garland Encyclopedia of World Music*, pp. 319–323. New York: Garland.

Kvitka, Klyment. 1917. *Narodni melodii z holosu Lesi Ukrainky*. Kiev: Slovo.

Kymlicka, Will. 2000. *Politics in the Vernacular: Nationalism, Multiculturalism, and Citizenship*. Oxford: Oxford University Press.

Laborde, Denis. 2000. "Basque Music." In Timothy Rice, James Porter, and Chris Goertzen, eds., *Europe*. Vol. 8: *The Garland Encyclopedia of World Music*, pp. 309–318. New York: Garland.

Ladd, Brian. 1997. *The Ghosts of Berlin: Confronting German History in the Urban Landscape*. Chicago: University of Chicago Press.

*Lagerliederbuch, Das: Lieder, gesungen, gesammelt und geschrieben im Konzentrationslager Sachsenhausen bei Berlin 1942*. 1980 [1942]. Dortmund: Verlag "pläne."

Laitin, David D. 1998. *Identity in Formation: The Russian-Speaking Populations in the Near Abroad*. Ithaca, N.Y.: Cornell University Press.

Lampland, Martha. 2000. "An Anthropology of Postsocialism." In Daphne Berdahl, Matti Bunzl, and Martha Lampland, eds., *Altering States: Ethnographies of Transition in Eastern Europe and the Former Soviet Union*, pp. 1–13. Ann Arbor: University of Michigan Press.

Lane, Eric, and Ian Brenson. 1984. *The Complete Text in English of the Oberammergau Passion Play*. London: Dedalus.

Lange, Barbara Rose. 2003. *Holy Brotherhood: Romani Music in a Hungarian Pentecostal Church*. New York: Oxford University Press.

Lanner-Strauss-Compagnie, ed. 1992. *Von den Linzer Tänzen zum Wiener Walzer*. Linz: Rudolf Trauner.

Larkey, Edward. 1992. "Austropop: Popular Music and National Identity in Austria." *Popular Music* 12 (2): 151–185.

_____. 1993. *Pungent Sounds: Constructing Identity with Popular Music in Austria*. New York: Peter Lang. (Austrian Culture, 9.)

Latzina, Anemone. 1999. "Csikszereda—Miercurea Diuc." In Georg Aescht, ed., *Siebenbürgen: Europa erlesen*, p. 167. Orig. publ. 1978. Klagenfurt: Wieser.

Lauristin, Marju, and Peeter Vihalemm, eds. 1997. *Return to the Western World: Cultural and Political Perspectives on the Estonian Post-Communist Transition*. Tartu: Tartu University Press.

Lausevic, Mirjana. 1996. "The *Ilahiya* as a Symbol of Bosnian National Identity." In Mark Slobin, ed., *Retuning Culture: Musical Changes in Central and Eastern Europe*, pp. 117–135. Durham, N.C.: Duke University Press.

Lavie, Smadar, and Ted Swedenburg, eds. 1996. *Displacement, Diaspora, and Geographies of Identity.* Durham, N.C.: Duke University Press.

Lazarus, Neil. 1999. *Nationalism and Cultural Practice in the Postcolonial World.* Cambridge: Cambridge University Press.

Leggewie, Claus. 1990. *Multi Kulti: Spielregeln für die Vielvölkerrepublik.* Berlin: Rotbuch Verlag.

Lemon, Alaina. 2000. *Between Two Fires: Gypsy Performance and Romani Memory from Pushkin to Postsocialism.* Durham, N.C.: Duke University Press.

Lesser, Jeffrey. 1999. *Negotiating National Identity: Immigrants, Minorities, and the Struggle for Ethnicity in Brazil.* Durham, N.C.: Duke University Press.

Levin, Theodore. 1993. "The Reterritorialization of Culture in the New Central Asian States: A Report from Uzbekistan." *Yearbook for Traditional Music* 25: 51–59.

Levy, Alan Howard. 1983. *Musical Nationalism: American Composers' Search for Identity.* Westport, Conn.: Greenwood.

Lieven, Anatol. 1993. *The Baltic Revolution: Estonia, Latvia, Lithuania and the Path to Independence.* New Haven, Conn.: Yale University Press.

Ling, Jan. 1986. "Folk Music Revival in Sweden: The Lille Edet Fiddle Club." *Yearbook for Traditional Music* 18: 1–8.

————. 1997. *A History of European Folk Music.* Rochester, N.Y.: University of Rochester Press.

Linke, Uli. 1999. *Blood and Nation: The European Aesthetics of Race.* Philadelphia, Pa.: University of Pennsylvania Press.

Lipp, Wolfgang. 1994. "Die Wiederkehr des Volkes—Erscheinungsformen und Klärungen: Zum volkskundlichen, politikwissenschaftlichen und soziologischen Befund." In Walter Deutsch and Maria Walcher, eds., *Sommerakademie Volkskultur 1993,* pp. 12–28. Vienna: Österreichisches Volksliedwerk.

Lissa, Zofia. 1964. "Über die nationalen Stile." *Beiträge zur Musikwissenschaft* 6: 187–214.

List, George. 1979. "The Distribution of a Melodic Formula: Diffusion of Polygenesis?" *Yearbook of the International Folk Music Council* 10: 33–52.

Liszt, Franz. 1926 [1859]. *The Gipsy in Music.* Trans. by Edwin Evans. London: William Reeves.

Livingston, Tamara E. 1999. "Music Revivals: Towards a General Theory." *Ethnomusicology* 43 (1): 66–85.

Lloyd, A. L. 1967. *Folk Song in England.* London: Lawrence and Wishart.

Lomax, Alan. 1976. *Cantometrics: A Method of Musical Anthropology.* Berkeley: University of California Extension Media Center.

Longinović, Tomislav. 2000. "Music Wars: Blood and Song at the End of Yugoslavia." In Ronald Radano and Philip V. Bohlman, eds., *Music and the Racial Imagination,* pp. 622–643. Chicago: University of Chicago Press.

Lönnrot, Elias. 1989. *The Kalevala: An Epic Poem after Oral Tradition.* Trans. by Keith Bosley. Oxford: Oxford University Press. (Oxford World's Classics.)

Loos, Helmut, ed. 1997. *Musikgeschichte zwischen Ost- und Westeuropa: Symphonik, Musiksammlungen.* Sankt Augustin: Academia.

Lord, Albert B. 1960. *The Singer of Tales.* Cambridge, Mass.: Harvard University Press.

Lortat-Jacob, Bernard. 1995. *Sardinian Chronicles.* Trans. by Teresa Lavender Fagan. Chicago: University of Chicago Press. (Chicago Studies in Ethnomusicology.)

Lützler, Paul Michael, ed. 1982. *Europa: Analysen und Visionen der Romantiker.* Frankfurt am Main: Insel Verlag.

L'vov, Nikolai, and Ivan Prach. 1790. *Sobraniie narodnikh russkikh pesen s ikh golosami* ("Collection of Russian Folk Songs with Their Melodies"). St. Petersburg: A. S. Suvorin.

Mačák, Ivan. 1995. *Dedičstvo hudobných nástrojov* ("The Heritage of Musical Instruments"). Bratislava: Slovenské národné múzeum, Hudobné múzeum.

Macedo, Catharine. 2002. "Music and Catalan Nationalism in Fin-de-siècle Barcelona." Ph.D. dissertation, University of Oxford.

Mach, Zdzisław. 1994. "National Anthems: The Case of Chopin as a National Composer." In Martin Stokes, ed., *Ethnicity, Identity and Music: The Musical Construction of Place,* pp. 61–70. Oxford: Berg.

Magrini, Tullia, ed. 1992. *Il maggio drammatico: Una tradizione di teatro in musica.* Bologna: Analisi.

———, ed. 1993. *Antropologia dell musica e culture Mediterranee.* Bologna: Il Mulino.

Mahr, Roland. 2002. "Von der Aufwärmrunde bis ins Ziel—Der 'Grand Prix der Volksmusik': Eine musikwissenschaftliche Untersuchung des Wettbewerbs als Schlüsselstelle zum Karrieresprung in der volkstümlichen Unterhaltungsbranche." Master's thesis, University of Vienna.

Maier, Charles S. 1997. *Dissolution: The Crisis of Communism and the End of East Germany.* Princeton, N.J.: Princeton University Press.

Mäkelä, Tomi, ed. 1997. *Music and Nationalism in 20th-Century Great Britain and Finland.* Hamburg: Von Bockel.

Malino, Frances, and David Sorkin, eds. 1990. *Profiles in Diversity: Jews in a Changing Europe, 1750–1870.* Oxford: Blackwell.

Malm, Krister. 1993. "Music on the Move: Traditions and Mass Media." *Ethnomusicology* 37 (3): 339–352.

Manuel, David. 1992. *Medjugorje under Siege.* Orleans, Mass.: Paraclete Press.

Manuel, Peter. 1989. "Andalusian, Gypsy, and Class Identity in the Contemporary Flamenco Complex." *Ethnomusicology* 33 (1): 47–65.

———. 1993. *Cassette Culture: Popular Music and Culture in North India.* Chicago: University of Chicago Press.

———. 2000. "Ethnic Identity, National Identity, and Music in Indo-Trinidadian

Culture." In Ronald Radano and Philip V. Bohlman, eds., *Music and the Racial Imagination,* pp. 318–345. Chicago: University of Chicago Press.

Marcu, George. 1977. *Folclor muzical aromân* ("Arumanian Musical Folklore"). Bucharest: Editura Muzicala.

Marcus, George E., ed. 1993. *Perilous States: Conversations on Culture, Politics, and Nation.* Chicago: University of Chicago Press. (Late Editions, 1.)

———, ed. 1997. *Cultural Producers in Perilous States: Editing Events, Documenting Change.* Chicago: University of Chicago Press. (Late Editions, 4.)

Mathieson, Kenny, ed. 2001. *Celtic Music.* San Francisco: Backbeat Books.

Mautner, Konrad. 1910. *Das steyerische Rasplwerk: Vierzeiler, Lieder, und Gasslreime aus Gößl am Grundlsee.* Vienna: Stählein & Lauenstein.

Mazower, Mark. 2000. *The Balkans: A Short History.* New York: Modern Library. (Modern Library Chronicles Books, 3.)

McCann, May. 1995. "Music and Politics in Ireland: The Specificity of the Folk Revival in Belfast." *British Journal of Ethnomusicology* 4: 51–75.

McNeill, William H. 1995. *Keeping Together in Time: Dance and Drill in Human History.* Cambridge, Mass.: Harvard University Press.

Menasse, Robert. 1992. *Das Land ohne Eigenschaften: Essay zur österreichischen Identität.* Frankfurt am Main: Suhrkamp.

———. 2000. *Erklär mir Österreich.* Frankfurt am Main: Suhrkamp.

Metil, Robert Carl. 2000. "Post-Velvet Revolutionary Cultural Activism and Rusyn Song in the Prešov Region of Eastern Slovakia, 1989–2000." Ph.D. dissertation, University of Pittsburgh.

Metz, Franz. 1996. *Die Kirchenmusik der Donauschwaben.* Sankt Augustin: Academia Verlag. (Deutsche Musik im Osten, 7.)

Miles, Elizabeth J. 2000. "Immigrant Music in Europe." In Timothy Rice, James Porter, and Chris Goertzen, eds., *Europe.* Vol. 8: *The Garland Encyclopedia of World Music,* pp. 231–243. New York: Garland.

Miller, David. 1995. *On Nationality.* Oxford: Oxford University Press.

Milojković-Djurić, Jelena. 1984. *Tradition and Avant-Garde: The Arts in Serbian Culture between the Two World Wars.* Boulder, Colo.: East European Monographs.

Mintz, Jerome. 1997. *Carnival Song and Society: Gossip, Sexuality and Creativity in Andalusia.* Oxford: Berg.

Mitchell, Tony. 1996. *Popular Music and Local Identity.* London: Leicester University Press.

———, ed. 2001. *Global Noise: Rap and Hip-Hop outside the USA.* Middletown, Conn.: Wesleyan University Press. (Music/Culture.)

Modood, Tariq, and Pnina Werbner, eds. 1997. *The Politics of Multiculturalism in the New Europe: Racism, Identity and Community.* London: Zed Books.

Montagu, Jeremy, et al. 2001. "Military Music." In Stanley Sadie, ed., *The New Grove Dictionary of Music and Musicians.* 2d ed. Vol. 16: 683–690. London: Macmillan.

Móricz, Klára. 1999. "Jewish Nationalism in Twentieth-Century Music." Ph.D. dissertation, University of California, Berkeley.

Moser, Hans Joachim. 1960. *Die Tonsprachen des Abendlandes: Zehn Essais als Wesenskunde der europäischen Musik.* Berlin: Merseburger.

Mosse, George L. 1985. *Nationalism and Sexuality: Respectability and Abnormal Sexuality in Modern Europe.* New York: Howard Fertig.

Mraz, Gerda, ed. 1997. *Österreich-Ungarn in Lied und Bild: Ein Hochzeitsgeschenk an Kaiserin Elisabeth 1854.* Vienna: Christian Brandstätter.

Mu, Yang. 1994. "Academic Ignorance or Political Taboo? Some Issues in China's Study of Its Folk Song Culture." *Ethnomusicology* 38 (2): 303–320.

Müller, Herta. 1984. *Niederungen.* Berlin: Rotbuch Verlag.

Murillo, Ernesto, ed. 1935. *National Anthems of the Countries of North, Central and South America.* Chicago/New York: Clayton F. Summy.

*Musica imperialis: 500 Jahre Hofmusikkapelle in Wien, 1498–1998.* Tutzing: Hans Schneider.

Nairn, Tom. 1977. *The Breakup of Britain: Crisis and Neonationalism.* London: New Left Books.

Narayan, Kirin. 1996. "Songs Lodged in Some Hearts: Displacements of Women's Knowledge in Kangra." In Smadar Lavie and Ted Swedenburg, eds., *Displacement, Diaspora, and Geographies of Identity,* pp. 181–214. Durham, N.C.: Duke University Press.

Nathan, Hans, ed. 1994. *Israeli Folk Music: Songs of the Pioneers.* Madison, Wisc.: A-R Editions. (Recent Researches in the Oral Traditions of Music, 4.)

*Nationalhymnen.* 1982. *Nationalhymnen: Texte und Melodien.* Stuttgart: Reclam.

*Nationalism and Music.* 1996. *Nationalism and Music.* Special edition of *Repercussions* 5 (1 and 2).

Nettl, Bruno. 1990. *Folk and Traditional Music of the Western Continents.* 3d ed. Englewood Cliffs, N.J.: Prentice Hall.

Nettl, Paul. 1967. *National Anthems.* Trans. by Alexander Gode. 2d, enlarged ed. New York: Frederick Ungar.

Nielsen, Svend. 1982. *Stability in Improvisation: A Repertoire of Icelandic Epic Songs (Rímur).* Trans. by Kale Mahaffy. Copenhagen: Forlaget Kragen.

Nixon, Paul. 1998. *Sociality—Music—Dance: Human Figurations in a Transylvanian Valley.* Göteborg: Skrifter från Institutionen för musikvetenskap, Göteborgs universitet.

Noll, William. 1991. "Music Institutions and National Consciousness among Polish and Ukrainian Peasants." In Stephen Blum, Philip V. Bohlman, and Daniel M. Neuman, eds., *Ethnomusicology and Modern Music History,* pp. 139–158. Urbana: University of Illinois Press.

Nooteboom, Cees. 1993. *Wie wird man Europäer?* Trans. by Helga van Beuningen. Frankfurt am Main: Suhrkamp.

Nußbaumer, Thomas. 2000. "Das Ostmärkische Volksliedunternehmen und die ostmärkischen Gauausschüsse für Volksmusik: Ein Beitrag zur

Geschichte des Österreichischen Volksliedwerkes." In Gerlinde Haid, Ursula Hemetek, and Rudolf Pietsch, eds., *Volksmusik—Wandel und Deutung: Festschrift Walter Deutsch zum 75. Geburtstag*, pp. 149–172. Vienna: Böhlau.

Okely, Judith. 1983. *The Traveller-Gypsies*. Cambridge: Cambridge University Press.

Oliver, Paul, ed. 1990. *Black Music in Britain: Essays on the Afro-Asian Contribution to Popular Music*. Milton Keynes: Open University Press.

O'Neill, Francis. 1903. *O'Neill's Music of Ireland: Eighteen Hundred and Fifty Melodies, Airs, Jigs, Reels, Hornpipes, Long Dances, Marches Etc*. Chicago: Lyon & Healy.

———. *The Dance Music of Ireland: 1001 Gems, Double Jigs, Single Jigs, Hop or Slip Jigs, Reels, Hornpipes, Long Dances, Set Dances Etc*. Chicago: Lyon & Healy.

———. 1908. *O'Neill's Irish Music: 250 Choice Selections Arranged for Piano and Violin*. Chicago: Lyon & Healy.

———. 1913. *Irish Minstrels and Musicians, with Numerous Dissertations on Related Subjects*. Chicago: Lyon & Healy; Dublin: M. H. Gill.

———. 1922. *Waifs and Strays of Gaelic Melody, Comprising Forgotten Favorites, Worthy Variants, and Tunes Not Previously Printed*. 2d ed. 1927. Chicago: Lyon & Healy.

*Österreichisch-ungarische Cantoren-Zeitung*. 1881–1891. 11 vols.

*Osterreichisch-ungarische Monarchie in Wort und Bild, Die*. 1886–1902. 24 vols. Vienna: Kaiserlich-königliche Hof- und Staatsdruckerei.

O'Sullivan, Donal. 1960. *Carolan: The Life and Times of an Irish Harper*. London: Routledge and Kegan Paul.

Ottens, Rita, and Joel Rubin. 1999. *Klezmer-Musik*. Cassel: Bärenreiter.

Özdogan, Selim. 2000. *Im Juli*. Hamburg and Vienna: Europa Verlag.

Pallmann, Gerhard. 1940. *Soldatenlieder von Front und Heimat: 1914/1939*. Leipzig: N. Simrock.

Parakilas, James. 1992. "Political Representation and the Chorus in Nineteenth-Century Opera." *19th Century Music* 16 (2): 181–202.

Parker, Andrew, et al., eds. 1992. *Nationalisms and Sexualities*. New York: Routledge.

Paulus, Irena. 1999. "Music in Krzysztof Kieslowski's Film *Three Colors: Blue*. A Rhapsody in Shades of Blue: The Reflections of a Musician." *International Review of the Aesthetics and Sociology of Music* 30 (1): 65–91.

Pederson, Sonya. 1993–1994. "A. B. Marx, Berlin Concert Life, and German National Identity." *19th Century Music* 18: 87–107.

Pekić, Borislav. 2001. "Spieler aus Goldener Zeit." In Jörg Schulte, *Europa erlesen: Belgrad*, pp. 37–44. Klagenfurt: Wieser.

Pennay, Mark. 2001. "Rap in Germany: The Birth of a Genre." In Tony Mitchell, ed., *Global Noise: Rap and Hip-Hop outside the USA*, pp. 111–133. Middletown, Conn.: Wesleyan University Press.

Periwal, Sukumar, ed. 1995. *Notions of Nationalism.* Budapest: Central
European University Press.

Pettan, Svanibor. 1996. "Gypsies, Music, and Politics in the Balkans: A Case
Study from Kosovo." *The World of Music* 38 (1): 33–62.

———, ed. 1998. *Music, Politics, and War: Views from Croatia.* Zagreb: Institute
of Ethnology and Folklore Research.

Pietsch, Rudolf. 1999. "Between Romas and Jews: An Ethnomusicological
Field Expedition to Romania." *East European Meetings in Ethnomusicology* 6:
3–10.

Pika, Aleksandr, ed. 1999. *Neotraditionalism in the Russian North: Indigenous
Peoples and the Legacy of Perestroika.* Edmonton and Seattle: Canadian
Circumpolar Institute Press and University of Washington Press.

Pilzer, Joshua D. 2002. "'Inwazja Waranów': Apocalypse and Social Critique in
Polish Rock." *European Meetings in Ethnomusicology* 9: 227–235.

Pinck, Louis. 1926–1962. *Verklingende Weisen: Lothringer Volkslieder.* 5 vols. Metz:
Lothringer Verlags- und Hilfsverein, and other publishers.

———, ed. 1937. *Lothringer Volkslieder.* Cassel: Bärenreiter. (Landschaftliche
Volkslieder, 31.)

Pinder, John. 2001. *The European Union: A Very Short Introduction.* Oxford:
Oxford University Press. (Very Short Introductions, 36.)

Plantinga, Leon. 1996. "Dvořák and the Meaning of Nationalism in Music."
In David R. Beveridge, ed., *Rethinking Dvořák: Views from Five Countries,* pp.
117–123. Oxford: Oxford University Press.

Plastino, Goffredo, ed. 2003. *Mediterranean Mosaic: Popular Music and Global
Sounds.* New York: Routledge. (Perspectives on Global Pop.)

Polec, Andrzej. 1997. *Distant Glens and Moors: The Hutsuls Today.* Trans. by
Jacek Buras et al. Warsaw: Wydawnictwo A. P.

Popa, Steluta. 1996. "The Romanian Revolution of December 1989 and Its
Reflection in Musical Folklore." In Mark Slobin, ed., *Retuning Culture:
Musical Changes in Central and Eastern Europe,* 156–175. Durham, N.C.:
Duke University Press.

Porter, Cecilia. 1979–1980. "The New Public and the Reordering of the
Musical Establishment: The Lower Rhein Music Festivals, 1818–1867."
*19th Century Music* 3: 211–224.

———. 1996. *The Rhine as Musical Metaphor: Cultural Identity in German
Romantic Music.* Boston: Northeastern University Press.

Porter, James. 1977. "Prolegomena to a Comparative Study of European Folk
Music." *Ethnomusicology* 21 (3): 435–451.

———. 2000. "Travellers' Music." In Timothy Rice, James Porter, and Chris
Goertzen, eds., *Europe.* Vol. 8: *The Garland Encyclopedia of World Music,* pp.
294–298. New York: Garland.

———, and Herschel Gower. 1995. *Jeannie Robertson: Emergent Singer,
Transformative Voice.* Knoxville: University of Tennessee Press.

Potter, Pamela M. 1998. *Most German of the Arts: Musicology and Society from the Weimar Republic to the End of Hitler's Reich.* New Haven, Conn.: Yale University Press.

Prahbu, R. K., ed. 1967. *Songs of Freedom: An Anthology of National and International Songs from Various Countries of the World.* Bombay: Popular Prakashan.

Radano, Ronald, and Philip V. Bohlman, eds. 2000. *Music and the Racial Imagination.* Chicago: University of Chicago Press. (Chicago Studies in Ethnomusicology.)

Ragozat, Ulrich. 1982. *Die Nationalhymnen der Welt: Ein kulturgeschichtliches Lexikon.* Freiburg im Breisgau: Herder.

Ramet, Sabrina Petra. 1997. *Whose Democracy? Nationalism, Religion, and the Doctrine of Collective Rights in Post-1989 Eastern Europe.* New York: Rowman and Littlefield.

———, ed. 1994. *Rocking the State: Rock Music and Politics in Eastern Europe and Russia.* Boulder, Colo.: Westview Press.

———, James R. Felak, and Herbert J. Ellison, eds. 2002. *Nations and Nationalisms in East-Central Europe, 1806–1948: A Memorial to Peter F. Sugar.* Columbus, Ohio: Slavica.

Ramnarine, Tina K. 2003. *Ilmatar's Inspirations: Nationalism, Globalization, and the Changing Soundscapes of Finnish Folk Music.* (Chicago Studies in Ethnomusicology.)

Rasmussen, Ljerka. 1996. "The Southern Wind of Change: Style and the Politics of Identity in Prewar Yugoslavia." In Mark Slobin, ed., *Retuning Culture: Musical Changes in Central and Eastern Europe,* pp. 99–116. Durham, N.C.: Duke University Press.

———. 2002. *Newly Composed Folk Music of Yugoslavia.* New York: Routledge. (Current Research in Ethnomusicology.)

Raun, Toivo. 1991. *Estonia and the Estonians.* Stanford, Cal.: Hoover Institution Press.

Raupp, Jan. 1963. *Sorbische Volksmusikanten und Musikinstrumente.* Bautzen: VEB Domowina-Verlag. (Schriftenreihe des Instituts für sorbische Volksforschung, 17.)

Reemtsma, Katrin. 1996. *Sinti und Roma: Geschichte, Kultur, Gegenwart.* Munich: C. H. Beck.

Rehding, Alexander. 2000. "The Quest for the Origins of Music in Germany Circa 1900." *Journal of the American Musicological Society* 53 (2): 345–386.

Reimann, Jacob Friedrich. 1709. *Versuch einer Einleitung in die historiam literariam derer Teutschen.* Vol. 3. Halle an der Saale: Renger.

Rein, Kurt, and Reiner Hildebrandt, eds. 1979. *Siebenbürgisch-deutsches Wörterbuch.* Marburg: N. G. Elwert Verlag.

Renner, Erich. 1997. *"Und wir waren auch Naturmenschen": Der autobiographische Bericht des Sinti-Musikers und Geigenbauers Adolf Boko Winterstein und andere*

*persönliche Dokumente von und über Sinti und Roma.* Frankfurt am Main: Peter
   Lang. (Studien zur Tsiganologie und Folkloristik, 22.)
Rexroth, Dieter, ed. 1979. *Zwischen den Grenzen: Zum Aspekt des Nationalen in
   der neuen Musik.* Mainz: B. Schott's Söhne. (Frankfurter Studien, 3.)
Rice, Timothy. 1994. *May It Fill Your Soul: Experiencing Bulgarian Music.*
   Chicago: University of Chicago Press. (Chicago Studies in
   Ethnomusicology.)
_____. 2000. "The Music of Europe: Unity and Diversity." In Timothy Rice,
   James Porter, and Chris Goertzen, eds., *The Garland Encyclopedia of World
   Music,* vol. 8, *Europe,* pp. 2–15. New York: Garland.
_____. 2002. "Bulgaria or Chalgaria: The Attenuation of Bulgarian
   Nationalism in a Mass-Mediated Popular Music." *Yearbook for Traditional
   Music* 34: 25–46.
Rice, Timothy, James Porter, and Chris Goertzen, eds. 2000. *Europe.* Vol. 8:
   *The Garland Encyclopedia of World Music.* New York: Garland.
Riethmüller, Albrecht. 1993. *Die Walhalla und ihre Musiker.* Laaber: Laaber-
   Verlag.
_____. 1995. "Musik, die 'deutscheste' Kunst." In Joachim Braun, Vladimir
   Karbusický, and Heidi Tamar-Hoffmann, eds., *Verfemte Musik: Komponisten
   in den Diktaturen unseres Jahrhunderts,* pp. 91–104. Frankfurt am Main: Peter
   Lang.
Ringer, Alexander L., et al. 1995. "Nationalsozialismus–Stalinismus: Eine
   vergleichende Diskussion." In Joachim Braun, Vladimir Karbusický, and
   Heidi Tamar-Hoffmann, eds., *Verfemte Musik: Komponisten in den Diktaturen
   unseres Jahrhunderts,* pp. 1–28. Frankfurt am Main: Peter Lang.
Roessingh, Martijn A. 1996. *Ethnonationalism and Political Systems in Europe: A
   State of Tension.* Amsterdam: Amsterdam University Press.
Rohr, Auguste. N.d. *Trilogie: Chansons et documents en français, allemand et
   dialekte.* Freyming-Merlebach: Petits Chanteurs Lorrains.
Ronström, Owe. 1996. "Revival Reconsidered." *The World of Music* 38 (3):
   5–20.
Rose, Paul Lawrence. 1992. *Wagner, Race, and Revolution.* New Haven, Conn.:
   Yale University Press.
Rosenberg, Tina. 1995. *The Haunted Land: Facing Europe's Ghosts after
   Communism.* New York: Random House.
Roth, Joseph. 1983 [1932]. *The Radetzky March.* Trans. by Eva Tucker.
   Woodstock, N.Y.: Overlook Press.
_____. 1999 [1929]. *Hotel Savoy: Ein Roman.* Cologne: Kiepenheuer &
   Witsch.
Rousseau, Jean-Jacques. 1753. *Lettre sur la musique française.* 2d ed. Paris: N.p.
_____. 1977. *A Complete Dictionary of Music.* Reprint of the 1779 edition. New
   York: AMS Press.
Rubtsov, Feodosy. 1962. *Intonnacionoye siazi o pesennom tvorchestve slavianskikh*

*narodov* ("Intonational Connections in the Song Art of the Slavic People"). Leningrad: Sovetskii Kompozitor.

Rupcić, Ljudevit. 1989. *Erscheinungen unserer lieben Frau zu Medjugorje.* 3d ed. Jestetten: Miriam-Verlag.

Rupp-Eisenreich, Britta, and Justin Stagl, eds. 1995. *Kulturwissenschaft im Vielvölkerstaat: Zur Geschichte der Ethnologie und verwandter Gebiete in Österreich, ca. 1780–1918.* Vienna: Böhlau. (Ethnologia Austriaca, 1.)

Ryback, Timothy W. 1990. *Rock around the Bloc: A History of Rock Music in Eastern Europe and the Soviet Union, 1954–1988.* New York: Oxford University Press.

Said, Edward W. 1978. *Orientalism.* New York: Pantheon.

SakoHoess, Renata, and Rotraut Hackermüller, eds. 2001. *Europa erlesen: Bratislava.* Klagenfurt: Wieser. (Europa erlesen.)

Sandrow, Nahma. 1977. *Vagabond Stars: A World History of Yiddish Theater.* New York: Harper & Row.

Santino, Jack. 2001. *Signs of War and Peace: Social Conflict and the Use of Public Symbols in Northern Ireland.* New York: Palgrave.

Sárosi, Bálint. 1967. *Die Volksmusikinstrumente Ungarns.* Leipzig: Deutscher Verlag für Musik.

_____. 1971. *Gypsy Music.* Budapest: Corvina.

_____. 1990. *Volksmusik: Das ungarische Erbe.* Budapest: Corvina.

Schade, Ernst. 1990. "Volkslied-Editionen zwischen Transkription, Manipulation, Rekonstruktion und Dokumentation." *Jahrbuch für Volksliedforschung* 35: 44–63.

Scheierling, Konrad. 1987– . *Geistliche Lieder der Deutschen aus Südosteuropa.* 6 vols. Kludenbach: Gehann.

Schlegel, Hans-Joachim. 1999. "Das stalinistische Hollywood: Zu Grigorij Aleksandrovs Musikfilmkomödien." In Malte Hagener and Jan Hans, eds., *Als die Filme singen lernten: Innovation und Tradition im Musikfilm 1928–1938,* pp. 138–149. Munich: edition film + kritik.

Schmidt, Esther. 2000–2001. "Nationalism and the Creation of Jewish Music: The Politicization of Music and Language in the German-Jewish Press Prior to the Second World War." *Musica Judaica* 15: 1–31.

_____. 2003. "From the Ghetto to the Conservatoire: The Professionalisation of Jewish Cantors in the Austro-Hungarian Empire (1826–1918)." Ph.D. dissertation, University of Oxford.

Schmitter, Philippe C. 2000. *How to Democratize the European Union . . . and Why Bother?* Lanham, Md.: Rowman and Littlefield. (Governance in Europe.)

Schneider, Lothar, ed. 1999. *Europa erlesen: Lappland.* Klagenfurt: Wieser. (Europa erlesen.)

Schneider, Marius. 1934, 1935, and 1968. *Geschichte der Mehrstimmigkeit.* 3 vols. Tutzing: Schneider.

Schoenberg, Arnold. 1975. "National Music." In Leonard Stein, ed., *Style and*

*Idea: Selected Writings of Arnold Schoenberg*, pp. 169–174. Trans. by Leo Black. New York: St. Martins.

Schönfellinger, Nora, ed. 1999. *"Conrad Mautner, Großes Talent": Ein Wiener Volkskundler aus dem Ausseer Land*. Grundlsee: Kulturelle Arbeitsgemeinschaft Grundlsee. (Grundlseer Schriften, 3.)

Schorske, Carl E. 1981. *Fin-de-siècle Vienna: Politics and Culture*. New York: Vintage.

_____. 1998. *Thinking with History: Explorations in the Passage to Modernism*. Princeton, N.J.: Princeton University Press.

Schulhoff, Erwin. 1995. *Erwin Schulhoff: Schriften*. Ed. by Tobias Widmaier. Hamburg: Von Bockel. (Verdrängte Musik, 7.)

Schulte, Jörg, ed. 2001. *Europa erlesen: Belgrad*. Klagenfurt: Wieser. (Europa erlesen.)

Schulze, Erich. 1984. "Die Aktion der Europäischen Gemeinschaft im kulturellen Bereich." In Elisabeth Haselauer and Karl-Josef Müller, eds., *Europäische Gegenwartsmusik: Einflüsse und Wandlungen*, pp. 13–20. Mainz: Schott.

Schulze, Hagen. 1999. *Staat und Nation in der europäischen Geschichte*. Munich: C. H. Beck. (Europa bauen.)

Schünemann, Georg. 1923. *Das Lied der deutschen Kolonisten in Russland*. Munich: Drei Masken Verlag. (Sammelbände für vergleichende Musikwissenschaft, 3.)

_____, ed. 1936. *Trompeterfanfaren, Sonaten, und Feldstücke, nach Aufzeichnungen deutscher Hoftrompeter des 16./17. Jahrhunderts*. Cassel: Bärenreiter. (Das Erbe deutscher Musik, Series 1, Reichsdenkmale, 7.)

Sciolino, Elaine. 2002. "Visions of a Union: Europe Struggles to Define Its Identity." *The New York Times* (on-line). 15 December.

Scott, James C. 1990. *Domination and the Arts of Resistance: Hidden Transcripts*. New Haven, Conn.: Yale University Press.

Scruggs, T. M. 1999. "'Let's Enjoy as Nicaraguans': The Use of Music in the Construction of a Nicaraguan National Consciousness." *Ethnomusicology* 43 (2): 297–321.

Sebald, W. G. 2001. *Austerlitz*. Trans. by Anthea Bell. New York: Random House.

Seebass, Tilman. 2000. "Notation and Transmission in European Music History." In Timothy Rice, James Porter, and Chris Goertzen, eds., *Europe*. Vol. 8: *The Garland Encyclopedia of World Music*, pp. 49–57. New York: Garland.

Seemann, Wilhelm. 1973. "Die europäische Volksballade." In Rolf Wilhelm Brednich, Lutz Röhrich, and Wolfgang Suppan, eds., *Handbuch des Volksliedes*. Vol. 1: *Die Gattungen des Volksliedes*, pp. 37–56. Munich: Wilhelm Fink.

Shafir, Gershon. 1995. *Immigrants and Nationalists: Ethnic Conflict and*

*Accommodation in Catalonia, the Basque Country, Latvia, and Estonia.* Albany: State University of New York Press.

Shapiro, James S. 2000. *Oberammergau: The Troubling Story of the World's Most Famous Passion Play.* New York: Pantheon.

Shapiro, Susan E. 1994. "*Écriture judaïque:* Where Are the Jews in Western Discourse?" In Angelika Bammer, ed., *Displacements: Cultural Identities in Question,* pp. 182–201. Bloomington: Indiana University Press.

Sharma, Sanjay, John Hutnyk, and Ashwani Sharm, eds. 1996. *Disorienting Rhythms: The Politics of the New Asian Dance Music.* Atlantic Highlands, N.J.: Zed Books.

Sharp, Cecil J. 1907. *English Folk-Song: Some Conclusions.* London: Simpkins and Novello.

Shaw, Martin, Henry Coleman, and T. M. Cartledge, eds. 1969. *National Anthems of the World.* New York: Pitman.

Shields, Hugh. 1993. *Narrative Singing in Ireland.* Dublin: Irish Academic Press.

Shore, Cris. 1993. "Inventing the 'People's Europe': Critical Perspectives on European Community Cultural Policy." *Man: Journal of the Royal Anthropological Institute* 28 (4): 779–800.

_____. 1997. "Metaphors of Europe: Integration and the Politics of Language." In S. Nugent and Chris Shore, eds., *Anthropology and Cultural Studies,* pp. 126–159. London: Pluto Press.

_____. 2000. *Building Europe: The Cultural Politics of European Integration.* London and New York: Routledge.

Sibelius, Jean. 1961. *Kullervo: Tondichtung, op. 7.* Wiesbaden: Breitkopf & Härtel.

Siebs, Theodor, and Max Schneider, eds. 1924. *Schlesische Volkslieder mit Bildern und Weisen.* Breslau: Bergstadtverlag. (Landschaftliche Volkslieder, 1.)

Silverman, Carol. 2000. "Rom (Gypsy) Music." In Timothy Rice, James Porter, and Chris Goertzen, eds., *Europe.* Vol. 8: *The Garland Encyclopedia of World Music,* pp. 270–293. New York: Garland.

Singer, Regis. 1986. *Les hymnes nationaux du monde.* Paris: Aug Zurfluh.

Slobin, Mark. 1992. "Micromusics of the West: A Comparative Approach." *Ethnomusicology* 36 (1): 1–88.

_____. 1993. *Subcultural Sounds: Micromusics of the West.* Hanover, N.H.: University Press of New England. (Music and Culture.)

_____, ed. 1996. *Retuning Culture: Musical Changes in Central and Eastern Europe.* Durham, N.C.: Duke University Press.

Slonimsky, Nicolas. 1950. "The Changing Styles of Soviet Music." *Journal of the American Musicological Society* 3 (3): 236–255.

Smadar, Lavie, and Ted Swedenburg, eds. 1996. *Displacement, Diaspora, and Geographies of Identity.* Durham, N.C.: Duke University Press.

Smidchens, Guntis. 1996. *A Baltic Music: The Folklore Movement in Lithuania, Latvia, and Estonia, 1968–1991.* Ph.D. dissertation, Indiana University.

Smith, Anthony D. 1979. *Nationalism in the Twentieth Century.* New York: New York University Press.

――――. 1983. *Theories of Nationalism.* 2d ed. New York: Holmes & Meier.

――――. 1986. *The Ethnic Origin of Nations.* Oxford: Blackwell.

――――. 2000. *The Nation in History: Historiographical Debates about Ethnicity and Nationalism.* Hanover, N.H.: University Press of New England. (The Menachem Stern Jerusalem Lectures.)

Smith, Graham, et al., eds. 1998. *Nation-Building in the Post-Soviet Borderlands: The Politics of National Identities.* Cambridge: Cambridge University Press.

Sorce Keller, Marcello. 2000. "Popular Music in Europe." In Timothy Rice, James Porter, and Chris Goertzen, eds., *Europe.* Vol. 8: *The Garland Encyclopedia of World Music,* pp. 204–213. New York: Garland.

Sousa, John Philip. 1890. *National, Patriotic and Typical Airs of All Lands.* Philadelphia: H. Coleman.

Soysal, Yasemin Nuhoğlu. 1994. *Limits of Citizenship: Migrants and Postnational Membership in Europe.* Chicago: University of Chicago Press.

Starkie, Walter. 1933. *Raggle-Taggle: Adventures with a Fiddle in Hungary and Roumania.* London: John Murray.

Steinberg, Michael P. 1990. *The Meaning of the Salzburg Festival: Austria as Theater and Ideology, 1890–1938.* Ithaca, N.Y.: Cornell University Press.

Steinitz, Wolfgang. 1978. *Deutsche Volkslieder demokratischen Charakters aus sechs Jahrhunderten.* Berlin: Akademie-Verlag.

Sternhell, Zeev. 1998. *The Founding Myths of Israel: Nationalism, Socialism, and the Making of the Jewish State.* Princeton, N.J.: Princeton University Press.

Stocking, George W., Jr. 1968. *Race, Culture and Evolution: Essays in the History of Anthropology.* Chicago: University of Chicago Press.

――――. 1994. "The Turn-of-the-Century Concept of Race." *Modernism/ Modernity* 1 (1): 4–16.

Stöckl, Ernst. 1993. *Musikgeschichte der Rußlanddeutschen.* Dülmen: Laumann-Verlag. (Die Musik der deutschen im Osten Mitteleuropas, 5.)

Stokes, Martin. 1992. *The Arabesk Debate: Music and Musicians in Modern Turkey.* Oxford: Oxford University Press.

――――. 1997. "Voices and Places: History, Repetition and the Musical Imagination." *The Journal of the Royal Anthropological Institute* 3 (4): 675–691.

――――. 1999. "Music, Travel, Tourism: An Afterword." *The World of Music* 41 (3): 141–155.

――――. 2003. "Globalization and the Politics of World Music." In Martin Clayton, Trevor Herbert, and Richard Middleton, eds., *The Cultural Study of Music: A Critical Introduction,* pp. 297–308. New York: Routledge.

――――, ed. 1994. *Ethnicity, Identity and Music: The Musical Construction of Place.* Oxford: Berg.

_____, and Philip V. Bohlman, eds. 2003. *Celtic Modern: Music at the Global Fringe*. Lanham, Md.: Scarecrow Press. (Europea: Ethnomusicologies and Modernities, 1.)

Strauss, Johann, Jr. N.d. "Wiener Blut Walzer." Vienna: C. Z. Spina's Nachfolger.

Strauss, Josef. N.d. "Dorfschwalben aus Österreich." Vienna: C. A. Spina.

Strohm, Reinhard. 1993. *The Rise of European Music, 1380–1500*. Cambridge: Cambridge University Press.

Suchoff, Benjamin. 1972. "Bartók and Serbo-Croatian Folk Music." *The Musical Quarterly* 58 (4): 557–571.

Sugarman, Jane C. 1997. *Engendering Song: Singing and Subjectivity at Prespa Albanian Weddings*. Chicago: University of Chicago Press. (Chicago Studies in Ethnomusicology.)

_____. 1999. "Imagining the Homeland: Poetry, Songs, and the Discourses of Albanian Nationalism." *Ethnomusicology* 43 (3): 419–458.

Sulițeana, Gisela. 2000. "On the 'Hascala' Movement and the Traditional Music of Jews in Romania." *East European Meetings in Ethnomusicology* 7: 48–66.

Sulz, Josef, Johanna Blum, Gretl Brugger, and Stefan Demetz. 1986. *Kommt zum Singen: Liederbuch aus Südtirol*. 2d ed. Bolzano: Verlagsanstalt Athesia.

Suny, Ronald Grigor, and Michael D. Kennedy, eds. 1999. *Intellectuals and the Articulation of the Nation*. Ann Arbor: University of Michigan Press.

Suojanen, Päivikki. 1984. *Finnish Folk Hymn Singing: Study in Music Anthropology*. Tampere: University of Tampere Institute for Folk Tradition.

Suppan, Wolfgang, and Wiegand Stief. 1976. *Melodietypen des deutschen Volksgesanges*. Tutzing: Schneider.

Survilla, Paula. 2002. *Of Mermaids and Rock Singers: Placing the Self and Constructing the Nation through Belarusan Contemporary Music*. New York: Routledge.

Swedenburg, Ted. 1997. "Saida Sultan/Danna International: Transgender Pop and the Polysemiotics of Sex, Nation, and Ethnicity on the Israeli-Egyptian Border." *The Musical Quarterly* 81 (1): 81–108.

Tägil, Sven, ed. 1995. *Ethnicity and Nation Building in the Nordic World*. Carbondale: Southern Illinois University Press.

Tappert, Wilhelm. 1890. *Wandernde Melodien*. 2d ed., enlarged. Leipzig: List und Francke.

Taruskin, Richard. 1983. "Some Thoughts on the History and Historiography of Russian Music." *The Journal of Musicology* 3 (4): 321–339.

_____. 1996. *Stravinsky and the Russian Traditions*. Berkeley: University of California Press.

_____. 1997. *Defining Russia Musically: Historical and Hermeneutical Essays*. Princeton, N.J.: Princeton University Press.

_____. 2001. "Nationalism." In Stanley, ed., *The New Grove Dictionary of Music and Musicians.* 2d ed., vol. 17: pp. 689–706. London: Macmillan.

Taussig, Michael. 1987. *Shamanism, Colonialism and the Wild Man: A Study in Terror and Healing.* Chicago: University of Chicago Press.

Taylor, Julie M. 1976. "Tango: Theme of Class and Nation." *Ethnomusicology* 20 (2): 273–292.

Taylor, Timothy D. 1997. *Global Pop: World Music, World Markets.* New York: Routledge.

Teutsch, Karl, ed. 1997. *Siebenbürgen und das Banat: Zentren deutschen Musiklebens im Südosten Europas.* Sankt Augustin: Academia Verlag. (Deutsche Musik im Osten, 9.)

Tibi, Bassam. 2001. *Europa ohne Identität? Leitkultur oder Wertebeliebigkeit.* 2d ed. Munich: Siedler.

Tiersky, Ronald, ed. 1999. *Europe Today: National Politics, European Integration, and European Society.* Lanham, Md.: Rowman and Littlefield. (Europe Today.)

Todorov, Tzvetan. 1993. *On Human Diversity: Nationalism, Racism, and Exoticism in French Thought.* Cambridge, Mass.: Harvard University Press.

Trochimczyk, Maja. 2002. "Passion, Mourning, and the Black Angels: Ewa Demarczyk as the Voice of the Nation." *European Meetings in Ethnomusicology* 9: 236–260.

Tromholt, Sophus. 1999 [1885]. "Das Jodeln der Lappen." In Lothar Schneider, ed., *Europa erlesen: Lappland,* pp. 149–150. Klagenfurt: Wieser.

Trumpener, Katie. 1995. "The Time of the Gypsies: A 'People without History' in the Narratives of the West." In Kwame Anthony Appiah and Henry Louis Gates, Jr., eds., *Identities.* Chicago: University of Chicago Press.

_____. 1996. "Imperial Marches and Mouse Singers: Nationalist Mythology in Central European Modernity." In Laura Garcia-Moreno and Peter C. Pfeiffer, eds., *Text and Nation: Debates on Cultures in Conflict,* pp. 67–90. Rochester, N.Y.: Camden House.

_____. 1997. *Bardic Nationalism: The Romantic Novel and the British Empire.* Princeton, N.J.: Princeton University Press.

_____. 2000. "Béla Bartók and the Rise of Comparative Ethnomusicology: Nationalism, Race Purity, and the Legacy of the Austro-Hungarian Empire." In Ronald Radano and Philip V. Bohlman, eds., *Music and the Racial Imagination,* pp. 403–434. Chicago: University of Chicago Press.

Tsenova, Valerie, ed. 1998. *Underground Music from the Former USSR.* Trans. by Romela Kohanovskaya. New York: Routledge.

Turi, Johan. 1999. "Der Gesang der Lappen." In Lothar Schneider, ed., *Europa erlesen: Lappland,* pp. 152–154. Klagenfurt: Wieser.

Turino, Thomas. 2000. "Race, Class, and Musical Nationalism in Zimbabwe." In Ronald Radano and Philip V. Bohlman, eds., *Music and the Racial Imagination,* pp. 554–584. Chicago: University of Chicago Press.

Turner, Victor, and Edith Turner. 1978. "St. Patrick's Purgatory: Religion and Nationalism in an Archaic Pilgrimage." In Victor Turner and Edith Turner, *Image and Pilgrimage in Christian Culture: Anthropological Perspectives*, pp. 104–139. New York: Columbia University Press.

Tyrrell, John. 1988. *Czech Opera*. Cambridge: Cambridge University Press.

Uhland, Ludwig. 1844–1845. *Alte hoch- und niederdeutsche Volkslieder*. 2 vols. Stuttgart and Tübingen: J. G. Cotta'scher Verlag.

Ungar-Klein, Brigitte, ed. 2000. *Jüdische Gemeinden in Europa: Zwischen Aufbruch und Kontinuität*. Vienna: Picus.

Urla, Jacqueline. 2001. "'We Are All Malcolm X!': Negu Gorriak, Hip-Hop, and the Basque Political Imaginary." In Tony Mitchell, ed., *Global Noise: Rap and Hip-Hop outside the USA*, pp. 171–193. Middletown, Conn.: Wesleyan University Press.

Utsi, Paulus. 1999. "Der Joik ist eine Freistätte des Gedankens." In Lothar Schneider, ed., *Europa erlesen: Lappland*, p. 149. Klagenfurt: Wieser.

Valkeapää, Nils Aslak. 1999. "Der Joik." In Lothar Schneider, ed., *Europa erlesen: Lappland*, pp. 154–156. Klagenfurt: Wieser.

Vallely, Fintan, ed. 1999. *The Companion to Irish Traditional Music*. Cork: Cork University Press.

van de Port, Mattijs. 1998. *Gypsies, Wars and Other Instances of the Wild: Civilisation and Its Malcontents in a Serbian Town*. Amsterdam: Amsterdam University Press.

van der Veer, Peter. 1994. *Religious Nationalism: Hindus and Muslims in India*. Berkeley: University of California Press.

Vargyas, Lajos. 1941. *Aj falu zenei élete* ("The Musical Life of the Village of Aj"). Budapest: Akadémai Kiadó.

———. 1983. *Hungarian Ballads and the European Ballad Tradition*. 2 vols. Trans. by Imre Gombos. Budapest: Akadémiai Kiadó.

Vaughan, C. E., ed. 1915. *The Political Writings of Rousseau*. 2 vols. Cambridge: Cambridge University Press.

Vaughan Williams, Ralph. 1934. *National Music*. London: Oxford University Press.

———. 1996. *National Music and Other Essays*. 2d ed. Oxford: Clarendon.

Veidlinger, Jeffrey. 2000. *The Moscow State Yiddish Theater: Jewish Culture on the Soviet Stage*. Bloomington: Indiana University Press. (Jewish Literature and Culture.)

Verdery, Katherine. 1983. *Transylvanian Villagers*. Berkeley and Los Angeles: University of California Press.

———. 1991. *National Ideology under Socialism: Identity and Cultural Politics in Ceauşescu's Romania*. Berkeley and Los Angeles: University of California Press.

———. 1996. *What Was Socialism, and What Comes Next?* Princeton, N.J.: Princeton University Press.

Vernon, Paul. 1998. *A History of the Portuguese Fado.* Aldershot: Ashgate.

Vertkov, Konstantin, et al. 1975 [1963]. *Atlas of Musical Instruments of the Peoples Inhabiting the USSR.* Moscow: Muzyka.

Vital, David. 1999. *A People Apart: The Jews in Europe, 1789–1939.* Oxford: Oxford University Press. (The Oxford History of Modern Europe.)

von Hallberg, Robert, ed. 1996. *Literary Intellectuals and the Dissolution of the State.* Chicago: University of Chicago Press.

Wachtel, Andrew Baruch. 1998. *Making a Nation, Breaking a Nation: Literature and Cultural Politics in Yugoslavia.* Stanford, Cal.: Stanford University Press. (Cultural Memory in the Present.)

Wackenroder, Wilhelm Heinrich, and Ludwig Tieck. 1979 [1797]. *Herzensergießungen eines kunstliebenden Klosterbruders.* Stuttgart: Reclam.

Wagner, Manfred. 1996. "Response to Bryan Gilliam Regarding Bruckner and National Socialism." *The Musical Quarterly* 80 (1): 118–123.

Wagner, Richard. 1869 [1850]. *Das Judenthum in der Musik.* Leipzig: J. J. Weber.

———. 1983. "Über deutsches Musikwesen." In Richard Wagner, *Richard Wagner Werke.* Vol. 5, pp. 151–170. Frankfurt am Main: Insel.

Wagner, Richard. 1999. "Auf ungarisch." In Georg Aescht, ed., *Siebenbürgen: Europa erlesen,* pp. 171–172. Klagenfurt: Wieser Verlag.

Waldmann, Guido, ed. 1938. *Zur Tonalität des deutschen Volksliedes.* Wolfenbüttel and Berlin: Georg Kallmeyer.

Walicki, A. 1982. *Philosophy and Romantic Nationalism: The Case of Poland.* Oxford: Oxford University Press.

Wallaschek, Richard. 1893. *Primitive Music: An Inquiry into the Origin and Development of Music, Song, Instruments, Dances and Pantomimes of Savage Races.* London: Longmans, Green.

Wallis, Roger, and Krister Malm. 1984. *Big Sounds from Small Peoples: The Music Industry in Small Countries.* New York: Pendragon Press.

Wanner, Catherine. 1996. "Nationalism on Stage: Music and Change in Soviet Ukraine." In Mark Slobin, ed., *Retuning Culture: Musical Changes in Central and Eastern Europe,* pp. 136–156. Durham, N.C.: Duke University Press.

Waschabaugh, William. 1996. *Flamenco: Passion, Politics and Popular Culture.* Oxford: Berg.

Weber, Michael. 1998. "Zu den Grundsätzen der Kulturpolitik der Europäischen Union: Eine einführende Betrachtung." In Elisabeth Theresia Hilscher, ed., *Österreichische Musik, Musik in Österreich: Beiträge zur Musikgeschichte Mitteleuropas,* pp. 703–722. Tutzing: Hans Schneider.

———. 1999. "Signs of 'Home' in Austrian 'New Folk Music'." In Ioannis Zannos, ed., *Music and Signs: Semiotic and Cognitive Studies in Music,* pp. 435–458. Bratislava: ASCO Art and Science.

Weber-Kellermann, Ingeborg. 1978. *Zur Interethnik: Donauschwaben, Siebenbürger Sachsen und ihre Nachbarn.* Frankfurt am Main: Suhrkamp.

Weiner, Marc. 1993. *Undertones of Insurrection: Music, Politics and the Social Sphere in the Modern German Narrative.* Lincoln: University of Nebraska Press.

Weisser, Albert. 1954. *The Modern Renaissance of Jewish Music: Events and Figures, Eastern Europe and America.* New York: Bloch.

Wellner, Christoph. 2002. "Pluralismus in Nordeuropa." *Österreichische Musikzeitschrift* 57 (3/4): 33–40.

Wicker, Hans-Rudolf, ed. 1997. *Rethinking Nationalism and Ethnicity: The Struggle for Meaning and Order in Europe.* Oxford: Berg. (Nationalism and Internationalism.)

Wieser, Lojze. 2001. "Ante scriptum." In Renata SakoHoess and Rotraut Hackermüller, eds., *Europa erlesen: Bratislava,* pp. 5–7. Klagenfurt: Wieser.

Wilkinson, Iren Kertész. 1997. *The Fair Is Ahead of Me: Individual Creativity and Social Contexts in the Performances of a Southern Hungarian Vlach Gypsy Slow Song.* In Hungarian and English. Budapest: Institute for Musicology of the Hungarian Academy of Sciences. (Gypsy Folk Music of Europe, 4.)

Wilson, Thomas M., and Hastings Donnan, eds. 1998. *Border Identities: Nation and State at International Frontiers.* Cambridge: Cambridge University Press.

Wilson, William A. 1976. *Folklore and Nationalism in Modern Finland.* Bloomington: Indiana University Press.

Winock, Michel. 1998. *Nationalism, Anti-Semitism, and Fascism in France.* Trans. by Jane Marie Todd. Stanford, Cal.: Stanford University Press.

Wiora, Walter. 1957. *Europäische Volksmusik und abendländische Tonkunst.* Cassel: J. P. Hinnenthal.

———. 1962. *Das echte Volkslied.* Heidelberg: Müller-Thiergarten Verlag.

———. 1966. *European Folk Song: Common Forms in Characteristic Modification.* Cologne: Arno Volk.

Wischenbart, Rüdiger. 1992. *Karpaten: Die dunkle Seite Europas.* Vienna: Kreymayr & Scheriau.

Witzmann, Reingard. 1976. *Der Ländler in Wien: Ein Beitrag zur Entwicklungsgeschichte des Wiener Walzers bis in die Zeit des Wiener Kongresses.* Vienna: Arbeitsstelle für den Volkskundeatlas in Österreich.

Wolff, Larry. 1994. *Inventing Eastern Europe: The Map of Civilization on the Mind of the Enlightenment.* Stanford, Cal.: Stanford University Press.

Young, James E. 1993. *The Texture of Memory: Holocaust Memorials and Meaning.* New Haven, Conn.: Yale University Press.

Zemtsovsky, Izaly. 1995. "Underground Styles as a Feature of a Totalitarian Culture: The Case of Russian Music." In Joachim Braun, Vladimir Karbusický, and Heidi Tamar-Hoffmann, eds., *Verfemte Musik: Komponisten in den Diktaturen unseres Jahrhunderts,* pp. 195–204. Frankfurt am Main: Peter Lang.

_____. 2000. "'Jiddischismus' in der Music: Bewegung und Phänomen." In *Jüdische Musik in Sowjetrußland: Die "jüdische Nationale Schule" der zwanziger Jahre*, pp. 1–21. Berlin: Ernst Kuhn. (Studia Slavica Musicologica: Texte und Abhandlungen zur osteuropäischen Musik, 15.)

Zerubavel, Yael. 1994. *Recovered Roots: Collective Memory and the Making of Israeli National Traditions*. Chicago: University of Chicago Press.

Zuck, Barbara A. 1980. *A History of Musical Americanism*. Ann Arbor, Mich.: UMI Research Press.

Zulaika, Joseba. 1988. *Basque Violence: Metaphor and Sacrament*. Reno: University of Nevada Press.

## DISCOGRAPHY

*10 Jahre Wiener Jüdischer Chor: Jiddische, sephardische und hebräische Lieder*. N.d. CSM 9911-F1.

". . . åba lustig san d'Leit!" 1996. ". . . åba lustig san d'Leit!": Eine musikalische Reise durch die Pyhrn-Eisenwurzen*. BRE-PRO MdR 04 Au Me. (Musik der Regionen, 4.)

Adler, Abraham. n.d. *Oberkantor of the Great Synagogue of Vienna*. n.p.

*Bannal*. 1996. *Bannal: Waulking Songs*. Greentrax CDTRAX 099.

Bajrektarević, Sofija, and Ursula Hemetek, eds. 1996. *Sevdah in Wien: Eine Dokumentation bosnischer Liedkultur in Österreich*. Vol. 5: *Bosnische Musik*. RST 91615-2. (Tondokumente zur Volksmusik in Österreich, 5.)

Barzilai, Shmuel. 1996. *Schir Zion: Kompositionen der Wiener Kantoren*. ORF CD 62.

*Basque Country: Traditional and Contemporary Songs*. N.d. Ocora C 559083.

*Béla Bartók: Turkish Folk Music Collection*. 1996. 2 CDs. Hungaroton Classics HCD 18218–19.

Berke, Steven C., Elizabeth S. Berke, and the Madrigalchor of the Hochschule für Musik in München. 1996. *Jewish Masterworks of the Synagogue Liturgy: A Concert in Honor of the Re-Establishment of Liberal Judaism in Germany*. Deutsche harmonia mundi 05472 7738 2.

*Berlin Lounge*. 2001. 2 CDs. Wagram 3069692.

Beth Hatefutsoth. 1989. *Masoret kehillit Danzig* ("The Danzig Tradition"). Beth Hatefutsoth BTR 8901.

_____. 1997. *Ha-masoret ha-musikalit shel ha-kehilla ha-reformit shel Berlin* ("The Musical Tradition of the Jewish Reform Congregation in Berlin"). 2 CDs and a booklet. Beth Hatefutsoth BTR 9702.

Bezirk Oberbayern. 1998. *"Alpenrosen": Zwölf Gebirgslieder aus der gleichnamigen Liedhandschrift aus Grassau im Chiemgau um 1840*. WRB 1054 DSP.

*Bosnia*. 1993. *Bosnia: Echoes from an Endangered World*. Smithsonian Folkways SF 40407.

*Botschaften der Muttergottes in Medjugorje.* N.d. Augustinus MC 3886.

Bowen, Robin Hue. 1993. *Telyn Berseiniol fy Ngwlad/The Sweet Harp of My Land.* Flying Fish FF 70610.

Brăiloiu, Constantin, ed. 1958. *Norvegiens.* UNESCO Conseil Internationale de la Musique A1 108/109.

Bruji. N.d. *Kein Wort Deutsch.* Extraplatte EX 341–2.

*Burgenländische Volksmusik.* 1991. *Burgenländische Volksmusik.* SSM-Records CD 020 124–2.

Chandra, Sheila. 1992. *Weaving My Ancestors' Voices.* Real World Records Carol 2322–2.

_____. 1994. *The Zen Kiss.* Real World Records Carol 2342–2.

_____. 1995. *Roots and Wings.* Caroline Carol 1779–2.

*Chants du pays basque.* 1993. Arion ARN 64223.

*Chants populaires yiddish.* N.d. Buda 92595–2. (Music of the World.)

Chieftains, The. 1996. *Santiago.* RCA BMG 09026 68602.

Citoller Tanzgeiger, Die. 2000. *Am Tanzboden belauscht.* Die Citoller Tanzgeiger CD 23456.

Courlander, Edward, ed. 1954. *Songs and Dances of Norway.* Folkways FW 04008 (rereleased on CD by Smithsonian Folkways).

Dahle, Johannes, and Knut Dahle. 1993. *Griegslåttene.* Musikhuset Forlag M-H 2642 CD.

*Das ist mein Österreich: Das Zeitalter Franz Josephs und Elisabeths – volkstümlich.* N.d. GMM 980 402.

Deutsches Volksliedarchiv, ed. 1998. *1848– ". . . weil jetzt die Freiheit blüht": Lieder aus der Revolution von 1848/49.* Südwest SWR 104–98 CD.

*England.* 1998. *World Library of Folk and Primitive Music.* Comp. by Alan Lomax et al. Vol. 1. Rounder ROUN 1741.

*English Roots Music.* N.d. *English Roots Music: The Rough Guide.* Rough Guide/World Music Network RGNET 1018CD.

Erkose Ensemble. 1991. *Tzigane: The Gypsy Music of Turkey.* CMP CD 3010.

*Es wird nicht untergehen: Jüdisch-liturgische Gesänge aus Berlin.* 1996. Edition Barbarossa EdBa 01317–2.

Europäisches Parlament. N.d. *Europa—da is Musik drin!* Deutsche Grammophon 445 492–2.

*Europe.* 1994. The World of Traditional Musics, 6. ed. by Christian Poché. Ocora C 560066.

*Eurovision.* 1998. Nash' Didan Studios. S-cd-178.

*Eurovision Song Contest 1956–1999.* 2000. 2 CDs. Universal 541 347–2.

*Eurovision Song Contest Kopenhagen 2001.* 2001. BMG 74321 78583 2.

*Eurovision Song Contest Stockholm 2000.* 2000. BMG 74321 76587 2.

*Eurovision Song Contest Tallinn 2002.* 2002. BMG 74321 [] 2.

*Eurovision Song Contest Riga 2003.* 2003. EMI CMC 5843942.

*From Galway to Dublin: Early Recordings of Traditional Irish Music.* 1993. Rounder CD 1087.

Garfein, Rebecca, Arnold Ostlund, Jr., and the Pestalozzistrasse Synagogue Choir. 1998. *Sacred Chants of the Contemporary Synagogue.* New York: Bari Productions.

Gmasz, Sepp, Gerlinde Haid, and Rudolf Pietsch, eds. 1993. *Tondokumente zur Volksmusik in Österreich.* Vol. 1: *Burgenland.* Vienna: Institut für Volksmusikforschung. RST-91557-2.

———. 1993. *Tondokumente zur Volksmusik in Österreich.* Vol. 2: *Niederösterreich.* Vienna: Institut für Volksmusikforschung. RST-91558-2.

Goldmark Choir of the Rabbinical Seminar. 1993. *Eljött ax ének ideje.* Biem-Artisjus PRECD 9305.

*Gypsy Dances.* 1999. *Gypsy Dances.* Easydisc 12136-9017-2.

Haid, Gerlinde, and Hans Haid, eds. 1993. *Musica alpina, I & II.* 2 CDs and book. Innsbruck and Vienna: Institut für Volkskultur und Kulturentwicklung and Institut für Volksmusikforschung. Extraplatte FR-930923.

———. 1999. *Musica alpina, III & IV.* 2 CDs and book. Innsbruck and Vienna: Pro Vita Alpina Alpenakademie, Arunda, and Institut für Volksmusikforschung. Extraplatte 91705-2 and 91 706-2.

Heanzenquartett. 1996. *20 Jahre Heanzenquartett.* RST Records 91619-2.

Hedningarna. 1998. *Trä.* Northside NSD6008.

*Heideboden und Seewinkel.* 1997. *Heideboden und Seewinkel: Dorfmusik und Volksgesang aus dem nördlichen Burgenland.* BRE-PRO MdR 09 Au Me. (Musik der Regionen, 9.)

*Im steirischen Ennstal.* 1996. *Im steirischen Ennstal: Jodler, Lieder, Geschichten und Musik—das Klangbild einer Landschaft.* BRE-PRO MdR 01 Au Me. (Musik der Regionen, 1.)

*Irish Music.* N.d. *Irish Music: The Rough Guide.* Rough Guide/World Music Network RGNET 1006CD.

Italian Treasury. 1999a. *Callabria.* Rounder 11661-1803-2. (The Alan Lomax Collection.)

———. 1999b. *Folk Music and Song of Italy.* Rounder 11661-1801-2. (The Alan Lomax Collection.)

———. 1999c. *The Trallaleri of Genoa.* Rounder 11661-1802-2. (The Alan Lomax Collection.)

———. 2000. *Sicily.* Rounder 11661-1808-2. (The Alan Lomax Collection.)

———. 2001a. *Abruzzo.* Rounder 11661-1811-2. (The Alan Lomax Collection.)

———. 2001b. *Emiglia-Romagna.* Rounder 11661-1804-2. (The Alan Lomax Collection.)

———. 2002c. *Liguria: Baiardo and Imperia.* Rounder 82161-1816-2. (The Alan Lomax Collection.)

_____. 2002d. *Liguria: Polyphony of Ceriana*. Rounder 82161–1817–2. (The Alan Lomax Collection.)

Kalaniemi, Maria, and Aldargaz. 1997. *Iho*. Hannibal HNCD 1396.

Karelia. 1990. *The Best of Karelia*. BBCD 5007.

Karelian Folk Music Ensemble. 2001. *From the Land of the Kalevala*. Gadfly 511.

Kavkasia. 1995. *Songs of the Caucasus*. Well-Tempered Productions WTP 5178.

Khevrisa. 2000. *European Klezmer Music*. Smithsonian Folkways Recordings SFW CD 40486.

Kiss, Ferenc. 1999. *Nagyvárosi bujdosók*. Etnofon Zenei Társulás ER-CD 020.

*Klanggesetz*. N.d. *Klanggesetz: 14 Klangbilder zum Minderheiten-Artikel 7*. Extraplatte EX-468–2.

*Klezmer à la russe: Musiques juives d'Europe orientale*. 1996. Maison des Cultures du Monde W260066.

*Klezmer Music*. 1996. *Klezmer Music: A Marriage of Heaven and Earth*. Ellipsis Arts 4090.

Klotz, Helmut, and the Leipziger Synagogalchor. 1995. *Jewish Chants and Songs*. Berlin Classics 0090762 BC.

Kovács, Sándor. 1994. *Liturgy of the Dohány Street Synagogue*. Hungaroton HCD 18134.

Lanner Struass Compagnie. 1992. *Von den Linzer Tänze zum Wiener Walzer*. Studio Weinberg Nr. SW 1.

*Latcho drom*. 1993. *Latcho drom: La musique des Tsiganes du monde de l'Inde a l'Espagne*. Caroline Carol 1776–2.

Laxblech. 2001. *Laxblech*. BMG Ariola Austria RST 91729.

*Legends of Gypsy Flamenco*. 2000. *Legends of Gypsy Flamenco*. ARC EUCD 1624.

Lemper, Ute. 1996. *Berlin Cabaret Songs*. London 452 601–2.

Lomax, Alan, ed. 2001. *Yugoslavia*. Vol. 5: *World Library of Folk and Primitive Music*. 2 CDs. Rounder 11661–1745–2.

Male Choir of the Cantor Art Academy. N.d. *Tikvatenu*. N.p.

*Märche aus der Kaiserzeit*. Austro Mechana CD 156.437.

Matter, Max, ed. 1998. *1848 – ". . . weil jetzt die Freiheit blüht": Lieder aus der Revolution von 1848/49*. Freiburg im Breisgau: Deutsches Volksliedarchiv. Südwest SWR 104–98 CD.

*Medjugorje: Ereignis und Wirkung*. N.d. Augustinus MC 8986.

*Mei Schätz is mei Schicksål*. 1996. *Mei Schätz is mei Schicksål: Klingende Kostbarkeiten aus dem Mariazellerland*. BRE-PRO MdR 03 Au Me. (Musik der Regionen, 3.)

*Muckle Sangs, The*. 1992. *The Muckle Sangs: Classic Scots Ballads*. Greentrax Records CDTRAX 9005. (Scottish Tradition Series, 5.)

*Music from Austria*. 1999. *Music from Austria—Vol. 3: Jazz and Folk Music*. Music Information Center Austria (mica) 2 CDs, LC7918.

*Music from the Edge of Europe: Portugal*. 1998. Hemisphere 7243 8 59270 2 7.

Musica Svediae. 1995. *Folk Music in Sweden—Låtar från Orsa och Älvdalen.* Caprice CAP21476.

*Musical Tradition of the Jewish Reform Congregation of Berlin, The.* 1997. Book and two CDs. Beth Hatefutsoth BTR 9702.

Muzsikás. 1993. *The Lost Jewish Music of Transylvania.* Hannibal HNCD 1373.

Naidoo, Xavier. 1998. *Nicht von dieser Welt.* Pelham Power Productions 3P 489869 6.

Najma. 1990. *Atish.* Shanachie 64026.

Naokolo, Varošaić. *Das Städtchen drumherum: Ein musikalisches Märchen.* Vienna: Viktory Musikverlag. CSM 9936-F2.

Nelipolviset. 1979. *Kalevalaisia Lauluja* ["Kalevala Songs"]. Suomalaisen Kirjallisuuden Seura SKSK2.

Népzenei Kiadó Folklórachívum. 1996. *Elveszett* ["Lost Eden"]. 2 discs. Etnofon ED-CD 009–10.

New Budapest Orpheum Society. 2002. *Dancing on the Edge of a Volcano: Jewish Cabaret, Popular, and Political Songs, 1900–1945.* Cedille Records CDR 90000 065.

Nikolić-Lakatos, Ruža. N.d. *Amare gila—Unsere Lieder.* Ed. by Ursula Hemetek. Vol. 4: *Romamusik 1.* RST-91571–2. (Tondokumente zur Volksmusik in Österreich, 4.)

*Nordic Roots: A Northside Collection.* 1998. Northside NSD6016.

*Nordic Roots 3.* 2001. Northside NSD6060.

Odessa Klezmer Band. 2000. *Izsák száraz fája* ["Isaac's dry rice"]. Etnofon ER-CD 022.

Ógáin, Rionach Ui, ed. 1997. *Ireland/Irlande.* Auvidis and Unesco D 8271. (Traditional Musics of Today/UNESCO Collection).

*One World, One Voice.* 1990. Virgin Records CDV 1632.

Országos rabbiképző intézet kórusa. N.d. *És felnyitod az emlékesek könyvét . . .* Artisjus PREMC 9615.

Paulsen, Ståle. 1993. *Slåtter frå Helgeland.* Heilo HCD 7082.

Pietsch, Rudolf, ed. 1995. *Die Zwanzger spiel'n auf. . . .* Vol. 3: *Tondokumente zur Volksmusik in Österreich.* Book and CD. Trans. by Philip V. Bohlman. Institut für Volksmusikforschung an der Hochschule für Musik und darstellende Kunst in Wien. RST-91570–2.

Plastino, Goffredo, comp. 2001. *Tambores del Bajo Aragón.* CD and book. Aragón LCD Prames D.L. Z-635–2001. (Archivo de Tradición Oral, 17.)

Pliss, Vladimir, and Alexander Tsalyuk. N.d. *The Male Choir of Academia Cantorial Art* [sic]. Joint.

Ponitran. 1999. *Zahraj mi, gajdoško: Gajdošské piesne a tance z Nitry a Tekova.* Rádio Bratislava RB 0218–2711.

Prague Choir Mishpaha. 1991. *Zpívá chasidské písne.* ARTeM 9101 CD.

Preisner, Zbigniew. 1993. *Bande originale du film* Trois Couleurs, Bleu. Virgin Records America 7243 8 39027 2 9.

*Rilke Projekt.* 2001. *Rilke Projekt: "Bis an alle Sterne."* RCA Victor BMG CD 74321 78280 2.

Rödelheim Hartreim Projekt. 1996. *Zurück nach Rödelheim.* MCA MCD 70000.

Rough Guide, The, ed. 1999. *The Rough Guide Music of the Gypsies.* The Rough Guide RGNET 1034 CD.

———. 2000. *The Rough Guide to the Music of Scandinavia.* The Rough Guide RGNET 1051 CD.

———. 2002a. *Arabic Electronica: Traditional Roots Meet Modern Beats—The Rough Guide to Arabesque.* The Rough Guide RGNET 1093 CD.

———. 2002b. *Emerging Sounds: Bards and Balalaikas—The Rough Guide to the Music of Russia.* The Rough Guide RGNET 1107 CD.

*Roumanie.* 1983. *Roumanie—polyphonie vocale des Aroumains/Romania—Vocal Polyphony of Arumanians.* Le Chant du Monde LDX 74803.

*Saami Music and Change.* 1988. Ole Edstrom Caprice 1351.

*Scottish Music.* N.d. *Scottish Music: The Rough Guide.* Rough Guide/World Music Network RGNET 1004CD.

*Scotland.* 1995. *Scotland: Tunes from the Lowlands, Highlands, and Islands.* World Network WDR 58.394.

Shej, Ruzsa. N.d. *Ruzsa N. Lakatos and the Gypsy Family.* CSM 9944-M7.

Skaličan. 1999. *Poprvé . . . : L'udová hudba.* Mikula.

*So geht's zua bei uns in Wean.* 1994. *So geht's zua bei uns in Wean: Wiener Instrumentalmusik (1895–1935).* Basilisk Records DOCD-3013.

*Songs of the Travelling People.* 1994. *Songs of the Travelling People: Music of the Tinkers, Gipsies and Other Travelling People of England, Scotland and Ireland.* Saydisc CD-SDL 407.

*St. Petersburg School.* 1998. *The St. Petersburg School: Music for Cello and Piano.* Beth Hatefutsoth BTR 9801.

Sürpriz. 1999. *Reise nach Jerusalem—Kudüs'e Seyahat—Journey to Jerusalem.* BMG 74321 65392 2.

Swarovski Musik Wattens. 1993. *25 europäische Hymnen.* Koch International 340 102 F1.

*Synagogální zpevy.* 1996 [1956 and 1960]. Supraphon SU 3073-2.

Tanzgeiger, The. 1994. *Die Tanzgeiger.* RST Records RST-91589-2.

Taraf de Haïdouks. 1991. *Musique des Tziganes de Roumanie.* Crammed Discs CRAW 2 CD.

———. 1994. *Honourable Brigands, Magic Horses and Evil Eye.* Cram World CRAW 13. (Musiques des Tsiganes de Roumanie, 2.)

———. 2001. *Band of Gypsies.* Nonesuch 79641-2.

Taraful din Baia. 2000. *Gypsies of Romania: Transylvania—Banat.* ARC EUCD 1618.

Tarkan. 1998. *Tarkan.* Polygram 559 981-2.

Tekameli. 1999. *Ida y vuelta.* Epic EPC 493333 2.

Transjoik. N.d. *Mahkalahke.* Warner/Atrium.

*Unblocked: Music of Eastern Europe.* 1997. Three-CD set, with accompanying booklet. Ellipsis Arts CD3570.

———. 1998. Ellipsis Arts CD3574.

Värttinä. 1996. *Kokko* ["Bonfire"]. Nonesuch 19429–2.

Veřa Bílá and Kale. 1997. *Rom-Pop.* RCA Victor 74321–27910–2.

*Voices of Europe.* 2000. *Voices of Europe: Concert in Hallgrímskirkja Church Reykjavik, August 27th 2000.* RUV Iceland.

von Goisern, Hubert, und die Alpinkatzen. 1995. *Wia die Zeit vergeht.* . . . 2 CDs. BMG 74321 263 262.

*Wånn i vo Puachberg.* 1996. *"Wånn i vo Puachberg auf Miesenbåch geh,* . . .*": Das Schneeberggebiet, eine einzigartige Musiklandschaft—in Niederösterreich.* BRE-PRO MdR 05 Au Me. (Musik der Regionen, 5.)

*What Is Bhangra?* 1994. IRS Records 7243 8 29242 27.

*Wienermusik.* 1996. *Wienermusik—Zwischen Gürtel und Wienerwald: Seltenes, Vergessenes und gern Gehörtes aus der Wiener Tradition.* BRE-PRO MdR 02 Au Me. (Musik der Regionen, 2.)

Wiener Tschuschenkapelle. 1994. *G'rebelt: Live.* Extraplatte EX 205–2.

Wimme. 2000. *Cugu.* Northside NSD6048.

*World of Gypsies.* 2000. *World of Gypsies.* ARC EUCD 1613.

*Yoik: A Presentation of Saami Folk Music.* N.d. Caprice.

Zawinul, Joe. 2000. *Mauthausen:* . . . *vom großen Sterben hören—Chronicles from the Ashes.* ESC Records EFA 03666–2.

Zemel Choir, The. 1996. *Louis Lewandowski (1821–1894): Choral and Cantorial Works.* Olympia OCD 347.

Ziegler, Clément. 1992. *Musiciens Manouches en Roussillon/Gypsy Manouches from Roussillon: Zaïti.* Al Sur ALCD 107.

Zoltan and His Gypsy Ensemble. N.d. *Traditional Gypsy Music from the Balkans.* Legacy International CD 434.

## FILMOGRAPHY

N.B.: For the most part these are educational and documentary films, available from distributors of such films.

Alexandrov, Grigori. 1938. *Volga, Volga.*

*Antonio and Rosario.* 1961. Janus Films, Pennsylvania State University.

Arnberg, Matts, and Pål-Nils Nilsson. 1965–66. *Jojk: Da, när var mannen pa Oulavuoli.* Stockholm: Swedish Broadcasting.

*Ashkenaz.* 1993. *Ashkenaz: The Music of the Jews from Eastern Europe.* Jerusalem: Israel Music Heritage Project. (A People and Its Music, 3.)

Berlet, Walter H. 1973. *La guitarra española.* Boston: Boston University.

Bhattacharya, Deben. 1992. *Village Life and Music in Hungary.* Guilford, Conn.: Audio-Forum.

Brian, Julian, Kenneth Richter, and Shirley Richter. N.d. *Dances of Macedonia.* Contemporary Films.

Corti, Alex. 1994. *Radetzkymarsch.* Satel Films, with ORF/BR/Progefi.

*Danzas regionales españolas.* 1966. Berkeley: Extension Media Center, University of California. (*Encyclopaedia Britannica* Educational Corporation.)

*Discovering Russian Folk Music.* 1975. BFA Educational Media.

Egler, Lars, and Bengt Nordwall. 1963. *Bingsjölåtar i Pekkosgården.* Stockholm: Swedish Broadcasting Corporation.

———. 1964. *Leticke, Leticke, Korna är hemma.* Stockholm: Swedish Broadcasting Corporation.

Elias, Erik. 1966. *Bryllup i bjergene.* Copenhagen: Erik Elias Film Production.

Fajardo, Rafael, and Pilar Perez de Guzman. 1994. *Fiesta gitana!* New York: Alegrías Productions.

*Flamenco.* 1995. *Flamenco.* Princeton, N.J.: Films for the Humanities and Sciences.

Hammond, David, and Derek Bailey. 1991. *The Story of the Clancy Brothers and Tommy Makem.* Newton, N.J.: Shanachie Records.

Haramis, Peter. 1969a. *Anastenaria.* Berkeley: Extension Media Center, University of California.

———. 1969b. *Kalogeros.* Berkeley: Extension Media Center, University of California.

*Hassidut.* 1994. *Hassidut: The Music of the Hassidic Community.* Jerusalem: Israel Music Heritage Project. (A People and Its Music, 6.)

*La jota aragonesa.* 1996. Madrid: Videos de la Luz.

*JVC/Smithsonian Folkways Video Anthology of Music and Dances of Europe.* 1995. *Europe.* Vol. 1: *Iceland, Denmark, Ireland, Scotland, England, Czech Republic, Hungary, Belgium.* Tokyo and Washington, D.C.: JVC and the Smithsonian Institution.

———. 1996. *Europe.* Vol. 2: *France, Spain, Italy, Serbia, Romania.* Tokyo and Washington, D.C.: JVC and the Smithsonian Institution.

*JVC Video Anthology of World Music and Dance.* 1990a. Vol. 20: *Europe I: Ireland, England, France, Switzerland, West Germany, Spain, Italy, Greece.* Tokyo: JVC.

———. 1990b. Vol. 21: *Europe II: Poland, Czechoslovakia, Hungary.* Tokyo: JVC.

———. 1990c. Vol. 22: *Europe III: Romania, Yugoslavia, Bulgaria, Albania.* Tokyo: JVC.

*Jugoslav Folk Dances.* 1965. Berkeley: Extension Media Center, University of California. (Dennis Boxell Films.)

Kennedy, Peter, Alan Lomax, and George Pickow. N.d. *'Oss, 'Oss, Wee 'Oss.* Bloomington: Indiana University.

Kuter, Lois, Michael Bailey, and Gei Zantzinger. 1997. *Of Pipers and Wrens: De souffle et de roseau.* Devault, Pa.: Constant Spring Productions.

Lappalainen, Heimo, and Jouko Aaltonen. 1991. *Taiga Nomads: The School and the Village.* Helsinki: Fin Image.

Lemon, Alaina, and Midori Nakamura. 1996. *T'an Bakhtale! (Good Fortune to You!): Roma (Gypsies) in Russia.* New York: Documentary Educational Resources.

Luneau, Georges. 1990. *Musica sarda.* Paris: Centre National de la Recherche Scientifique.

Marre, Jeremy. 1992. *The Romany Trail.* Vol. 2: *Gypsy Music into Europe.* Newton, N.J.: Shanachie Records.

Maton, Gérard. 1963. *Le carnaval de Binche.* Studio de Balenfer.

McColgan, John. 1994. *Riverdance: The Show.* Tyrone/RTE Video.

*Message from Gyimes.* 1996. Győr: Jeno Hartyandi.

*My Blood, Your Blood: The Rock Generation in Today's Poland.* N.d. New York: Brighton Video.

*Other Voices, Other Songs: The Greeks.* N.d. New York: Sapphire Productions.

Perez de Guzman, Pilar. 1991. *Danza flamenco de hoy.* New York: Alegrías Productions.

Piechura, Sabine, and Eckhard Schenke. 1994. *Beruf—Wandermusiker.* Göttingen: Institut für Wissenschaftlichen Film.

*Purimshpiler, Der.* 1937. Directed by Joseph Green. Available as video. Teaneck, N.J.: Ergo Films.

Rudavsky, Oren, and Yale Strom. 1990. *At the Crossroads: Jews in Eastern Europe Today.* New York: Arthur Cantor Productions.

Segler, Helmut. 1993. *Kindertänze türkischer Kinder in Deutschland.* Göttingen: Institut für den Wissenschaftlichen Film.

*Sepharad.* 1993. *Sepharad: The Music of the Jews from Spain.* Jerusalem: Israel Music Heritage Project. (A People and Its Music, 2.)

Sevikova, Jana. 1992a. *Jakub.* Watertown, Mass.: Documentary Educational Resources.

———. 1992b. *Piemule.* Watertown, Mass.: Documentary Educational Resources.

*Sing of the Border.* 1967. Berkeley: Extension Media Center, University of California.

Sjarov, Plamen. 1991. *The Mask of the Other Face.* Prague: Plamen Sjarov.

*Song of Seasons.* 1978. New York: Canadian Travel Film Library.

*Soviet Union: Epic Land.* 1971. Berkeley: Extension Media Center, University of California. (*Encyclopaedia Britannica* Educational Corporation.)

Strom, Yale, and Bernard Berkin. 1995. *The Last Klezmer: His Life and His Music.* New York: Maelström Films.

Thurlbek, Ken. N.d. *USSR and R: Rock on a Red Horse.* New York: Tapestry International.

*Voices from Heaven.* 2000. *Voices from Heaven: The Religious Music of Europe in the Middle Ages.* Princeton, N.J.: Films for the Humanities and Sciences.

Wickbor, Jan. 1962. *Norwegian Folk Dances.* Oslo: National Film Board of Norway and Dance Films.

*Yugoslav National Folk Ballet.* 1965. Berkeley: Extension Media Center, University of California. (Dennis Boxell Films.)

# Index

# About the Author

Philip V. Bohlman is Mary Werkman Professor of the Humanities and of Music and chair of Jewish studies at the University of Chicago, where he is also a member of the Center for Middle Eastern Studies and of the Committee on Southern Asian Studies, and where he is an Adjunct Faculty Member in the Department of Germanic Studies.